Mary Helen Allies

The Life of Pope Pius the Seventh

Mary Helen Allies

The Life of Pope Pius the Seventh

ISBN/EAN: 9783743307018

Manufactured in Europe, USA, Canada, Australia, Japa

Cover: Foto ©ninafisch / pixelio.de

Manufactured and distributed by brebook publishing software (www.brebook.com)

Mary Helen Allies

The Life of Pope Pius the Seventh

Quarterly Series.

SIXTEENTH VOLUME.

---

*THE LIFE OF
POPE PIUS THE SEVENTH.*

THE LIFE OF POPE PIUS THE SEVENTH.

BY

MARY H. ALLIES.

LONDON:
BURNS AND OATES, PORTMAN STREET
AND PATERNOSTER ROW.
1875.

TO THE MEMORY OF PIUS VII.,

WHO IN EVIL TIMES,

AGAINST THE DESPOTISM OF A CÆSAR

IN MIGHT AS IN GENIUS GREATEST OF HIS KIND,

ALONE, BY THE SOLE POWER OF RIGHT,

AND THE RING OF THE FISHERMAN,

DEFENDED THE CHURCH'S INDEPENDENCE,

AND HANDED IT DOWN UNIMPAIRED;

WHO RULED IN MEEKNESS,

WHO CONQUERED BY SUFFERING,

AND WHOSE SEPULCHRE IS GLORIOUS.

Christmas Day, 1875.

PREFACE

Two Cardinals, eye-witnesses of the highest credit, Consalvi in his *Mémoires*, and Pacca in his *Memorie Storiche*, have supplied valuable materials for the following narrative: and the dry *Histoire de Pie VII.* by Artaud de Montor, is supplemented by d'Haussonville's late work of conspicuous merit, *l'Eglise Romaine et le Premier Empire*. The main staple of facts is drawn from these sources: the Author's task has been to weave out of them a life of the Pope in very moderate compass, but sufficient, it is hoped, to give a clear notion of the greatness of his Pontificate as well as the purity and delicacy of his personal character.

The picture, if I mistake not, is one of rare, almost unique interest. A simple Benedictine monk is placed by the Divine Providence on the Chair of Peter, when an universal deluge cast forth by the anti-Christian Revolution threatens to destroy the Church. At that moment rises a great warrior, a splendid genius, a remarkable legislator, who presumes that by setting himself at the head of the Revolution he can control and guide its forces. He seats himself on the throne of the eldest Son of the Church, and forthwith seeks to raise again her altars. But soon appears in him the spirit not of a son, but of one who, himself enthroned above the kings of the earth, would make the Church his footstool. He proceeds from victory to victory: and in the height of his power, he lays his hands upon the Vicar of Christ, who had consecrated his throne, seizes him in his Apostolic Palace, drags him like a gagged criminal through the length of Italy and France, confines him in a small episcopal residence of a provincial town, and pronounces that the States of the Church form departments of his Empire. The Vicar of Christ utters his protest in the name of Him Who in his person is insulted, imprisoned, and dethroned. At this the crowned Son of the Revolution, who has just trampled Prussia into the dust, snorting with anger, exclaims:

'What does Pius VII. mean by denouncing me to Christendom? Would he put my throne under an interdict or excommunicate me? Does he imagine that their arms will fall from the hands of my soldiers?'

In the meantime Europe crouches before him in silence. It seems not even to be indignant at the dethronement, the captivity of the Vicar of Christ. Napoleon having incarcerated the Head of the Church, proceeds in the sight of all men to dishonour publicly one of her sacraments: and Austria and Russia vie with each other for the honour of introducing a daughter into a marriage-chamber not vacant. From that point the retribution begins. Napoleon cannot marry two daughters of sovereigns at once, and the disappointed monarch becomes an enemy. Within three years from the date of the pseudo-marriage the arms fall from the hands of hundreds of thousands of soldiers marshalled in vain against the snows of Russia. From his own palace of Fontainebleau the Emperor sends back the Pope to his States, and Pius enters Rome in triumph, as Napoleon descends from his throne.

But more than this. The expiation is not yet made. The Rock of St. Helena has to atone for Savona and Fontainebleau, and a gaoler is found who repeats in some measure upon Napoleon the insults but not the cruelties which gaolers of his own appointing had practised upon the Vicar of Christ. Moreover, the period of Napoleon's captivity, terminated by his death a discrowned outcast, coincides with the period of the Pope's dethronement and captivity terminated by his triumphant restoration.

Such were the consequences of making the Quirinal a prison in 1808. Two generations have passed, the same battle is now waging : a royal locksmith has again taken possession of the Quirinal: another Emperor mocks the Vicar of Christ : and the last quarter of the century will witness the consequences of fraud and violence imitating, with the distance which becomes their several authors, the fraud and violence of Napoleon, and exercised upon one who bears the name and repeats without a blemish the constancy of Pius VII.

T. W. A.

CONTENTS.

CHAPTER I.

The Revolution and the See of Peter.

	PAGE
Actual meaning of the word *State*	1
Mission of the Church in Society	2
Relations of Church and State	3
Two principles represented by Pius VII. and Napoleon	4
Pitt's notion of opposing the Revolution	5
Jansenists false friends of the Church	7
Fénelon's view of the sect	8
Republican principles applied to the Church	9
Gallicanism second great enemy of principle of authority	10
Joseph II. and his system	11
Mediation of Pius VI. to Belgians	14
The social revolution of 1789	15
Its results in France	16
Treaty of Tolentino	17
Exile and testament of Pius VI.	18
The Conclave of 1799-1800	19
Election of Barnaba Chiaramonti	20
Policy of German Cabinet	21
Negotiations with Pius VII.	23
Battle of Marengo	24
The Holy Father's voyage in the *Bellona*	25
His entrance into Rome	26

CHAPTER II.

The Sovereign and the Minister.

	PAGE
Choice of Consalvi as Secretary of State	27
Antecedents of the 'great Cardinal'	28
His character	29
Reforms in Papal administration	30
Bonaparte's notion of utilizing the Church	31
His Allocution at Milan	32
Bonaparte's Ministers	33
Bernier, his man of business	34
Cacault at Rome	35
Consalvi's departure for Paris	36

CHAPTER III.

Two Cardinals: Strength and Weakness.

Aspirations of the spiritual and temporal Powers	37
Substance of the Concordat	38
Bonaparte's religion	39
Consalvi's audience at the Tuileries	40
Attitude of First Consul	41
Herculean labours	42
A snare	44
The First Consul and the Roman plenipotentiary at dinner	45
Consalvi's battle	46
Unpleasant surprises	47
A last assault	48

	PAGE		PAGE
Cardinal Caprara	49	The Avignon scheme rejected by the Holy Father	86
His line of conduct with Bonaparte	50	Imperial jealousy a fruit of ambition	87
An intriguing abbé and a Gallican counsellor	52	Proclamation of new kingdom of Italy	87
Discussions	53	Return to Rome	88
Obstinacy of constitutional bishops	54	The Holy Father's experiences of French enthusiasm	89
Useless concessions	55		
Publication of Concordat	57		
The Organic Articles	58		

CHAPTER IV.

Pius the Seventh at the Tuileries, 1804-1805.

Text of Concordat	59		
Substance of Organic Articles	62		

CHAPTER V.

The Apple of Discord, 1805-1806.

		Pius VII.'s ruling thought	91
		Napoleon's domestic tyranny	92
Anticipations of Pius VII.	66	Expectations from a 'green blossom'	93
The first results of publication of Organic Articles	68	Napoleon's letter to Pius concerning Jerome Bonaparte	94
Napoleon seconded by Portalis, Minister of Worship	69	Validity of Jerome's marriage to Miss Patterson	95
The Emperor's views as to Gospel morality	70	Immediate result of the Holy Father's decision	96
First appearance of Cardinal Fesch	71	General aspect of Europe	97
Napoleon voted Emperor by the Senate	72	New allotments of European territory	98
Policy of Papal Legate in Paris	73	Napoleon's schemes respecting England and Germany	99
Reasons and conditions for the Coronation	74	Occupation of Ancona	99
Talleyrand's empty promises	75	Influence of human glory on Napoleon	100
A premature breach of faith	76	His letter to Pius	101
Meeting of Pope and Emperor	77	Gentleness and long-suffering opposed to insulting language	103
Convenience of a huntsman's garb	78		
Efforts to beguile Pius	79	Threats	104
Josephine's secret visit to the Holy Father	80	Self-illusion of a wayward genius	105
The Coronation	81	Erroneous opinion of an English peer	107
Mutual appreciation of Pius and Napoleon	82	Reply of Pius invited to accede to Continental Blockade	108
Demand of Pius in favour of Temporal Power	83	Ambition necessarily inconsistent	109
Nature of Napoleon's answer	84		
Solitary advantage reaped by Pius VII. at Paris	85	Fesch endeavours successfully to play a double part	110

Consalvi's retirement from the Ministry	111
Danger of Pius from his devotion to duty	112

CHAPTER VI.

The position assumed by Napoleon as a Ruler towards the Church.

Napoleon's advances to religion prompted by policy	113
The Holy Father's estimation of the Concordat	114
The Organic Articles	115
Napoleon's programme with regard to religion	116
His notion of profiting by spiritual things	117
The constitutional clergy gradually discarded	118
The imperially ordered *Te Deums* and pastorals	119
His views about 'heretical England'	120
Measure of praise expected from bishops	120
State despotism compared with Catholic liberty of Rome	121
The 15th of August given to St. Napoleon	122
Ignorance as to the Emperor's patron saint	123
Caprara and Consalvi on the Imperial Catechism	123
Why the Catechism was called into existence	124
Its commentary of the Fourth Commandment	125
Caprara's compliance duly appreciated by Napoleon	127

CHAPTER VII.

The Quirinal a Prison, 1806–1809.

A one-sided view	128
Cardinal Casoni as Secretary of State	129
A Papal Legate at an imperial reception	130
Napoleon's plans specified to Caprara	131
M. Alquier's *Ultimatum*	132
Servile notion of 'rights'	132
Resistance and expectations of Pius	133
His letter to Caprara	134
The difference between 'cannot' and 'will not'	136
Napoleon at Berlin	137
The Emperor's demand of an extraordinary Legate	138
The communication from Dresden	139
Napoleon's conviction that he is a 'pillar of the faith'	140
Napoleon unconsciously a true prophet	141
Foresees the time when he may call a general council	142
M. de Talleyrand succeeded by M. de Champagny for a motive	143
Pius' letter of invitation to the Emperor	144
Its answer	145
A useless condescension	146
The essence of the Catholic Religion opposed to State supervision	147
The Holy Father's letter to Caprara respecting imperial requirements	148
Plan of approaching invasion of Rome	149
The shadow of what was to come	150
The Feast of the Purification at Rome in 1808	151
French monopoly of the Post and Press	152
Pius VII. a close prisoner in the Quirinal	153
Ministry of Pacca	154

	PAGE		PAGE
Brigandage tolerated by invaders	155	Effects of State-legislation on the Church	185
Attempts to exile Pacca	156	Roman Court transferred to Paris	186
Intervention of the Holy Father	157	Religious aspect of Italy	187
Friendly disposition of Cabinet of St. James	158	Results of State interference	189
Napoleon's letter to M. de Champagny	159		
Consummatum est	160		

CHAPTER VIII.

Savona, 1809–1810.

CHAPTER IX.

Strife through Woman, 1810.

	PAGE		PAGE
Publication of Bull of Excommunication	161	Domestic life of Napoleon and Josephine	190
Its results	163	Divorce prompted by ambition	191
Terms of conflict between Pope and Emperor	165	Result of imperial disclosure on Josephine	192
Armed force at the Quirinal	166	The Empress' farewell to the Tuileries	193
The Holy Father found at his post	167	Conversation of two courtiers	194
Pius' answer to General Radet's notification	168	Difficulties as to religious marriage	195
His testament to the Romans	169	Napoleon's arguments	196
Apostolic poverty	170	Pius VII. excluded from the whole question of new marriage	197
The Chartreuse at Florence and its Bonaparte ruler	171	Glory not infallibly conducive to happiness	198
Progress of Pius VII. and sojourn at Grenoble	172	Consalvi's second appearance in Paris	199
Aim of Napoleon	173	Another audience	200
Servility a result of despotism	174	Demeanour of Consalvi in imperial marriage	201
Ignoble similitude adopted in *Moniteur*	175	Opinions of the Sacred College	202
Life of Pius at Savona	176	Assaults directed against Consalvi's conscience	203
His gaolers	177	The religious marriage	204
Importance of the Holy See proved by circumstances	178	The Black and Red Cardinals	205
Remonstrances of courtier prelates	179	A deputy from Austria at Savona	206
Pius' letter to Caprara	180	Desires of Pius VII.	207
Maury's expedient to supply a spiritual need	181	Negotiations of Spina and Caselli with the Holy Father	208
The new Minister of Worship	182	The Emperor strengthened in his evil resolutions	209
Imperial acts of spiritual jurisdiction	183		
M. Emery's audience with Napoleon	184		

CHAPTER X.
The Ring of the Fisherman, 1810-1811.

	PAGE
The government of the Church monarchical	211
Schism essentially inconsistent	212
Maury named Archbishop of Paris by Napoleon	213
The Abbé d'Astros at Notre Dame	214
The Holy Father's protest against Maury's election	215
The Minister of Police's weapons against conscience	216
Tyrannical measures and their fruits	217
Napoleon's directions to M. Bigot	218
Search at the Holy Father's prison	220
Pius divested of the Ring of the Fisherman	221
Address of Metropolitan Canons drawn up by Napoleon and Maury	222
Bossuet erroneously cited as a Gallican champion	223
Capitulary addresses, a new seduction used by Napoleon	224
Bishop of Savona rewarded by imperial gratitude	225
Ecclesiastical Commission to solve an impossible riddle	226
Its decision	227
Independence of the Holy Father necessary for his spiritual liberty	228
Ground for National Council	229
Degeneration	230
An extraordinary sitting at the Tuileries	231
Emery's defence of the Temporal Power	232
The Sulpician's defence of truth to Napoleon	233
Emery's advice not acted upon	234

CHAPTER XI.
A Gallican Council, 1811.

	PAGE
Death of M. Emery	236
Peculiar character of Napoleon's National Council	237
Ignorance of bishops as to the state of things	238
Value of the Council viewed as a resisting body	239
Deputation to Savona	240
Emperor and Minister of Worship controlling the bishops	241
Bribing of the Pope's doctor	242
M. de Chabrol's notion of confessors	243
The Holy Father's attitude with regard to Deputation	245
Misdirected energy of M. de Chabrol	246
Alarming state of Pius VII.	247
Feeble advantage wrenched from him by Deputation	247
Results of Deputation	249
The real president of the Council	250
The Bishop of Séez and his Vicar-General	251
Opening of the National Council	253
Situation prepared by Gallicanism	254
Inaugural oration	255
Demeanour of presiding Prelate	256
The Ministers of Worship at the First General Congregation	257
Napoleon's will notified to National Council	258
Fesch's interview at St. Cloud	260
Motion of Council in favour of Pius VII.	261
Bishop of Chambéry's speech	262
Worldly prudence of Fesch	263
Authority of Council of Trent invoked by Mgr. d'Aviau	264

Contents.

	PAGE
Impotence of Council displeasing to Napoleon	265
Holy Father's interference solicited by helpless bishops	266
Napoleon's decree	267
Bishops beguiled	268
Partial retractation	269
Arrest of opposing prelates	270
Despotism not propitious to moral courage	271
M. Bigot's operations	272
Attempt at resurrection, and its fruits	273
Summing up of Council	274

CHAPTER XII.
From Savona to Fontainebleau, 1811–1812.

A novel negotiation	275
Capital made of the Holy Father's ignorance	276
Members of the new Deputation	277
Solitude in the midst of unfaithful friends	278
Deceitful conduct of Deputation	279
M. de Chabrol's notions of liberty and the truth	280
The Papal Brief of September, 1811	281
Napoleon's absorption in Russian Campaign	282
Dissatisfied ambition	283
A pictured elysium of earthly glory	285
Emperor's communication to Deputation	286
Disenchantment	287
Letter of Pius to Napoleon	288
Its answer	289
Aggravated severity of Holy Father's imprisonment	291
Napoleon's ground for removing the Pope to Fontainebleau	292
Farewell to Savona	293
Sufferings of Pius VII.	294
His reception at Fontainebleau	295
New weapons in the conflict	296
The Holy Father's arms	297
Simplicity and nobility of his conduct	298
Condition of French Church	299
Napoleon's new device for punishing bishops	300
Result of Emperor's expedients in spiritual administration	301
What is involved in Gallican system	302
Protestation of Chapter of Ghent	303
The Man of the Iron Mask supplied with a successor	304

CHAPTER XIII.
Greatness in Humility, 1813.

Last ordeal of Pius VII.	305
Aspect of social and religious horizon	306
Napoleon's renewed negotiations with the Holy Father	307
Primary scheme of Concordat of Fontainebleau	308
Fontainebleau a new Savona	309
Mgr. Duvoisin's admission concerning Pius VII.	310
The huntsman's second appearance	311
Conferences	312
False counsellors	313
Text of Concordat of Fontainebleau	314
Formality of signing	315
Its value as a treaty	317
Sadness and remorse of the Holy Father	318
Pacca's journey and arrival at Fontainebleau	319
Pius VII. a sovereign without a kingdom	320

His fixed idea	321
Division amongst the Black Cardinals	322
Retractation decided upon	323
Its arduous process	324
Letter of Pius to Emperor	325
Allocution to Sacred College	327
Retractation ignored by Napoleon	328
Vain attempts of Cardinal Maury	329
Arrest of Cardinal di Pietro	330
Evils resulting from double administration of a diocese	331
Napoleon's dealings with Catholic Flanders	332
Voice from a death-bed	333
Emperor's chances with the French Church	334
Cardinal Fesch's prediction	335

CHAPTER XIV.

The Fallen Emperor and the Restored Pontiff.

The secret of resistance offered by Pius VII.	336
The Church must triumph	337
Waning of the Emperor's star	338
Marie Louise's notification to the Holy Father	339
Negotiators, male and female	340
Reasons for inactivity of the Holy Father	341
An interested offer of restitution	342
Once more an Apostolic Pilgrim	343
Napoleon's policy with regard to Pius VII.	344
The Holy Father's confidence in God	345
A tardy restitution viewed as a hateful necessity	346
Homeward journey of Pius VII.	347
Entry into Rome	348
The Holy Father's prayer at St. Peter's	349
Another signing at Fontainebleau	350
Vengeance of Pius VII.	351
Gratitude expressed by Napoleon's mother	353

CHAPTER XV.

'*They who sow in tears shall reap in joy.*'

Europe in 1814	354
Re-establishment of the Society of Jesus	355
The Holy Father's estimation of its services	356
The Congress and Treaty of Vienna	357
Temporary exile	358
Napoleon's final sentence	359
Consalvi Secretary of State again	360
The Holy Father's important *motu proprio*	361
Another concordat for France	362
Difficulties with French bishops	363
Policy of French Legislative Assemblies	364
New Archbishop of Paris	365
An age of concordats	365
Calm after the storm	366
Corpus Domini at Rome	367
Roman hospitality freely shown to house of Bonaparte	368
Napoleon's death as a humble son of the Church	369
1808 — 1814: 1815 — 1821, viewed together	370
A few parting words about the 'great Cardinal'	371
Protest of Pius against Carbonari and secret societies	372
Death of Pius VII.	373

CHAPTER I.

The Revolution and the See of Peter. The Conclave of 1799—1800.

'Beata quippe vita est gaudium de veritate.'—S. Aug. in Ps. 118.

As liberty is a divine gift to man, and yet many a thoughtful mind in this nineteenth century is wary of pronouncing the word owing to the excesses of unbridled licence to which it has lent the support of its name, so in the same way the word *State*, which ought simply to denote a divine institution, actually brings before the mind under an unfavourable aspect the relation of the natural to the supernatural order. Society is the natural communion of mankind assembled on the earth to accomplish all those works which belong to man as not only a rational, but a social animal. It is an ordination of God, for in the beginning we read that He said: 'It is not good for man to be alone.'[1] He had made man with a heart which could not even naturally suffice to itself. Eve first supplied this want and met this need, and through her children were born unto Adam, and the world became gradually inhabited. But it would seem that the word *State*, in its present signification, is an offspring of our own times. Thus considered, it seems to mean a material power having no soul, as it were, and possessing no aspirations beyond this world. As we view the whole

[1] Genesis ii. 18.

subject-matter implied in the word, it may perhaps be defined to be the effort of the secular authority to predominate, and to overrule that supernatural authority, which was likewise an ordination of God in society, in order to be the guardian of the soul's liberties. The most superficial knowledge of the question would prompt a man to own at once in theory the superiority of the Church over the State, one representing temporary, the other eternal interests. But in practice this is often denied. The claims of Almighty God are found to be too many and too pressing; and the State, which personifies to us a power which we can almost grasp with the senses, is always at hand inviting us to throw off the yoke, to eat, drink, and be merry, for to-morrow we die. When such a voice is listened to by men, they are unconsciously led to the most grievous of despotisms; for may not that be called grievous which is the destruction of a divine law and the marring of the divine idea?

God, Who willed that each man should help and soothe his fellow-man in the common bond of society, instituted the Church as the guardian of the higher and nobler part of His creatures. This world, fleeting and full of sorrow as it is, is singularly attractive, and the human heart cleaves to its pleasant places, and eagerly drinks of the cup of life. This is an inordinate attachment whose weakness God stooped to consider, and together with the natural society, or rather over this natural society, He gave to a divine religion a working organization in time. When the secular power pressed heavily on man he was to refresh himself by inhaling the higher atmosphere of an institution presenting, it is true, a certain appearance of material structure, but whose last word is in eternity, and whose daily admonition is *Sursum corda!* God and Cæsar, or, to express the respective claims of each in the familiar phrase, Church and State, are not antagonistic, but in obedience to the divine law must fulfil their respective ends. As the secular power watches over the material, so the divine power guards the spiritual life of man; but dealing as they do with the same persons, under the same conditions of time and place, the course productive of true peace and happiness is found in the perfect harmony of the two. History tells us that concord has only been attained and preserved through the submission of the minor and temporary interests to the greater and eternal. Too often the *non serviam* of the State has called forth, as its necessary echo, the *non possum* of the Church. It is a fact which explains to us many otherwise incomprehensible pages in the world's annals. God has given an innate force to this legitimate *non possum*, a strength more divine than human, as He has proved it to be by the dearth of natural means, and yet by the never-failing endurance of His cause through His all-sufficing power. When a full comprehension is arrived at of the nature of the struggle provoked by the attempts of pride to resist the control involved in the teaching of the Church, to own no superior, and to invade the territory of religion, the divine institution, which, as we know, mere natural reason had condemned as 'folly,' stands out in clearer beauty. We see a reason for the contest waged from the beginning of the Christian era. The seed which the Divine Truth sowed in person blossomed in simplicity and purity. But as the contest between Church and State had begun, martyrs were its fruit, and catacombs its first resting-place on earth. What can we expect when we contemplate beginnings so contrary to all human ideas of greatness? We can look for weakness triumphing over material force by a divine strength which is not from men, but from God. It is the reverse of all our preconceived notions of power and magnificence, and by this very mark we acknowledge the parentage and mission of the Church, and we say the more: truly the finger of God is here. As on Mount Calvary, the centurion who looked upon a poor, mangled Body, distorted by terrible suffering, cried out, against the dictates of human reason as it might seem, truly this Man was the Son of God; so it is through all the ages of the Christian history.

Thus also in this instance of Pius the Seventh and Napoleon. On the one side, we are to see the most splendid conqueror of modern times, revelling in genius, empire, and riches. In the pride of his dream of universal dominion, he forgot the respect due to the limits which a Divine Legislator had set up; he passed beyond them, and proclaimed that there should be no more distinction between the kingdom of God and that of Cæsar, but that he himself should become the magnificent sovereign of both. But where was the champion on the other side bold enough to confront the desire and the power of one who ruled absolutely sixty millions of subjects? An old man whose outward circumstances were in all things opposed to those of the Conqueror, but who carried in his person the principle of divine authority. Here we see not lands, riches, empire, or even sparkling and wonderful natural gifts, but a Pontiff who was meek and humble of heart, and whose hope, as the Successor of Peter, was founded upon the Rock of the divine promises. These were his arms, yet Napoleon died an exile from his land and his own people, whilst from the depths of humiliation Pius VII. was led back in triumph to his capital. In patience he had awaited God's time. The issue of the contest causes a well of gladness to spring up in our hearts. May not all who suffer in defence of the truth and of justice look for something of the reward of Pius VII.? May they not expect to see truth and justice, after a temporary humiliation, exalted?

A Catholic mind and appreciation of events were by no means necessary in order, towards the end of the last century, to arrive at this conclusion, for the human sagacity of a great statesman saw that the Papacy alone had power to impede the growth of the Revolution, the Papacy though separate from the splendour of the middle ages. The Pope was still the Pope, but Europe was no longer the Europe of Urban II. or St. Gregory VII. We find the Bishop of Arras, a prelate who had emigrated to England during the Revolution, writing to Cardinal de Bernis in May 1794, at the instigation of Pitt, and thus rendering an account of an interview with England's great Minister. 'Mr. Pitt expressed a deep and sincere admiration for the vigour of the Court of Rome; but he also told me very plainly, that without wishing to make a vast monarchical coalition an affair of religion, he believed the intervention of the Pope to be more than ever essential under existing circumstances.... He is of opinion that the revolutionary torrent is only to be stemmed by opposing to it, as a dyke, Europe armed for the combat. These are his notions of such a coalition. "I do not ask," he said, "the Pope to put himself in person at the head of a political crusade, or to preach it as Urban II. did. Those days are over; and, if as an Anglican I do not regret them, I may well be allowed, under existing circumstances, to be of one opinion as an individual and of another as a statesman of Great Britain, having at heart the disturbed state of Europe. Particular interests cross and disarm the coalitions we are organizing in the name of social tranquillity. More than once, I have seen continental courts draw back before the diversity of opinion and religion which separates us; I think that a bond common to all should unite us. The Pope alone can be such a bond. He has Italy, Spain, Austria, and part of Germany in his power. His authority, temporarily weakened from regrettable causes, can easily recover its prestige, especially when Prussia and Russia in conjunction with England set themselves to work together. . . . Society is divided by personal interests and political views, Rome alone can speak with an impartial voice free from all external pre-occupation. . . . A Papal Bull, presented to Catholic Courts by legates *a latere*, announcing a holy war, war to anarchy, would produce a great and salutary effect. It would arm sovereigns and nations, founding an indissoluble alliance, which is the only means of resisting the fierce enthusiasm of democracy. . . . Differences of religion are forgotten in a vast and common peril. If the Pope consents to publish a Bull of coalition, an English fleet shall be sent to protect the Roman States, and it shall carry with it an extraordinary ambassador from his Majesty to the Holy See, to honour the visible chief of this indispensable alliance." [2]

Now it was that Europe reaped what she had sown. The one aim of her cabinets had been to misrepresent the Papacy and to weaken its action. A few years later the Revolution hurrying Pius VI. as a dethroned sovereign to die in exile proclaimed that the reign of the Popes was at an end, and so Pitt's notion of placing Rome at the head of an European coalition to stem democracy could meet with no response. They who had disarmed the man turned round at the eleventh hour and asked him to make their cause his own. Pius VI. answered Pitt's advances through Cardinal de Bernis by saying that for such a plan to succeed the

[2] Quoted by M. Crétineau-Joly. See his book, *L'Eglise Romaine en face de la Révolution*, t. i. p. 189.

necessary unity and homogeneity were wanting in the counsels of sovereigns. He had in fact ceased to count as a political personage and could only enlighten Europe in his *spiritual* character as the common Father. To how great an extent the spiritual element remained in the eighteenth century, we can judge by taking a retrospective view of some of the causes which had been at work to weaken the action of the Church, and if we say the Church, we mean both the principle of authority and the guardian of all liberties in the secular and religious order.

False friends are more to be feared than open enemies. Luther, renouncing his Augustinian habit and cowl to take to himself a nun for a wife, proclaimed himself what he was—a victim to pride of intellect and sensuality. But Luther in the Church, professing himself a devout son of the Roman Pontiff, a strenuous upholder of discipline, pious and mortified, this was the phenomenon special to Jansenism, that disloyal heresy whose missiles were aimed at the centre of authority and unity under cover of apparent rigorism and austerity, and mournful cries against abuse and relaxation. The primary idea of Jansenism consisted in confounding in the first man nature and grace, reason and revelation. In consequence of this principle, there was not in Adam the supernatural end of glory, nor the supernatural end of grace, but an end and means belonging strictly to the natural order. It was a misapprehension of the Fall. It saw in Adam a fallen man henceforth incapable of using his free will in the choice of good. His salvation, therefore did not depend upon his use of grace but upon whether, as the sect expressed it, he belonged to the *number of the elect*. It is easy to discern the perniciousness of a doctrine which made the grace of God play a false part, acting in the place of man's free will, and God Himself (if we may so speak) a capricious Creator and Redeemer, Who should have predestined many of His creatures to eternal damnation, and only died for a chosen few. This was the theory of Jansenism. What were its great practical results? The honour (it cannot be called love) of an impossible God, Whom only the perfect could be allowed to approach in the Sacrament which is essentially the sacrament of love and mercy—an impossible morality connected with unapproachable sacraments. The Jansenists were constantly thanking God they were not as other men, and despising their weaker brethren who could be Christians without shedding tears of pity over the innovations of Rome; but in very truth, the most prominent character of their own sect was laxity, an incorrigible laxity, since it affected the frequenting the means of grace. Mobility of impressions is proper to error, and whatever may have been the primary scheme of the Jansenists, at least of those among them who were in good faith as to their mission of reforming relaxed morals, Fénelon, with his keen appreciation of men and things could thus signalize the venom of the doctrine which had not recognized Rome's interpretation of St. Paul's *Oportet sapere ad sobrietatem*. 'I perceive,' he wrote, 'a great number of impious men, who although despising all religion, become nevertheless enamoured of Jansenism. It is not to be wondered at. The fundamental principle of Jansenism is that *it behoves every man to seek the gratification of his greatest passion incessantly*, which passion must inevitably rule over him, determining him invincibly either to good or evil. Licentious men are delighted with a principle so flattering to the most shameful passions. They say, we can well feel that the pleasure of what is called evil is incomparably greater than the feeble pleasure of a sad, mortifying, moral system. We, then, will follow the principle of St. Augustine and his most learned disciples, giving ourselves up without shame or remorse to sensual pleasures. Is an inevitable attraction to be avoided? ... Such impious men as these favour Jansenism through animosity towards religion.'[3]

And Fénelon spoke the truth. But this was not all. In their machinations against the Church, the Jansenists did not spare the State. In a word, they prepared the downfall of both by creating a Church in the Church, an independent State in the very heart of the State. Their destiny was that of all false reformations. When the religious character of the sect had become a thing of the past, they remained a political party whose spirit manifested itself in hatred of all authority. They applied republican principles to the Church. According to them the power of excommunication belonged not to Peter's Successor, not even to the Bishops, but to the whole Church, that is, to each one of the faithful. The French Parliaments were tired of playing a subordinate part under Louis XIV. Jansenism was conveniently at hand. It could have an eye to its interests, feather its own nest, and give the magistracy just that measure of importance for which it pined, especially after being borne down by a despot of Louis XIV. calibre. Thus Jansenism, in its religious character presented to the popular mind an image of Jeremias, but Jeremias with a secret watchword which any true prophet would disown. To Church and State alike it refused obedience.

To the truly Catholic mind, the Church, with Peter for her mouthpiece, presents the embodiment of truth. All dogmas accepted save one—the infallible prerogative of the Great Chair and Centre of Truth—are as scattered members of one body. Who shall use the hand that

[3] *Lettre* 263, t. iii.

has been severed from the body, or walk with the foot that no longer forms part of a living organization? It was a wrong appreciation, or perhaps a certain jealousy of the high office of Peter, which produced Gallicanism. This, in a few words, may be said to consist in a strong tendency to nationalism in religion, to weaken the power of the Head by increasing that of the second order of the Church. Jansenism was the Republic, Gallicanism the Limited Monarchy, which error tried to set up in Christ's kingdom on earth. It is one of the glories of the Catholic Church that she bears the name of no nation; but if, by impossibility, Gallican principles could have prevailed, we might have seen a Spanish Church, an Italian Church, or a German Church, as we know there is a Russian Church and an Anglican Church. Their pet theory was the importance of the General Council, to which they could appeal against the Pope's decisions. 'Take away the queen-bee from the swarm of bees,' remarks Joseph de Maistre, 'and you may have as many bees as you wish, but you will never have a hive.'[4] This tendency to jealousy of Rome, and to suspicion of Rome's decisions, had been a production of the great schism of the West, itself a result of the papal banishment at Avignon. It had grown gradually, and developed, and now, at the close of the eighteenth century, helped on that thirst after a new order of things, that groping in the dark for which both sovereigns and subjects left the ground of positive belief. Throughout Europe the wind of revolt was blowing. The Jansenists had carried their work of destruction into Belgium, Spain, Portugal, and Italy. To those who were tired of obedience they supplied an outward religious system, a certain colouring of religion which implied little or nothing in the right direction. In Holland they made

[4] *Du Pape.*

common cause with the Huguenots and Freethinkers. Calling themselves Catholics, they flooded Europe with irreligious books, created bishops and rebellious priests for themselves, always, however, able to explain their rebellion to those who were contented to accept their elucidations. Here, one party substituting a sectary for the Supreme Pontiff, and the other putting man above God and the State before the Church, prepared the ruin of all power save that which is founded on the Rock. They counted as partisans certain ministers of kings, Manuel de Roda in Spain, Pombal in Portugal, Tanucci at Naples, and everywhere the enemies of the Society of Jesus. The fall of the Jesuits led as a matter of necessity to the teaching of youth being entrusted to the Universities; hence the predominance of the secular element in Central Europe. Gallicanism was not more Catholic than the times. In the midst of the Revolution in 1795, the title of a book published at Frankfort gives us the measure of its capabilities: 'Le système gallican atteint et convaincu d'avoir été la première et la principale cause de la révolution qui vient de décatholiciser et de dissoudre la monarchie très chrétienne, et d'être aujourd'hui le plus grand obstacle à la contre-révolution en faveur de cette monarchie.'[5]

But the Revolution, always inconsistent, sought a sovereign whom it might lead, and at the same time might dupe into believing that he was not being led. Joseph II. of Hapsburg-Lorraine, was the victim of his own reforms, and the sad glory which lives after him is only that of having given his name to a system of State-encroachment. A modern German writer of thought[6] says that all the struggle of latter times has been to put

---

[5] Quoted by M. Crétineau-Joly, *L'Eglise Romaine en face de la Révolution*, t. i. p. 61.
[6] Möhler, *Kirchengeschichte*, t. iii. p. 305.

the State, and only the State, into the place left vacant by the Pope. For this purpose, Joseph II. was all that philosophy in its alliance with revolt could desire. Whilst he declared Catholicism to be the religion of the State, it was, in fact, the only religion which he did *not* tolerate. Liberty of conscience was the never-ceasing cry of this blinded sovereign, and reform his all-engrossing passion. He was a man of extremes. But still it is hard to imagine that he could have effected what he did, had not the situation been, as it were, prepared. He found cooperators amongst the clergy and the magistracy; he had at his side the infidel Kaunitz, whose all but sovereign power was not powerful enough to bear the mention of death. Josephism was a struggle to combine Catholicism with Gallican principles, an attempt on the part of the sovereign to unite in his own person the spiritual and the temporal power; for it was the great aim of Joseph II. to cut off all appeal to Rome, and to exercise supremacy in the wide arena comprised between the nomination of bishops down to that of the precise number of candles required for Benediction. This was the man ironically called by Frederick of Prussia, '*mon frère le Sacristain!*' The great battery of Joseph's persecution was directed against the Catholic education of youth, the rights of bishops, religious orders, while he struck at Christian marriage by sanctioning divorce. After publishing in 1781 an edict of universal tolerance, he soon made it felt that the Pope alone was excluded. The primary idea of his system of education was materialism and religious indifference. The Society of Jesus had been temporarily swept away, and could no longer supply the rising generation with masters versed alike in secular and ecclesiastical lore. Their places were filled by Jansenists, whose whole religious code was hatred of Rome and so-called liberalism. A general seminary was established in every great centre of the Empire, at Vienna, Prague, Olmutz, Inspruck, Pavia, Louvain, and Pesth. Theology was to be learned there, and there only, and no bishop could ordain a man who had not passed five years in one of these seminaries. Persecution, then as now, disclaimed with a magnanimous untruthfulness any notion of prejudicing Catholic doctrine at the precise time it was waging war against the very heart of the Church. It would have imposed the third century upon the eighteenth, making no account of the development of history, and forgetting that, if certain outward forms have been changed in ecclesiastical discipline, they rather tend to prove the vitality of the Body which can alter external points without touching its essence and the core of its doctrine.

Jansenist and Gallican principles had penetrated into Germany and familiarized the notion of national religious independence. There were prelates such as Maximilian, Archduke of Austria, and the Archbishops of Mayence, Cologne, Salzburg, and Treves, quite prepared to become popes in their own dioceses, and to dispense entirely with the Apostolic See. In the name of universal tolerance Joseph confiscated the revenues of religious houses, made the reception of novices in orders of both sexes an illegal proceeding, forbade his bishops to have any intercourse with Rome, and opposed two obnoxious Papal Bulls—*Unigenitus* and *In Cœna Domini*—with a warrant of arrestation. Josephism tended to make every priest a kind of machine at the mercy of the State, the bishops rulers subordinate only to Cæsar, and the Pope a mere bishop who should exercise his episcopal faculties within the limits of the Roman Campagna. By tolerating other religions, that is to say, renouncing that claim to authority which is so essential to Catholicity, it prepared generations of freethinkers and of philosophers,

with, at best, a dreary materialism for creed, and a
secret society for church. But it prepared more. The
arms which Joseph II. had used against the Church
were to turn against himself, and he lived to accuse
Belgium of his premature death. Catholic Belgium, then
a part of his hereditary States, broke out in insurrection
on the suppression of the University of Louvain, and
on the appointment of a Jansenist, Stoegger, as director
of theology at the new general seminary. In defence
of the Belgians it may be said, that they had as much
right to refuse obedience to Joseph II. as he had to
oppress the religious faith of their consciences. There
was only one Voice on earth disinterested enough to
make itself heard in defence of a fallen cause, and
against its teaching and claims he had directed the
efforts of his power and intelligence as a man and as
a sovereign. Joseph II. knew with whom he had to
deal; he felt that an appeal to Rome would not be vain,
and Pius VI. did not fail him. A letter of the Pontiff
to the Belgian bishops, dated January 23, 1790, remains
to prove how the last request of an ungrateful son
was answered. 'We make haste,' Pius says, 'to offer
our mediation to dissipate this fatal division. We owe
it to our love for our dear son Joseph, Emperor Elect
of the Romans and your sovereign, who himself,
animated with the spirit of concord, desires this step
on our part; we owe it to our affection for the illustrious
States and to the people of these provinces, who have
always deserved well of the Catholic religion, and have
always been considered the most dear children of the
Holy See.'[6] 'Be not afraid of them who kill the body,
and after that have no more that they can do.'[7] The
reign of Pius VI. was a living realization of these words.

[6] *L'Eglise Romaine en face de la Révolution*, t. i. 112.
[7] St. Luke xii. 4.

As a mere temporal sovereign, in the actual state of Europe, he had full grounds for fearing the worst, but not so as the Successor of Peter, for the cause of One greater than he was at stake, and God would defend His own. In other times particular dogmas had been attacked, and Peter, guardian of the true doctrine, had refuted them all. But now it was the reign of a false philosophy, which aimed at dethroning not merely the Vicar of Christ, but Christ Himself. The Revolution of 1789, which has been called the French Revolution, but which was in fact an universal revolution, began its operations on the ideas, the customs, laws, and government of nations before it took to itself flesh and blood by outward acts. Every obstacle was swept up and hurried away by the raging torrent which came in the name of liberty, to leave behind it a vast and dreary doubt as the world's coming state. In certain countries, liberty meant nothing else but a capability of rendering obedience, perhaps even to a despot. A middle course seemed an impossibility; it was a choice of two evils—despotism and democracy. This secret became palpable every time the multitude of the people in France rose up to give, if it were possible, the lie to their own history. In 1789 the Assembly began its work of destruction by oppressing the Church in the name of tolerance. Tithes and monastic vows were suppressed; sacred vessels belonging to the service of the altar were confiscated, and the Nation was declared to inherit the goods of the clergy. 'Let the Church return to her primitive state of evangelical poverty;' this was the cry uttered by men who believed neither in the Apostles nor in the Church, and whose hands were soon to be steeped in the blood of their fellow men. And their good faith was trusted, or rather, a people half mad before the vision of an impossible dream broke the bonds which an all-seeing Providence had made. It was as if the sea, forgetful of the divine commands, was to carry with its waters desolation far and wide on the dry land. The clergy, moreover, was civilly constituted; indeed, this constitution was the special feat of the Revolution. In virtue of it bishops were henceforth to be elected by the people, hence what need of the Pope? Every priest was to swear fidelity to this priceless constitution—which made Rome a dead letter—or else be prepared to face death or exile. It was introducing Presbyterianism into the Catholic Monarchy. By its fruits we are able to form some idea of the origin of a thing or state of things. If then we view France some few years after the Reign of Terror had been proclaimed, and the hypocritical efforts of certain party leaders to 'bring back the Church to her primitive state' had more or less succeeded, what do we find? A guillotine in good working order set up in every possible place, mowing away human life as if it were grass, accustoming the people to see and delight in blood. God was treated as an outlaw; the places once made sacred by His presence were dedicated to Reason, Commerce, or Hymen; it was almost a crime to pronounce His Name. We find that the lust of the flesh was a secret reason behind many an oath of fidelity to the constitution, and that apostate priests did not scruple to seek a blasphemous sanction to their marriage by causing it to be celebrated in their parish church transformed into a temple of Reason. But the French Republic, 'one and indivisible,' passing through the different phases of the directory and the consulate, was ill content to rule at home. Bonaparte, its most brilliant son, was beginning to display his military genius, and Europe, viewing his exploits, asked itself where and when were to be drawn the limits of the glory of France. What kingdom should be sacrificed next? Was this a logical putting into practice of the immortal watchword—liberty, equality, and fraternity? The chambermaid who becomes suddenly a lady makes an insolent mistress! But Bonaparte eluded the order to march upon Rome. A certain religious feeling prompted him to write these words to Cardinal Mattei—'Save the Pope from the greatest of evils; be persuaded that I need only the will in order to destroy his power.'[8] The Treaty of Tolentino was the expedient resorted to by Bonaparte to conciliate two difficult questions—the orders of the French Republic and the respect of Catholics, the respect almost in spite of himself which he entertained for the Principle and the Person represented by that *materially* powerless old man at Rome.

Forced to submit to the violation and confiscation of his territory by France, Pius VI. signed, in February, 1797, a treaty with the French Republic to the following effect. He revoked all treaties contrary to the French alliance, acknowledged the Republic, and himself to be at peace and on a peaceful footing with it. He ceded to it all his rights to the Comtat Venaissin, abandoned to the Cispadane Republic the legations of Bologna and Ferrara and the province of Romagna. The city and important fortress of Ancona remained in the power of France till the general peace. The two provinces of the duchy of Urbino and Macerata, invaded by a French army, were restored to the Pope on payment of fifteen million francs. The same sum was to be paid according to the armistice of Bologna, still unexecuted. The thirty millions were payable, two-thirds in money and one-third in diamonds or other precious stones. The Pope was called upon besides to provide eight hundred cavalry horses and eight hundred draught horses, buffaloes, and other productions of Church territory. He was to

[8] *L'Eglise Romaine en face de la Révolution*, t. i. p. 203.

disclaim the assassination of Basseville, and cause three hundred thousand francs to be paid to the heirs of the victim and to those who had suffered from the event. All works of art and manuscripts ceded to France by the armistice of Bologna were to be immediately transferred to Paris.[9]

Still more ignominy was reserved for Pius VI. The assassination in a popular riot of Duphot, a hot-headed republican, who encouraged the Romans to revolt against the Papal Government, was the signal for the French invasion and occupation of the Eternal City under General Berthier, in February, 1798. The reign of the Popes was declared to be at an end; it was to yield to the Roman Republic which was inaugurated by the most complete violation of the law of nations. Pius VI. might well have trembled at the burden of the persecuted Church which weighed on his feeble shoulders. But in that hour of exceeding darkness, when his very garments were portioned out and distributed in his presence, and the Sacred College with himself were condemned to exile, he was strong with the immortal power of suffering in a just and noble cause—the greatest of all causes. The words of St. Paul were in his heart, 'I can do all things in Him Who strengtheneth me;' and as a testament he left the people of Rome that outspoken conviction which every age has confirmed, a generous protest in the face of material power, addressed to the Revolution. 'Destroy if you will the dwellings of the living, the tombs of the dead; the Catholic Faith is eternal. This Faith, which existed before you, will live after you, and its reign shall last until the end of all time.'[10] At Valence, the inexorable Directory grudged waiting for the hand of death. Doctors declared that Pius VI. had

---

[9] Thiers, *Histoire de la Révolution*, t. iv. p. 76.
[10] *L'Eglise Romaine en face de la Révolution*, t. i. p. 213.

but a few days to live, and there indeed, on the 29th August, 1799, expired the Successor of Peter, whose sole arms had been prayer, and whose sole sufferings had been those of the Church. Valence did not bury a fallen cause. Out of that tomb, and in virtue of the tomb raised in exile, came forth strength and power for future generations of pontiffs. The Revolution indeed said — 'There is no more Pope; let us rejoice and be glad, for he who alone could have opposed our course has descended into an ignominious grave.' But in the things of God humiliation generates strength, and sorrow joy. A long vacancy, it is true, followed the death of Pius VI. At that time the natural order seemed inverted, and it was chiefly the victorious arms of heretical and infidel nations that opened the doors of the Conclave —Russia, England, and Turkey in conjunction with Austria. The Roman prelate Consalvi, who had received his spoken will from the almost dying lips of Pius VI. at Florence, was naturally designated as secretary to the assembly which met so entirely without any preconcerted arrangements.

The Conclave, composed of thirty-five Cardinals out of the whole number living—forty-six—opened in the Benedictine monastery of the little island of St. George at Venice, on the 30th November, 1799, at the expense of the German Emperor. For a long time the votes were divided between Cardinals Bellisoni and Mattei. Bellisoni was opposed by Austria, whose chief aim was to secure a Pope willing to consent to its continued possession of the three legations. But all such interested foresight, which represented rather the tendencies of the German Cabinet than the personal sentiments of the Emperor, was baffled in the ultimate result of the Conclave. On the 14th March, 1800, the new Pontiff was proclaimed to the world; he who was to be prepared not for the delights of sovereignty but for suffering, that mysterious suffering which is the inheritance of the great Cause. Barnaba Chiaramonti, Cardinal-Bishop of Imola, who took the name of Pius on his accession, out of gratitude to the memory of Pius VI., was born at Cesena in 1742, of an illustrious family. His mother was a Ghini, a woman of remarkable sanctity. She became a Carmelite at Fano in 1763, where her memory is still cherished, and it was there that she foretold his election to Pius VII. and the suffering he would have to undergo. It seems that only the opposition of the son, who dreaded nepotism, prevented the beatification of the mother. At the age of sixteen, Barnaba Chiaramonti entered the Benedictine Monastery of Sta. Maria del Monte, near Cesena, as a novice, and took the name of Gregory. It would certainly appear that in the case of this youthful son of St. Benedict, 'future events cast their shadow before.' Anxious on the accession of Clement XIV. to witness the benediction given from the *loggia*, he leapt up behind an empty carriage. The coachman turning round, far from resenting this intrusion, said good-naturedly, 'My dear little monk, why are you so anxious to see a function which one day will fall to your lot?'[11] When Pius VI. became Pope, Dom Chiaramonti held the office of Professor of Theology in the Benedictine Convent of St. Calisto. As a kind of compensation to him for some shabby treatment from his fellow-monks, Gregorio received the title of *abbate*, which signified that he had a right to certain privileges, such as the ring and mitre and other honourable distinctions, but conferred no power of jurisdiction. From *abbate*, the future Pope rose to the dignity of bishop, and finally to that of Cardinal in 1785. He governed successively the dioceses of Tivoli and Imola. It was

---

[11] Wiseman, *Recollections of the Four Last Popes.*

at Imola, in 1798, in the midst of the trouble and alarm caused by the French invasion of Rome and the Papal States, that the Cardinal Bishop published a homily which men recalled to mind at the moment of his election to the See of Peter. The object of this homily was possibly to prevent a popular insurrection in favour of Pius VI., whose cause would rather have suffered than have benefited by such a step. That certain sentiments somewhat savoured of an excessive pandering to the unlawful but overwhelming power of the French Republic cannot be denied, but do not subsequent events give us full reason to suppose that any such excess of language was rather the work of the counsellors of the Cardinal than a spontaneous production of his own pen? The style of the homily also naturally leads to this conclusion.

The coronation of the Pope is the manifestation and consecration of his temporal power. It took place, contrary to all expectation, in the church of the Monastery of St. George, and not in St. Mark's, the faithful Venetians generously incurring all the expenses attendant upon such an occasion. The conduct and policy of Austria became palpable after the event; and let us remember that we must attribute to the powerful traditions of Josephism the ignoble treatment which Austria inflicted on the Holy Father, upon the new Pontiff who had been sent to build up ruins, and to restore a cause that men had thought to bury at Valence with Pius VI. Before the result of the Conclave had become known, fear and hope lurked in the German Cabinet. It had left no means untried to secure the election of a Pope willing to further its views upon the three legations (Romagna, Bologna, and Ferrara), and the States in Lombardy ceded by the French Republic. Now that the Conclave had been ruled by a higher power, and had freely chosen as Pope Cardinal Chiaramonti, Austria would at least abstain from compromising itself by sanctioning publicly the Temporal Power. Bonaparte's arms were achieving fresh victories every day. Who could say what changes of territory at the expense of the Pope might be the result. This being far from an improbable hypothesis, it was absolutely necessary to give no official recognition of the new Pope as a temporal sovereign. At the time that Austria was acting this selfish part, the troops of the King of Naples occupied Rome, the administration was carried on in the name of Ferdinand, and re-modelled after that of Naples. Ignorant of none of the designs of Austria upon the Eternal City, the Neapolitans were only 'guarding Rome for its true sovereign,' a protestation which did not number many dupes. In the face of present difficulties, Austria resorted to compromises. The Cardinal Bishop of Imola had been no politician; for many years he had lived as a simple, humble monk of St. Benedict. But Cæsar had yet to learn that obedience is the best school for future sovereigns. A pressing invitation to go to Vienna was sent to Pius VII., together with a demand that he would choose a certain Cardinal Flangini, who being a Venetian was a subject of his Imperial Majesty, as his Secretary of State. In vain Cardinal Herzan, who had appeared in the Conclave as the envoy of Austria, urged upon Pius VII. the importance of this journey and the good that might follow for the Church. The Pontiff refused with that gentle firmness which formed the principal trait in his character and furnished him with a peculiar charm and an irresistible force. Time pressed, and he must return to his flock and to his people. Every Pope has in his heart this instinct; Rome is his true home, his true home now as it was in the days of the exile of Avignon, when the Romans longed for his face among them, and when the great Catholic

Father was for seventy years in danger of becoming, as it were, a mere nominal sovereign, with an authority hampered or even controlled by that of his keeper, the King of France. As to a Secretary of State, the demand was a strange one, since, as Pius remarked, he owned no State. But to elude taking a creature of the Emperor's, he continued to employ as pro-Secretary the Secretary of the Conclave, Hercules Consalvi, who is to play so great a part in this Pontificate. Only at Rome, free from all undue influence, would the Pope nominate his principal officers. Austria could gain nothing.

As a last resource, Vienna bethought itself of an extraordinary ambassador, one who should come fresh from de Thugut, a Minister carrying on in some measure at the Austrian Court the ideas and the work of Kaunitz. The Marquis Ghislieri was the chosen man. He communicated his orders to Consalvi, as pro-Secretary of State. His Imperial Majesty would magnanimously concede to the Pope the territory in Lombardy recently won by his arms, but he would keep the three legations. He moreover demanded that the Pope should accede to the spoliation of his territory. Consalvi, although he guessed instinctively the intentions of Austria, was astonished beyond measure at the shamefaced way in which they were specified. He answered that he would act conformably to the orders of His Holiness, though persuaded that Pius VII. would never consent to such a transaction.[12] Surely enough, the answer was as negative as Consalvi had expected. Then it was that Ghislieri somewhat relented. The Emperor, his master, would only keep two legations and would cede the third, that of Romagna, to the Pope. This was positively the final word of Austria, and Ghislieri, not content with his high-flown

[12] D'Haussonville, *L'Eglise Romaine et le Premier Empire*, t. i. pp. 39, 40.

conditions, passed to threats. Pius took no account of them, but caused an official letter to be written from the pro-Secretary to Baron de Thugut, and penned himself two letters, one to the Emperor the other to his Minister, in which he claimed his rights to the invaded provinces. Neither ever received an answer, for what reason is not clearly known. Consalvi supposes that Thugut intercepted the papal letter, and that he made all applications to the Emperor in this question an impossibility. However this may be, it seems pretty certain that the spoliation of the Pope was to be attributed rather to the manœuvres of the minister than the will of the master.[13] The Pope continued to demand justice from Ghislieri, and one day, wearied with the Ambassador's solicitations, he made this prophetic speech: 'Since the Emperor obstinately refused a restitution which both religion and justice required, he (Pius) knew not what more he could allege to convince him, having exhausted the most pressing arguments; nevertheless, let his Majesty look to himself, and be careful not to place in his wardrobe clothes not belonging to him but to the Church, for so far from enjoying them, they were capable of communicating rust to his own clothes, that is, to his hereditary States.' Ghislieri could hardly contain his anger, but he vented his feelings to Consalvi. 'The new Pontiff is young in the trade; he proves that he knows nothing of the power of Austria. Very great events would be requisite before the hereditary States could be touched.' These *very great events* were nearer than could have been supposed. It was then the end of May, and on the 14th of June the battle of Marengo was fought, which decided the fate of Italy, and we may add, of Austria.

In the meantime Pius VII. expressed his wish and

---

[13] See *Mémoires de Consalvi*, t. i. p. 282.

determination to return to Rome. Austria felt what danger would result if this desire were carried into effect. The Pope would have to traverse two at least of the three legations, following the natural overland route, but they were disputed territory, or rather the Catholic feelings of the population were apprehended, and yet, how forbid such demonstrations towards the Successor of Peter? There was only one course open to Austria, and Austria did not scruple to follow it. The Vicar of Christ was to be embarked in a wretched frigate called the *Bellona*, wanting in all the ordinary conveniences of life, with a crew too few to manage a vessel even if they had not been besides unskilful, and to disembark at Pesaro, a place with no port, but possessing the merit of not being situated in the legations. Here with four Cardinals, Consalvi, and a few other prelates, Pius VII. passed twelve days instead of twenty-four hours in very close quarters with Ghislieri, who by way of doing the honours of the *Bellona*, was in reality his gaoler. At Ancona news of the Battle of Marengo, with its tremendous consequences for Austria, startled them both. Indeed the 'rust' had lost no time in doing the work assigned to it by the Holy Father. In one day Austria was doomed to lose, not only the stolen goods, but even part of its hereditary States, by the cession to France of Piedmont, Liguria, Lombardy, and the country as far as the Adige. Under these circumstances, Ghislieri could no longer have any objection to the lawful restitution of the papal territory, and at Foligno he notified his forced agreement to the Holy Father. Naples, by interested policy, was moving in the same direction. All things considered, the Pope was a pleasanter neighbour than Austria, whose close vicinity might become dangerous. Until the Peace of Florence, concluded some months after the return to

Rome of Pius VII., Neapolitan troops continued to occupy Rome and Terracina. The Sovereign Pontiff entered Rome on the 3rd of July, 1800, in the midst of universal joy, and his first act in his own city was to visit the shrine of the holy Apostles. Nominally, he was a temporal sovereign; the rising star of France had taken away from Austria the power ill-used in the cause of the Church, and as a more striking humiliation, the power had gone whilst the will to harm remained. Naples, with a keen eye to its own interests, had preferred the neighbourhood of the Pope as a lesser evil. Such being the ungracious attitude of two great Catholic Powers, we can almost foretell the trials and struggles of Pius VII. in the cause of his temporal sovereignty. Crowned heads and princes demurred to recognize the great axiom which is its basis, that the entire independence of the Holy Father is only to be attained by the possession of a territory 'large enough for liberty, too small for domination!'[14]

[14] Lacordaire, 4ème Conférence de N.D. de Paris, t. i.

CHAPTER II.

The Sovereign and the Minister.

'Est autem amicitia nihil aliud nisi omnium divinarum humanarumque rerum cum benevolentia et caritate summa consensio.'—Cic. *De Amicitia.*

Now that Pius VII. had returned to Rome, his natural home, the first part of the work before him was to consolidate his government by the choice of an able Minister. None appeared to unite greater qualifications for the post of Secretary of State than Hercules Consalvi, the Secretary of the Conclave, who had had a great share in the election of Pius. This prelate, hitherto, to use his own expression, only a 'pro,' was confirmed in his appointment on the return of the Pope to Rome, and created a Cardinal Deacon. The very fact of his being a 'pro' at all had been a middle course adopted by Pius VII. to avoid, in a matter of extreme importance, obeying the imperious dictates of Austria. Many things might be said of Consalvi, and it would be hard to speak too favourably of one who in times so perilous and critical was so completely the man of the situation. Indeed, to comprehend Pius VII. fully, we must also study his Secretary of State, for the sympathy which existed between the Pope and his Minister constituted one of those very rare friendships that traverse the vicissitudes of time entirely uninfluenced by external causes of temporary discord or misunderstanding. They had, as a German proverb says, 'one soul in two bodies.'

What had brought them so closely together? Perhaps the echo which one generous soul finds in another; the love of a great cause and devotion to it; but more than this—the one completed the other. In a word, Pius retained of his primitive vocation a certain tendency to disbelieve in the proverbial degeneracy of the human race. He would have liked to think men better than they are. Consalvi, on the contrary, was a man of the world, that is, not that he had the sentiments or the standard of a worldling, but that he possessed a very considerable knowledge of men and of things. A few words as to the antecedents of the 'great Cardinal' will not be out of place in this history. He was born in 1757. Brunacci, not Consalvi, had been the name of his family, and this was not unimportant at a time when to own a pedigree was still a title to consideration, for the Consalvis, though enjoying a certain position, did not belong to the Roman nobility. His grandfather, a Brunacci, had changed his name on inheriting the fortune of a Consalvi, to whom he was related. Cardinal Consalvi was above disputing with the world on the subject of his family; he never cared to set right the erroneous popular opinion that he came of new blood. Educated at Frascati, he turned his thoughts to the prelature and made it his career, without however taking Orders. He occupied several posts in the household of Pius VI., until in 1792 he became Auditor of the Rota. This last appointment led on of itself in due time to the Cardinalate. Pius VI., who had laughingly promised Consalvi that he should be employed rather in diplomacy than in material administration,[1] could not, in the face of the Revolution, act up to his assurance. The Auditor of the Rota suddenly became Minister of War at the disastrous period of the French

[1] 'Al tavolino e non in bottega.'

invasion of Rome, and as such unfortunately implicated in the affair of the assassination of Duphot, or rather was punished for an event in which he had had no part by a temporary imprisonment in the citadel of Sant' Angelo. Transferred from place to place by the jealousy of the French Government, who probably suspected his genuinely Roman and anti-republican sentiments, Consalvi's one desire was to soothe the anxious moments of the Holy Father his Sovereign, then a prisoner at the Chartreuse at Florence. He did indeed, as we have said, contrive to see Pius VI. and obtain his instructions for the Sacred College, which, with his last blessing, constituted all the testamentary riches of the Pontiff. Truly, Consalvi seems to have gloried in honouring fallen causes with a disinterestedness as noble as it is rare. The last of the Stuarts, the Cardinal of York, acted as his patron, but only on one condition would Consalvi become his executor, that all clauses in the will tending to his personal advantage should be effaced. In his memoirs he particularly insists on his conduct in refusing gifts. A ring, he says, presented by a friend is all that he would consent to receive.[2] But the man so jealous of his reputation, so averse to currying favour for himself, possessed a magic charm of attraction which few could withstand, and employed it, be it said to his glory, in the service of the Catholic Church. With him this charm of his personal presence was not only a great quality, but a power, allied as it was to true independence and nobility of character. He has been called the 'Roman siren,' and his capability of creeping into the caskets and strong boxes of human hearts likened to a sweet perfume. Such attributes were peculiarly advantageous to the Minister whose chief duty at that period seemed to be to throw oil on the troubled waters.

[2] *Mémoires*, t. ii. p. 112.

The first few months of Consalvi's administration were, as he tells us himself, full of anxieties, arising from the reformatory measures which he set on foot. Two departments claimed his especial attention, and one, free trade, which he introduced into the Papal States, provoked the enmity of Cardinal Braschi, nephew of Pius VI. and a loser by the new system. It was, however, a necessity, due to justice and economy. The papal treasury was exhausted with contributions levied upon it, the loss of provinces, and the abolition of paper money (*cedole*), while the common and pressing actual needs absorbed the small State revenue. All these causes prevented the sale of provisions under cost price. But free trade would put an end to certain privileges, prerogatives, rights, and also abuses. The Cardinal Camerlingo, Braschi, who presided over the old system and superintended the transmission of licences for purchase of grain, for exportation, and even for circulation in the State, did not submit with a very good grace to the new order, but finally Consalvi by his conciliatory and gentle demeanour won back the affection of one so nearly allied to Pius VI., and whose enmity consequently could not fail to be particularly felt. The second great administrative reform was directed to the suppression of bad money, which had become current in the Papal States. In virtue of it, six Roman scudi were only worth three in good coin. Pius VII. directed particular attention to this, and although it cost his Government fifteen hundred thousand scudi to purge trade completely of the surreptitious element, he was often known to rejoice over what had been so important a reform introduced for the welfare of his subjects.[3]

At Rome, the Sovereign and the Minister were employing their energies for the public weal, when the eyes

---

[3] Artaud de Montor, *Histoire de Pie VII.* t. i. p. 114.

of Europe were fixed upon one man, in whose policy after the Battle of Marengo a notable change was displayed. Bonaparte having conquered Austria, set himself to win public opinion by making advances to the representatives of religion. At this stage of his career his one aim was to impose his own cause on the multitude as that of the Church. Before the people of France would honour him as their sovereign, they must see in him the patron and defender of religion. Such long-sightedness was characteristic of Bonaparte, and we cannot doubt that universal empire was the object he had in view from the first, or rather, perhaps his mighty genius impelled him to say in his heart, long before he wore an imperial crown: My work is to reign. With these aspirations and tendencies, he would have supported anything that pointed to the bourn his mind contemplated in the far distance. In France, for their realization, it was necessary to befriend the Catholic Church: more than this, to reorganize its worship as a mark of the respect attached to it as a religious and national institution—the growth of fourteen centuries. All this he did—with a view to the end to be attained! His expressions of attachment to religion covered a deep policy. The great mass of the French people in the beginning of this century, spiritually famished as they had been, saw principally in Napoleon a great man who had taken away the interdict of Revolution, and lent his mighty arm to replace God on their empty altars.

Bonaparte was leading his victorious troops across the Alps in May, 1800, as Pius VII. announced his accession to all the bishops of the Universal Church. Arrived at Milan, the General, who in Egypt had flattered Mussulman vanity by speaking of Christ and Mahomet in pretty nearly the same terms,[5] ordered a *Te Deum* in thanksgiving for the deliverance of Italy from heretics and infidels. This was an allusion to the assistance lent to Austria by the subjects of the Great Turk and those of his Britannic Majesty. We find in an allocution addressed to the clergy of Milan, a sketch of the future Concordat. 'My intention,' Bonaparte says, 'is that the Christian, Catholic, and Roman religion be maintained in all its purity, practised publicly, and that it may enjoy this freedom with the same extensive, entire, and inviolable liberty as at the time of my first visit to these smiling countries. . . . France, having acquired experience through its misfortunes, has awakened to a true knowledge of the state of the case, and now sees in the Catholic religion an unfailing support, which alone possesses power to quiet internal struggles and to rescue it from the results of the storm. . . . When I am able to confer with the Pope, I shall, I hope, succeed in levelling all obstacles in the way of an entire reconciliation between France and the Head of the Church.'[6] Bonaparte craving a blessing for his victorious arms in the Ambrosian Cathedral presented a spectacle likely enough to find an echo not only in the hearts of Italians, but what was far more to his purpose, in those of the French. He sent his good deeds before him; the fame of his doings for religion in Italy crossed the Alps and prepared the way for the great Concordat. Shortly after the allocution above mentioned, the First Consul charged Cardinal Martiniani to inform Pius VII. of his wish to open preliminary negotiations for the arrangement of religious matters, and to ask that Spina, Archbishop of Corinth *in partibus*, might be sent to him as an envoy from the Court of Rome.

[5] See *Mémoires de Napoléon*, part concerning Egyptian campaign dictated to General Bertrand.
L'Eglise Romaine et le Premier Empire, t. i. pp. 65, 66.

The artificial manner of acting peculiar to Bonaparte became, according to Consalvi, evident for the first time in this circumstance. Spina, who had had orders to confer with the First Consul at Turin, suddenly received a summons to Paris. Bonaparte had already calculated the magical effect as to his own exaltation of a papal envoy soliciting an audience amongst the crowd of petitioners at the Tuileries. Spina, arming himself with the presence and assistance of a consummate theologian, Father Caselli, General of the Servites, reached Paris about the middle of July, 1800. It becomes necessary to study the surroundings, we will not say the auxiliaries, of Bonaparte, as they give us a very deep insight into his motives, and will help us to know this extraordinary man. In the first place he intended to have his own way, and to dominate as negotiator in chief over all others whose opinion he made a pretence of asking. His Minister of Foreign Affairs, M. de Talleyrand, the ex-Bishop of Autun, was frequently consulted in questions touching upon the conciliation of the new with the old régime. But in this matter de Talleyrand might have showed one of two dispositions: either great hostility to a Church which he had publicly left, or excessive servility in order to obtain a formal secularization. Bonaparte was quite shrewd enough to feel the force of this, and even the ex-Bishop half guessed it, and restricted himself quietly to the official exercise of his charge, asking no questions. But the presence of other persons was absolutely necessary for the form of the thing, however little for the substance, and Bonaparte consequently selected the best Gallicans he could find in his Council of State, Bigot de Préameneu, Portalis, and Cretet. M. Bigot especially possessed a conscience which Gallicanism had endowed with elasticity for all future dealings with the Holy See.

D

He is a very fair specimen of the powerful French magistracy of the seventeenth and eighteenth centuries, which certainly exerted its utmost ingenuity to make laws both for Church and State. To these the First Consul adjoined the Abbé Bernier, as a man representing the religious element on his side, but with flexible views, and who would consent to play a part that, to the multitude, might seem to offer an appearance of piety. The antecedents of the future Bishop of Orleans did not bear witness to an excess of loyalty. Bonaparte had made his acquaintance in Brittany before the last Italian campaign. Bernier was then a curé, with immense popular influence, and desiring nothing so much as to become a great man. The fusion of the Republican Generals with the Catholic clergy of La Vendée was the plan which offered itself to the aspiring, ambitious, and—let us say the word—intriguing Bernier, as the means of making himself important. He betrayed these motives when he said, in a letter of December, 1799—'Talk of me and get others to talk, that my name may become known.' In the eyes of the Republican Government, he was a priest belonging to the old régime by birth and education, but to the new order of things by his sympathies. However this may be, he was playing into the hands of both parties, making pretence on the one side to leave the Royalists, and on the other, seeking to ingratiate himself with the emigrant Princes by demanding of and receiving from them a mark of confidence. In 1800 he seems to have gone over entirely to Bonaparte, and to have found grace with the First Consul. Probably he pleased by his absence of refinement and unscrupulous adoration of persons rather than principles. Then he was not a superior-minded man, and this was greatly relished by a restless and ardent genius bent on ruling. It must be acknowledged, however, that if Bonaparte had really condescended to be counselled in the matter of the Concordat, Bernier was not the priest Catholic hearts would have selected.

In the meantime, poor Spina whose mission in going to Paris had been to hear and to report (*con ordine di sentire e di riferire*) found himself engaged in a very difficult matter. He complained that everything was changed in France, and especially that the notion of any one particular exterior form of religion had become almost a thing of the past. Either the First Consul presented him impossible sketches of a Concordat, totally opposed to the most fundamental principles of religion, or those issuing from the Government which Spina found less obnoxious were judged inadmissible by the Court of Rome. At this moment of wearisome uncertainty, M. Cacault, an envoy from the First Consul, without however the character or name of an ambassador, arrived in Rome to treat with the Holy See. Consalvi laconically says of him, 'that he had an admirable knowledge of customs, men, and things in the Court of Rome.' He was a frank, honest, large-minded Breton, a 'corrected republican,' and he soon won for himself the esteem and affection of Pius VII. and the Sacred College. With such a man for negotiator, Consalvi hoped Rome and Paris might soon come to an understanding, but Bonaparte intended to finish the matter by a stroke of his own policy and an abrupt conclusion which nobody had expected. He now required the acceptance of the last projected Concordat which had been judged by the Pope and the Cardinals contrary to the principles and honour of the Holy See. If it was not signed without alteration five days after this intimation, he would withdraw Cacault, and declare all negotiations to be at an end. Under these trying circumstances, the Minister of France suggested a middle course; Consalvi must start immediately for Paris and treat personally with Bonaparte. 'The Roman siren,' in his capacity of Prime Minister to Pius VII. would be irresistible. What food for the vanity of the First Consul! Cacault seized the thing at once in all its bearings. The Pope still hesitated. 'Most Holy Father,' was the significant answer, 'Consalvi must start immediately, he must be the bearer of your reply. He will negotiate in Paris with the power you give him here. I am fifty-nine years old, and have seen many things since the *Etats de Bretagne*, which were beyond a doubt the most unmanageable of *Etats*. Take my word, something stronger than cold-blooded reason, an instinct prompts me to speak, a foolish instinct if you will, but a sure one. In sending Consalvi, you appear as it were yourself. People wish for a religious Concordat. Here it is.' Pius VII.'s opposition was conquered. It had become a question of clearing himself in the eyes of the First Consul from a charge of obstinacy and personal ill-will, whereas duty alone had prompted his conduct and his constant refusal to bend to terms injurious and dishonourable to the Holy See.

Cacault's orders to leave Rome were positive, although his absence was a temporary one. As far as Florence, the two ministers travelled together. Consalvi, in some trepidation at the thought of confronting *l'homme terrible*, thus expressed his private conviction to the King of Naples. 'The good of religion demands a victim. I am going to see the First Consul. I am walking to martyrdom. The will of God be done.'[7] We shall see how far these sentiments of the great Cardinal were exaggerated.

[7] *L'Eglise Romaine et le Premier Empire*, t. i. p. 90.

CHAPTER III.

Two Cardinals: Strength and Weakness.

'Lend not to a man that is mightier than thyself: and if thou lendest, count it as lost.'—Ecclus. viii. 15.

BEFORE following the Secretary of State of Pius VII. in his arduous journey to Paris in the summer of 1801, it may be well to form a clear notion of the points about to be discussed; the motives which actuated the Holy Father; the policy of Bonaparte; the allies of Rome and of Paris. There was to be a struggle, or rather the old, old struggle was to be renewed, between the City of God on earth, materially powerless, but with an invincible moral strength, and the State represented by restless, aspiring, and encroaching Bonaparte. Napoleon found the Empire of Europe a poor thing because he could not command the souls of men. Ambition with him took the place of conscience. The notion of duty was perfectly foreign to him, and in his dealings with Rome he never could or would understand that there was a point where all concession must stop, and where he must remain purely and entirely the 'devout son of the Church.' In a few words, the Concordat may be said to have represented to the Holy Father the total extinction of schism and the deposition of the constitutional clergy. The end justified many, indeed all possible concessions, and Pius VII. was prepared to go as far as a conscientious regard for the rights of the Holy

See would let him. He banished all interested motives from a transaction of such importance; it was to treat exclusively of religious matters. To regain Catholic France great sacrifices were asked of him; he was called upon to depose the emigrant bishops who had borne the burden and the heat of the day, and perhaps in their estimation to pass for a Pontiff more anxious to ingratiate himself with the First Consul, than to reward the well-tried fidelity of sons. The Concordat, after declaring the Catholic religion to be that of the great majority of the French people, re-established the hierarchy in France on a new footing. It curtailed one hundred and thirty-five bishoprics to sixty, deposed the actual bishops, placed the nomination of bishops in the hands of the First Consul, and their confirmation in those of the Pope. It required a promise of submission from them to the established Government. The clergy was to be supported by the revenues of the State, and a renunciation demanded from the Church of all alienated possessions. This was the substance of the convention, and to carry it out fully, Consalvi needed other qualifications than those of a siren. The article contained in the very proclamation of the Concordat, namely, that concerning the public exercise of the Catholic religion, was the subject of a hot dispute. And again the whole matter of the constitutional bishops gives us great insight into the motives of acting of the First Consul. Outwardly, he appeared to have yielded the point that they should not be appointed to the new dioceses, but it was with the secret resolution to take back at whatever price it might be that which he had granted openly. To spare him the semblance of weakness attached to submission, no means were too low in the opinion of Bonaparte. During Consalvi's sojourn in Paris, he affected indifference as to the ultimate success of the

Concordat, when in point of fact it was a matter of the very greatest consequence to him, of which he was fully aware, to act as the restorer of religion in France. A contemporary writer[1] speaks with some enthusiasm of Bonaparte's scanty religious creed. Under the starry firmament in the park at La Malmaison, he who believed in no outward form of religion, professed his conviction in the existence of God. This proves one of two things. Either that M. Thiers, in the wish to see a kindred spirit in Napoleon, underrated his religious convictions with respect to positive dogma, which would seem to be the fact if Napoleon's death may be allowed to give us a key to his whole life — or else, that he found little practical importance in belief in God. But if we view Napoleon as a man who concentrated all the powers of his mind and body on one object—universal empire and the foundation of a new dynasty based on his personal glory—we shall have some notion of the part occupied by religion in his heart. No man can have two chief loves. In all cases, a great passion is only checked by a good practical Christianity, and where this does not exist, the passion soon takes the proportions of a mania, and consumes the physical and mental powers. So it was with Napoleon. He was essentially a man of one idea, and when we grasp this fully we are able to explain to ourselves wayward and capricious freaks in his dealings with Consalvi and Rome, or, which is identical, a childish irritability of temper, and a want of straightforwardness and loyalty particularly painful in a great man. With the speciality of genius looking a long way before it, he grasped the end, and for its attainment used all means indifferently.

After a fatiguing journey of fifteen days, Cardinal Consalvi arrived in Paris, and joined Spina and the

[1] M. Thiers.

theologian Caselli. The Revolution at that time still displayed its ensigns abroad, still, outwardly at least, predominated in places once made sacred by the presence of God. Catholic churches were dedicated to friendship, commerce, fraternity, or liberty, whilst the revolutionary mode of address, *citoyen*, was gratuitously bestowed upon all, even upon Consalvi himself. The Abbé Bernier, who was Bonaparte's man of business in the affair of the Concordat, hastened to visit the Cardinal, and upon the inquiry of the latter, at what hour and in what costume he should be admitted to see the First Consul, was the bearer of the reply: 'I was to go at two o'clock that very afternoon, Consalvi tells us, *le plus en Cardinal que je pourrais*.'² Having arrived on the previous night only, he was thus summoned to the Tuileries, weary and jaded, and without the necessary leisure to look about him, and accustom himself to the extraordinary situation. He reflected, however, that a Cardinal appeared before the Pope alone in full dress, and contented himself with scarlet stockings, biretta, and collar, as adequate indications of his rank. At the appointed time the master of ceremonies came to take the Cardinal to the Tuileries, and he was ushered into a room on the ground-floor called the ambassador's room, a silent nook of the palace, where he waited several minutes quite alone. There was a design in this. The bustle and turmoil of a brilliant Court were to break suddenly as a bewildering vision upon eyes unprepared for grandeur. He was directed by the master of ceremonies to open a little door leading to the great staircase of the palace, on doing which he likens his surprize to the astonishment produced at a theatre by the sudden transformation of the scene 'from a cottage, a wood, or a prison, to the most

² *Mémoires*, t. 1. p. 328.

splendid and dazzling regal pomp.'³ Through a levy of statesmen, senators, dignitaries of the household, ministers, generals, and an immense crowd of troops and idle spectators, the astonished Cardinal passed to an interview with the man who was not too great to excite by such means the wonder, perhaps the fear, of the Roman plenipotentiary. Consalvi could hardly believe that his first audience was to be a public one. He imagined, therefore, in his ignorance, that the crowd had been attracted to witness his presentation, whereas it was *jour de parade*, a formality renewed every fortnight at the Tuileries. Conducted at length by M. de Talleyrand to the culminating point of display, he innocently hoped that he was going to be alone with the First Consul. Not at all. A room filled with an immense number of people, arranged as if for effect, opened before him. There were the Senate, the Tribunate, the Legislative body, and the higher magistracy, surrounded by generals, officers of all kinds, and dignitaries of every degree, and lastly, three persons standing by themselves in a marked position—the three Consuls of the French Republic.

Bonaparte, who held the place of honour in the middle, left the Cardinal no time to speak, but began immediately in a tone 'neither affable nor the contrary:' 'I know what brings you to France. I wish the negotiations to begin at once. I give you five days, and I warn you that, if at the end of the fifth day matters are not arranged, you must return to Rome, seeing that for my own part, I have already provided against such an hypothesis.'⁴ The first point that Bonaparte wished to lay down in this speech was, that he had no need of Rome. Perceiving, however, that Consalvi was neither over-awed by the pomp purposely displayed, nor filled

³ *Mémoires* t. i. p. 329.   ⁴ *Ibid.*, t. i. p. 332.

with astonishment at the notion of five days terminating all negotiations, he was probably impressed favourably with the ability of the Cardinal, and conversed upon various topics connected with the great question of the Concordat, for more than half an hour. An abrupt nod from the First Consul brought the interview to a close, and then began the hard work for Consalvi, who at great personal sacrifices of time and the rest so much needed after a long journey set himself immediately to carry out, if possible, the imperious commands of Bonaparte, reserving his refusals for points which touched the honour of the Church. He consecrated one night's labour to a memoir justifying the Holy Father's refusal of the former scheme of Concordat submitted by the French Government, on the plea that principles at least, where so many minor sacrifices were incurred, were sacred ground. The result was not satisfactory, and M. de Talleyrand's report of the memoir only served to foster Bonaparte's notion that Consalvi bore personal ill-will to the French Government. The conferences took place at the Cardinal's hotel. Instead of five, they lasted twenty-five days, during which he worked in common with Spina and Caselli, and received a daily visit from Bernier. It was a time not only of struggle, but of intense anxiety. In the difficulties that arose, Bernier would decide nothing without having recourse to the First Consul, but when Consalvi would have wished for the same liberty on his side, he was told that a plenipotentiary was capable of acting upon his own responsibility. The orders of Pius VII. sustained his Minister through this delicate negotiation, and they explain to us the persevering efforts of Consalvi in a cause rendered so difficult by the domineering spirit of Bonaparte. In his memoirs, after relating the feeling expressed to him by the Austrian and Spanish Ministers in favour of the

Concordat, and after telling us how they pressed him to conclude it almost at any price, Consalvi says: 'Their pressure only served to confirm me in the determination which the Pope's orders imposed upon me, namely, that I should neither break off negotiations nor refuse the Concordat, because the latter is not as favourable as it might have been, but that I should not conclude it by going further than the instructions given to me.' It was beyond a doubt an exceedingly trying step for the Pope to depose the actual bishops, but in spite of the herculean labours of Consalvi (this allusion, as he says, is a play upon his name), and his remonstrances with the First Consul, nothing further could be obtained than that Pius VII. should word the Brief of Deposition. Bonaparte's reasons for the non-concession were political. The motto of the *Ancien Régime* was indeed even for bishops *le trône et l'autel*, but at the same time, as Consalvi endeavoured to point out, he was inflicting a wound on Gallican sensibility by calling upon the Pope to depose from eighty to a hundred bishops without cause or legal procedure of any kind. But other points lay just then nearer the heart of the First Consul than the Gallican Church. In the first place, he could not bear the thought of concession, and was determined to regain by stratagem what he had granted to Consalvi's immutable principles—we say principles, for only as to them had the Cardinal insisted on the right of the cause he represented. At length, on the 13th of July, the Abbé Bernier reported that the First Consul accepted all the discussed points, and was ready to ratify the Concordat. Three persons were to sign for Pius VII., Consalvi, Spina, and Caselli: and three for the French Government, the *citoyen* Joseph Bonaparte, brother of the First Consul, Bernier, and Cretet. At the suggestion of Bernier, they adjourned to Joseph's house, seeing that an ordinary hotel was no fitting place for so important a consummation. Bernier arrived at four o'clock with a roll of paper in his hand, which he said was the Concordat, but did not unfold. When the Cardinal had claimed the right of signing first, this roll of paper was produced, and Bernier seemed anxious that Consalvi should sign it at once, and without examination. A glance cast by him over the very first lines revealed the stratagem. This was not only the plan rejected by the Holy Father, but it contained moreover other points declared wholly inadmissible at Rome. 'Such a proceeding speaks for itself,' is the comment of Consalvi in his memoirs.[5] It was a last attempt on the part of Bonaparte to enforce his will. The Cardinal was painfully surprized, but he could not lend his name to such a plan. It was evident that Bernier alone had been in the secret. Joseph was innocent of all connivance, if his perfectly natural astonishment could be trusted, and Cretet affirmed that he was entirely ignorant of the fraud. With the vision of the First Consul's anger, and Consalvi's inflexibility, there was only one course open, to recommence discussions, since on the following day, 14th of July, the signing of the Concordat was to be proclaimed by Bonaparte as an accomplished fact at a patriotic dinner of more than three hundred covers. This sitting, provoked by the urgency of the circumstances, lasted from four p.m. till four the following day, that is, twenty-four consecutive hours. 'We thus passed the whole night,' Consalvi says, ' sending away neither our servants nor the carriages which had brought us, imagining that every hour would be the last.' One point, however, surpassed the plenipotential powers of Consalvi. In order not to disappoint the First Consul, he would sign all the rest, and refer that point to the Holy Father.

[5] *Mémoires*, t. i. p. 355.

In the meantime five o'clock was the hour fixed for the dinner, and Consalvi with Spina and Caselli were bound to appear. The speech which greeted the Cardinal proved the extent of the First Consul's anger. 'As soon as he saw me, he called out in a mocking tone, "So you wish to break with me, Monsieur le Cardinal. Well, be it so! I have no need of Rome! I can act by myself. I have no need of the Pope! If Henry VIII. without the twentieth part of my power, was able successfully to change the religion of his country, how much more have not *I* the same power and will. In changing the religion of France, I shall change it in all Europe, in all places where my power is felt. Rome shall feel the losses she has caused; she shall mourn over them, but it will be too late. You may go, indeed it is the best thing you can do. By your own will, you have broken off negotiations with me. Well, be it so, since you have wished it! When will you go?"

"After dinner, General," I replied in a calm tone.'[6]

The perfect self-possession of the reply cooled the anger of the First Consul. Consalvi tried to make him view the point in its true bearings; principle was at stake, therefore why urge an impossible concession, why treat honourable and conscientious resistance as obstinacy? Finally, Bonaparte showed an astonishing inconsistency by agreeing to a new discussion. The contracting parties could meet again, but the disputed article must remain as he, Bonaparte, wished and would have it remain. The Cardinal gives us a key to the question which called forth the full exertion of his ability. He strove to render the Catholic Faith, which the Concordat restored in France, as independent as possible of the secular power, and to protect the Church, if possible, from becoming

[6] *Mémoires*, t. i. pp. 365, 366.

tied hand and foot by the State. Rome had regarded the liberty and the publicity of Catholic worship as the two pivots of the Concordat, but the Government objected the susceptibility of its non-Catholic population. Such a regulation carried, would be contrary to that universal equality proclaimed by the Constitution. Consalvi was wise enough to measure the capabilities of so-called universal tolerance, remembering that Joseph II. had been a liberal religious sovereign, and had persecuted no other denomination but the Catholic Church. The proposed article ran, 'Worship shall be public, but conformable to the regulations of the police.' This was a vague phrase, under shadow of which the liberty of the Church might sustain numerous fetters: it was inadmissible in a written Concordat. Spina and Caselli were weary of resisting, and agreed to sign the article. Consalvi, preferring a total rupture to illegitimate conditions, pursued the fight alone and unaided. Once more, the discussion opened at Joseph Bonaparte's hotel, and the sitting this time lasted twelve hours, from mid-day to midnight. The article was finally settled by defining the terms of *the restriction:* the Government, seeking *merely* public order and tranquillity by its phrase, 'conformable to the regulations of the police,' consented to express clearly, that it did *not* aspire to enslave the Church to the secular power. Joseph, as the most fitting person to meet his brother's very probable wrath, proposed to carry the Concordat signed to the First Consul, whose consent might possibly be quietly obtained if he found that the step had been already taken. The great man whose *placet* was thus, as it were, to be carried by storm, greeted Joseph's information by tearing the minute of the treaty into a hundred pieces, and declaring that he could accept it at no price. But second thoughts brought reflection and prudence.

Bonaparte ended by yielding, or seeming to yield, and Joseph was able to transmit an affirmative answer to Consalvi. The popular joy at the happy termination of negotiations was very great. Bonaparte officially restored the fallen altars, and the publication of the Concordat would once more render the exercise of the Catholic Faith a legal proceeding. In one word, Almighty God was no longer an outlaw, for, however strange the phrase may sound, to render Him such had been the fruitless attempt of the Revolution. God and the Church are too nearly allied ever to be separated by triumphant infidelity.

Consalvi had accomplished the object of his mission, and was eager to return to Rome, where as Prime Minister to Pius VII. his presence could ill be spared. Before leaving Paris, he had two significant audiences with Bonaparte. To the first, a private one, he was called unexpectedly, and did not at once perceive the drift of the First Consul. Many points foreign to the Concordat were discussed, and at length, as if by accident, Bonaparte announced his embarrassment at having to choose the new bishops from the constitutional as well as the non-constitutional clergy. This was a blow to Consalvi. The principal aim of the Holy See in conceding so much had been to secure the total extinction of schism. Bonaparte's policy was stronger in his own opinion than the religious reason urged by Consalvi, that the popular Faith would be scandalized at such nominations, and that no constitutional priest could be accepted without retracting his errors. To the First Consul, who wished above all things to conciliate the body who represented a strong party, it was a matter of comparatively very small importance whether they were perfectly orthodox or not. Their feelings must be spared the humiliation of a public acknowledgment of the Holy

See's decisions as to the civil constitution. In vain Consalvi urged that it would be far better to dispense with them entirely in the new nomination. Bonaparte, after promising again and again to give them up, now manifestly intended to do nothing of the kind. The second audience was a diplomatic one at which Consalvi held the first rank, but as if wishing to prove to the public that he held in no high account a Cardinal, and the Holy See, after he had arranged his private concerns with both, Bonaparte did not once address the Envoy of Rome. Purposely, as it seemed to the Cardinal, he avoided any display of the most ordinary courtesy, and purposely too engaged in a long conversation upon indifferent topics with Cobentzel, the Austrian Ambassador, who was standing near, giving Consalvi nothing but looks.[7] A last assault on the part of Bonaparte was attempted just as Consalvi was on the point of getting into the carriage which was to take him away. Bernier appeared and announced that the First Consul wished positively to know the substance of the Bull accompanying, according to custom, the Concordat. Poor Consalvi had indeed need to be a Hercules! A Bull is not the mechanical work of a few hours, and he was not authorized to compose it, putting aside the mode in which he was called upon at all hours and seasons to propound the most weighty statements. 'The First Consul hoped to surprize me in the hurry of the last moments,' says the Cardinal in his invaluable memoirs, 'he hoped in this way to prevent the insertion of certain things that did not quite please him in the Bull.'[8] But the indefatigable Consalvi immediately set to work, and we may hope that eight consecutive hours spent on this his last labour in Paris baffled the disloyal attempt of Bonaparte. With the understanding that the Concordat

---

[7] *Mémoires*, t. i. p. 394.   [8] *Ibid.* t. i. p. 395.

would only wait for its ratification from Rome, Consalvi used the greatest speed on his journey, stopping but three times on the way, at Lyons, Milan, and Parma. The Pope welcomed back his Minister with the greatest tenderness, and the Cardinals met immediately in Consistory to discuss the Concordat. Two points alone raised some difficulties: that which concerned the publicity of worship, and the article regarding the promise given by the Church not to reclaim alienated possessions. The Holy Father, having listened in silence to the expressed opinions of the Sacred College, spoke last to the effect, that although the liberty of the Church was not respected as much as he could wish, still under the circumstances, no more could be obtained by expostulations, therefore he ratified what had been done. The Court of Rome, so cautious and so prudent, was expeditious in this instance, for thirty-five days after the signing of the Concordat the official approbation of the Holy See arrived by an extraordinary courier in Paris.[9]

After the signing of the Concordat in Paris, and before its publication, Bonaparte particularly requested the presence of a legate, who should in fact lend himself to the modification of some of the terms imposed by Consalvi, and judged too exacting by the First Consul and his shadow, the Abbé Bernier. He singled out Cardinal Caprara by name, showing a choice which proved him to be as usual, a keen observer of men. Pius VII., who had made it his rule of conduct to bend to Bonaparte's will in all things lawful, yielded in this matter, though not without foreseeing that his own cause might suffer by the concession. Caprara had been Papal Nuncio at Vienna under Joseph II. and Kaunitz, a position wherein he had managed to remain on good terms with the Emperor and his Minister, and

[9] *Mémoires*, t. i. p. 402.

had excited by that very fact the suspicions of Rome. His opinions had, however, always remained perfectly orthodox, although his line with secular power had been one of weak concession and compromises. Not always possessing the courage of his convictions, he has described himself admirably in these few words: 'Seeing the man with whom we have to deal (Bonaparte) and his universally acknowledged power, we must at all costs keep on our legs, for once fallen, there will be no resurrection.' This being his axiom, Consalvi says in his Memoirs, that Caprara sanctioned many things that Rome would have wished him never to sanction. With good intentions, he often acted without consulting the Pope, and sometimes, imagining that he was doing the right thing, against the orders he had received from Rome. That which he thus effected could not be undone, and the Holy Father's remonstrances were of no avail. More than once we were determined to recall him, a decision upon which we could never act.[10] Caprara was evidently far from being the right man in the right place. He was from the beginning entwined in the nets of the First Consul, charmed and awed at the same time. Without the perspicacity of Consalvi, he looked upon the warmth of manner displayed by Bonaparte in a first interview as a personal compliment, whereas it was an artful attempt to place him under an obligation, and to make him accede to the nomination of the constitutional bishops. Pius VII. had placed before the Legate when he left Rome two primary objects which he was to have in view: one, the nearest and dearest to the heart of the Holy Father, regarded this very point: Caprara was to throw all the weight of his authority against the constitutional bishops. In the second place, he was to negotiate for the restoration of

[10] *Mémoires de Consalvi*, t. i. p. 405.

the three legations. Bonaparte had his own views upon the subject; but until the favourable moment arrived when he might declare his will with authority, it suited him to follow a middle course. He would flatter the hopes of the Holy Father, neither granting nor refusing what he asked. Caprara's entry into Paris is a revelation in itself of Bonaparte's tactics. It was effected by night in a sort of incognito, which was an expedient of the First Consul's to prevent any noisy demonstrations. The First Consul was in fact a greater moral coward than he liked to admit.

Caprara arrived in Paris on the 4th October, 1801. With the Cardinal Legate, as with Consalvi, there were the same stormy interviews at unwonted times, the same almost compulsory measures taken for the enforcement of that iron will which had so soon and easily learned to carry all before its commands. The stereotyped phrase: 'If you refuse me such a thing, I will do without your consent, and break with Rome,' filled with terror the Legate who above all things wished, as he said, 'to keep on his legs.' At his side, there were not wanting those who prophesied a kind of universal schism if he should really come to a rupture with Bonaparte, so that to his somewhat feeble mind the choice may have often seemed to lie between two evils of which he could but take the lesser. In a word, it may often happen that the situation is more vicious than the individual.

Caprara's official correspondence to Consalvi may be summed up in a few words. As he was a spirit of an inferior order to the First Consul, Bonaparte lorded it over him, awing and charming him at the same time, using the natural power of genius to elicit unlawful concessions. When the Legate would have urged principle, he was not believed. Indeed, as has been said before, Bonaparte had no notion of a moral obstacle when he commanded a thing. Those who had, were, in his eyes, either obstinate or acting from personal ill-will towards himself. In the petty war carried on against an unfortunately weak Papal Legate, Portalis, Counsellor of State, and Bernier, the intriguing abbé, played an important part. Portalis was a conscientious Catholic in many respects, but Gallicanism had given him a religious twist, that is, a tendency to see in the power of the State something more than its proper temporal authority. Early education and prejudices were perhaps to blame that his mind did not embrace the Catholic notion of the prerogatives of the Holy See in all their plenitude. Caprara wrote to Consalvi on the 13th of March, 1802, that not a single constitutional priest was on the list for nomination. A few days later, he began to entertain doubts on the subject, for the First Consul required a formal declaration from him as to whether or not the constitutional clergy could be nominated. At this stage of the question, the Peace of Amiens was signed, and Bonaparte determined that the Legate's scruples should not long stand in the way of the public *Te Deum* at Notre Dame, which, thus connected with great national events, would more surely find an echo in all hearts. A single interview between Caprara, Portalis, and Bernier, will give some idea of the violent mode of acting peculiar to Bonaparte. At five o'clock one afternoon the Counsellor of State and the *ci-devant* Vendean curé waited upon the Legate. Portalis opened the conversation by declaring that at the approaching *Te Deum* the First Consul would make use of both constitutional and non-constitutional clergy. The Cardinal remonstrated vehemently against the notion. But a negative answer to this imperative intimation, represented Portalis, would undo all the good accomplished, and serve to prolong the schism. Caprara thought that non-compliance with an impossible order ought to produce no such effect. 'Ah!' exclaimed the Counsellor of State, 'you don't know him (Bonaparte), or you pretend not to know him. He wishes the clergy to gather together in great numbers at the *Te Deum*, in order to render the ceremony as impressive as possible.' Portalis had orders to arrange matters speedily, as the answer was required before seven o'clock! The Legate replied with firmness, 'that if he could once obtain the conviction that the rights of principle would be respected, he would willingly listen to reasonable propositions; but that nobody could wish to exact of him that which was contrary to his conscience, and in direct opposition to his duty.' So far, so good. But now it was Bernier's turn to step forward. He had foreseen the Cardinal's resistance, and, to shorten matters, had concerted a fitting answer to the First Consul, with Portalis. Saying this, he drew a paper from his pocket, containing 'nothing that could in any way wound either the Legate's feelings or his duty.' This memorandum propounded in substance five propositions which Caprara had already refused to sign when they had been submitted to him on a former occasion by the Counsellor of State. Now he was somewhat wearied with the struggle (a disposition of mind which had been adroitly foreseen, and devoutly hoped for), and his unfortunate view that he must gain all or lose all, impelled him to reply to Bernier, 'You have had time to examine the memorandum. If, therefore, you can give me your conscientious word that it contains nothing contrary to our maxims and principles, I see no reason why I should not sign it, and return it to you signed, with the simple intention of avoiding a greater evil which you both say is so imminent and so fatal.' Thus Caprara appended his signature to the deed which Bonaparte needed as a preliminary to the nomination of the constitutional clergy, who now possessed an official attestation that Rome did not deny their fitness for the episcopal dignity.[11] Very superficial knowledge must Caprara have had of the First Consul, if he imagined that he could with impunity in their mutual dealings sign a deed in the dark. Three days after this preconcerted interview, the Cardinal Legate learned from Bonaparte that ten bishops, two of the number being archbishops, were to be nominated from the constitutional clergy. It was 'this or nothing.' Caprara, whose remonstrances were vain, would at least, he said, submit the constitutional priests elected to a severe examination. But in point of fact, he took upon himself to acquiesce in their nomination. The Holy Father's instructions had been positive, limiting his powers to admitting the schismatic clergy to lay communion. The Pope had never consented that the constitutional bishops should be re-established in their episcopal functions; the extent of indulgence, as far as they were concerned, was to consist in reconciling them with the Church.

With Bonaparte more than any other man, perhaps, it was necessary never to begin making attempts at unlawful concession. Such a course is open to two serious objections. Going back is soon an impossibility, and the conceder loses ground in the moral estimation of the man to whom he concedes. Caprara then agreed, though with impotent tears, to confirm the new constitutional bishops, but he stipulated that they should first make an act of submission to the Holy See. When they met at the Legate's house, they positively and unanimously refused to accede to the formula drawn up by him to that effect, but rather chose to sign a letter whose substance had been furnished by Bonaparte, Portalis, and Bernier. On Palm Sunday, Caprara had installed Mgr. Belloy, named as Archbishop of Paris, at Notre

[11] *L' Eglise Romaine et le Premier Empire*, t. i. pp. 185—191.

Dame, and consecrated Mgr. Cambacérès for Rouen, Bernier for Orleans, and Pancemont for Vannes. The following Friday, that is, Good Friday, he received a serious visit from the new Bishop of Orleans. The preparations for the *Te Deum* on Easter Sunday were all suspended, and the only course open to the Legate, if he wished to see them renewed, was to accept the letter to Rome proposed by the constitutional bishops. Poor Caprara's trouble and perplexity were extreme, but finally he found that concession was an unwise policy. When once he had entered on such a path, there was no standing still. Now he humbled himself, and, we may add, his office of Legate, so far as to go the length urged by Bernier, though he made a condition. He demanded that the submission of the constitutional bishops to Rome should be made public through the press, and, moreover, that the bishops elect should in presence of Mgr. Bernier and Mgr. de Pancemont, explicitly confess their participation in schism, and renounce their former errors. At this point of the transaction the want of loyalty and good faith in those whose sacred character would have seemed to guarantee at least honourable dealing is inexpressibly painful. Caprara was given to believe that the constitutional bishops had submitted themselves to Rome with tears in their eyes, for the bishops of Orleans and Vannes reported that they had received from them a sincere retractation. How can we reconcile this assertion with the fact that only a few days later the constitutional bishops were heard to boast not only that they had persisted in their opinion, but also that they had indignantly torn up the formula of the proposed letter to Rome.[12] In the correspondence of Napoleon I. we unfortunately find two letters which very probably give us the reason for the unintelligible behaviour of Bernier

---

[12] *L'Eglise Romaine et le Premier Empire*, t. i. p. 205.

and Pancemont, or which, at all events, throw light upon it. One is addressed to M. de Talleyrand, recommending the transmittal of thirty thousand francs to Mgr. Bernier as a subsidy for the entertainment of the Legate. The other, to M. Portalis, contains a similar order in behalf of Mgr. de Pancemont, but this time it is fifty thousand francs, which the Bishop of Vannes is to receive with as little publicity as possible.[13] By means so ignoble all obstacles to the proclamation of the Concordat were swept away. The 18th of April, 1802, dawned with a double brightness on Paris and on all France. *Resurrexi, et adhuc sum tecum!* It was in very truth the Resurrection of God in France by His Church, the beginning of a new era of comparative religious freedom for those whose faith had not suffered shipwreck in the dreadful storm of revolution. Contemporary documents bear witness to the fact that more curiosity than devotion was displayed on this occasion; but may not the attitude of the principal personages of the scene have been made to represent popular opinion? It cannot be denied that many were at Notre Dame on that morning of the Resurrection who saw with displeasure any sort of compact with religion. An old and a young France stood there in opposition: one which had owned for king the eldest son of the Church, the other an offspring of the Voltairian school, indifferent, disdainful, or jeering in opposition when any divine religion was concerned.

Splendid preparations were on foot at the Tuileries; the gala carriages of the Court of Louis XVI. had been repaired for the use of less aristocratic occupants, but adorned with youthful and elegant beauties, they answered all purposes sufficiently well. It was rumoured that the First Consul desired the presence of ladies in full dress,

---

[13] See *La Correspondance de Nap. I.* t. vii. p. 269 and t. viii. p. 99.

and those who formed the circle of Madame Bonaparte had been invited to start from the Tuileries in these official equipages. After the absence of all pomp and pageant since the terrible event of 1793 at the Place Louis XV., such details were not lost upon the multitude. They eagerly drank in the spectacle presented by the *cortège*, in which the Bonaparte family played a semi-royal part. From eight o'clock in the morning M. Réal, Prefect of Police, accompanied by his civil officers, paraded the streets to proclaim publicly the different legal articles connected with the Concordat. At eleven o'clock the Cardinal Legate in his scarlet robes, followed by the new archbishops and bishops, entered the Cathedral of Notre Dame. Then came the first and last grand mustering of the French Republic. But even at that time it was only outwardly a Republic. One great man's victorious sword had stemmed democracy, and he now lent it to the outward glorification of religion, more with a view to what that restored religion would profit him, than what he could profit it. Willingly or unwillingly the civil and military officers of Bonaparte must follow him to Notre Dame. An ingenious manœuvre of Berthier, the Minister of the War Department, had triumphed over the resistance offered by the Republican generals. Invited to partake of a military breakfast at his house, they had been conducted to the Tuileries as it were by accident, just as the procession was moving away to the Cathedral. As may be imagined, no one of them found courage to say no when Bonaparte said yes, and they were carried off to cast their particular splendour around the First Consul. During the ceremony the behaviour of such heterogeneous elements was what might have been expected, for the French Revolution had done a great deal towards destroying religious conviction. The members of the Council of State showed manifest disdain, the officials generally a sneering levity, or an utter want of attention. As for the attitude of the First Consul, he gave men the impression of performing, by a stern act of will, a necessary duty. His whole deportment was grave, but without a shadow of recollection or piety, and the announcement conveyed to Rome by Caprara, and too easily believed, that he had the intention of receiving the sacraments at Easter, was a pure fable.[15]

Soon after the festivities of the Concordat another concession was wrung from the Cardinal Legate. It concerned the reconciliation of the second order of the clergy, the constitutional priests. The First Consul demanded that no further retractation should be required from them beyond submission to their legitimate bishop. As usual, a vivid picture of the evils that would befall the Church if he did not consent, moved Caprara to sanction this step; but he felt that he was losing ground, and earnestly prayed for his recall. The truth of the matter was simply that the Legate had placed himself in a false position by accepting the rich archbishopric of Milan from the First Consul as head of the Italian Republic. The title of benefactor gave a certain weight to the exactions of Bonaparte. When now the Cardinal objected his want of power, the reply was: 'Bah, this is one of your usual tricks.'[16] Caprara awoke gradually to realize what were the fruits of his faculty in concession. In a great measure, he had lost the confidence of Pius VII. and of Consalvi, and gained, on the other hand, no influence over the mind of the First Consul.

The joy of the Holy Father at the accomplishment of the Concordat was marred by the simultaneous publication of certain Organic Articles, as if they too had received

---

[15] *L'Eglise Romaine et le Premier Empire*, t. i. p. 216.
[1] *Correspondance du Card. Caprara au Card. Consalvi*, 3 juillet, 1802.

his approbation. So far from this being the case, Consalvi tells us that they were 'constitutional laws,' which pretty nearly undid the good effected by the Concordat.

To form an accurate judgment as to the truth of this observation we subjoin the text of the Concordat, and add to it an abstract of those important points in which the Organic Articles went outside and beyond the solemn compact publicly entered into by the First Consul with the Holy Father. The Concordat runs as follows :

'The First Consul of the French Republic, and His Holiness, the Sovereign Pontiff, Pius VII., have named for their respective plenipotentiaries; the First Consul, the citizens, Joseph Bonaparte, Counsellor of State; Cretet, Counsellor of State; and Bernier, Doctor of Theology, Curé of St. Laud d'Angers, provided with full powers; His Holiness, His Eminence the Lord Hercules Consalvi, Cardinal of the Holy Roman Church, Deacon of St. Agatha ad Suburram, his Secretary of State; Joseph Spina, Archbishop of Corinth, domestic prelate of His Holiness, assisting at the Pontifical Throne; and Father Caselli, consulting theologian of His Holiness, provided equally with full powers in good and due form. The aforesaid, after exchange of their respective full powers, have made the following convention.

'Convention between the French Government and His Holiness Pius VII.

'The Government of the Republic recognizes that the Catholic Apostolic and Roman religion is the religion of the great majority of French citizens.

'His Holiness likewise recognizes that the said religion has received, and further at this time expects the greatest good and the greatest honour from the establishment of the Catholic worship in France, and from the particular profession of it made by the Consuls of the Republic.

'Consequently, after this mutual recognition, they

have agreed upon what follows as well for the good of religion as for the maintenance of internal tranquillity.

'Art. 1. The Catholic, Apostolic, and Roman religion shall be freely exercised in France. Its worship shall be public, but in conformity with the rules of police which the Government shall judge necessary for public tranquillity.

'2. A new circumscription of French dioceses shall be made by the Holy See in concert with the Government.

'3. His Holiness shall declare to the titularies of the French sees, that he expects of them with a firm confidence every sort of sacrifice, even that of their sees, for the good of peace and unity.

'After this exhortation, should they refuse this sacrifice required by the good of the Church, a refusal nevertheless which His Holiness does not expect, provision shall be made by new titularies for the government of the bishoprics of the new circumscription, as follows.

'4. The First Consul of the Republic shall name, within the three months following the publication of the Bull of His Holiness, Archbishops and Bishops of the new circumscription. His Holiness will confer canonical institution according to the forms established in respect of France before the change of Government.

'5. Nominations to bishoprics, which afterwards become vacant, shall also be made by the First Consul, and canonical institution shall be given by the Holy See, in conformity with the preceding Article.

'6. The bishops, before entering upon their office, shall make direct to the First Consul the oath of fidelity which was in use before the change of Government, as follows :

'"I swear and promise to God, upon the holy Gospels, to maintain obedience and fidelity to the Government established by the Constitution of the French Republic.

I promise likewise not to hold any communication, not to be present at any design, nor to enter into any engagement, whether within or without, which is contrary to the public tranquillity: and if in my diocese or elsewhere I learn of any design to the prejudice of the State, I will make it known to the Government."

'7. Ecclesiastics of the second order shall make the same oath to the civil authorities designated by the Government.

'8. The following prayer shall be recited at the end of the Divine Office in all the Catholic churches of France:

'"Domine, salvam fac rempublicam; Domine, salvos fac consules."

'9. The bishops shall make a new circumscription of the parishes of their dioceses, which shall not take effect until it has received the consent of the Government.

'10. The bishops shall appoint the curés. Their choice can only fall on persons accepted by the Government.

'11. The bishops may have a Chapter for their cathedral, and a seminary for their diocese, without obligation on the part of the Government to endow them.

'12. All metropolitan, cathedral, parochial, and other churches not alienated, which are necessary for worship, shall be put at the disposition of the bishops.

'13. His Holiness, for the good of peace and the happy re-establishment of the Catholic religion, declares that neither he nor his successors shall in any way trouble those who have acquired alienated ecclesiastical goods, and that in consequence the property of these goods, the rights and revenues attached to them, shall remain unchanged in their hands and in those of their representatives.

'14. The Government will assure a suitable support to the bishops and the curés, whose dioceses and cures shall be comprised in the new circumscription.

'15. The Government will likewise take measures in order that French Catholics may, if they choose, make endowments in favour of the churches.

'16. His Holiness recognizes in the First Consul of the French Republic the same rights and prerogatives as the old Government enjoyed in regard to the Holy See.

'17. It is agreed between the contracting parties that in case any one of the successors of the actual First Consul should not be Catholic, the rights and prerogatives mentioned in the article above and the appointment of bishops shall be regulated in respect to him by a new convention.

'Ratifications shall be exchanged at Paris within forty days.

'Done at Paris, the 26th messidor of the 9th year of the French Republic, 15th July, 1801.'

The following are the enactments of the Organic Articles which we wish to put alongside of the above Concordat. They were presented for acceptance to the French Legislature at the same time as the Concordat, being called 'the Organic Articles of the said Convention,' and were promulgated with it as a 'Law of the Republic.'

As to the liberty of the Church in the important point of intercourse between the Head and the members, the Organic Articles laid down that no bull, brief, or other communication from the Holy See, even if it regarded only individuals, should be received, published, printed, or put into execution without the authorization of the Government. Further, that no nuncio, legate, or any other officer, should, without the same authorization, exercise, on French soil or elsewhere, any function respecting the affairs of the Gallican Church. With regard to the Church as the one divine kingdom of God upon earth, the Organic Articles laid down that no decrees of foreign synods, not even of general councils, could be published in France before the Government had examined their form, their conformity with the laws, rights, and franchises of the French Republic, and all that in their publication could affect the public tranquillity. That no national or metropolitan council, no diocesan synod, no deliberative assembly, should take place without express permission of the Government. The Articles created an appeal to the Council of State in all cases of abuse on the part of ecclesiastical superiors or other persons. And cases of abuse were defined to be usurpation, or excess of power; contravention of the laws and regulations of the Republic; infraction of rules established by the canons received in France; infringement of the liberties, practices, and customs of the Gallican Church; and every attempt or procedure in the exercise of worship which may affect the honour of citizens, arbitrarily trouble their conscience, degenerate into oppression of them, or into public scandal. As to the ministry of the Church, three articles of very pregnant meaning ran thus: 'The Catholic worship shall be exercised under the direction of archbishops and bishops in their dioceses, and under that of curés in their parishes. Every privilege carrying with it either exemption from episcopal jurisdiction, or possession of it, is abolished. Archbishops and bishops shall be able, upon authorization of the Government, to establish in their dioceses cathedral chapters and seminaries. All other ecclesiastical establishments are suppressed.'

The bishops were to name and institute the curés:

but were not to declare their nomination, nor to give them canonical institution, before that nomination had been accepted by the First Consul. They were bound to reside in their dioceses, out of which they were not allowed to go without the First Consul's permission. They were charged with the organization of their seminaries, the rules of such organization being submitted to the approbation of the First Consul.

Those who were selected to teach in the seminaries were bound to subscribe the declaration made by the clergy of France in 1682, and to consent to teach the doctrine therein contained; and the bishops must address a formal statement of this consent to the Counsellor of State charged with every matter which concerns worship. 'The bishops shall send every year to this counsellor the names of the persons studying in the seminaries and intended for the ecclesiastical state.' 'The bishops shall hold no ordination before the number of the persons to be ordained has been submitted to the Government and approved by it.' 'No foreigner can be employed in the functions of the ecclesiastical ministry without permission of the Government.' 'The curés in giving instruction shall not permit themselves to use any inculpation, direct or indirect, either against persons, or against other worships authorized in the State.'

It is especially to be noted that the Organic Articles in requiring that all teachers in seminaries should profess their adherence to the four articles of the declaration of 1682, and promise to teach the doctrine contained in them, required as a law of the French State that those teachers should profess and teach two doctrines which lay under the censure of the Holy See. The one doctrine concerned the power of the Holy See in respect to a general council; the other the due relation between the spiritual and the temporal powers.

It will be seen that Bonaparte at the moment that he was entering into a Concordat with the Holy Father, every article and even every word of which had been carefully examined by the Cardinal Plenipotentiary, lest the liberty of the Church should receive any injury, was imposing as a law of the State articles upon the Catholics of his empire, by the tenor of which not only was a complete captivity inflicted upon the Church, but the teaching of false doctrine was enjoined on the educators of the clergy. To this he added the falsehood of representing these articles as 'Organic Articles of the Convention made with Pius VII.'[16]

The Organic Articles and the nomination of constitutional bishops were the two thorns which pressed into the heart of Pius VII. For three years after the publication of the Concordat, he spared neither labour, trouble, nor fatigue to bring about either the revocation or the revision of the Organic Articles, and the retractation of the constitutional bishops.[17]

But other frauds and sorrows were reserved for Pius VII. His great natural charm was to be enhanced and idealized by the supernatural power of suffering for justice' sake. His history is that oft-repeated one in the annals of the Church of God: of physical weakness coupled with spiritual strength, of persecution producing renewed life and vigour. To betray indeed the rights of a great cause, or to permit them to be trampled on in ignominious silence, is as dangerous as it is unworthy, while to suffer for them is the surest means of attracting to that injured cause the sympathies and hearts of those who love upon earth with the deepest and truest love.

---

[16] For the text of the Concordat and the Organic Articles see *Portalis sur le Concordat de 1801*. Paris, 1845. Pp. 58—77.

[17] *Mémoires de Consalvi*, t. i. p. 406—410.

CHAPTER IV.

Pius the Seventh at the Tuileries.

'Cum autem duobis modis, id est, aut vi, aut fraude, fit injuria; fraus quasi vulpeculæ, vis leonis videtur; utrumque homine alienissimum: sed fraus odio digna majore.'—Cic. *De Officiis.*

THE tone of mind of Pius VII. at this time (the summer of 1802) is best rendered in his own words. It seems that even then he had a sort of instinctive feeling as to what would present the peculiar trial of his long and arduous pontificate. Concession after concession would be torn from him, each one accompanied by the untruthful assertion that it was the last, as well as imperatively demanded for the good of the Church. But worse than concession to the heart of the sensitive Pontiff was the disloyal behaviour of Bonaparte. The tacking on the Organic Articles to the Concordat acted as a first intimation to the Holy Father that the First Consul did not always deal openly in his transactions with the Church. A breach of trust and of honourable confidence produced a stifled sadness and a melancholy discouragement that alarmed Consalvi. 'Alas,' Pius had said to M. Cacault in July, 1802, 'we find true peace and repose only in those Governments where Catholics are subject to infidels and heretics. The Catholics of Russia, England, Prussia, and the Levant, are no subject of pain to us. They ask for Bulls, and for necessary counsels, and then they go their way peaceably in perfect conformity to the laws of the Church. But you know what our predecessor suffered through the changes operated by the Emperors Joseph and Leopold. You are witness of the daily assaults of the Spanish and Neapolitan courts. At this present moment, no man is so unfortunate as the Sovereign Pontiff. He is the guardian and supreme chief of religion and of its divine ordinances. Religion itself is a structure which men wish to demolish entirely, although they say at the same moment that they respect its laws. They pretend to have need of us to carry on their ever-recurring attempts at social changes, without considering that it is our conscience and our honour which are powerless in the matter. Our objections are passed over with ill-feeling and anger, and in nearly all cases, the demands submitted to us are accompanied with threats.' Then, with the sad wisdom of a disenchantment, and before the prospect of what would ensue from the Italian Concordat now proposed to him, the Holy Father added, 'We had flattered ourself that France, actually possessing what constitutes the ambition of other powers, would remain in perpetual harmony with the Holy See. . . . But if the First Consul bring innovations into Italy, it will no longer be possible for us to hold our own at Rome. He has surely no design to ruin us, or to draw upon us the reproaches of the whole Church of which we are the Head.'[1]

Though the Organic Articles were opposed to the compact made, the Emperor considered that the Pope committed an unpardonable liberty in denouncing them in Consistory and in profiting by his newly acquired experience in treating for the Italian Concordat, which nearly followed the great French Convention. Pius made the special stipulation that, in ecclesiastical matters, nothing should be settled without the consent of the Holy See.[2]

[1] *Histoire de Pie VII.* t. i. pp. 319, 320.
[2] *Mémoires de Consalvi*, t. ii. p. 381.

The Organic Articles carried into effect explain the attitude of Bonaparte, as one act of dishonesty calls for another, or one abyss invites a greater abyss. They had been published under the shadow of the Holy Father's name, and thus it became necessary to distort his words in order that they should not belie too strongly the acceptance imputed to him. The insertion, moreover, of an unmistakable bit of Gallicanism in so important an official treaty strengthened Bonaparte in his determination to carry out to the utmost the so-called Gallican liberties, to exercise a petty tyranny over the bishops, and to display a marked preference for the constitutional clergy. In support of this, we need only consult contemporary testimony, or better still, his own correspondence. Thus although the papal protest against the Organic Articles was published in the *Moniteur*, its energy was considerably weakened by the observation which accompanied its appearance, and which was contrary to all truth. It was remarked that such reserves were habitual to the Court of Rome as an arm against Gallican liberties. The same paper translated from the Bull which confirmed the 'Concordat: "*Deus . . . eadem cupiditate finem tot malis imponendi inflammavit eum,*" as "God has put into the generous heart of the great and illustrious man, the same desires."' . . . A nomination of Cardinals occurred soon afterwards, and Bonaparte demanded imperiously that the five vacant hats should be given to France. The tone of his despatch on the subject to M. de Talleyrand, is as that of a monarch crowned doubly by hereditary right and the will of his people. 'You will inform the *citoyen* Cacault that I desire that these places be given to France. . . . If my just request is uncomplied with, I renounce from this moment all nomination of Cardinals, preferring that France should have nothing to do with the Sacred College, than that it should be treated with less distinction than other powers.[3]

Before speaking of the evil results produced by the State's intrusion in matters which are the special province of the Church, it is well to recognize Bonaparte's misfortune in that he had no one amongst his courtiers or his bishops bold enough or honest enough to tell him that he was encroaching on forbidden territory, and so in danger of not, 'rendering to God those things which are His,' in his eagerness to further the omnipotence of the State at that time represented by himself. He was surrounded by creatures, courtier-bishops, and Gallican ministers. In this instance, it was Portalis, the Counsellor of State, and later the Minister of Worship (a title fitly suited to his functions), who became at his master's bidding a sort of controller general of the French bishops. Under the supervision of this exemplary Gallican, it devolved upon the bishops to submit their pastorals, letters, and all other official documents issuing from their pen to secular censure. They were moreover forbidden to publish anything that was not printed at their respective prefecture. This system engendered results so ridiculous, that M. Portalis was constrained at last to transfer the censure from the various provincial prefectures to one central bureau in Paris, unfortunate enough to attract the particular attention of Bonaparte. From this office, there issued for the benefit of prelates particularly zealous in the imperial cause, bulletins from the army to be read in church, as well as sketches of pastorals which needed only a little ecclesiastical colouring to be fit for use.[4] Political questions in the pulpit were forbidden ground. M. Portalis further announced in a circular of June, 1802, 'that divorce is admissible by the civil law, and that conse-

---

[3] *Correspondance de Napoléon I.* 8 juillet, 1802.
[4] See *La Vie de Mgr. d'Osmond, évêque de Nancy.*

quently it would be unjust as well as imprudent to refuse the nuptial benediction to those who wish to contract a second marriage after divorce.'[5] A little extract from the correspondence of the First Consul will show us whether or not he had learnt the wisdom of the ancient motto, *in medio stat virtus*. 'I send you, *citoyen* Counsellor of State,' he writes to Portalis, 'a memorandum which comes to me from the Inspector of Police, about the Bishop of Rennes. It is my wish that you should write and tell the Bishop, that it is time to put an end to such conduct, that he is in the wrong to have displaced a constitutional priest without my permission for a priest recently returned from emigration. . . . If Gospel morality is not a sufficient check upon his passions, he ought to act from policy, from fear of the Government, which might pursue him as a disturber of the public peace. Write less harshly to the Bishop of Clermont. His diocese is filled with constitutional priests, who are the friends of order and enjoy the popular confidence. It is both impolitic and immoral to banish such useful men from the State and from the Church. . . . Write to the Bishop of Bayeux, that in the commune of Balleroy he has illegally displaced a curé, a step which is contrary to my intention. . . . Impress upon all the bishops as a lasting disposition, *that I wish for constitutional priests as curés, vicar generals, and canons.*' At another time, he wanted to punish some unfortunate priests who had corresponded with the 'infamous' Bishop of Arras. 'I wish to know (to M. Portalis), what the canonical form of degradation for them would be, in order that they may be delivered over to justice, for I think an example is necessary to strike the clergy forcibly. I am no longer pleased with the vicaire of S. Sulpice. Here is another fit subject for degradation.' Then, after giving an

[5] *Circulaire de M. Portalis*, 19 prairial an x. (juin, 1802).

order of arrest, he expresses anxiety to ascertain the proper punishment for a priest who separates himself from his bishop, since, as Bonaparte remarks, 'God will certainly punish him (the refractory priest), in the next world, but Cæsar must punish him in this.'[6]

In July, 1803, a new personage comes before us, as one who is to figure with some importance in the Pontificate of Pius VII. It is he who was styled the Cardinal Oncle, or the Cardinal of Lyons, Fesch, uncle to Napoleon Bonaparte; the possessor of certain noble qualities, considerably marred, however, by extreme obstinacy and total want of tact. It seems strange that a man of this calibre should have been used by his imperial nephew as an instrument; yet his obstinacy was perhaps rather the offspring of narrow-mindedness than of any great determination of character. At a time when the more immediate relations of the First Consul were in ignorance of the design he was meditating—his coronation by the Holy Father—Cardinal Fesch alone was let into the secret, and sent to Rome to replace Cacault, who had said with some truth : 'How men have spoilt my General and my First Consul for me! He listens to me no longer. He has made me a senator and silenced me.'[7] From the first instant that he appeared in Rome, Fesch made an unfavourable impression. He was haughty and far from conciliating in his official demeanour, possessing, moreover, no experience of the situation. But his position had been marked out for him beforehand by the First Consul, whose policy it was ever to solicit special favours of Rome with more pride than lowliness, and by intimidation rather than any excess of flattering compliance. The Holy Father had protected a certain Comte de Vernègues, a Russian, accused by the French Embassy

---

[6] *Correspondance de Napoléon I.* t. vii. p. 28, t. ix. pp. 4, 74, 310.
[7] *Histoire de Pie VII.*, t. i. p. 483.

of plotting and intriguing against their Government. Bonaparte, in an imperious and menacing letter to M. de Talleyrand, urged him to require absolutely that the unfortunate count should be delivered over to France; and Consalvi, who had resisted long and bravely, suddenly consented to a step which was only a prelude to still greater concessions. On the 16th of May, 1804, the Senate voted and determined that Napoleon should take the title of Emperor; but on March 21st, before this resolution had passed, the last of the Condés had perished by his orders at Vincennes. It has been said with truth that every heresy has a political reason, and we make the same remark upon all the deeds of blood perpetrated by Bonaparte. This assassination was not a mere act of violence committed in a momentary fit of anger, but a design meditated in cold blood, as an act of useful policy.[8] Once for all, Napoleon would if possible crush out the Royalist party. To give him his due, certain flimsy and badly-organized plots directed in their name against his person had called forth the lion's wrath, but retaliation such as the premeditated murder of the Duc d'Enghien was unworthy of a hero who should have been great even in his revenge. It is recorded that Pius VII. alone, of all contemporary sovereigns, shed tears over the grave so inopportunely opened, and that he would have wished to refuse to crown the exterminator of the last Condé.[9] How, then, it may be asked, did he so speedily and so easily reduce to silence his religious scruples on this point? The question is best answered by studying the attitude of the principal actors at Rome and Paris during the months immediately preceding the Coronation. If Pius VII. sympathized with the wrongs of each one of

---

[8] *L'Eglise Romaine et le Premier Empire*, t. i. p. 308.
[9] *Mémoires de Consalvi*, t. ii. p. 387.

his children individually, he never forgot that he was charged to 'feed the lambs with the sheep;' he had wedded the Universal Church, and must henceforth view all things in the light of the one great Cause. Napoleon, since he had sullied his fair fame, was on his side the more anxious to obtain for his crown the outward sanction of the Holy Father. Who, after this, could taunt him with the murder of the Duc d'Enghien?

The policy of the Papal Legate at Paris was still unaspiring in its tendency. Napoleon must be humoured by the Holy Father as long as it was not a question of principle. The announcement sent by Caprara to Consalvi paints very graphically the extent of these modest desires. 'The monarch whom it has become a question of crowning,' he writes, 'would take it very ill from His Holiness, and would look upon it as an injury if any difficulties were raised by him, or if he sought to compromise, or refused to lend himself to the Coronation. The Emperor's resentment would be all the stronger in that the Holy Father, as Head of the Church, has the power, more than any one else, of consolidating the succession in the family of a man who has just re-established and reorganized religious and Catholic worship. . . . No excuse would be accepted as legitimate, were it even confirmed by the testimony of Cardinal Fesch. It would only be looked upon as a pretext. . . . I limit myself, then, to beseech of your Eminence, not even to hint in your answer at the most distant idea of any difficulty, be it of age, of health, or any other pretence whatever.'[10] The enthusiasm of Caprara was not shared by the Court of Rome. The crowning of a new Emperor by the Pope must present some very deep and weighty religious reasons to justify it, and Pius VII. needed to treat tenderly the jealous susceptibility of other European Cabinets, whose

---

[10] *Le Card. Caprara au Card. Consalvi*, 10 mai, 1804.

ambassadors, obsequious enough in Paris in presence of the new imperial power, revenged themselves by the title of Chaplain to the Emperor (Bonaparte) jeeringly conferred upon Pius VII. by their ministers in Rome. Consalvi was not slow to grasp the whole bearings of the question. Napoleon would not suffer the Sovereign Pontiff to remain neutral, and Rome must consent either to take up his cause, or to wound his pride by an open and flat refusal. A middle course was no longer possible; and perhaps this yielding to circumstances, rendered obligatory by the peculiar nature of events, has not been sufficiently taken into account by those who have been too ready to blame Pius VII. for sanctioning by his presence the coronation of Napoleon. The conditions specified by Consalvi to justify so grave a step on the part of the Holy Father, were the retractation of the constitutional bishops and the repeal of the Organic Articles. Furthermore, in the ceremony itself the due and customary amount of respect was to be paid to the character of the Vicar of Christ. The sincere fulfilment of these conditions could alone prevent the scandal and stop the reproaches of contemporaries and of posterity; for both had a right to expect great and solid advantages for the Church from a condescension so unwonted in a Sovereign Pontiff. The substance of the oath which the First Consul purposed to pronounce at his coronation was also judged inadmissible at Rome. Caprara was dismayed. Again Consalvi, to his consternation, wrote that 'the essence of the Catholic Church is to be intolerant,'[11] in the sense that the one only true religion must proclaim itself infallible, and teach 'with authority.'

Cardinal Fesch now intervened to conciliate, if possible, the scruples of Rome with the desires of his imperial nephew. A cool and calm self-possession and

---

[11] *Consalvi à Caprara*, 6 juin, 1804.

a great clearness of purpose go to make up a wise negotiator. These qualities were not remarkable in Fesch. It is related of him that coming one day from a stormy interview with Consalvi on the subject of the Coronation he had lost his head so far as to reply to his chief footman when asked where to drive: *Al casa del diavolo*.[13] His fixed idea was that the Holy Father should improve the occasion to obtain the restoration of the Three Legations. But as in the Concordat, so in this circumstance Pius VII. banished all temporal interests. No material consideration should weigh in his decision.[14] It is curious that the French Ambassador, and not the Holy Father, should have urged the question of the Temporal Power. It serves as another proof of the disinterestedness of purpose which many are too slow to acknowledge in the dealings of the Head of the Church with secular power. A contemporary writer[15] seems to say that no formal written statement was ever obtained by Rome to the effect that Napoleon would yield the disputed points. But Cardinal Consalvi, who is beyond a doubt the greatest authority on the subject, thus expresses himself in his memoirs: 'We at length wrested an official note from M. de Talleyrand, addressed to the Cardinal Legate for transmission to Rome. It contained the most positive assurances that the Pope should receive full satisfaction as to the Organic Articles. ... M. de Talleyrand's note promised a great deal about the constitutional bishops. But it seemed to us that the purport and also the vagueness of these latter promises did not offer to the Holy Father that assurance of redress which he could have desired.' Consalvi pursued negotiations with Fesch, determined to obtain as to the constitutional

---

[13] *Histoire de Pie VII.* t. i. p. 489.
[14] *Mémoires de Consalvi*, t. ii. p. 392.
[15] M. le Comte d'Haussonville.

clergy the promise already granted as to the Organic Articles. 'Finally Cardinal Fesch gave us in writing, in the Emperor's name, the assurance that the constitutional clergy should make their retractation in the Pope's hands, in the form prescribed by him; that for this end, they would profit by his presence in Paris, and that supposing the improbable possibility of the refusal of a constitutional bishop to retract, he should be deposed from his see by the Government.' This statement was confirmed by M. de Talleyrand; but Consalvi says: 'All the efforts made by the French Government tended solely to obtain the Pope's presence in Paris, for it had not the smallest intention of keeping one of its promises.'[15] Apart from France, Pius VII. had to weigh all the results of a negative determination. The enemies of the Church would not fail to lay to his account the good left undone and the evil effected, and perhaps reproach him for attaching too much importance to the jeers of those who saw the rise of a new Empire with ill-concealed jealousy. In face of very possible advantages and the prevention of future evils, the Holy Father consented to sanction, by his august presence, the Coronation of the Emperor of the French. But as if, his ends once attained, he wished to deprive Pius VII. of the reverence due to the Vicar of Christ, Napoleon intrusted his official invitation not to the highest Church dignitary of his Empire, but to a general of brigade, Caffarelli, the letter itself being so shabby in every respect, that the Pope was on the point of ending all negotiations by a final refusal. He had required that two bishops should present this note, and if Napoleon began so soon to prove faithless to his word, what might not be expected later? The Cardinals, however, having been consulted on this point, were of opinion that the

[15] *Mémoires de Consalvi*, t. ii. pp. 394, 398.

journey to Paris having been agreed to entirely from religious motives, everything must be sacrificed to the same end.[16]

The Holy Father left Rome on the 2nd of November, 1804, accompanied by six Cardinals only, although the French Government would have desired a larger number, to enhance the splendour of the occasion for the benefit of Napoleon. The faithful Secretary of State remained behind, for the Romans could not be called upon to endure the simultaneous absence of the Pope and of his Chief Minister. The journey was accomplished with unfitting speed. Not content with goading on Pius VII. by couriers sent repeatedly for the sole end of impressing haste on the traveller, Napoleon would not suffer him to stop more than twice, that is, once at Florence, and once at Turin. No regard was shown for his feeble health, nor was he consulted as to the day of the ceremony, a deference which seemed only due to the most ordinary politeness. In a word, the Holy Father was summoned to Paris much in the same way as a chaplain may be called upon to say Mass by his employer.[17] The Pope and the Emperor met for the first time in the open country between Fontainebleau and Nemours. This was a trick of Napoleon. As a sovereign elect, it would have been a terrible trial to his pride to meet another crowned head half-way. In the case of the Pope, he, as an outward Catholic at least, must have given that sort of homage which is hallowed by custom and revential faith; he must have fallen on his knees in homage, not to the man indeed, but to the Divine Person Whom that man represented, and so have proclaimed before his Court that there existed one on earth greater than he. To spare himself in this particular Napoleon had arranged the scene, which presented all

[16] *Mémoires de Consalvi*, t. ii. p. 402.   [17] *Ibid.* t. ii. p. 403.

the appearances of a natural encounter. He was there in his attire of huntsman, booted, spurred, and surrounded by a pack of hounds. The Holy Father's carriage stopped as soon as he saw the Emperor. It was a wet, muddy November day, and the white silk shoe of Pius had to encounter the dirt of the road in order to walk across the measured distance which Napoleon had settled should be traversed before he would make any advances. When both Pope and Emperor had taken a certain number of steps towards each other, they met and embraced. The imperial carriage was to conduct Pius to the Palace of Foutainebleau, and he should naturally have taken precedence of his host. Here too a graceful manœuvre had been pre-concerted out of regard for the Emperor. The carriage drew up in such a way as to separate him from the Pope. Two footmen on either side opened the respective doors simultaneously. The Emperor taking the right and leaving the left for his august visitor, they entered together. Unfortunately, as a zealous imperialist [18] remarked, this first precedence determined the Holy Father's position for the rest of his stay in France, where he was all along made to feel that he was but a secondary personage. The solitary occasion when Napoleon ceded to him the place of honour was the entry into Paris, but this (as that of the Cardinal Legate) was effected by night, that the people might not witness what their new sovereign evidently deemed his degradation. Installed at the Pavillon de Flore at the Tuileries, Pius VII. endeared himself to all French hearts by the sweetness which was his true character. To the people of Paris whom revolution had all but shipwrecked he proved by a near contact that the Father at Rome was no idle word, and that he loved each one who sought him out with something of a

[18] Le Duc de Rovigo.

father's love. It seems that no time was lost to beguile the Holy Father into accepting what proved to be an insincere retractation from the constitutional Bishop of Besançon, Lecoy, designated as a man of party spirit by Bernier of Orleans. The Pope had arrived at Paris on the 28th of November. On the 30th, Napoleon, after reading the document in a great hurry aloud to the Holy Father, left it in his hands. The next day Pius VII. thought it necessary to write as follows to the Emperor:

'Last night, as soon as we had a spare minute, we considered the declaration of the Bishop Lecoy, which your Majesty had the goodness to bring to us yourself. Looking over it, we perceived a point which had escaped our notice in the very rapid reading of your Majesty. The said Bishop has altered the original words of the formula minuted by Cardinal Fesch and M. Portalis, *Submission to his decisions in the ecclesiastical affairs of France*, to, *in the canonical affairs of France*. We can appreciate the meaning of the change, and do not admit it. We have considered ourself bound to tell your Majesty this without delay, because we are pressed for time, nothing having as yet been obtained from a small number of obstinate refractories. We have a sufficient knowledge of the piety and discerning wisdom of your Majesty to feel sure you will deign to take the necessary measures that we may not find ourselves compromised, and that nothing may disturb or mar the solemn function of to-morrow morning. We pray God to pour His choicest blessings on your Imperial Majesty, to whom we heartily give the Apostolical benediction.

'From our house, the 1st of December of the year 1804, and the fifth of our Pontificate.

'PIUS P.P. VII.'[19]

[19] *Histoire de Pie VII*, t. i. p. 517.

On the eve of the Coronation, Pius VII. received a curious and touching visit from the Empress Josephine. At that time Napoleon would not listen to the remonstrances of his family, who urged a separation, for although the prospect of a royal alliance befitting his new rank did not displease him, he still retained a great regard (if it was no more) for Josephine. But he wished all liberty to be left for future possibilities, and would not in consequence compromise himself by a public religious union with her. She went in tears to disburden her heart to the Holy Father. The Church had never blessed her marriage with Napoleon, and whatever Catholic instincts she had combined to make her feel what a false position she would occupy on the morrow. Although immeasurably shocked, Pius answered the Empress' communication with infinite tact. Wounded to the heart by Napoleon's duplicity, he seemed to Josephine to feel her wrongs still more deeply than his own. Rigorously speaking, he had nothing to do with the conscience of the Emperor, but as Sovereign Pontiff, he could not, with the knowledge he now possessed, crown Josephine with Napoleon, if before the morrow, a Catholic priest had not given the sanction of the Church to their marriage. The anger of Napoleon was obliged to yield to the calm determination of Pius, for duty and principle were at stake. During the night preceding the Coronation, Cardinal Fesch privately united Napoleon and Josephine in the chapel of the Tuileries, M. de Talleyrand and General Berthier acting as witnesses. The Holy Father was never known to make the simplest allusion to Josephine's painful avowal. He acted as though he had never heard it, because to him it was a confidence deposed in the heart of the Sovereign Pontiff and therefore sacred.

Two incidents strike us in the Coronation itself. From

whatever cause it may have been, perhaps simple mismanagement—though appearances go far to accuse Napoleon of wilful disregard—the Holy Father was kept waiting an hour and a half at Notre Dame, in a state of manifest anxiety. When the moment of the actual crowning came, Napoleon, as if impatient of receiving his imperial diadem from another, took it himself from the altar, and placed it on his own head. At the public banquet following the ceremony the Pope occupied a third rank after both Emperor and Empress. Then, contrary to the stipulation exacted by Consalvi, there was a second coronation in the Champ de Mars. These latter are incidents which would be trifling in themselves did they not touch the question of that respect and loyal treatment, due to all men, and most of all to a Sovereign Pontiff. Napoleon had given his word that there should be only one coronation, but unfortunately he attached very little importance to any obstacle, whether moral or otherwise, in contradiction with his wishes. Pius did not complain, reserving his energies for more vital points, but out of a certain respect for his office, he felt himself obliged to oppose the publication in the newspapers of anything which would prove that that office had not received its due. He declared that, if the account of the ceremony differed in any point from the ceremonial previously agreed upon, he would protest that he had not acted freely. To this reason is to be attributed the dead silence kept by the *Moniteur* on the whole subject of the Coronation, an event which filled the newspapers of other countries. Napoleon preferred even this to a semblance of submission.

As to the interviews between Pope and Emperor, it must be gathered from various recorded impressions that very little was gained by the Holy Father in favour of the cause which he had hoped to further by a

sovereign act of condescension. The Emperor, as long
as it was not a question of religion, knew how to appear
the most amiable of men. No doubt, he exercised a
great charm over Pius, which must probably date from this
visit to Paris. It is a strange fact that this affection
for the Emperor really did exist, in spite of the humiliating treatment which he inflicted on his visitor. It only
serves to prove Napoleon's magnificent capabilities,
whether for good or for evil. The man with whom he
was trifling, and whose confidence he had already so
often abused, loved him as a father! But his personal
affection for Napoleon did not blind Pius VII. He
was obliged to own to his Cardinals that he could obtain
nothing in religious matters. The Emperor, on his side,
had hoped, by coming into daily contact with the Pope,
to do with him much as he pleased, for, as has been
said, principle was a word possessing very little meaning
with Napoleon. He had flattered himself that it would
be with the Pope as with those courtier bishops whom
he could turn round his thumb, but now came the
disenchantment, for the Holy Father was decidedly
'narrow-minded and obstinate.' Moreover,—for these
interviews had their ludicrous side—the Emperor's knowledge of Church history was not the growth of early
teaching. He had been prepared for the occasion by
Portalis, and unfortunately was not able to confront the
double difficulty presented by the superior learning, in
this particular, of the Holy Father, and his own dislike
of correction. One day, he angrily exclaimed, 'Does
your Holiness take me for a *Charles IV?*' [20] The first
memoir drawn up and addressed by Pius VII. to the
French Government, on the subject nearest his heart
—the Church—met with so small a result that it was
with hesitation that he broached the temporal interests

[20] *L'Eglise Romaine et le Premier Empire*, t. ii. p. 360.

of the Holy See. Naturally enough, it was only to be expected that they would not obtain a more favourable hearing than the spiritual points which were of far greater importance in the eyes of the Sovereign Pontiff. It was with timidity then that he finally resolved to demand a restitution of his patrimony from Napoleon. This memoir, breathing a gentle resignation, presented perhaps a certain exaggeration of language as far as the Emperor's person was concerned. The Pope did not escape the erroneous popular view that Napoleon was, in some degree, a second Charlemagne.

'The sincere admirers of your glory are pleased to find a resemblance between the ancient founder and the present restorer of the French monarchy. To make the parallel perfect, may it please your Majesty to imitate in this instance the spontaneous and celebrated action whereby Charlemagne gave back to Peter whatever his victorious arms had recovered from the donation previously conferred upon our predecessor by his father, Pepin. The Lombards had invaded Peter's territory, and Charlemagne conquered them. We mean the Exarchate and the Pentapolis, with certain other domains, and in particular, the duchies of Spoleto and Benevento. It would be another trait in common with Charlemagne, who was possessed of a never-tiring zeal to defend and even to augment the rights and prerogatives of the Holy See, if, on every occasion, and more especially in the case of a congress for the establishment of public peace, your Majesty would assure your protection to the Holy See, and could procure that we might be represented at the congress, not that our ambassador should implicate himself in temporal matters, but guarantee by an efficacious mediation the rights and possessions of the Roman See.' [21] M. de Talleyrand was charged to reply to this

---

[21] *L'Eglise Romaine et le Premier Empire*, t. i. p. 370.

appeal, and his answer is a model specimen of its kind, full of courtesy and vague politeness, speaking in a flattering way of the Pope's personal qualities but conceding nothing to his *office*. It was not in fact a plain answer to a plain question, because however much Napoleon might have been touched by the Pope's tender confidence, he had long ago determined not to restore the temporal power. M. de Talleyrand adroitly introduced this sentence into his reply. 'Against the attacks of such an enemy (the Revolution) power and riches are impotent.' But the Holy Father had not asked for power or riches, only for the rights of his See, which, on his accession, he had sworn to protect. However well the ex-bishop had worded this meaningless answer to a conscientious demand, it did not quite satisfy Napoleon, and with the resolution which we know he even then had formed, he did not scruple to dictate the following paragraph to his docile minister. 'If God gives to us the ordinary years of man, we hope to meet with circumstances which will permit us to consolidate and extend the domain of the Holy Father, and even now we have it in our power, and we wish to lend a willing hand to help the Sovereign Pontiff out of the chaos and the difficulties brought upon him by the catastrophes of the late war, thus proving to the world our veneration for the Holy Father, our care for the Capital of Christendom, and finally our constant desire to see our religion holding the first rank as to ceremonial pomp, the splendour of its churches, and all that outward magnificence which claims the respect of nations. We have charged our uncle, the Cardinal Grand-Almoner, to explain our intentions to the Holy Father, and that which we mean to do.' The memoir finished in the words of Talleyrand. 'Always faithful to the rule which he imposed upon himself from the very beginning of negotiations, the Emperor will make it his glory and his happiness to support the Holy See with unsurpassed constancy, and to be a sincere protector of the prosperity of Christian nations. Amongst the actions which have shed splendour on his life, he wishes the respect he has always manifested for the Roman Church to hold a place, and also his efforts to reconcile to that Church the conviction and the affections of the first nation of the universe.'[22] Such expressions as these were gratifying to the Holy Father, but in reality they were big words and no more. The only real advantage reaped by Pius VII. in Paris was, not the work of the Government, but the effect of his own personal influence. His countenance lit up with a constant though rather melancholy smile, his mature age which shed a pleasant gravity over his whole aspect his presence imprinted with the double force of extreme suavity and gentle firmness, rendered him irresistible to those whose instincts and hearts were still profoundly Catholic. The constitutional bishops made an entire retractation of their errors, and perhaps the Holy Father, in joy at this event, deemed his journey to Paris and the affronts he had received, in some measure compensated by the attainment of so desired an end.

Napoleon was already weighing in his mind the advantages of keeping the Pope in France, as Popes had once been kept at Avignon. Strange it is that heresy and ambition both tend in the same direction. It is always Rome, Catholic Rome, which they would wish to strike out from the annals of the world, and their instinct is sure. They know that the independence of the Pope has always been necessary for the proper exercise of his spiritual functions, and Rome represents this independence. One day, an important member of the Imperial

[22] *Histoire de Pie VII.* t. ii. p. 34.

Court, who had the reputation of trying beforehand how far certain ideas of Napoleon would be relished, introduced before Pius VII. the question or possibility of the Pope once more taking up his abode either at Avignon or Paris. Supposing the latter, the part of Paris occupied by the archiepiscopal palace was to be exclusively devoted to the Diplomatic Body accredited to the Pontifical Government. The Holy Father, alarmed at the bare notion of such a probability, hastened to reply to what had been rather an insinuation than a question, although its drift could not escape Pius VII. 'The report has been spread that we are willing to remain in France. Well, then, all possibilities have been provided for. Before leaving Rome, we signed a formal abdication, supposing the case of our imprisonment. The act is out of the reach of the French. Cardinal Pignatelli is in possession of it at Palermo, and when the plan now meditated is signified to us, he, who is now in your power, will be nothing but a poor simple monk called Barnaba Chiaramonti.'[23] The nobleman in question, whose name Pius VII. would never mention, could only report to his master, that in spite of the suavity of the Pontiff, he was not one to lend himself to any such arrangement as that which Napoleon meditated. If this scheme had approved itself to the Holy Father, and had been realized under an emperor of Napoleon's character and tendencies, it is easy to understand what the Pope's position would have become in a very short space of time. Napoleon, who professed a great regard for Gallicanism, would have carried out what may be called its essential idea, making the Catholic Church subordinate to the State, and using the Pope as the chief instrument for enslaving the Church in a national system of religion. More than any

---

[23] *Histoire de Pie VII.* t. ii. p. 45.

other man of modern times, it was his will to reign absolutely over his subjects. He saw with displeasure the popularity of Pius VII., and as the surest means of remaining master of the hearts of his subjects, he would not consent to the splendour of a Pontifical High Mass at Notre Dame. On Christmas Day, the Holy Father said Mass in an obscure parish church, and for the same reason — Napoleon's susceptible jealousy of rival power or attraction—was constrained to leave Paris before Easter. On Easter Day itself, it was contrived that he should stop at Mâcon (as a town of less importance) rather than Lyons, for fear that he might eclipse the Emperor.

Napoleon was so possessed, indeed, on the one hand with this hunger and thirst after glory, and on the other, with the fear of being surpassed, that he was led away by his passion to commit acts which he might have condemned in another. In recording them, we fear to seem too ready to load his memory with reproaches, whereas the main force of history lies in a true and dispassionate narration of the circumstances in the world's social course, and of the human lives which Divine Providence wills to put into contact with each other. Greatness based on Christianity is, after all, the only greatness possessing solid strength even in the eyes of critical and anti-religious men.

Napoleon chose the time of the Pope's sojourn at the Tuileries to proclaim in the Senate the new kingdom of Italy. Such conduct needs no comment, but we can sympathize with the feelings of Pius VII., who had undertaken a journey without precedent for the purpose of bestowing the highest of all favours on the rapacious man who, foreshadowing his future absorption of the sovereignty of Peter, caused the Papal keys to figure with the conquered Venetian lion on his new escutcheon!

What is almost more incredible was the invitation conveyed to Pius VII. shortly after Easter, that his presence would be much appreciated at the ceremony of the Emperor's coronation at Milan as King of Italy. The Holy Father, however, remained utterly and resolutely deaf to such an astounding proposal.[24]

The return to Rome was not wanting in the humiliations which had been lavished on the journey to Paris. The Pope and the Emperor were both leaving the capital about the same time, but Napoleon, with what we may call his usual want of courtesy, started the first, without any regard for the rank of the visitor who occupied the same palace. The Holy Father was not only forced to follow him, but to wait at each relay for the horses which had already served the Emperor.

The Catholic population of France compensated in some measure for this treatment. Wherever he passed, Pius was greeted with an enthusiasm which proved that Napoleon's wish to degrade the office of the Successor of Peter, was not shared by his subjects. The Holy Father thus described in his own words to M. Artaud, Secretary of the French Legation at Rome, some of the emotions he had experienced on his return through France: 'At Châlons-sur-Saône, we were on the point of leaving a house we had inhabited for a few days; it was to Lyons we were going; it became an impossibility for us to traverse the crowd. More than two thousand women and children, old men and young men, separated us from the carriage, which could not pull up. Two dragoons (the Pope thus designated our mounted police, because the only mounted officers that he owned himself were dragoons), two dragoons to whom our escort was intrusted, conducted us on foot to the carriage, causing us to walk between their horses in a very narrow

---

[24] *Mémoires de Consalvi*, t. ii. pp. 410, 412.

space. These dragoons seemed proud of this thought of theirs, and of having greater power of invention than the crowd. Having gained the carriage in an almost stifled condition, we were just about to jump in as quickly and cleverly as possible, for it really was a work of skill, when a young girl, who possessed more intelligence than we and the two dragoons put together, got between the legs of one of the horses, took hold of our foot to kiss it, and would not leave go her hold of it, because she wanted to pass it to her mother, who reached us by the same means. Almost losing our equilibrium, we leaned our hand on one of the dragoons, him who appeared from his face to be the least pious of the two, begging of him to hold us up. We said to him, "Signor dragone, have pity upon us." Upon which the good soldier (see whether we are to judge by faces!) instead of sympathizing with our embarrassment, took hold in his turn of our hands more than once to kiss them. So between the young girl (*la ragazza*) and your soldier, we remained suspended for more than half a quarter of an hour, asking for ourself back again, and moved to tears of emotion. Ah! how pleased we were with your people.'[25] The Holy Father distinguished then between the people and the sovereign. In the letters written by him at this time to the Emperor there is no trace of bitterness or anger. Probably, after his experiences at Paris, knowing now somewhat of the man with whom he had to deal, he resigned himself to all future possibilities, but determined to act as if he ignored them. Whithersoever it pleased Divine Providence to guide Peter's Bark, it was for Pius to watch and to pray, for 'Lo, He will not slumber nor sleep, Who keepeth Israel.'[26]

[25] *Histoire de Pie VII.* 50. [26] Psalm cxx.

CHAPTER V.

The Apple of Discord.

'Les personnes ne sont quelque chose que par leur relation avec les principes, tandis que les principes subsistent en eux-mêmes, dans l'éternelle vérité de Dieu.'—Père Lacordaire.

DISAPPOINTMENT, not as yet total discouragement, was the result of the negotiations in Paris in the mind of the Holy Father. He had hoped for a great deal from the action of his personal influence over Napoleon, and however his illusions had been dispelled, it seems that what Consalvi calls his 'serenity' never left him. When in addressing the Sacred College, he declared that he had brought back more than 'mere hopes' from Paris, he was probably expressing a sanguine confidence which he did not feel. However true it may be and is that the Emperor in treating with the Pope officially had not spared him humiliation, it is no less certain that Pius had been captivated, he had in some degree yielded to the charm of the man whose great gift it was to inspire powerful affection even in those who should have been his enemies. Attracted by the natural qualities of Napoleon, the Holy Father experienced at the same time a bitter disappointment that so little had been gained by his journey to Paris. This feeling lay, as it were, at the bottom of his heart, as one which he shrunk from analyzing—a nameless fear which future Catholic generations rather than his contemporaries were to perceive. For a most striking feature in Pius VII. is the daily practical realization of those words of our Lord, 'Seek first the kingdom of God and His justice, and all these things shall be added unto you.'[1] Firmly and gently he suffered affronts directed not only against his person but against his office, when such sufferings did not imply a sacrifice of principle. Principle was the battle in which by 'the grace of God he would not be found wanting.' He had hardly regained Rome when a domestic incident in the Bonaparte family became the immediate cause of that struggle between Pope and Emperor which only ended with the downfall of Napoleon's power. This apple of discord was the outraged honour of a Protestant girl, which the Holy Father maintained in the face of her angered Imperial brother-in-law.

If devotion to principle through better and through worse was remarkable in Pius VII., the thirst after glory and domination was no less so in Napoleon. With him there was only the choice between submission to his will in all matters, or open war. In this respect, nations do not differ from individuals; generally they prefer an easy-going docility to a wearying and incessant strife, and so it was that Napoleon was asserting every day more loudly his pretensions to universal empire. Each day, the position of contemporary European powers became more precarious, as each day they saw more clearly that it was impossible to preserve an inoffensive neutrality with Napoleon Bonaparte. The Pope had been the first to yield to this material superiority of the Emperor, but because, as the Head of the Body which constitutes the highest authority upon earth, his dignity was secondary to that of no man, he must also accept a conflict long as the passion which provoked it. Before,

[1] St. Matt. iv. 33.

however, Napoleon proclaimed his ambitious dreams to the world, he had acted as a domestic tyrant. With his family too it had been, 'You must go with me or against me. You must consent to do as I wish, or retire into the obscurity of private life.' Few men will resist a diadem under the hardest conditions, fewer still when it only necessitates a little bending to a mightier will, for in spite of abstract stoical theories in the absence of opportunity, human nature in the mass loves to reign. Three then of Napoleon's brothers consented to receive crowns at his hand. The second, Lucien, was kept at a distance. He lived in Rome, principally it seems to intrigue against his brother, by whom he was feared.[2] Joseph, the eldest, enjoyed more power, but he was not to be allowed to employ his authority as an imperial prince against the Government, and Napoleon called upon him to choose a definite course of action. 'If you adopt private life, let it be without noise. Retire to Morfontaine, I will give you a million francs for revenue, two millions if necessary. You have nothing to fear from me. I am not the tyrant of my family.' How was Joseph to help himself? 'Where are your means of resistance? Where is the army which you can oppose to my course? Where the auxiliaries with whom you can dispute me the Empire? You are helpless in every way, and I will destroy you, for after all you will be obliged to show yourself at the Tuileries. . . It is not a bad thing to be the second man in France, perhaps in Europe. . . I am called to renovate the social world, at least I think so, and this very confidence ensures my success.' It had been Napoleon's wish to establish the succession in the family of his brother Louis, conferring upon the father the Crown of Italy till the majority of his son. This plan not unnaturally

[2] *Mémoires du Comte Miot de Melito*, t. i. p. 238.

appeared to Louis derogatory to his own dignity, and although Napoleon had deep reasons for not over-favouring Josephine's family, he ended by making Eugène de Beauharnais Viceroy of Italy. On his side, Joseph would not relinquish his claims to the imperial throne, and his pertinacity produced an ill-feeling between himself and Napoleon, who became all the more anxious to rule the destiny of his younger brother Jerome. Unfortunately, this green blossom menaced a blight, for Jerome who, as a simple sailor, had crossed the Atlantic in an admiral's squadron, had married at Baltimore, Miss Patterson, a Protestant, daughter of a rich and well-known citizen of the United States. With the ardour of youth, Jerome had not waited for his mother's consent to the match; and although in a country constituted as the United States, this neglect together with the difference of religion had presented no effective obstacle to the Bishop of Baltimore who performed the ceremony, Madame Bonaparte's ignorance was afterwards brought forward by Napoleon as after all the only reason possessing any weight against the validity of the marriage. Miss Patterson was not to be recognized in France as Jerome's wife. Orders were given that should she succeed in landing there, she was to be immediately sent to Amsterdam, and from thence to the United States by the first opportunity.[3] Napoleon could and did annul the civil marriage by imperial decree, but the Catholic marriage still remained, and what God had put together, the Church could not part. There was only one course open to the Emperor if he wished to keep up appearances with Catholics—recourse to Rome. He forgot or did not wish to remember that the power of binding and loosing is only applicable to the law of the Church, not to the law of God, and that

[3] Lettre de Nap. I. à M. Decrès (23 avril, 1805).

the dissolution of legitimate marriage surpasses even the supreme powers of the Successor of Peter. On the 24th of May, he addressed a letter to the Holy Father which was faithful to his usual mode of attack, introducing the question of the marriage almost indifferently, as if it was the easiest thing in the world to obtain the sentence of dissolution. After other matters, he said:

'I have spoken several times to Your Holiness of a young brother of nineteen, whom I sent to America in a frigate, and who, although a minor, has married a Protestant, the daughter of a merchant of the United States, after a month's sojourn at Baltimore. He has just come back. He is aware of his fault. I have sent back Miss Patterson, his so-called wife, to America. According to our laws, the marriage is invalid. A Spanish priest was so far forgetful of his duty as to give the nuptial benediction. I wish for a Bull from Your Holiness, annulling the marriage. I send Your Holiness several memorandums, one by Cardinal Caselli, which will enlighten Your Holiness. It would be easy for me to have the marriage annulled, as the Gallican Church recognizes (declares) the non-validity of such marriages. But it would be better effected at Rome were it only to serve as an example to members of reigning houses who contract marriage with Protestants. I would urge great secrecy in this proceeding on Your Holiness. Only when I learn that you consent to this step will I cause the marriage to be civilly annulled. It is important, even in France, that no Protestant girl should be so nearly related to me. It is dangerous that a minor of nineteen years of age, of prominent position, should be exposed to so great a seduction, contrary to civil laws, and every sort of propriety.

'With this, I pray that God may preserve you many

years, most Holy Father, to the Government of our Mother Holy Church.

'Your devoted son,

'NAPOLEON.'[4]

Pius VII., the simple but learned Benedictine monk of former years, had no need of the counsels of the Sacred College, nor even of those of his faithful friend Consalvi, to determine a question so nearly touching imperial susceptibility, but so strictly, too, within the limits of his own theological science. Four obstacles had been submitted to the Holy Father's consideration in the different memorandums: disparity of religion; absence of the maternal consent; seduction employed; the absence of the curé or rector involving the non-fulfilment of a necessary formality, and rendering the marriage clandestine. In all countries where the decree of the Council of Trent known as *de Reformatione matrimonii* had been published, the latter point was binding; this alone then, of all the four gave some colour to the alleged non-validity. The Holy Father consequently directed particular attention to the question whether or not the decree had been published at Baltimore. The result of his diligent researches went to prove that no such publication had been made, and the dissolution of the marriage was therefore an impossibility. He gave a detailed reply to Napoleon, exposing his reasons, to convince the Emperor that he refused only in face of a moral obstacle. The letter ends with these noble words:

'If we usurped an authority which we did not possess, we should be guilty before the tribunal of God, and before the whole Church, of the most crying abuse of our sacred ministry. For this reason, we earnestly hope

[4] Quoted by M. Artaud, t. ii. p. 57.

that your Majesty will feel assured that our ardent desire to gratify you in those things which particularly touch your Majesty's august person and your family is in this case simply powerless. We therefore pray you to accept this our declaration as a proof of our paternal affection. We most heartily give you the Apostolical benediction.

'Pius, P.P. VII.'[5]

Napoleon failed to see the point of this letter. According to him, it was not a reply prompted by an upright devotion to principle, but a revenge on the part of the Pope for the non-restoration of the three legations. To refuse what to the Emperor seemed so simple a thing merely because a decree of the Council of Trent had not been published at Baltimore was preposterous in his eyes. It was astonishing that the Sovereign Pontiff should lend a hand towards legitimatizing the position of a Protestant as sister-in-law to the man who had raised the fallen altars of France. Unfortunately, Napoleon forgot all these scruples when it became a question of marrying his brother Jerome to the Protestant daughter of the King of Wurtemburg.

The immediate effect of the papal decision was to produce a state of things painful to the Catholic feelings of the Holy Father in the new kingdom of Italy. By the Italian Concordat the Catholic religion had been proclaimed the religion of the State, but now, in direct opposition with one point at least of the highest importance in the eyes of that religion—the sacred character of marriage—divorce was recognized by the Code Napoleon. The Emperor had been legislating for the Italian clergy somewhat after the fashion of Joseph II., and as an excuse for such intrusion, he alleged to the Holy Father, 'that the Court of Rome

[5] *Histoire de Pie VII.* t. ii. p. 65.

was too slow, and that it followed a policy which might have been wise in other days, but was no longer adapted to the times.' His whole crime consisted in having acted as he had acted 'without the cooperation of the Holy See.' He knew by experience that 'Rome would have employed three or four years to settle Italian affairs, and that they might have collapsed altogether had he not lent a speedy succour.'[6] This letter, despite the imperious character of these remarks, was the last courteous one penned by Napoleon to Pius VII. It pleased the Pope by its details on ecclesiastical matters, for a direct answer to a definite reclamation was a favour which the Emperor too rarely conferred upon the Head of the Church. Cardinal Fesch was charged to discuss the objections raised by the Holy See with those whom Pius VII. should designate for such an end, after which Napoleon would lend himself to any possible modifications.

For the full comprehension of future events it becomes necessary to examine a little the general aspect of Europe, and the policy of Napoleon with regard to the secular powers and to Christ's representative on earth. It was an inconsistency in the Emperor to separate in the person of the Pope the spiritual from the temporal authority, whilst requiring at the same time that he should side with France in all temporal questions. He was to have no weight as an independent sovereign. He was to live by the strength and by the sword of France, but in return he was to make common cause with the country whose arms shielded him from the assaults of other powers. Napoleon perhaps fancied that his scheme was entirely novel in the world's annals. It was true that the Pope would be required to sacrifice the two points which, humanly speaking, have conduced to

---

[6] *Histoire de Pie VII.* t. ii. p. 75.

render him the Universal Father, ruling and guiding the Church without fear of adverse nationalities—his neutrality and his independence. But then he received in exchange the victorious sword of the most invincible conqueror of modern times. It was laid at his feet with all the material wealth which that sword could command. In face of these conditions, and to avoid becoming not the ally only, but the tool of a secular power, the Holy Father accepted the struggle.

During his sojourn in Italy for his coronation at Milan Napoleon had found time to make various new allotments of Italian territory. Genoa was united to the French Empire, Lucca was given to Elisa Bonaparte, his sister, and the State of Parma organized as a dependance of the French crown. Austria saw these changes with jealousy, for they rendered its own hope of re-conquering the Lombard States more distant. The Cabinet of St. James profited by this discontent to draw Austria into an alliance, a long wished for consummation which Austrian timidity had hitherto opposed. Russia, Austria, and England united in the common interest of dislike and dread of France, constituted a coalition whose existence Napoleon could not disregard. Prussia, as the fourth great power, wished for nothing better than a favourable opportunity for declaring itself against the murderer of the Duc d'Enghien. But England, and England's Minister, Pitt, were the heart and soul of the anti-Napoleonic movement in Europe. Pitt not only directed these plans and intrigues on the Continent, but supported them with English gold. England then should suffer; England, Napoleon's mortal enemy, who could only thank her own 'strip of silver sea' that she was not swallowed up in the great French Empire, and used as a convenient prey for a new Bonaparte sovereign. Napoleon had prepared a fleet to carry across the Channel that invincible army already fired with warlike ardour at the mere thought of a second conquest of England. But his design was nipped in the bud, and then with the capability which he possessed in so peculiar a manner, of transferring his energies where they were most needed, he directed his attention to Germany. The campaign was thrown off almost in a breath, and presented a wonderful compendium of military genius. The sum and substance of this project was to humble the 'odious house of Austria,' and to make Bavaria an interposing State between Austria and France. The crowning point was the peace which he promised himself that he would sign in the palace of the Emperor of Germany. On the Italian side of the Alps the French troops were commanded by Massena. These, facing the Austrian army on the Adige, were to preserve a merely defensive attitude. On the other hand, some twenty thousand French soldiers, under General Gouvion Saint-Cyr, were garrisoned in Otranto. The object of the campaign being to bring two armies to bear upon the enemy's city, Vienna, it became necessary that the latter troops should take up a position in Lombardy. For this it was indispensable to traverse the States of the Church, and then it was that Napoleon commanded the violent occupation of Ancona, which he had had the generosity to restore unconditionally to the Pope. He now repented of his liberality. It was the first aggressive step taken against the Temporal Power, for the case of the legations did not present the same character of violence. The Holy Father's conscientious refusal in the matter of Jerome's marriage had probably a great deal to do with this beginning of open hostility.

It is strange that at this very time Pius VII. should have incurred the universal reproach of partiality for Napoleon. In vain the Sovereign Pontiff protested that a strict neutrality was the natural result of his position. In the midst of the various petty intrigues of European Cabinets, all burning to further their own interests, his disinterested assurances were received with outward respect, but not believed. The occupation of Ancona effected this good. Inasmuch as it was an act of violence, it served to justify the assertions of the Holy Father, and alas, to dispel also whatever illusions he still retained as to the friendly dispositions of Napoleon. On the 13th of November, 1805, he placed a sealed letter for the Emperor in the hands of Fesch. It was an expostulation full of pained surprise, and an expression of grief to find that Napoleon was not corresponding as he might and ought to have done to the marks of confidence bestowed upon him by the Holy Father. Moreover, if Ancona were not evacuated by the French troops, Pius intimated the impropriety of the continued mission of Fesch, that is of his official relations with the Roman Court. Not until the 7th of January, 1806, could Napoleon find time to answer his injured correspondent. During those two months, he had gone from glory to glory. He had conquered two Emperors and dictated his own terms to them. He could now afford to bestow crowns on those who had the privilege of belonging to him by the ties of blood, or on those whose bravery he wished to reward. Magnificent in his conquests, he could dispose of what had once constituted the hereditary possessions of his enemies. Caroline of Naples was rewarded for her intrigues by the announcement that 'the Bourbons of Naples had ceased to reign.' The Elector of Bavaria received the title of King; the Grand Duke of Baden was rewarded with the hand of Stéphanie de Beauharnais. Louis Bonaparte was called to reign over Holland, and Joseph at Naples. A prince or a princess of royal blood must be found for those members of the Bonaparte family who lacked a husband or a wife, as the case might be, and unfortunately in one instance for a certain minor already too well provided for in this respect. A marriage was concluded between Eugène de Beauharnais and Augusta, Princess of Bavaria, and one was talked of between Jerome (the legitimate husband of the Protestant Miss Patterson), and the daughter of the Protestant King of Wurtemburg. No discordant note had marred this triumph of Napoleon till he opened the papal letter, and discovered that in the universal hymn of flattery, there still remained one who dared to force an unpleasant truth upon him. In his wrath, he penned from Munich the following reply to the Holy Father—

'Most Holy Father,

'I am in receipt of a letter from Your Holiness, dated November 13th. It has been impossible for me to help feeling deeply that, at a time when the Powers of Europe were united in a coalition against me by the gold of England, Your Holiness should have listened to bad advice, and written me so blunt a letter. Your Holiness is perfectly free to keep or to send away my Minister from Rome. The occupation of Ancona is an immediate and necessary consequence of the badly organized military arrangements of the Holy See. The true interest of Your Holiness was to see this fortress in my possession rather than in that of the Turk or of the English. Your Holiness complains that, since your return to Rome, you have had no other but painful experiences. The reason of this is, that since then, all those who feared my power or expressed friendship for me have changed their opinion, thanks to the material power of the coalition, and also that during that time, I myself have experienced nothing but refusals, even on points of first-class importance in religious matters, such for instance as the question of preventing Protestantism from raising its head in France. I have looked upon myself as the protector of the Holy See, and on this ground have occupied Ancona. As my predecessors of the second and third race, I have considered myself the eldest son of the Church, as alone possessing a sword powerful enough to protect her from the insults of Greeks and Mussulmen. I will always protect the Holy See, in spite of the disloyal steps, the ingratitude and the evil disposition of men who have appeared in their true colours during the last three months. They thought all was over for me: God has manifestly shown, by the success with which He has favoured my arms, the protection which He gives to my cause. I shall be the friend of Your Holiness as often as you consult only your own heart and the true friends of religion. I repeat, if Your Holiness wishes to send away my Minister, you are free to give the preference to the English, and the Caliph of Constantinople; but not wishing to expose Cardinal Fesch to such outrages, I shall replace him by a secular. The hatred too of Cardinal Consalvi is such, that he (Cardinal Fesch) has experienced nothing but refusals, whereas the preference has been given to my enemies. God is judge as to who has done the most for religion of all reigning princes.

'With this, I pray that God, most Holy Father, may give you many more years to govern our mother Holy Church.

'The Emperor of the French, King of Italy,

'NAPOLEON.[7]

'Munich, 7th January, 1806.'

---

[7] *Histoire de Pie VII.* t. ii. p. 106.

The strange logic of this letter is evident. Because Napoleon was the Protector of the Holy See, he had a right to occupy Ancona with French troops. Pius VII. was specially grieved at the reproaches inflicted on his Minister's conduct, and he could not rest till an answer was sent. Does not the gentle and long-suffering Pontiff faithfully render the character of his feelings, which should be that of all who suffer injustice, when he says in closing his reply—

'This liberty of language will be an earnest of the confidence which We feel in your Majesty. If the tribulation that God has reserved for Us in our dolorous pontificate should reach its final point, if We were to see ourself deprived of what is so precious in our sight—the friendship and the goodwill of your Majesty—the Priest of Jesus Christ, who has the truth in his heart and on his lips, will suffer all with fearless resignation. By his constancy, his tribulation itself will furnish him with comfort. He hopes that the reward not offered to him in this world is reserved for him in heaven, where it will be sure and lasting?'[8]

The same day, January 7th, Napoleon had addressed Cardinal Fesch in language still more injurious to the feelings of Pius VII., with the recommendation to publish the letter at the Vatican.

'The Pope has written me a most ridiculous, a most foolish letter. These people thought I was dead. I have caused the occupation of Ancona because, in spite of your remonstrances, nothing had been done for its fortification, and also because the organization is so miserably bad that no efforts could have carried on a resistance. Make it well understood that I will no longer endure this child's play, and that I do not wish representatives of Russia and Sardinia to find a place at

[8] *Histoire de Pie VII.* t. ii. p. 112.

Rome. My intention is to recall you and to replace you by a secular. Since these idiots do not object to the possibility of a Protestant occupying the throne of France, I will send them a Protestant ambassador. . . . I am a Christian, but I am not sanctimonious. Constantine separated the civil from the military power, and I also can name a senator who shall command at Rome in my name. It is a fine thing indeed for those who have admitted Russians, rejected Malta, and who wish now to send away my Minister, to talk about religion. It is they who defame religion. . . . Tell Consalvi, tell the Pope, that as he wishes to send away my Minister from Rome, I am quite capable of going there myself to re-establish him. Nothing is to be done with such men. . . . They are becoming the laughing-stock of courts and of nations. I gave them advice, which they would never take. They imagined that Russians, English, and Neapolitans would respect the Pope's neutrality. To the Pope I represent Charlemagne, because as Charlemagne did, I unite the French and Lombard crowns, and my Empire stretches to the East. It must be understood, then, that we come to an understanding on these points. I will change nothing outwardly, if people behave themselves properly with me. But otherwise, I shall reduce the Pope to be Bishop of Rome. . . . Really, nothing is so wanting in sense as the Court of Rome.'[9]

Protestation against injustice and insult was the only arm left to the Sovereign Pontiff. The States of the Church, serving as they did to separate the two French armies camped in Italy, the one under Eugène de Beauharnais, and the other under Joseph, King of Naples by the grace of Napoleon Bonaparte, presented no difficulties to the imperial conqueror. All he had to do was to

---

[9] *L'Eglise Romaine et le Premier Empire*, t. ii. p. 77.

bring material power to bear upon a weak adversary, and this adversary, as the Vicar of Christ, would be released from the cares of temporal sovereignty with full leisure and tranquillity of mind for those weightier spiritual questions which essentially pertain to the office of Supreme Pontiff. If Napoleon could only succeed in rendering Pius VII. the Spiritual Father of the faithful, without the burden of material anxieties, would he not be doing a work worthy of being classed by posterity with the foundation of the French Empire? It was impossible for a great genius to carry self-illusion further. He would have had his ideal Pope consent to receive a lesson in ecclesiastical government from himself, to submit in all things to his will; for though in theory he professed to rest content with temporal sovereignty, who that had seen him, the enactor of the Organic Articles, domineering over the French bishops through a Minister of Worship, could give any weight to his protestations? No pen but his own can adequately render the tone of command which he now adopted in writing to the Holy Father. The letter of February 13th, 1806, is besides so characteristic that no excuse is needed for giving it in full.

'Most Holy Father,

'I have received the letter of your Holiness, dated January 29th. I share all your troubles; I can imagine that obstacles are not wanting to you. You can escape both by walking on a straight path, by avoiding the intricacies of politics and the question of consideration for those powers who with regard to religion are heretical or outside the Church, and who with regard to politics are far from your States, incapable of protecting you, and only powerful for evil. All Italy shall acknowledge my government. I shall not touch the independence of the Holy See. I will even be at the expense of the movements of my army in your territory. But these must be our conditions. Your Holiness must profess the same regard for me in the temporal order as I profess for you in the spiritual order. You must discontinue an excess of useless caring for heretics who are enemies of the Church, and for European powers who are incapable of benefiting your cause. Your Holiness is the Sovereign, but I am the Emperor, of Rome. All my enemies must be your enemies. That an Englishman, a Russian, a Swede, or a Minister of the Sardinian King should henceforth reside in Rome or in any part of your States, is entirely unfitting. No vessel belonging to any of these nations should enter your ports. As hitherto, I shall always manifest a filial respect for your Holiness as Head of our faith. But I am answerable before God for religion, which He has willed to restore through my means. How can I then, without deep lamentation, see it compromised by the tardy proceedings of the Court of Rome, where nothing is completed, where the true basis of religion—souls—are allowed to perish, all through certain worldly interests, or foolish disputes founded on the prerogatives of the tiara? They who leave Germany in anarchy, who so zealously protect Protestant marriages, and wish to oblige me to unite my family with Protestant princes, who keep back the Bulls of my bishops, and deliver up my dioceses to anarchy, will be accountable to God for such conduct. Six months are necessary to supply a bishop with working powers, when it might be done in eight days. As to Italian affairs, I have done everything for the bishops. I have consolidated the interests of the Church, and not meddled in spiritual matters. What I have done for Milan, I will do for Naples, and for every other place within my dominion. I do not refuse the assistance of men who are inspired with true zeal for religion, nor to come to an understanding with them. But since God has chosen me to watch over religion after such tremendous catastrophes, and if at Rome time is wasted in a guilty indifference, I can neither become nor remain heedless as to what might endanger the prosperity and the good of my subjects. I know, most Holy Father, that your Holiness wishes to do right, but you are surrounded by men who have no such wish, who have erroneous principles, and who aggravate present evils instead of endeavouring to remedy them. If your Holiness would be mindful of what I told you in Paris, religion in Germany would be organized, and not remain in its present miserable condition. . . . But I cannot let a thing which might be done in a fortnight last a whole year. It is not by sleeping away the time that I have raised the state of the clergy and the publicity of worship to its high actual level, that I have reorganized religion in France on such a footing that no country exists where it works so much good, is more respected, or enjoys greater consideration. Those who speak a different language to your Holiness deceive you and are your enemies; they will bring down misfortunes which will end by proving fatal to themselves.

'With this, I pray that God, most Holy Father, may give you many years to govern our mother, Holy Church.

'Your devoted son,

'NAPOLEON.[10]

'Paris, 13th February, 1806.'

In the parliamentary discussions raised in 1805 in England, on the subject of Catholic Emancipation, a member of the House of Lords gave utterance to a view of the reigning Sovereign Pontiff, which it may be well to mention. 'I think,' he said, 'indeed, I am certain, that

[10] *Histoire de Pie VII.* t. ii. p. 113.

the Pope is nothing but a miserable puppet in the hands of the usurper of the Bourbon throne; that he does not dare to take the simplest step without the order of Napoleon, and that if the Emperor asked for a Bull which should authorize the priests of Ireland to provoke the popular rebellion against the Government, the Pope would not refuse the tyrant.'[11] The answer made by the 'miserable puppet,' who was summoned by a mighty Emperor to accede to the continental system as the most effectual means of diminishing the maritime power of our own country, will best tell us how far the speaker in question had measured the character of Pius VII.

'As Vicar of that Eternal Word,' were his meek words, 'Who is not the God of dissension, but the God of peace, Who came to blot out our iniquities, and to preach peace to those who are near, and to those who are far off (these are the Apostle's expressions), how can We deviate from the teaching of our Divine Founder? How can We act in contradiction with the mission for which We have been destined? It is not our will, but that of God, Whose place We occupy on earth, which lays down the duty of peace towards all men, without distinction of Catholics and heretics, of vicinity or distance, without forethought as to those from whom We may expect good or evil. We cannot betray the office entrusted to Us by Almighty God, and We should betray it, if, for the motives alleged by your Majesty—as, for instance, in the case of heretical powers who can work Us no good (these are your Majesty's own words)—We consented to demands which would force Us to take active part in a war against them. The sheer necessity of combating hostile aggression, or the defence of endangered religion, may have given a just ground for the non-continuance of neutrality to some of our pre-

---

[11] See *Du Pape*, J. de Maistre, t. i. p. 267.

decessors. If any one among them, through human frailty, ever departed from these principles, We do not hesitate to say that his conduct could never serve as an example to Us. You say further, that your enemies must be our enemies. This is opposed to the character of our divine mission, which owns no enmities, not even with those who have departed from the centre of our unity.'[12]

The Holy Father had called a Congregation (not a Consistory), of the Sacred College, to discuss the two points officially communicated to him by Fesch.

1. 'The expulsion of Russians, English, Swedes, and Sardinians, from Rome and the Papal States.

2. The closing of the Papal ports to English, Russian, and Swedish vessels.

Thus the Sovereign who recommended the Pope to hold aloof from politics, would have drawn him into an inconsistency ill-becoming his dignity, by causing him to adopt the cause of France to the prejudice of three powerful nations of Europe. Fesch, in his quality of French Ambassador had consented to absent himself from the Congregation, for as Consalvi urged, his presence would have fettered the liberty of the Cardinals. Only one, a French Cardinal, voted in favour of the Emperor's demands. After the event, Fesch bitterly complained that he had been kept at a distance. He had been unable to use that personal influence from which the Emperor pretended to expect so much. He was irritated and distressed at the result of the Congregation, and he seemed determined to find a personal grievance in the matter. With an ill-will for Consalvi which he had never attempted to master, he used every means to bring the imperial displeasure on the devoted Minister. It seems that Catholic posterity has a right to be hard upon the conduct of Cardinal Fesch at this time, but

[12] *Histoire de Pie VII.* t. ii. pp. 122, 123, 128,

the real evil of it lay in the impossible game that he was trying to play. 'No man can serve God and Mammon,' but this is precisely what Fesch was striving after at Rome. He had a conscience, and he was a Prince of the Church, it is probable then, that he secretly thought that things were going a great deal too far, and his own part was distasteful to his Catholic feelings. On the other hand, he was uncle to the man who was causing Europe to tremble, who was crowning and uncrowning kings as if it were child's play. He had not the moral courage to shut his eyes to the alluring imperial pomp, to side with the weak against the strong, or to proclaim, in a word, that he was one of two things: a zealous Cardinal, or a devoted courtier. Because he tried to conciliate God and the world, he failed to please either,

> Incontanente intesi e certo fui
> Che quest'era la setta dei cattivi,
> A Dio spiacenti, ed ai nemici sui.[12]

Thus his position at Rome was full of thorns. His conscience was uncomfortable, and this made itself felt by extreme sensitiveness, a great capacity for taking offence, and no less for giving it by his restless meddling and his want of tact. Later on in his career he redeemed the period of his ambassadorship, the vice of which was certainly before all things the cruel necessity of a false position. In the beginning of 1806, he was recalled and replaced by M. Alquier, who was rather an ex-republican than a 'corrected' one. The parting words of Pius VII. to Fesch were that 'although the Emperor ill-treated him exceedingly, he remained firmly attached to the imperial person, and to the French nation.'

To Consalvi, however, beyond a doubt, was attributed by Napoleon, the Pope's firm resistance to his wishes,

---

[12] Dante, *Inferno*, canto iii. 61.

and for this reason, he determined to overthrow the Secretary of State. 'Tell him' (Consalvi), he wrote to Fesch, 'that only two courses remain open to him: always to do what I wish, or to quit the ministry.' Later on, Alquier was charged to signify to the Cardinal that none of his movements escaped the Emperor, and that for the first compromising act, he should answer with his head. Napoleon would cause him to be arrested in the middle of Rome.[13] Pius VII. for a long time opposed Consalvi's representations as to leaving the ministry. Consent on his part to such a step, would have seemed to imply that he believed the slanderous accusations made by the Cardinal's enemies. But this resignation had at least one advantage. It would prove to France—to Europe, that Pius VII. was acting freely, and that he was not ruled by the Prime Minister, when instead of what would have been unlawful submission, he accepted the combat. The Holy Father was wont to say sometimes, 'Will those people (the French Cabinet) persist in believing that I am a mere puppet (*fantoccino*)? I shall show them that is far from being the case.'[14] Cardinal Consalvi retired from the Ministry at a critical moment, June 1806. The struggle daily took a more definite shape. Not satisfied with the violent occupation of Ancona, Napoleon alienated the Pope's possessions in favour of his particular friends. Benevento was bestowed upon the ex-bishop of Autun, Talleyrand; and Ponte-Corvo was allotted to General Bernadotte. Napoleon would be Emperor of the West, but at the very zenith of his glory, when he had accomplished his dream, history does not record of him that he revelled in his self-acquired fame. There was no peace for him as the Sovereign of mere matter. He coveted that empire over

---

[13] *Correspondance de Napoléon I.* t. xii. p. 402.
[14] *L'Eglise Romaine et le Premier Empire*, t. ii. p. 202.

the nobler part of man, and angrily said of priests, 'they keep the soul for themselves and throw me the carcass.'

But this was not the prize for such ambition as his. That empire is in the hands of God, and becomes the inheritance only of those who have sought to be despised, and have esteemed themselves blessed to suffer ignominy for the name of Jesus. 'The bodies of the saints are buried in peace, and their names shall live for evermore.'

By a singular disposition of Providence, the Head of the Catholic Church had estranged the Emperor of French Democracy, because he had fearlessly defended the honour of a Protestant girl, the daughter of a simple citizen of the United States, against the attacks of pretensions marked with the extremest pride of the old regime. And now he was destined to witness the gradual deprivation of the remaining fragments of his temporal power, because at a time of peace he refused to close his ports against England.[15]

---

[15] *L'Eglise Romaine et le Premier Empire*, t. ii. p. 44.

CHAPTER VI.

The position assumed by Napoleon as a Ruler towards the Church.

Two powers are there, O Emperor, by which in chief this world is ruled: the sacred authority of Pontiffs, and the royal power. And in these two the weight of the Pontiffs is in so far the heavier, in that they will have in the judgment to render an account to the Lord even for kings themselves.'—Pope Gelasius to the Emperor Anastasius, A.D. 494.

THE position which Bonaparte assumed towards the Church is one sufficiently remarkable to claim a distinct consideration. The civil part which he came to carry out was to terminate the revolution by setting himself at the head of it. With the intuitive glance of genius he discerned that he could never accomplish his purpose without the aid of religion. Hence, while the men about him were almost all involved in that gross disregard of the Church and all its offices which the impiety of the times had generated, the First Consul of his own accord approached the Sovereign Pontiff, and proposed a visible re-establishment of religion. Here it is to be noted that he not only treated the Pope as the sole and absolute representative of the Church, but even called upon him for an exercise of spiritual authority such as in its extent and absolute character the eighteen preceding centuries could not show. The First Consul, himself still a Republican officer, invited the Pope to extinguish the jurisdiction of all remaining among the one hundred and thirty-five legitimate bishops, confessors for the Faith, to erect in the stead of one hundred and thirty-five bishoprics in old France, and twenty-four in the annexed provinces, sixty new sees, and to fill those sees with new occupants. No proceeding can be conceived which would cut away more completely from its root the whole growth of so-called Gallican liberties. Yet this proceeding was the basis of the Concordat which he made with the Holy Father. The sufferings and losses of the Church in the ten preceding years had been so great that the Pope considered an agreement made with the civil power, even on such a basis, to be a great gain. How carefully and conscientiously, in this Concordat, Cardinal Consalvi pondered every word, how he tempered every concession, and how he bore in mind every subject which was omitted, for there are cases in which omission carries liberty, has been seen from the preceding narrative. The result may be stated in the fact that the Concordat of 1801, while it consented to a vast diminution of sees, and to the alienation of great endowments, yet granted to the First Consul, as chief of the State, a privilege which had only been conceded as a special favour to the eldest son of the Church, in a country wherein the Church was established on a scale of wonderful splendour and possessed of innumerable rights. Nor did it stop here. But to the nomination of bishops was also added the privilege that the curés whom the bishops themselves were to nominate should be first presented for approval to the First Consul.

It is plain that the man who demanded such terms approached the Church not so much as a mother having claim to his reverence, but rather as an unquestionable power in human society which he needed and which he was bent upon using for his own end. But it shows the inmost nature of the man, utterly devoid of truth and honour, that when dealing, as the chief of a great commonwealth, with one whom he recognized to be the Head of Christendom, after all had been agreed upon by the respective parties, and only the signing of a solemn treaty remained to be performed, he instructed his agent Bernier to bring in his pocket and present for signature a counterfeit document, in the hope that it might escape the vigilance of the Cardinal. Who could imagine that the conqueror of Marengo and the restorer of religion, would descend to be a forger and thimble-rigger?

But the imposture which Consalvi had detected and frustrated was to be made up by another expedient, scarcely less discreditable.

When the Concordat had been ratified at Rome, it was presented, by order of the First Consul, to the Legislature, in order that it might be enacted as a law of the French Republic; but with it was presented likewise another scheme of laws, which were termed Organic Articles of the Convention, entered into between the French Government and His Holiness Pius VII. These articles at once and largely encroached upon the region left outside of the Concordat. They submitted every act of the Holy See and every decree of a General Council to the control of the civil power before execution. They tacitly abolished all religious Orders of both sexes, by declaring that with the exception of cathedral chapters and seminaries all other ecclesiastical establishments were suppressed. Even with regard to their seminaries, the Bishops were to submit to the Government the rules for their organization, as well as the names of the persons studying in them, and the number of those whom they should ordain; and they were to compel all the teachers in their seminaries, the educators of the clergy, to profess themselves and to teach to others the four articles of

1682, whose erroneous doctrines the Pope had condemned and had caused Louis XIV. to withdraw.

To present the Concordat in one hand, and these articles in the other, as the common result of an agreement with the Holy See, was to carry into his legislation the fraud of the sharper detected by Consalvi. It showed the despotic temper of the man who was about to seat himself on the throne of the eldest Son of the Church, not as one who recognized by the loyalty of his conduct Him Who said: 'By Me kings reign and princes decree justice,' but as one who thought in his heart: 'My people will reverence my throne if they see my feet set upon the Church as a footstool.'

This is not the place to show the wonderful action of Divine Providence by which the good which the Pope hoped for from the Concordat has been obtained, and the captivity which the First Consul, in the Organic Articles, sought to impose on her, has been changed for the glorious liberty of a Church rich in multiplied daily sacrifices of self-denial, and abounding also in the labours of devoted religious bodies, while she pours out the exuberance of her life in missionary enterprize.

Now let us pass from the spiritual prerogatives claimed by Napoleon's legislation to his practical conduct as an every-day ruler. From his living tomb of St. Helena the Emperor dictated the words: 'Napoleon did not wish to change the creed of his subjects; he respected that which pertained to religion, and wished to be master without meddling therein. He wanted to square religion to his views and to his policy, but through temporal means."[1]

Did he speak truth? Or do not these sentiments express rather what he would wish to have done than what he did? In the abstract, he recognized in the Sovereign Pontiff the Spiritual Father of Christendom;

---
[1] *Mémoires de Napoléon*, t. iv. p. 236.

in the concrete, he did not scruple to strip the Holy Father of the territory which he held in trust for that same Christendom, and to reduce him to become the first of his subjects. In his eyes the Church was a wide domain, which tempted him to exercise his innate propensity to reign in it as he did over his vast material empire. When therefore Napoleon spoke of 'being master without meddling,' we naturally ask ourselves where he drew the line, what he considered 'being master,' and what 'meddling.' The true state of the case was that, as he had been the tyrant of his family whilst disclaiming all notion of domestic tyranny, so now he meant to be somewhat more than even a Gallican Head of the State in all dealings with the French Church. His power nowhere savoured more forcibly of an usurpation than here; and consequently nowhere was it more despotic. He had used temporal things in order to reign, and his new dignity of Cæsar somewhat justified the step; but when he turned to spiritual things, and sought to make profit of them for his own ends, we vainly look for an attenuating circumstance. When he told the Holy Father, bluntly enough, that he alone possessed the art of ecclesiastical government, that the Court of Rome was too slow, that the Pope's Ministers were 'idiots' whose narrow minds could not keep pace with the age, we might fully expect to see established over the French clergy in all its details a system of State intrusion, with full powers to govern, or to dictate to them, their minutest movements. Was it Napoleon's misfortune, or his fault, that wherever he ruled it was as a tyrant? To the Holy Father, to the French clergy, to his own family, to each and all, he could have applied the well-known sentiments of Louis XIV.: '*L'état c'est moi.*' For to him ruling and despotism were synonymous. The one followed the other as surely as the bud expands into the flower. The king of men would in no case content himself with less than the lion's part. Who knows whether, if his petty tyranny of the clergy had lasted longer, it might not have drawn Catholic France into schism? He was pushing Gallicanism to its farthest limits, concentrating both spiritual and temporal authority in the person of the Head of the State. From the Concordat till 1814, the French clergy endured a system of secular intrusion of which it would be instructive to form an adequate notion. Some priests suffered imprisonment, others groaned in a passive, yet enforced inaction; but perhaps the majority resorted to compromises, to silent compacts with their conscience, under the view that as long as Napoleon respected the ground of positive dogma, their wisest course was a timid silence. It was not agreeable to be interfered with in the discharge of their pastoral duties, or to be obliged to sing the Emperor's praises from the pulpit; but at this price they bought a kind of peace which is an offspring and a result of weak submission. Perhaps they flattered themselves that so long as peace was maintained, religion was advancing.

After the Holy Father had given the highest religious sanction to Napoleon's crown, the Emperor's policy with regard to the nomination of bishops visibly changed. He seemed to have broken with his old notions in discarding gradually the constitutional clergy. Hitherto, as a son of the Revolution, he had needed them; now, as the founder of a new dynasty, he rather sought out those who by birth and education should have belonged to the old royalty. The question had been viewed in all its aspects by Bonaparte as First Consul. The sympathies of the constitutional clergy went, for the most part, with the movement of 1789. The Revolution, in wearying them with its excesses, did not inspire them with any desire for the return of the Bourbons, and they were ready to adore the star of glory and fame which, rising out of liberty, equality, and fraternity, decorated the forehead of a conqueror who ended by exacting of them humble obedience.

Napoleon, as Emperor, considered that he had taken the place of the old dynasty, and to make this a conviction with his subjects, he began, after his coronation, openly to favour its friends. They who had frequented Trianon and Versailles were to introduce tone and etiquette into the new court. None, according to Napoleon, were so capable of obedience as they who had passed through a docile apprenticeship in the school of the ancient royalty. Thus amongst his bishops, Mgr. de Boulogne had been designated to the see of Trojes, chiefly because he had preached the funeral oration of Louis Dauphin, son of Lous XV., and the last sermons listened to at the Tuileries by Louis XVI. A similar motive had dictated the choice of Mgr. de Boisgelin as preacher on the Easter Sunday of 1802 at Notre Dame. He had performed the same office at the coronation of the Martyr King.

Napoleon had said that he wished to 'be master of that which pertains to religion, but without meddling therein.' It was therefore his will to endeavour to associate his own cause to that of religion, and so strenuous were his efforts in this particular, that they are calculated to excite the ridicule of posterity. After each great victory, he wrote in pressing and edifying terms to the archbishops and bishops of his empire, to order a *Te Deum* in thanksgiving to the God of Armies, for his success. These *Te Deums* were generally accompanied by an episcopal exhortation or a pastoral, for which M. Portalis, sometimes the Emperor himself, furnished the subject, and which varied according to the direction of the imperial arms. While the Prussians were the objects of attack, great lamentations were poured forth on the impropriety of their state of schism and separation from Rome. The bishops were specially recommended to feed the national hatred against England on the ground of the perfidious heresy of Albion. 'Monsieur Portalis,' the Emperor wrote on the 21st April, 1807, 'it would be well, especially in Brittany and La Vendée, if some bishop would take it upon himself to compose a pastoral on the persecutions inflicted on the Irish Catholics. He might recommend prayers to be said that our brothers, the persecuted Catholics of Ireland, may enjoy liberty of worship. For this, it would be necessary to read up the subject, and you might write a telling article in the *Moniteur*, which would furnish the text of a pastoral.'

But it was not enough to preach a passive crusade against the Emperor's enemies. His personal praises must resound in the pulpit, and in this respect, no half and half measures, but very ardent zeal alone could be tolerated. The Prefect of Police, M. Réal, one day said to Mgr. de Broglie: 'You must praise the Emperor more in your pastorals.' The Prelate had just reproduced Bossuet's expressions of joy on the birth of a grandson of Louis XIV., to honour the King of Rome, therefore this announcement astonished him. He replied: 'Give me the measure of praise that is expected from me.' 'I do not know it,' replied the functionary. The custom had been gradually adopted of reading from the altar the bulletins from the army. Naturally enough they were commented upon by the reader, and as long as Napoleon continued a magnificent and undisputed conqueror, this presented no difficulty. When, however, the issue of the battle was somewhat doubtful, the task was delicate. Napoleon suppressed it gradually on the ground that priests must not be made to feel their political importance. At the same time, he did not see the harm of the State's usurpation of an overwhelming authority in religious matters. Though the Church was to be kept under proper control of the secular power, he would extract all possible support for his own cause from the influence exercised by priests on the popular mind. To become a vicar-general, a canon, or the possessor of a first-class cure it was necessary to obtain degrees which were entirely in the gift of the imperial university. It need hardly be said, that those whom the Emperor honoured with suspicions of 'Ultramontane views or dangerous ideas' were kept in the shade. With a narrow-minded despotism very unlike the generous liberty of Catholic Rome he not only supervised the pastorals of the French clergy, but even the sermons of provincial curés. He writes: 'Inform M. Robert, a priest of Bourges, of my displeasure. He preached a very foolish sermon on the 15th of August. L'Abbé de Coucy is a great worry to me. He keeps up too great a correspondence. I wish him to be arrested, and put into a monastery. . . . It is most urgent that you should keep your eyes on the diocese of Poitiers. It is really shameful that you have not yet arrested M. Stevens. People are too sleepy, else how could a wretched priest have escaped? . . . I see from your letter that you have caused a curé of La Vendée to be arrested. You have acted very wisely. Keep him in prison.[2]

Prison and the press, these were two powerful arms which Napoleon did not disdain to use actively for his own ends. Priests of doubtful views were sent without legal formality of any kind to people Vincennes, the isles of St. Margaret, Fenestrello, and other political prisons. Generally, no crime could be imputed to them but Ultramontane zeal, and unfortunately, once in prison, their confinement was indefinitely prolonged, seeing that

[2] *Correspondance de Napoléon I.* 1805, 1807.

their release would probably have caused them to be viewed by the sympathizing public as heroes and confessors, since even under a despotism the people's compassion naturally goes with the wronged. It is a remarkable fact too, that the Holy See seldom suffers alone, but that the whole Church participates, to a certain degree, in the prosperity or adversity, as it may be, of the Successor of Peter. The Emperor, knowing the importance of the press, suppressed all newspapers of a religious tone save one, the *Journal des Curés*, whose publication was closely supervised, for Napoleon elegantly observed 'no priest should bother his head about the Church save in his sermons.'[3] The Emperor fully acted up to his convictions. We find that he suggested the number and nature of the feasts which his people might keep without fear of an excess of piety. In the year 1638, Louis XIII., upon the birth of a son, afterwards the Grand Monarque, chose the 15th August, the Feast of the Assumption, to place his person, his crown, and France, under the special protection of the Mother of God, and ordered that every year there should be made a solemn procession to Notre Dame of Paris and throughout the kingdom, in memory of that consecration. But now the 15th August was to have a St. Napoleon, who should recall upon that great festival the anniversary of the Emperor's birth to his subjects, as well as the new order of things by the ratification of the Concordat. The distinguishing feature of the day was to be, not the glory of the Mother of the Lord, but thanksgiving for the prosperity of the Empire, as redounding to the praise of the Emperor. Besides this, the first Sunday following the 11th Frimaire (December), was to be consecrated to commemorating the Coronation, and the successes of the *Grande Armée*. In the sermon preached on the

[3] Lettre de l'Empereur à M. Portalis, 14 aout, 1807.

occasion, particular mention should be made of those parishioners who had fallen at Austerlitz. To celebrate any feasts besides the two invented by Napoleon, would have been, according to him, an extravagant sanctioning of useless memories. But a new difficulty arose out of the very saint who had given his name to the Emperor. St. Napoleon was entirely unknown. M. Portalis was obliged to acknowledge his ignorance in the matter, to a distressed bishop,[4] who was in search of facts for the office of the saint so suddenly held up for public admiration. At length the much wished-for information was provided that, 'under the Emperors Diocletian and Maximian, a great number of courageous confessors had suffered martyrdom at Alexandria in Egypt, during the cruel persecution which they raised against the disciples of Jesus Christ. Amongst the martyrs, there was a certain *Neopolis* or *Neopolas*, a Greek name, which, according to the pronunciation introduced into Italy during the middle ages, would have gradually become *Napoleo*, and later, the Italian, *Napoleone*.'[5]

A paragraph concerning public worship, contained in the Organic Articles, had ordered that there should be but one liturgy, and one catechism in all France. In itself this unity could present nothing displeasing to the Holy Father, as long as the catechism was approved and sound in its teaching. In the autumn of 1805, Caprara had sent a sketch of the proposed compendium of doctrine to Rome, entreating for a decision from Pius VII. It was perhaps a question which Rome purposely delayed answering, but at length, pressed by the Legate, Consalvi, who evidently expected no good from the business, specified in his reply, that were the Government to choose or to compose a catechism, His

---

[4] Mgr. d'Osmond, of Nancy.
[5] *L'Eglise Romaine et le Premier Empire*, t. ii. p. 252.

Holiness would look upon the act as one injurious to the French episcopate. To the Apostles, and to their successors alone had the power of teaching been given.[6] This explicit answer was as if it had never been for the weak Legate. Not only in direct disobedience to his instructions did he consent to contribute personally towards the subject-matter of the catechism, but he kept the whole proceeding a secret from Pius VII. and from Consalvi, so that they first heard of its publication through a newspaper.

M. Portalis was charged with the preparation of the new Imperial Catechism. A commission of French ecclesiastics who were to work under his directions with the consent of Caprara was nominated. Amongst the number was M. Portalis' own nephew, the Abbé d'Astros, who later, found his way to nobler occupation. The preliminaries were satisfactorily terminated towards the end of 1803, but the position of Napoleon at that time was not definitely fixed. Unfortunately his correspondence proves that this was a grave obstacle in the way of the immediate publication of the catechism, for to him, the only importance of the whole matter was the degree of obsequious submission he could by its means exact from the French people. At a chance suggestion of M. Emery, Napoleon feigned to adopt for his work, the catechism of Bossuet. The name of the great Bishop of Meaux contained more than a superficial meaning for the Emperor. Had not Bossuet supported Louis XIV. in his differences with Pope Innocent XI.? But in this case, as in all others, Napoleon took and left what he pleased. Bossuet might be agreeable when he strove to defend scientifically the liberties of the Gallican Church, and lent the stores of his learning to the King against the Pope, but his text in defining the duties of

[6] *L'Eglise Romaine et le Premier Empire*, t. ii. p. 278.

subjects towards their sovereign was judged singularly barren. He had mingled Louis XIV. with the vulgar crowd, not even speaking of the monarch nominally in the chapter of the fourth commandment. Napoleon would be more explicit. In the private correspondence between the Emperor and M. Portalis it was no question of Bossuet, but only of determining the degree of submission and obedience which was due to Napoleon from the French nation. The catechism appeared in August 1806, and as a specimen of what Gallicanism can produce when it has bent a conscience to the most abject desires of a sovereign, we may quote the chapter relating to the fourth commandment:

'*Q.* What are the duties of Christians with regard to reigning princes, and what are our duties in particular, towards Napoleon, our Emperor?

'*A.* Christians are bound to give to their princes, and we, in particular, are bound to give love, respect, obedience, fidelity, military service, the taxes which are ordered for the preservation and defence of the Empire and of the throne, to Napoleon, our Emperor. We are bound, moreover, to give him our fervent prayers for the spiritual and temporal prosperity of the State.

'*Q.* Why are we so bound towards our Emperor?

'*A.* In the first place, because God, who creates and distributes empires according to His pleasure, has, in loading our Emperor with talents, both in war and peace, established him as our sovereign, and has made him the minister of almighty power, as well as the divine image upon earth. The honour, then, and the service of our Emperor is one and the same thing as the honour and service of God.

'Secondly, because our Lord Jesus Christ has Himself taught us, by His doctrine and His example, what we owe to our Sovereign. In His birth, He was obedient to the edict of Cæsar Augustus. He did not refuse the lawful tribute, and just as He commanded us to render to God those things which are God's, so He desired that we should render to Cæsar that which is Cæsar's.

'*Q.* Are there not particular reasons which should attach us to the person of Napoleon I. our Emperor?

'*A.* Yes, for he is the man raised by God in difficult circumstances to re-establish public worship, and the holy religion of our fathers, and to be its protector. He has consolidated public tranquillity by his consummate and active wisdom; he preserves the State with his mighty arm; he has become the Lord's Anointed by the consecration of the Supreme Pontiff and Head of the Universal Church.

'*Q.* What opinion is to be entertained of those who are wanting in their duty towards our Emperor?

'*A.* According to the Apostle St. Paul, they resist the order of things established by God Himself, and render themselves worthy of eternal damnation.

'*Q.* Will our duty towards our Emperor bind us equally in the case of his legitimate successors, as stipulated by the constitutions of the Empire?

'*A.* Yes, certainly; for we read in holy Scripture that God, Who is Lord of heaven and earth, gives empires by a disposition of His supreme will and providence, not merely to an individual but to a family.

'*Q.* What are our obligations towards our magistrates?

'*A.* We must honour, respect, and obey them, as depositaries of the authority of our Emperor.

'*Q.* What is forbidden by the fourth commandment?

'*A.* It forbids disobedience to our superiors, conduct prejudicial to them, or evil speaking of them.'[7]

---

[7] *L'Eglise Romaine et le Premier Empire,* t. ii. p. 268.

Is it astonishing that a Legate, who could have consented to a catechism so constructed, should have entirely lost the confidence of Pius VII. and of his Minister Consalvi? If the situation rendered protestation or the recall of Caprara imprudent or even impossible, the Legate was no longer viewed by the Holy Father otherwise than as a mere agent of Napoleon. That the Emperor appreciated Caprara's devotion to his cause is sufficiently proved by the following announcement contained in a letter to Prince Eugène. 'I will willingly purchase his palace at Bologna for Caprara. Even should it cost me a few thousand more francs, I will make the sacrifice in order to extricate Caprara from his grievous difficulties. Entrust this purchase to my steward. I will have the money paid by long interest of several years, giving securities to the creditors. I know Caprara's faults, and I recommend him to you. He is one of the first and the truest friends that I have had in Italy.'[8]

It would not be true to say that the French bishops accepted the Imperial Catechism without a murmur. There were a certain number, of course, wholly devoted to Napoleon, but many others, who in presence of innumerable difficulties and the threatening atmosphere of religious matters, submitted to silence as their wisest policy. At such moments, the bravest and the most conscientious sometimes shrink from compromising themselves, for it is a truism presented by the study of history, of ecclesiastical history as well as any other, that in our appreciation of the defective acts of men, a very large allowance must be made for human frailty.

[8] Lettre de l'Empereur au Prince Eugène, 23 Mars, 1806.

CHAPTER VII.

The Quirinal a Prison.

Pulchrior est miles in pugnæ prælio amissus, quam in fuga salvus.'—
Tert. *De Fuga in Persecutione.*

IN the conflict between the Pope and Emperor, it was Napoleon's error to treat, or think that he could with impunity treat, Pius VII. as an ordinary sovereign. Instead of viewing the subject of the Pontiff's temporal power in all its aspects, it pleased him to look at one side only, or rather to regard instead of it the material glory of his empire, to which the States of the Church, as long as they remained States of the Church, opposed what seemed to him an insuperable difficulty. While he was changing the face of Europe, there remained one Sovereign, whose territory not only formed a barrier against the accomplishment of his vast designs, but who by the very nature of a double authority, alike spiritual and temporal, would always stand outside and independent of political leagues and factions. If this territory had been the possession of a merely secular power, it must have succumbed, a victim to Napoleon's dream of forming a Western Empire. But 'not by bread alone does man live.' The Holy Father opposed the Emperor by the invincible strength of his moral character, which rested on his spiritual Headship, not as the owner of a material sovereignty. It was the very existence of his office which rendered him superior to Napoleon, and caused him to answer the propositions of the modern Cæsar not only with 'I will not,' but with 'I cannot.' This *non possum* it was that the Emperor either framed into a narrow-minded resentment entirely foreign to a Pontiff so loving and so full of patient endurance as Pius VII., or attributed to exterior influence. Too long he imagined that the conflict lay but between a feeble old man incapable of deciding the smallest question, and himself, a magnificent conqueror whose arms, he was pleased to think, God had crowned with unexampled triumph. Here in this narrow region of Italy, of which Rome is the great centre as it is the temporal home of Catholic hearts, there should be no army stretched in battle array, no sovereign humbly kneeling in the dust at his feet, but a Pontiff calm and peaceful, yet strong in his weakness, whom sheer force alone could tear from his capital, whose wrongs no bloody scenes nor angry words would revenge. But the protestation of Pius in face of violence has echoed through succeeding generations, whilst the material power and empire which called it forth have passed away, leaving in the minds of men only an evil memory of the abuse of noble gifts.

On the resignation of Consalvi, Pius VII., as if to repudiate all notion of undue external influence, chose in his place Cardinal Casoni, a mild and gentle old man, without strong political views, and whom nobody would have thought to designate as the Pope's chief Minister. The first act of the new Secretary of State was a circular addressed to the various Papal Nuncios of Europe, informing them of the fate of Benevento and Ponte-Corvo. The Pope's design in publishing this officially was less to obtain results than to prove how far he had been from being governed by Consalvi. Material help from European Cabinets he was very far from expecting, for the man who was persecuting him was humbling them, and diminishing every day their political importance. The state of the question between Pius VII. and Napoleon, in the summer of 1806, was this. Either the Pope must consent to belong to the French Federation, and as a temporal sovereign bind himself to a league, offensive and defensive, against all the enemies of the empire, or he must submit to the loss of his States. The Holy Father had thwarted Napoleon's ambitious designs, and hitherto all similar obstacles had been swept away. The Emperor therefore was determined to bring the Court of Rome to reason by fair means or by foul. It would have pleased him better to do it quietly (*sans secousse*), but if it became necessary to resort to violence against a weak, unarmed adversary, he would not hesitate as to his course of action. The end which he had in view, covered with Napoleon a multitude of sins—open violation of the right of nations, double dealing, falsehood. It so engrossed him that he took small account of these minor details. Sometimes it pleased him to inflict a scene half spontaneous, half preconcerted, on the bewildered Legate at Paris, the result of which would, he knew, be communicated to Pius VII., and perhaps produce complete adhesion to his extravagant demands. Caprara was in the habit of frequenting, nearly every evening, the small and select circle of Josephine. One day the Empress was slightly indisposed, and the Legate, as it happened, was taken to the Emperor's reception, whereat his own household and that of the Empress were present, together with the principal part of the Court. Hardly had Napoleon perceived the Legate, when he began to speak in a loud voice about Roman affairs, and to inveigh against the evil counsellors of the Holy Father. 'My demands,' he said, 'were entirely of a temporal and political nature. But the world shall be judge between the Pope and me. It shall see that I also am bound in conscience to ensure to my subjects whom God has given to me, those rights of which St. Louis was tenacious, and yet he was beatified by Rome.'

Caprara ventured some inoffensive remark, but Napoleon, with the impetuosity of a torrent, would not let him finish his sentence. 'Write to Rome,' he pursued vehemently, 'that I am resolved to prevent the English from effecting a diversion, and from cutting the communication between my troops of the kingdom of Italy and those of the kingdom of Naples. Write that I demand of His Holiness an unreserved and frank declaration to the effect that during the present war, and all future wars, all the ports of the Pontifical States shall be closed to all English men-of-war and merchant ships. Write this to the Pope, write it at once, because if within the shortest possible delay I do not receive the declaration which I demand, I shall cause the rest of the Pontifical territory to be occupied. I shall have the French eagles posted on the gates of all his cities and of all his domains, and I shall divide the Papal provinces into duchies and principalities, which I shall confer upon whom I please, as I have already done with Benevento and Ponte-Corvo. If the Pope persists in his refusal, I shall establish a Senate at Rome, and when once Rome and the Pontifical States are in my hands, they will stay there.[1] Write this explicitly; conceal nothing; I shall see, from the Pope's answer, whether you have been a faithful reporter.'[2] The time had come when Napoleon could reveal a long-meditated design without shame. No more was to be obtained from that Pope who in too sanguine a moment of confidence had consented to recognize his crown before the throne of God in sight of all the people. He

---

We are reminded here of a later power which has said: '*Ci siamo e ci staremo.*'
[2] *L'Eglise Romaine et le Premier Empire,* t. ii. p. 307.

was to be sacrificed because the Emperor willed it. Napoleon's determination was fixed, and what was still more, it had been expressed before his astonished Court. He rarely acted from impulse; but when a project had grown and worked in his mind to full maturity, it issued forth after the fashion of a mountain stream, *seemingly* the mere birth of hastiness or anger. The immediate effect of the scene inflicted on Caprara, which had lasted no less than an hour, was an ultimatum penned by Alquier to the Holy Father. It told Pius VII., in rude and offensive language, that he was on the way to lose his remaining provinces through his own fault, and that no letters written 'after the fashion of Boniface VIII. to Philippe le Bel' would avail to save his temporal power.[3] Secret instructions were given to the French troops stationed at Ancona and Città Vecchia, to seize the Papal revenues, and to incorporate the Pontifical troops with their army. The tax on salt and whatever available money remained to the account of the Roman Government passed likewise into the hands of the French. These violent aggressive acts, and the occupation of the Pope's territory, produced a state of penury in the Papal treasury, which was a subject of exultation to Napoleon. He purposely delayed repaying the expenses caused by the keep of his army, in order to bring the Holy Father to the last gasp, and so make him gladly submit on the hardest terms. Power is a weapon which few can wield without abuse. 'By what right do you act in this way,' a Roman officer attached to the Pope's Treasury asked one day, before the impending seizure of his money. 'You serve a small prince, and I a mighty sovereign: that is all my right,' replied the aggressor.

If we may believe Cardinal Casoni, the mental and physical anxiety of this downright persecution threatened

---

[3] Note de M. Alguier, 8 juillet, 1807.

to prove fatal to the Holy Father. But at a time when an active system of State usurpation thus disturbed the rest of Pius VII., there were not wanting those amongst his children who were disposed to complain of what they termed an imprudent resistance. Caprara represented in his despatches that his own sentiments, favourable to the Emperor's demands, were shared by the most prominent Catholics of France, and Spina besought the Holy Father not to persevere in a line of conduct which must draw down irreparable evils upon the Church.[4] At our actual distance from the events in question, it seems almost incredible that such advice could ever have been given. In weighing therefore all the difficulties which beset his path as Sovereign Pontiff, praise and heartfelt gratitude are due to the memory of Pius VII. Resistance was prompted by his conscience, and by no worldly motive of interest, and this is so true that, after writing with his own hand the following letter to Caprara, he expected with perfect serenity and resignation what afterwards really came to pass, the occupation of Rome.[5]

'We have earnestly commended ourself to God, Whose unworthy Vicar We are upon earth, and to the Apostle St. Peter, whose successor We are, in order to obtain the necessary light wherewith to answer your question. Here is this answer, which We write with our own hand, to give you a new proof of the importance which We attribute to questions so weighty, and to impress upon you still more the earnest and deep nature of the convictions which We feel bound to communicate to you. The reasons for which We have refused to make the desired declaration, are too weighty and too just to allow Us to change our opinion. They are founded, not

---

[4] Lettre du Card. Spina au Saint-Père, 1806.
[5] Pacca, *Memorie Storiche*, t. i. p. 68.

upon human motives, which is generally supposed, but upon the very basis of those duties which are ours as the common Father of the faithful and the minister of peace. It may be true, as his Majesty has told you, that the English will never believe that Rome has risked everything for them, and that they will never bear, in consequence, the least gratitude to the Holy See: this is not what We have to take into consideration. We have only consulted our duty, which imposes upon Us the obligation to cause no injury to religion by the interruption of communication between the Head and members of the Church in all places where Catholics exist. We should ourself provoke this interruption by the exercise of hostile acts against any nation whatever, and by taking part in a war against that nation. If the evil caused to religion proceeded from the conduct of another, such for instance as that which might result from any measures his Majesty might set on foot owing to our refusal, We should deplore it in the bitterness of our heart, and We should adore the judgments of God, Who permits such evil for the accomplishment of the inscrutable workings of His Providence. But if, betraying our character and the nature of our office, We consented to aggressive measures which proved the source of evil for the Church, We ourself should be the cause of such evil, and in this precisely consists the point of our refusal. We cannot, in the face of an evil which threatens Us, cause the Church to suffer in the way We have specified. But these very calamities with which We are threatened, are not necessary calamities. They depend entirely on the will of His Majesty, who is free either to put them into execution or not. We still venture to hope that his regard for religion, his equity, and his magnanimity, and the remembrance of all We have done for him, will speak to his heart, and will not allow him, before the world and before posterity, to prefer the name of persecutor of the Church to that of her protector and her benefactor. Whatever happens, We put our cause into the hands of God, Who is greater than We, greater than the most powerful monarchs, and We rely upon His Divine help, which will not fail Us at the moment foreseen by His wisdom. His Majesty has said to you, that when once Rome and the States of the Church are in his hands, they will stay there. His Majesty is free to believe this. But We frankly reply, that if his Majesty justly flatters himself that he has material power at his disposition, We too know that, above all kings, there reigns a God Who is the Avenger of justice and of innocent causes, and to Whom all human power is subject. You tell Us that the Emperor has remarked to you that the public nature of the question must render him inflexible. But We must remind his Majesty that he cannot lose in real greatness or true magnanimity, when he gives way, not to an earthly potentate nor to a rival, but to the representations and to the prayers of a priest of Jesus Christ, who is his friend and father. If this consideration fails to move him, We are bound to tell him with an Apostolical liberty, that if his Majesty's honour is engaged before men, our conscience is engaged before God, never, as Head of the Church, to take part in war. Certainly We have no intention of being the first to set the Church and the world an example which no one of our predecessors during the course of eighteen centuries has given, that of associating ourselves in a hostile attitude which is progressive, indefinite, and permanent, against any nation whatever. We cannot accede to the federative system of the French Empire. The territory transmitted to Us independent of all federation, must remain independent by the nature of our Apostolic liberty. If this independence were attacked, or if the threats which are addressed to Us without any regard for our dignity and for our friendship for his Majesty, received their fulfilment, We should see in the step the signal of open persecution, and We should refer to the judgment of God. Our determination is fixed. Nothing can change it, neither threats, nor their realization. . . . These are the feelings which you may look upon as our last will and testament, and We are ready, if need be, to sign it with our blood. If persecution comes upon Us, the words of our Divine Master are our strength: "Blessed are they who suffer persecution for justice' sake." Make this disposition fully known to His Majesty, We expressly command it. It is time to extricate oneself from an ocean so encumbered with pain and anguish that it causes Us each day to beseech of God to abridge this sad and bitter ending of our life. At the same time, be sure to tell the Emperor that We love him still, that We are disposed to give him all possible proofs of affection, and to continue to show ourself his best friend; but do not let him ask for what it is not in our power to bestow.'[6]

In this letter the Pontiff and the man comes before us in his full spiritual stature. The Pope says, I simply cannot do what you ask, and the man, who was so full of tenderness, cannot resist adding, *but*, I love you still. *I love you still*, it was a cry which produced small echo in the heart of Napoleon. The Holy Father had addressed himself to Caprara, because the Emperor, objecting that Pius VII. on a former occasion had betrayed his confidence by publishing his letter to the Sacred College, refused now to correspond directly with

---

[6] *L'Eglise Romaine et le Premier Empire*, t. ii. p. 321. Lettre de Pie VII. au Card. Caprara, le 31 juillet, 1806.

Rome. ' In this instance, the Legate in vain made weak attempts to ensure an audience for the perusal of the new document. Once he fancied that he had secured Napoleon, but just as he was about to begin: 'Monsieur le Cardinal, que vous sentez les clubs de Rome," was the laconic and by no means dignified answer, and the Emperor turned his back straight upon Caprara, as if he considered that the movement settled the question.[7]

In September, 1806, Napoleon's thoughts were not with Rome nor Roman affairs. France was on the eve of war with Prussia, then, as now, a great military power, and to Prussia he carried all his energies and the resources of his genius. For a time he seems to have forgotten almost the existence of Italy and the Sovereign Pontiff, but in truth, he was only awaiting a favourable moment to strike with a master hand. The annihilation of those wonderful troops of Frederick, and the temporary fall of the Prussian monarchy, were events which added fuel to the fire of Napoleon's ambition. From Frederick's palace at Berlin, he once more dictated his terms to the Holy Father. Mgr. Arezzo, Bishop of Seleucia, was deputed to 'signify peremptorily' to Pius VII. that he must accede to the confederation of the French Empire. Either the Pope would consent, in which case he should lose nothing, or he would refuse, and be subjected to the deprivation of his States. Napoleon's last words to Mgr. Arezzo possess, as it seems to us, a special meaning: 'Let the Pope do what I wish, and he will be repaid for the past and for the future.'[8] The Emperor demanded the presence of a new Legate at Paris, or rather he would have been too contented to treat with Caprara, if the Holy Father consented to give the weak Cardinal the necessary

---

[7] *L'Eglise Romaine et le Premier Empire*, t. ii. p. 325.
[8] *Ibid.* p. 341.

powers to discuss and resolve the points in question. He said to Mgr. Arezzo: 'Let the Holy Father intrust the affair to his Legate in Paris, who is a good man, or to Spina, with the necessary powers for treating, or to anybody else.' This 'anybody else' was highly ambiguous, for Napoleon had settled that the Cardinal de Bayane, and only he, should come to Paris. As a Frenchman, he alone of the Sacred College had voted in favour of the Emperor's extravagant demands, and it was therefore clear that something might be done with him. Before, however, the Prussian Campaign had surpassed probably even Napoleon's expectations by the magnificent results, among which were the Battle of Friedland and the Peace of Tilsitt, Pius VII. had been asserting his spiritual rights by refusing the confirmation of certain bishops nominated by the French Government to the vacant sees of the Duchy of Milan and the Venetian provinces annexed to the Empire in 1806. It will be remembered that shortly after the affair of Jerome's marriage Pius VII. had protested against the non-fulfilment of the Italian Concordat. The step, in spite of Napoleon's assurances, had produced no sort of effect. Putting aside, then, the question of mere material insults—and during the Prussian War they were not wanting on the part of the French troops to the Holy Father as a temporal sovereign[9]—the grave course of action adopted by Pius VII. in refusing his confirmation to the Italian bishops proposed to him was perfectly legitimate, nay, strictly, was even his bounden duty. In a treaty, as soon as one of the contracting parties refuses to fulfil his engagements, he releases, by the very fact, the other from his obligations. But this refusal was not wholly disagreeable to the Emperor, inasmuch as it furnished him with something to take hold of against the Holy Father. 'The Pope wishes me then no longer to

[9] Pacca, *Memorie Storiche*, t. i. p. 74.

have bishops in Italy' he wrote to Prince Eugène. 'All
the better! If that is benefiting religion, how must they
act who wish *to destroy it.*'[10] Pius VII. afterwards consented to nominate *motu proprio* the bishops already
proposed, but condescension was entirely useless where
the will to be conciliated was so utterly wanting. Napoleon had beaten all his enemies. Save England, Europe
was at his feet. Now was the moment to conquer the
obstinacy or the weakness of the Holy Father, for that
he alone should hold aloof from the European League,
or continue to defend the interests of a Protestant
country against the might of a second Charlemagne, was
an impossible hypothesis. It was against Napoleon's
dignity, as he judged, to renew a direct correspondence
with the Head of the Church, so that in order to speak
his mind to Pius VII. he had recourse to artifice. He
wrote a short letter from Dresden to Prince Eugène on
the 22nd July, 1807, containing two enclosures, (1) a
letter that the Viceroy of Italy was to write to the Holy
Father, as if coming from himself; (2) a letter which was
to have all the appearance of having been written by
Napoleon to Eugène, and spontaneously communicated
by the latter to the Holy Father.[11] The first was the
following:

'Most Holy Father,

'I communicated the letter of your Holiness to
my most honoured father and sovereign, who has sent
me a detailed reply from Dresden, of which I make an
extract. . . . Let your Holiness allow me to say that all
the discussions raised by the Court of Rome tend to
aggravate a great sovereign, who, penetrated with pious
feelings, is conscious of the invaluable aid he has been to

---

[10] Lettre de l'Emp. au Prince Eugène, 12 avril, 1807.
[11] *L'Eglise Romaine et le Premier Empire*, t. ii. p. 355.

religion in France, Italy, Germany, Poland, or Saxony, as the case may be. He knows that the world looks upon him as the pillar of the Christian Faith, and the enemies of religion, as a prince who has restored the supremacy (which it had lost) of Catholicity in Europe. Is the Court of Rome actuated by love of religion, when on frivolous pretences and in things which could be settled with a little moderation it makes use of threats derogatory to the rights of the throne, which are no less sacred than those of the tiara? If your Holiness is really moved by devotion to duty and love of religion, send plenipotential faculties to the Cardinal Legate in Paris, and in eight days all will be settled. If you do not agree to this step, your pontificate will be more fatal to the Court of Rome than that under which Germany and England broke off from its jurisdiction.'

Here the Emperor's letter (the second inclosure) began.

' My Son,

'I see in a letter from His Holiness, which certainly he never wrote, that he threatens me. Does he think then that the rights of the throne are less sacred than those of the tiara? There were kings before there were Popes. They say that they want to publish all the evil that I have committed against religion. The idiots! They ignore, then, that there does not exist a spot in Italy, Germany, or Poland, where I have not done more for religion than the Pope has done evil, not with a bad intention, but owing to the irascible counsels of a few narrow-minded men that surround him. They wish to denounce me to Christendom! So ridiculous an idea can only proceed from a dense ignorance of our century. It is a notion proper to a thousand years ago. A Pope who could lend himself to such a step, would cease to be Pope in my eyes. I should only consider him as Antichrist, sent to disturb the world and inflict evil on men, and I should thank God for his helplessness. If it were so, I would cut off my people from all communication with Rome, and establish a civil guard there. . . . What does Pius VII. mean by denouncing me to Christendom? Would he put my throne under an interdict, or excommunicate me? Does he imagine that their arms will fall from the hands of my soldiers,[12] or does he think to put a dagger wherewith to assassinate me, into my people's power? Some infuriated Popes have preached this doctrine. All that the Holy Father would have to do would be to cut off my hair, and to shut me up in a monastery! Does he take me for Louis le Débonnaire? . . . The present Pope is too powerful. Priests are not made to reign. Let them imitate St. Peter, St. Paul, and the holy Apostles, who are certainly worth a Julius, a Boniface, a Gregory, or a Leo. . . . It is disorder in the Church which renders a Court of Rome necessary, not the good of religion. Rome is interested in promoting discord, to assume an arbitrary power, and to confuse the limits of temporal and spiritual dominion. Really, I am beginning to blush and to feel humbled at the foolish conduct which Rome has inflicted upon me, and perhaps the time is not far off, when if this meddling in my affairs does not stop, I shall acknowledge the Pope to be nothing more than

---

[12] M. le comte de Ségur in his book, *Histoire de Napoléon et de la Grande Armée*, remarks, *à propos* of the Russian campaign. 'Their very arms (those of the French soldiers) turned against them. They seemed an insupportable weight to their numbed limbs. The men frequently stumbled down, and then the *arms fell from their hands*, or got broken or lost in the snow. If they managed to regain their legs, it was without arms. *They did not throw down* their weapons; hunger and cold caused them to drop. The fingers of many other soldiers froze on their gun which they still held, and so made movement impossible, which would have produced a little warmth and life' (t. 1. c. xi.).

Bishop of Rome, holding a rank similar in all respects to my bishops. I shall not fear to unite the Gallican, Italian, German, and Polish Churches in a Council, to despatch my business without the Pope, and deliver my people from the pretensions of Roman priests. . . . In two words, this is the last time that I consent to treat with these wretched priests of Rome. It is possible to despise and to disown them without deviating from the right path, and in point of fact, what is capable of saving in one country, is capable of saving in another. . . . I hold my crown from God, and from the will of my people. I shall always remain Charlemagne for the Court of Rome, never Louis le Débonnaire. I have never wished for anything but to come to an understanding with Rome. But if Rome has no such wish, let it not name any bishops. My people will dispense with bishops, and my churches with direction, until the interest of religion points to a course imperatively demanded for their good, and that of my crown.' Here Prince Eugène was to say, as if coming from himself: 'Most Holy Father, this letter was not written for the eyes of your Holiness. I beseech of you to put an end to these disputes, not to listen to the perfidious counsels of irascible men, who, blind to circumstances and to the true interests of religion, are animated by unworthy passions. . . . Men wish to equal in power, I make bold to say in haughtiness, a sovereign whom we can only compare to Cyrus or to Charlemagne. Did the Patriarch of Jerusalem so comport himself towards Cyrus, or the contemporary Pontiffs so act with Charlemagne? It is not fair that flies should attack a lion, or prick him with their tiny stings. They hardly penetrate his skin, but still they irritate him. . . . The Romans are in an unhappy plight: it is the doing of the counsellors of your Holiness. The Church is suffering; it is the

Sovereign Pontiff's fault who will not nominate bishops through a foolish caring for prerogatives. . . . For that matter, this is the last time that I am authorized to write to your Holiness. You will no longer hear of my sovereign nor of me. You are free to nominate bishops or not. If after this, anybody allows himself to advocate insubordination, or insurrection, he will be punished by the justice of the law, whose power likewise emanates from the Divinity.'

'Send this letter to the Pope,' was the final injunction of the enclosure from Dresden, 'and tell me when M. Alquier delivers it.'[13]

About this time, M. de Talleyrand was succeeded in his office of Minister of the Exterior, by M. de Champagny, a man whose intellectual inferiority to the Prince of Benevento exactly suited Napoleon at the height of his social and military glory. As the Emperor would have wished to despatch his business without the Pope, so in the material administration of his Empire he would henceforth only deal with men willing to be led and governed in the minutest details. The very capacity of the ex-bishop of Autun rendered his services obnoxious to Napoleon. Talleyrand had innocently imagined that he would in some measure direct the pen of the new Minister, but he discovered that the Emperor both could and intended to rule the Empire without his assistance. He wisely retired behind his dignity of grand elector and arch-chancellor of State, as on a former occasion he had learnt that silence is safer than indiscreet questions. But this change aggravated, if possible, or in any case did not tend to smooth matters between Pope and Emperor. M. de Champagny's first note was only an echo of the letter from Dresden, but curiously enough, Napoleon's strange tactics were baffled by a disposition in Pius VII.

[13] *L'Eglise Romaine et le Premier Empire*, t. ii. p. 3˜5.

more akin to a prudent simplicity than anything else. 'A mild answer turneth away wrath.' How press insult and violence upon the Sovereign Pontiff who would 'cede to no one the honour of receiving the Emperor' at Rome. Threats, menaces, an insane pride elated by unheard of military feats, were answered invincibly by a cordial letter of invitation. Pius VII. was no politician, but in the humility and sincerity of his heart he unconsciously offered an arm of resistance worthy of one versed in diplomatic lore. He simply took away all ground for the war which the Emperor was bent upon waging against his spiritual and temporal rights.

'Although your Majesty has left several of our letters unanswered,' he wrote to Napoleon, on the 11th of September, 1807, 'We nevertheless venture to address you once more. Not without pain have We learnt from our Cardinal Legate that your Majesty believes that our heart is estranged from you, and that We oppose you simply for the sake of opposing you. Your Majesty, God is our witness, He knows that We speak truth. It is not the wish to contradict you, but the conviction of duty which has obliged Us to refuse several of your demands. Nothing can be more agreeable to Us than to second your desires with all our power, and to prove this, We shall manifest our condescension by sending Cardinal de Bayane to Paris according to your wish. . . . It has been rumoured that your Majesty purposed visiting this country. Thus the satisfaction of so desirable an arrangement would be enhanced by the pleasure of seeing your Majesty. In this case, We shall cede to no one the honour of receiving so illustrious a guest: our right to the preference is indisputable. The Vatican Palace, which We will have set in order to the best of our power, will be at your disposal. After all the business has been despatched at Paris, We, at Rome, shall be at liberty to work for the Catholic religion, by obtaining for it those blessings, which your Majesty, as its protector, has promised to grant. In the meantime, may your Majesty feel confidence in our heart; as an earnest of its affection, We give you the Apostolical benediction."[14]

Pius VII., it will be seen, was not weary of condescension and concession wherever his conscience of Sovereign Pontiff could allow him to make it. But Napoleon, in pursuit of a chimera, was tired of encountering what must be an invincible obstacle to its realization, as long as a semblance of the temporal power remained; the Spiritual Father of the Faithful, possessing for domain an interposing State between the kingdom of the Two Sicilies and the French Empire, holding himself aloof from the confederative league of this or that nation, and profiting by the neutrality of his office to defend an injured people. The invitation to the Vatican sent to Napoleon by Pius VII. with so perfect a good faith, was answered by an order to Prince Eugène to cause the occupation of the Duchy of Urbino and of the provinces of Macerata, Fermo, and Spoleto by General Lemarrois. Napoleon was provoked rather than pleased at the prospect of having Cardinal de Bayane at Paris, and to render his mission an impossible one he dictated terms so haughty and so offensive, that the wish of Pius VII. to come to a final agreement must indeed have been sincere for his courage not even then to have failed. When the Pope was told that there existed in France no religious questions which required his intervention, that the Gallican Church was enjoying its privileges in a peace due to the Emperor, that monks were no longer wanted, but soldiers to fight infidels and heretics,[15] it

---

[14] *L'Eglise Romaine et le Premier Empire* t. ii. 367.
[15] Note de M. de Champagny à Son Eminence le Cardinal Caprara, 21 7bre.

K

seemed as though schism were already showing its face on the horizon. The dearly loved formula of Gallicanism was expressed. If ecclesiastical difficulties required it, the Emperor would call together a general council, the 'only organ of the Infallible Church and sovereign arbitrator of all religious discussions.' It is evident that, unless Cardinal de Bayane could bring faculties altogether extraordinary, his best course was to remain at Rome. This was precisely the conclusion for which Napoleon would have wished. Then he might have proclaimed to Europe that he had been forced to take strong measures against Rome by the untractableness of the Holy Father. When the news of the violent occupation of his fairest provinces reached Pius VII. Cardinal de Bayane had already started, and early in October the Pope had allowed himself to be convinced by M. Alquier's representations that 'too great importance was not to be attached to sentiments expressed by the Emperor to the Legate in a momentary fit of impatience, that in the official instructions which he, M. Alquier, had received from his Court, it was no question of obliging His Holiness to league against all the enemies of the Emperor, but only against heretics and the English.' The Holy Father then agreed to a final act of condescension, the precise nature of which is rendered by an official despatch of Casoni to the Cardinal de Bayane. 'The latest requests of his Imperial Majesty with regard to the English have been confined to the closing of the ports. The Holy Father has every reason to believe that this is all that is involved by his adhesion. But if anything more were asked of him, he would consent, *provided that it did not oblige him to present war, nor touch the independence of his pontifical sovereignty.*'[16] As a matter of fact, the closing of the ports to the English

[16] Lettre du Cardinal Casoni au Cardinal de Bayane, 14 8bre. 1107.

was by no means all that Napoleon required of Pius VII. The exactions of the Emperor would have involved a total sacrifice of the 'independence of the pontifical sovereignty,' and to this the Sovereign Pontiff never consented. What he said was, that, firmly resolved to bring about peace, he would concede all that could be conceded. Hardly however had he adopted this tone, when the Emperor again specified his former pretensions through M. de Champagny. In a peculiarly offensive memorandum the Minister of the Exterior signified to Pius VII. the *ultimatum* of the Emperor of the French. It was in reality a project for submitting the Sovereign Pontiff, as supreme arbitrator of Catholic doctrine, to the good pleasure of secular power; or, in other words, for rendering the spiritual power entirely subordinate to the State. It may be said in passing, that such a plan has a chance or probability of success with any other but the Catholic religion, whose very essence it is to recognize in the supremacy of the Apostolic See the embodiment, at once, of Catholic doctrine and government. The position of the Chief Pastor must be, to some extent, in accordance with his teaching and his pastoral charge, and as the Catholic Church as a whole is free and independent of nations or empires, so he, who has a mission to feed her with the truth, and to govern as a shepherd of souls, must possess a liberty of action outside of and apart from worldly crowns and sceptres. In lending himself to similar demands Pius VII. would have ceased to be the Head of the Universal Church. By his answer to Cardinal de Bayane, we see how he had understood the concession of the closing of the ports, and whether in taking this step he had ever intended to accede to a federative league. 'It is with great pain, my Lord Cardinal,' Pius wrote, 'that We learned from your letter of the 16th of last month, containing a sketch of the projected treaty, that other demands, which We did not expect, have been added to those specified in the memorandum of the French Ambassador, whilst this plan expresses neither of the two conditions in virtue of which alone, as our Secretary of State explained to you, We had consented to the prolongation of your faculties. Nothing in fact had been done to revoke the measures taken with regard to our four provinces, and the substance of the despatches communicated to you on the 12th and 14th of October is judged inadmissible at Paris. Consequently, and as the projected treaty does not confine itself to the closing of the ports, but the design to draw Us into a league, which would oblige Us to recognize as our friends and enemies those of France, is furthermore forced upon Us, with a state of perpetual war utterly incompatible with our character and with our ministry of peace, our adhesion is impossible. Upon what grounds are We to expose ourself to the danger or rather to the certainty of seeing all spiritual communications with English Catholics cut off, which We now carry on freely? This restriction would surely follow immediately, if We consented to a permanent system of enmity against a power, for a cause wholly foreign to Us? Upon what ground are We called upon to renounce the rights of the Holy See with regard to the investiture of the Kingdom of Naples, and to the jurisdiction of Benevento and Ponte-Corvo, without any compensation whatever, when the very decree of forfeiture promised Us an indemnity? Wherefore should We bind ourself to cause the French Cardinals to occupy a third of the Sacred College, thus reversing the fundamental constitutions of the Holy See, and paving the way to similar and proportional demands from other Catholic Courts, and to the consequences of such proceedings which the history of the Church tells Us are inevitable? Why should We burden ourself with so many expenses, and nominally with that of an annual payment of four hundred thousand francs for the clearing of the port at Ancona and the augmentation of the fortifications, doings which instead of being useful to Us would be positively prejudicial. . . . Lastly, We are grieved to see that the project does not mention those ecclesiastical matters which are the end of our demands and of your mission at Paris. In a word, We feel that We are treated as an enemy. This is the fruit of our journey to Paris, of our patience, of the long-suffering which has caused Us to make so many sacrifices, and to suffer so many humiliations ! In this state of things, and as the two conditions which We specified on the 11th of November, have not been adopted, but as new and inadmissible concessions, are almost forced upon Us, We cannot in any sort of way adhere to a treaty contrary to the liberty and independence of our sovereignty. If then such pretensions are not withdrawn, you must ask for your passport without delay and return. We also give notice to our Cardinal Legate for whom this letter is likewise intended, to hold himself ready to leave Paris at the first intimation that he may receive from Us to that effect.'[17]

A month after this letter, Napoleon wrote minute directions to the King of Naples and to the Viceroy of Italy, for the French occupation of Rome under General Miollis. The troops of Miollis and Lemarrois numbering six thousand men were to enter Rome the first under the pretext of joining the army at Naples. Those of Joseph were to wait for news of Miollis' arrival in Rome, as it was possible they might have to serve as a reserve, keeping at a distance of four or five leagues from the Eternal City. Once in Rome, General Miollis was

---

[17] *L'Eglise Romaine et le Premier Empire*, t. ii. p. 393. Lettre du 2 xbre. 1807.

ordered to occupy the citadel of Sant' Angelo, to arrest the Neapolitan and English consuls, and even the English residents at Rome. All operations were to be carried out with the greatest secrecy. The whole scheme presented the appearance of proceeding from the mind of a man who was somewhat ashamed of the business. The Emperor, in his directions to M. de Champagny, speaks of Miollis as of one who is using Rome as a half-way house to get to Naples. M. Alquier was to represent to the Holy Father, that the purpose of the General's visit to Rome was to cover the rear of the Neapolitan army, and that on his way to Naples he was to clear the city of brigands and of the enemies of France. A motive by which quiet inoffensive English residents were classed in the category of disturbers of the public peace could hardly commend itself to Pius VII. The same imperial memorandum contains however the following words in cipher—

'The intention of the Emperor in writing this memorandum and in taking these steps is to accustom the people of Rome and the French troops to live together, so that, if the Court of Rome continues to act as foolishly as hitherto, it may cease by such gradual degrees to exist, that the disappearance will cause no surprize.' But the measured nature of the process did not exclude capital punishment where refractory conduct seemed to call for it. 'The smallest insurrection must be put down with material force, if necessary, and with telling examples.'[18] '*To accustom the people of Rome and the French troops to live together.*' Napoleon fancied to incorporate the Eternal City to his Empire without noise, and by one and the same stroke to become in reality Emperor of Rome, and to efface the temporal action of the Sovereign Pontiff. He had not weighed

[18] Lettre de l'Empereur à M. de Champagny et au Prince Eugène, 1808.

his arms in a just balance, and they were to fall back upon himself to his own destruction.

But in 1808 such a consummation was in the distance. Anxiety and a troubled agitation reigned at Rome. No man knew what the morrow might bring, and for one moment the Holy Father manifested his intention of retiring to Sant' Angelo. The Sacred College dissuaded him from such a step, persuaded that the merest pretext would furnish Napoleon with ground to assert that he took possession of Rome as a right of conquest. On the 2nd of February, 1808, the French troops passed through the open gates of Rome, disarming the Pontifical guards on station there. A compact body of cavalry and infantry surrounded the Quirinal Palace, then inhabited by the Holy Father, whilst a huge battery was pointed at the windows of his apartments. The peaceful Sovereign whose city was thus ruthlessly invaded by armed force was celebrating in the Quirinal Chapel the feast of the Purification. Surrounded by the Sacred College, he was offering to God on that Altar of which the Temple was but the figure, the Child who had been set up for the ruin and for the salvation of many in Israel. 'The old man held the Child in his arms, but the Child was the old man's Lord.'[19] In the Holy Father's reception of the French, we find, as it were, a perfume of the spirit of the feast which he was keeping at the time of their invasion—humility, sweetness, and fortitude, but he might not yet sing his *Nunc Dimittis*. 'He could not complain of the French nation,' and he pushed condescension far enough to receive Miollis at the Quirinal with his ordinary affability, and to say with a smile on his lips that he still loved France. On the 3rd of February, M. de Champagny signified peremptorily that the French troops would remain at Rome until the Pope

From the Vesper Office of the Feast of the Purification.

consented to enter the Italian Federation, and to make common cause with those who belonged to it (that is, with Napoleon). The answer, printed secretly during the night at the Quirinal, mysteriously made its appearance on the walls of Rome in the form of a protestation from the Holy Father, in his own name and in that of his successors, against all usurpation of his domains. It enjoined the Romans to keep the peace, and to abstain from acts injurious to the French. They were to be mindful of the welcome and of the affection shown to Pius VII. by that nation, in other and happier days.[20]

The Holy Father was a prisoner in his own capital, and by the French monopoly of the post and of the press it became impossible for him to appeal to the feelings of Catholic Europe. This violent measure was indispensable in Napoleon's eyes, as to him it was of primary importance that France should be kept in ignorance of his doings at Rome. The Pope then could no longer protest by means of the press against his wrongs, for the Emperor would allow nothing to be wanting for the perfection, as he understood it, of this state of imprisonment. In February, all the Neapolitan Cardinals received orders to leave Rome in twenty-four hours; and as Pius VII., warned of the intention of the French Government, had forbidden them to obey, they were carried off by force. It has been said that the Holy See is the guardian of all liberty, and in this instance the outrageous treatment of the Cardinals was bestowed, in some degree, upon other diplomatic personages, to the utter disregard of the rights of nations.[21] A final and offensive measure enacted against the Cardinals at length roused the anger of Pius VII., for it was a direct wound inflicted on his spiritual authority.

[20] Pacca, *Memorie*, t. i. p. 107.
[21] *L'Eglise Romaine et le Premier Empire*, t. iii. p. 14.

The Prince had been long suffering, but now the Pontiff's holy wrath predominated. Early in March Prince Eugène was ordered to direct the dismissal of all Cardinals who were not native subjects of the Pope. The whole number was fourteen, and amongst them the Pro-Secretary of State, Doria, who had succeeded Casoni. The Neapolitan Cardinals had numbered seven, so that in all twenty-one members of the Sacred College, occupying important posts in Rome, had been taken away in one month, and by sheer force, from the scene of their labours. Three days were given to each Cardinal as the utmost delay. This order, inasmuch as it was derogatory to the Holy Father's spiritual dignity, produced the cessation of Caprara's faculties as Legate. No one knows how far Pius VII. might have stooped to endure humiliations directed merely against his temporal sovereignty; but in the violence employed against the Cardinals in office, he saw an affront which tampered with the free exercise of his mission of Chief Pastor. Submission to similar usurpation of authority would have been, not Christian meekness, but weak pusillanimity. With a persistence which sadly reminds us of the present Successor of Peter, our own Pius, he refused to leave his palace. He was truly a prisoner. His only resource as a protestation against outrages was personal communication with the Sacred College; yet thus deprived of all material power, he became untractable, for the honour of the Pontiff was seriously involved. 'We feel,' he said, 'that a great persecution is coming upon Us; but We are prepared, fortified by our Divine Master's words "Blessed are they who suffer persecution for justice."'

In the midst of the minute directions which he was constantly issuing to Rome, Napoleon found time to superintend a revolution in the fortunes of Spain. The man who could reconcile his conscience to the persecution of a Sovereign Pontiff, thought it not only lawful but natural, to organize an ambuscade against Charles IV. of Bourbon, and to put the crown of Spain on the head of his brother Joseph, *ci-devant* King of Naples. Certainly, the usurpation and the spoliation are in keeping with each other.

The Pontifical States were incorporated officially with the French Empire by a decree of April 2nd, 1808, which declared them to be irrevocably united to the Kingdom of Italy, in the form of three departments, and announced the publication of the Code-Napoleon. Fraud had been employed to effect the entry of armed force into the very palace of the Pope, for the purpose of disarming those within the Quirinal, who helped to keep up a certain semblance of a Court.[22] Miollis had likewise caused the Governor of Rome, Mgr. Cavalchini, a personal friend of Pius VII. to be arrested. Probably the General, who seems to have been well-meaning individually, disliked his position, and thought that strong measures would bring matters to a still more definite crisis. The Holy Father himself caused a circular, variously commented upon, to be sent to the bishops of the annexed provinces. It was a recommendation to them to hold aloof from any submission to their new government. The Pro-Secretary of State, Cardinal Gabrielli, justly suspected by Miollis of signing this document, was arrested, and conducted to his bishopric of Sinigaglia. We come at last to the ministry of Pacca, the faithful Cardinal, whose name is for ever bound up with the Pontificate of Pius, as the disinterested counsellor and devoted friend of a persecuted cause. He was chosen to take the place of Gabrielli, in June 1808, not, he says, with the composure of mind necessary for such an important post, but with the hourly fear of a visitation

---

[22] *L'Eglise Romaine et le Premier Empire*, t. iii. p. 46.

such as that which had been inflicted on his predecessor. He was obliged to find secret drawers for the weightier documents. A great part of the Sacred College had been expelled from Rome, so that forced to act on his own responsibility and by his own counsel, and discouraged at the prospect, Pacca inwardly exclaimed from the depths of his heart: *Transeat a me calix iste.* He belonged to the party who had opposed from the beginning concessions to France, but now in the irritated state of public feeling his ambition was to 'throw water on the fire,' which had broken out between the Pontifical Government and General Miollis. It seems that Pius VII., who, according to Pacca, 'was the meekest of men on the face of the earth,' was the first to tire of this patience. With his experience of the situation, he knew that it would avail nothing, and one day he observed to the Pro-Secretary, 'My Lord Cardinal, they say in Rome that we have been sleeping; we must prove that we are awake, and pen a vigorous note to the French general (Miollis) on the subject of the latest violent measures.'[23]

One of these measures, and a crying shame, had been the organization in the midst of the Pontifical States, of civil volunteers, the refuse of the people. They fomented discord, and constituted, beyond a doubt, all that is commonly understood by brigands. When Gabrielli had protested against this enrolment, the French Government had seemed to acknowledge his right only to favour secretly the proceedings of similar troops. At first, Pacca's moderation and patience had been turned into capital for the same end, until the Cardinal perceived the necessity of vigorous acting. In one of his remonstrances with Miollis, the General had allowed himself to express Napoleon's order to shoot or to hang

[23] *Memorie Storiche*, t. i. pp. 119, 124, 126, etc.

all persons in the Pontifical States, who were rash enough to oppose the imperial commands.

'General,' answered Pacca, quietly, 'during your stay in Rome, you must have seen that the Ministers of His Holiness are not to be cowed by threats. For my part, I shall faithfully execute the orders of my Sovereign, whatever may be the results.' 'I soon learned,' remarks the Cardinal, 'the uselessness of conciliation, and should have reproached myself with prevarication in the discharge of my office, had I not strengthened the Holy Father's resolution to give a public disapproval of the civil volunteers.'[24] This proclamation, issued on the 24th of August under the Pontifical seal, produced the determination on the part of Miollis to send Pacca into exile in his turn, a measure, however, which was thwarted by the courageous resistance of the Cardinal. A few days afterwards, on the 6th of September, 1808, whilst the Pro-Secretary was discussing affairs with a Roman prelate, two officers in the service of France entered his apartment, and signified an order from General Miollis, that Pacca should leave Rome in twenty-four hours. At the Porta di San Giovanni the Pope's Minister would find an escort of dragoons with the commission to take him back to his country, Benevento. Without the least perturbation, Pacca replied, that in Rome he took orders of no other but the Pope; that if His Holiness forbade him to go, he should not think of doing so, and he declared his intention of consulting the Holy Father. This was, however, entirely inadmissible, for the officers were not to let the Cardinal out of their sight. Pacca petitioned to send a note to Pius VII. and to this they consented. A few minutes afterwards the door was hastily opened. It was the Holy Father who had come to his Minister since his

[24] *Memorie*, t. i. pp. 140, 142.

Minister could not go to him. Pacca, for the first time in his life, was witness of one of the most startling effects of great anger. The hair of Pius VII. was positively standing on end, and the Pope, beside himself, did not recognize the Cardinal.

'Who is it, who is it?' he asked in a loud tone.

'I am the Cardinal,' replied Pacca, kissing his hand.

'Where is the official?' And turning to him, the Holy Father said, 'Go and tell your General that I am weary of suffering so many insults and outrages from a man who still has the effrontery to call himself a Catholic. I am aware of the end which these violent measures have in view. They wish, in separating me gradually from all my counsellors, to make the exercise of my ministry and the defence of my temporal sovereignty, impossible. I command my Minister not to obey the injunctions of illegitimate authority. Let your General know, that if force must be used to separate the Cardinal from me, he will be obliged first to break open all the doors, and will besides have the responsibility of so injurious a proceeding.'

When the purport of this speech had been faithfully rendered by Pacca to the officer (who did not understand Italian), the Holy Father took his Minister's hand, saying, 'Let us go, my Lord Cardinal' (Signor Cardinale, andiamo), and led him out through a crowd of applauding servants and friends to the papal apartment, where three rooms in close vicinity to Pius VII. were immediately assigned to the faithful Cardinal. 'Here,' remarks Pacca, 'I had the consolation and the special honour to live for ten whole months, until the fatal 6th of July, 1809.'[25]

Gabrielli had formed a design for the flight of the Holy Father, but Pius VII. had resolutely refused to leave Rome unless it were by force. To England alone,

[25] *Memorie*, t. i. p. 143.

or to a country in alliance with England, could he have turned, and such a step on the part of a Sovereign Pontiff would speak for itself. By a strange inconsistency, Pius VII. had been reproached with partiality for Napoleon, and with an excessive adhesion to the interests of England. It would then have been compromising to his dignity, had he accepted the offer of escape, which it seems was really made by the Cabinet of St. James. One evening, before he had taken refuge in the Pope's apartment, Pacca received a visit from a Franciscan friar, who had avowedly come from Sicily in an English frigate to contrive the flight of the Holy Father. The Cardinal answered the friar's advances very coldly, fearing him to be a spy, but many years afterwards, he learned that the Franciscan had spoken truth, that the frigate belonged to the English navy, and that it was sent by the connivance of the English Cabinet. It had been magnificently fitted up for the accommodation of the Pope and of an accompanying Cardinal.[26]

At that time, thrones seemed to follow the precarious fortunes of the Holy See. The crown of Naples had been given to Joachim Murat, and the new Neapolitan King proved a docile instrument in carrying out Napoleon's designs upon Rome. From Spain, whose affairs he had undertaken to unsettle, the Emperor wrote to Murat in November, 1808: 'The Code-Napoleon is adopted in all the kingdom of Italy. Florence has it, Rome will soon have it, and priests will be obliged to stop pandering to prejudices, and will be forced to mind their own business.' In a circular addressed in December to the bishops, he invited them 'to sing a *Te Deum* in their holy churches with their accustomed prayers, in order to obtain from God, Who possesses all things, that He would continue to bless the French arms, and that

[26] *Memorie.* See Note, t. i. p. 160.

He would preserve the Continent from the malignant influence of the English, the enemies of all religion, as they are of the peace and tranquillity of nations.[27] A gratuitously insulting letter, as it appears to us, was sent by Napoleon to M. de Champagny on the 1st of January, 1809, with regard to the approaching feast of Candlemas.

'Monsieur de Champagny, the Pope is accustomed to give candles to the different powers; write to my agent at Rome that I do not wish for any. Neither does the King of Spain. Write to Naples and to Holland, that they may be refused there too. None must be received, because last year they were insolent enough not to offer any. This is how I understand the business. My chargé d'affaires will make it known that on the Purification I receive blessed candles from my curé; that it is neither the purple nor power which give these kind of things their value; there may be Popes in hell as well as curés, so that the candle blessed by my curé can very well be as holy a thing as that blessed by the Pope. I will not receive those which the Pope gives, and all the princes of my family must act in like manner.

'With this, I pray that God may have you in His holy keeping.
'NAPOLEON.'[28]

M. Alquier had already left Rome. Miollis represented France too well as superintendent of both military and civil proceedings.

The decree of April, 1808, announcing the incorporation of the Pontifical States with the French Empire, had not materially altered the state of things at Rome. Two more specific decrees appeared in May, 1809. The

---

[27] Circulaire aux évêques d'Italie, 1808.
[28] *Histoire de Pie VII.* t. ii. p. 200.

first declared that the 'temporal pretensions of the Pope were irreconcilable with the safety, tranquillity, and prosperity of the Empire.' The second named a council to superintend the measures necessary to be taken for the peaceful introduction of the new order of things at Rome on the 1st of January, 1810.[29] The whole plan of attack was placed under the direction of Joachim Murat. The decree which dethroned the Sovereign who was already a prisoner in his own capital, was proclaimed in Rome with the sound of the trumpet on the 10th of June, 1809. The Pontifical arms disappeared from the summit of Sant' Angelo, and were replaced by the victorious tricolore, whose appearance was hailed by a military salute. The partisans of France openly exclaimed that all was over with the Pope. It was an hour of hopeless trial as far as short-sighted human prudence could tell, and the same words fell from the Holy Father and from his Minister as Pacca hurried into his room: *consummatum est*—all is consummated. The Cardinal endeavoured to overcome his emotion sufficiently to read the imperial decree. The deafening sound of the cannon, the sight of his Sovereign dethroned by sacrilege, on whose countenance signs of just indignation showed themselves, the offensive wording of the decree, made the task a very difficult and painful one. Having listened in silence, the Holy Father calmly affixed his signature to an Italian protestation, which appeared the same night on the walls of the Basilicas, and then Pacca broached the subject of the Bull of Excommunication. After the event of the 6th September, it had been prepared against two possible eventualities: the ground of the storming of the papal palace and the exile of the Holy Father, or simply on that of his deposition as a temporal sovereign. Both copies had been signed by Pius VII. as a provision

[29] *L'Eglise Romaine et le Premier Empire*, t. iii. p. 88.

against either emergency. Now, therefore, it would only become necessary to issue the latter formula. The Holy Father hesitated. In reading the Bull over again, he had 'found certain expressions against the French Government perhaps too severe.' Pacca represented that it was time to protest publicly against so many crimes and injuries.

'But what would you do?' asked Pius VII.

'Holy Father, after the threat of an act so important to your enemies who fear it, after the hope which you have given to your people, who desire and look for it, P should cause the Bull to be issued; but the question of your Holiness troubles me. Most Holy Father, lift up your heart to God, then give me your orders, and be assured that whatever falls from your lips will be in accordance with the divine will.'

After a moment of reflection, Pius VII. exclaimed, 'Well, issue the Bull (*Ebbene, le dia corso*), but let those who execute your orders look to themselves. Above all, let them avoid discovery, for they would be shot, and we should be inconsolable.'

Despite the vigilance of the French, the Bull beginning with the words, *Quum memoranda illa die*, was effectively placarded on the usual places, that is, on the walls of St. Peter, St. Mary Major, and St. John Lateran. After enumerating the indignities which had been for so long inflicted on the Church, the violation of the Concordat, the usurpation of authority, the tyranny exercised towards cardinals, bishops, and priests, and finally the destruction of the temporal authority of the Holy See, Pius VII. passed to the actual excommunication, which is naturally the most important passage in the Bull: 'The time for clemency is over. No man, unless he shuts his eyes to the light, can doubt the point to which such assaults tend and what the consequences will be, if preventive means are not used in time. Moreover, it is quite clear to all that We have no hope whatever of touching by our admonitions and counsels the authors of so much evil, or of inspiring them with more favourable sentiments towards the Church, by our prayers or by our demands. In other times, many Sovereign Pontiffs, whom holiness and learning rendered illustrious, were obliged, because the cause of the Church required it, to resort to similar extreme measures against rebellious kings and princes who had been guilty of only one or two of the crimes which the canons condemn with anathema; shall We then fear to follow their example after witnessing so many evil deeds, and sacrileges so heinous and so universally known? May We not, on the contrary, rather fear to be justly accused of weakness and procrastination, than of rashness or temerity, especially now that a recent outrage, more audacious than all the rest as far as our temporal authority is concerned, warns Us that henceforth We shall no longer be at liberty to exercise the most important and necessary duty of our Apostolic ministry. For these reasons, by the authority of Almighty God, and that of the Holy Apostles Peter and Paul, and our own, We declare that all those, who, after the invasion of Rome and the ecclesiastical territory, and the sacrilegious violation of St. Peter's Patrimony by French troops, have committed either at Rome or in the States of the Church, against ecclesiastical immunities, and against the simple temporal rights of the Church and Holy See, either all or any of the outrages which have provoked our complaints; all authors, promoters, counsellors, or adherents of similar doings; all those, finally, who have contributed to facilitate the realization of these violent acts or have accomplished them; We declare that all such have incurred the canonical excommunication, censure, and punishment, as decreed by the holy canons and by the

Apostolical constitutions, by the decrees of General Councils, and nominally, by the Holy Council of Trent, and if need be, We excommunicate and anathematize them again, declaring them by the very fact, deprived of any privileges or indults which may have been granted either by ourself or by our predecessors.'

The following paragraph was prompted by the peculiar character of the times, and doubtless also, out of regard for those whose duty or office would throw them into an indispensable contact with Napoleon. 'But notwithstanding the necessity We feel for using the spiritual arms of anathema, We may not forget that We, though unworthy, occupy on earth—the place of Him, Who, even when He acts according to His justice, is mindful of His mercy. For this reason, We desire and command our own subjects, in the first place, and in the next, all Christian people, in virtue of holy obedience, not to make these presents a pretence for injury, evil treatment, or damage towards the person, goods, or prerogatives of those who are attained by our censure. For in chastising them with the kind of punishment which God has put in our power, and in repaying thus injuries so great and so numerous against God and against His Church, We seek only one thing: to draw back to ourself those who afflict Us, and to obtain their participation in our sorrows, if God gives them the grace of repentance in order to arrive at the knowledge of the truth.'[30]

Although the Bull was only visible for a moment, and although it did not mention Napoleon by name, it decided, in all probability, the fate of the Holy Father. The arrest of the Pope reminds us so forcibly of a fact in our own history, that it is impossible not to be struck by the analogy. A King of England once said, 'Who will rid me of that troublesome Archbishop?' The

---

[30] Quoted from Laurentie, *Histoire de France*, t. vii. p. 268.

Sovereign was Henry II.; the Archbishop, St. Thomas of Canterbury. Four knights were found to execute their master's will by raising their hands against the Lord's Anointed. So Napoleon, to whom we do not pretend to ascribe any wishes so sanguinary, needed only to express a desire to see its accomplishment. At St. Helena, he denied having ever commanded the arrest of the Holy Father. His correspondence, however, tells another tale by justifying those (if they can indeed be justified) who were always too ready to act not only upon his commands but even upon his suggestions. In a letter to Joachim Murat, dated June 19, 1809 (nine days after the Bull of Excommunication had appeared), we read: 'I have already told you that it is my intention that Roman matters be vigorously managed, and that no sort of resistance be tolerated. If full submission is not given to my decrees, no place is to be respected, and under no excuse whatever must resistance be tolerated. If the Pope, contrary to the spirit of his ministry and of the Gospel, preaches revolt, and is willing to profit by the immunities of his position to print circulars, let him be arrested. The season of similar scenes is past and over. Philippe le Bel caused Boniface to be arrested, and Charles V. kept Clement VII. in a long imprisonment, and they (Boniface and Clement) had been less offensive (than Pius VII.). A priest who preaches discord and war to temporal powers instead of peace, abuses his office.'[31] As in the days of St. Thomas, listening ears had caught the imperial command, and willing hands failed not in its execution.

[31] *L'Eglise Romaine et le Premier Empire*, t. iii. p. 102.

CHAPTER VIII.

Savona.

'Super flumina Babylonis, illic sedimus et flevimus, cum recordaremur Sion.'—Psalm cxxxvi.

WHEN Napoleon said that he *would despatch his affairs without the Pope,* he gave us the reason of that long and weary exile of the Vicar of Christ at Savona. The two ideas which had expanded into huge developments in his brain—the foundation of a Western Empire, and dominion over Catholic consciences—had produced a combat of which the terms were these: on the one side, an immense preponderance of material force and power, and the obsequious homage of all Europe; on the other, a helpless and dispossessed Sovereign, commanding not the arms of men but their secret sympathy in the sacred sanctuary of heart and conscience. If Pius VII. ultimately triumphed, it was not, (as it might have been), merely by the strength of a righteous cause. The world has seen other just causes borne down by exulting iniquity, and great names hopelessly stamped out from the annals of history. Pius VII. defended God's rights upon earth, and he fought for a kingdom whose basis lies not in time but in eternity, since its corner-stone is the God-man Himself. The arms, the riches, the pride of man can avail but little against a kingdom whose laws and government partake of the double nature of its Founder. As our Lord, its Head, by dying conquered death, and afterwards rose again, so the Church passes through many tribulations to her resurrection. Not once, but many times in sight of the unwise, she has seemed to die in ignominy upon a cross. Gazing at her undaunted, the children of Mary and of John have calmly waited for the splendour of the First Day. Never yet have they looked in vain, and as it was with Napoleon, so it will always be with the man or the nation that measures itself with the Sovereign Pontiff. The struggle is not a material one, and God will protect His own.

During the night of the 5th of July, 1809, the suspicions of Pacca had been aroused by news of various detachments of troops pervading the streets of Rome. There was a vague movement in the Eternal City, which caused him to watch until dawn, when, deceived by the silence and hush of the immediate vicinity of the Quirinal, he thought the danger past once more, and went to seek a few hours of repose. But General Baron Radet, who was charged with the dishonourable mission of expelling the Pope from his own palace, had been watching for the disappearance of the last sentinel at the Quirinal. A little after half-past two he gave the signal of attack, thus setting in motion three separate detachments of troops, who by dividing for the invasion, wished to ensure greater success. Radet himself would confront the Holy Father in the midst of his private apartments. He was escorted by a wretched man who had lately been discharged by the Pope, for theft. The noise caused by the entrance among them of armed force, the breaking open of doors, and the cries of the French soldiers, awakened those in the palace who had betaken themselves to a tardy rest. Pacca had scarcely lain down when he was apprised of the invasion, and his first thought was to send Tiberius Pacca, his nephew, to call the Holy Father. Pius VII. was already up when the Cardinal entered his room. He had on the mozetta and stole, and was perfectly calm and serene. 'Now I am in company with my true friends,' he exclaimed, alluding to the presence of two cardinals, that of Pacca, and Despuig, a Spaniard, and Pro-Vicar of Rome. The troops announced their vicinity by the noise, growing louder every minute, of the doors which were being gradually forced in order to obtain access to the very chamber of the Pope. Cardinal Despuig urged that he should seek refuge in the domestic chapel which was near, but Pius VII. who had always rejected escape, would not, at this last moment, fly before his enemies. He seated himself on a sofa behind a table, and here with the Cardinals at his side, surrounded by the chief members of his household, he confronted Radet. The French formed a semicircle round the General. About eighteen officers had been introduced into the apartment, and now they stood with bared heads and naked swords in a respectful attitude, waiting to address the august prisoner. Both parties observed each other in silence for more than five minutes. In this curious scene, it was not the Holy Father, but Radet who lost courage, so that with great difficulty and evident embarrassment, he at length managed to broach the object of his visit to the Quirinal at so unseasonable an hour. He had 'a painful commission to fulfil, which was, however, imposed by the sacred duties of his place.' The Holy Father rose, and said with dignity: 'What do you want of me? And why do you come at such an hour to trouble my rest and my abode?'

'Most Holy Father, I come in the name of my Government to ask your Holiness once more formally to renounce the Temporal Power. If your Holiness consents, I do not doubt that all may still be arranged, and the Emperor will treat Your Holiness with the greatest consideration.'

'If you think yourself obliged to execute such orders of the Emperor because of your oath of fidelity and obedience to him, consider how much greater our duty is to defend the rights of the Holy See, to which so many oaths bind Us. We cannot give up that which is not ours. The Temporal Power, of which We are only the administrator, belongs to the Church. The Emperor may tear Us to pieces, but he will not succeed. After all that We have done for him, is this what We might have expected?'

'I know,' replied Radet much embarrassed, 'that the Emperor is very much indebted to you.'

'He is, and more than you can know, but what are your orders?'

'Most Holy Father, I am sorry to have such an instruction, but I have orders to take you away with me.'

Pius VII. turned to Radet with that tenderness which was so irresistible in him, and said gently: 'Truly, my son, this order will not draw down upon you the Divine blessing. This is then the gratitude bestowed upon me for all that I have done for your Emperor. This is the reward for my great condescension to him and to the Church of France. But perhaps I have been guilty in this respect before God, and He wishes to punish me. I resign myself in all humility.'[1]

In the meantime, the further orders of General Miollis had been ascertained; the Holy Father and Cardinal Pacca were to be immediately arrested and taken away from Rome. Pius VII. would have wished for at least two hours to make his preparations for that journey, but they were refused. He and Pacca must start at once, and other members of his household should follow.

[1] Account of the Italian MS. in British Museum, n. 8,387.

General Radet here relates that he helped the Holy Father, who was weak and ill, to reach his bedroom, and improved the occasion to assure the Pope that his things would not be touched. 'He who attaches no importance to his life,' was the reply of Pius VII., 'cares still less for what it offers.' And taking only his breviary and his crucifix, he descended the grand staircase of the Quirinal, followed by Pacca. It was four o'clock in the morning: there was no sign of life in the streets, and the Sovereign Pontiff, as he cast his eyes upon the familiar but strange spectacle presented by a perfect union of repose, on the one side, and armed force on the other, solemnly blessed Rome, which he was leaving for he knew not what. The blinds of the carriage, that was waiting to escort the Pope, had been firmly nailed down, and Radet caused both doors to be locked, after which, seating himself by the side of the driver, he ordered the postilions to leave Rome by the Porta Pia. A detachment of policemen accompanied the carriage. We are not at a loss to form some idea of the Holy Father's sentiments; they are portrayed in that outspoken benediction which he bequeathed to the Romans as a touching farewell: 'In this our anguish, We shed tears of happiness: blessing God, the Eternal Father of our Lord Jesus Christ, and God of all consolation, Who gives Us sweet comfort. It is to see the fulfilment in our person of that which was foretold by His Divine Son, our Redeemer, to the Prince of the Apostles, St. Peter, of whom, though unworthy, We are the successor. "When," our Lord said to him,[2] "thou shalt be old, thou shalt stretch forth thy hand and another shall gird thee, and lead thee whither thou wouldst not."'[3]

The first words which passed in the closed carriage

---

[2] St. John xxi. 18.
[3] Written Proclamation of the Holy Father, dated July 6, 1809.

that was conveying away Pius VII. and his Chief Minister, prove still better the Apostolic nature of the journey forced upon them. Upon the Holy Father's asking Pacca whether he had any money with him, they both produced their purses. That of Pius VII. contained one *papetto* (about 5d.); that of Pacca, three *grossi* (one shilling of our money), and notwithstanding present and oppressive trial, they could not help laughing at their combined riches. Pius VII. showed his *papetto* to Radet, saying: 'See, of all my States, this is all that I possess.' An anxiety of another kind secretly troubled Pacca. He feared that the Pope, the victim to such severe measures, would regret having issued the Bull of Excommunication, as likely to bring down still greater evils upon the Church, and he was therefore greatly relieved when the Holy Father said, with a smile upon his lips, 'Cardinal, we acted wisely in publishing the Bull of Excommunication on the 10th of June. Otherwise, what should We do now?'[4]

The journey was pursued to Florence as quickly as Radet could manage it. *His* business was to insure speed, and to prevent the recognition of the Holy Father, so that Pius VII. might be already far away before his arrest became generally known. The prisoner thus hurried on, was suffering very much from an infirmity which travelling greatly aggravated. Once he was so ill, that he declared he would wait for the arrival of his household, and Radet was obliged to consent. When the populations between Poggibonzi and Florence, having guessed the occupants of the dark and well guarded carriage, turned out to try and obtain a glimpse of the Holy Father, Radet resorted to the expedient of telling them to kneel down on each side for the Papal Benediction. 'They were still on their knees,' he remarks,

[4] *Memorie*, t. i. p. 219.

'whilst we had galloped on.'⁵ The Chartreuse at Florence was reached at midnight on the 8th of July. The Pope was so ill and extenuated with fatigue, that rest seemed imperatively demanded by his state. The same room was prepared for him that had formerly been occupied by Pius VI. The remembrance added to the affliction of Pacca, who saw the Pope in a state of dejection and sadness for which he possessed small means of alleviation. Elisa Bonaparte, as Grand Duchess of Tuscany, sent a chamberlain to compliment the Holy Father, who, overcome with fatigue and illness, answered in a scarcely articulate tone, without raising his head. Happily the Cardinal was at hand to speak for his suffering master. After partaking of the splendid supper which had been prepared for them, they retired to rest with the prospect of an undisturbed night. But at three, a.m., another envoy from Elisa urged the immediate departure of the Holy Father, for he was a dangerous guest. She feared her brother's anger far more than the suffering of the Sovereign Pontiff, and her only aim was to rid herself at the earliest opportunity of a weighty responsibility. Therefore she had decided that Pius VII. should proceed without further delay on his journey, no matter in what state, in spite too of the day being Sunday, which involved the impossibility of his saying or even hearing Mass, as he earnestly petitioned to do. Pacca went to warn him of the cruel order, and found him greatly depressed; his face had turned green, and he seemed immersed in pain. 'I see too well,' he said, 'that they wish to cause my death by bad treatment, and indeed I feel that in this way they will soon attain their object.'⁶

Le Général Radet au ministre de la guerre, 1809.
Memorie, t. i. p. 41.

It was important that Florence should not be traversed in broad daylight, as a hearty reception from the natives would have compromised the Grand Duchess. Separated momentarily from Pacca (which separation, however, prepared the Cardinal for what was afterwards to come), the Holy Father journeyed on to Genoa, another wearying three days with little rest. The Catholic feeling there was such as to necessitate another departure by night. The Holy Father, with Mgr. Doria, his high steward, were hurried away at dusk on litters to Alexandria, and from thence proceeded to Turin. Prince Borghese, who reigned at the Piedmontese capital, exhibited the same heartless feelings as his sister-in-law at Florence. The sooner the Pope could be conveyed out of his dominions the better, it appeared to him. Only by the special protection of God was the Holy Father's life preserved through the extreme fatigue inflicted upon one in his suffering condition, and the total want of even ordinary care for his state exhibited by the authorities of the countries through which he passed. At Mondovi, however, he experienced a real ovation. Clergy, religious Orders with their banners, went to meet him, in the midst of a joyful peal of bells; women and children offered him rosaries and flowers to bless. It is a remarkable fact that as the Holy Father neared France, the enthusiasm became greater. Whole villages awaited the Papal escort to obtain the Pope's blessing; and sometimes in their eagerness to kiss his hand, men, and even women, risked their lives to reach it whilst the carriage was in motion. At Grenoble, where Pacca was restored to him, the popular reception was equally hearty —but the authorities would have checked it, if possible. Notwithstanding, however, their orders, Pacca tells us that so far from bearing any resemblance to a prisoner conducted by his guards to the appointed place of confinement, Pius VII. might have been a 'happy father returning after a long absence to his loving family.'[7] But it is none the less true that the Holy Father was a strict prisoner at Grenoble. He occupied the Prefecture, and Pacca a separate house, for all communication between them was forbidden. The officials treated the Holy Father with perfect respect, but when they offered him carriages to visit the surrounding country, they were refused, because he considered himself a prisoner. He would only consent to take exercise in the garden of the Prefecture, and here the people, who soon learned the hour of his walks, manifested an ardour to see and receive his blessing, which never diminished during the ten days of his stay. As for Napoleon, who had just gained the battle of Wagram, he was somewhat distressed that his directions to Murat and Miollis had been so punctually obeyed. Elisa Bonaparte and Prince Borghese had manifested an alarmed and unnecessary speed, as it now appeared, to rid their States of the Holy Father. The Emperor's policy was rather to bury among his people the moral influence of the Pope, than to inflict violence on the person of Pius VII. What could be more opposed to such tactics than hurrying the Sovereign Pontiff from one French town to another? The effect had been exactly contrary to Napoleon's wishes. A persecuted cause, not to say that of the Papacy in Catholic France, has everywhere at least the merit of drawing to itself the popular sympathy, and of representing the persecutor in an unfavourable light. The Emperor regretted deeply that Pius VII. should have been brought into close contact with his people, and on the 18th of July he wrote to Fouché, that his arrest had been an act of 'great folly.' If he (the Pope) would now listen to reason, Napoleon had no objection to his

[7] *Memorie,* t, ii. p. 51.

returning to Rome, but in the meantime Savona would be the right place to receive him. The letter contains an injunction to look over the correspondence of the Holy Father, and to cause the imprisonment of Pacca at Fenestrello. 'Should a single Frenchman perish at the instigation of the Cardinal, he will pay for it with his head.'[8]

It was a sign of the times when one mighty arm held down the people of France in a despotism never equalled under a Bourbon king, that the enthusiasm caused by the Pope's appearance in the south should have had small echo in the rest of the country. No dearly loved sovereign, returning after a long exile to wield his hereditary sceptre, could have produced such an impression among his people as that of which Pius VII. found himself the object all the way from Grenoble to Savona, but in the northern provinces and in Paris, 'Where is the Pope?' was a question which no man *professed* to ask himself or his neighbours. One effect of despotism is to produce servility, vulgarity of sentiment, and to make a great people follow in the mass the lead of its master. At that time, too, the public attention in France was fully engrossed by the outward events which were unshaping the destinies of Europe. Whilst, then, whole populations poured out in the south to strew flowers before the Holy Father's passage, and bands of Italian peasants serenaded at his windows, whilst towns were festooned with garlands and illuminated as if to honour the triumphal march of a sovereign, France and Europe hardly ventured to express the smallest sympathy for his adverse fortunes. Individuals still loved and welcomed him, but nations, as nations, were engrossed and buried in material interests and spiritual indifference. It was the reign of universal egotism, which was not a

[8] Lettre de l'Empereur à Fouché (ministre de la police), 18 juillet, 1809.

production of speedy growth, but a situation gradually attained by the machinations of an infidelity daily showing itself with greater effrontery. Another tendency of despotism is to rule the Press. Not a word had been published concerning the assault of the Quirinal, the arrest of the Pope, or his journey through the southern populations, but it was tacitly known in the Council of State, and perhaps vaguely guessed in Paris, whose inhabitants had witnessed too many marvels to be henceforth astonished at anything. Fouché resorted to a vulgar expedient to quench whatever public curiosity might be felt concerning the Holy Father's movements, for the most indifferent might certainly wonder how the *Moniteur* would extricate itself from the difficulty of explaining such an unheard of proceeding as the employment of armed force to expel a Sovereign Pontiff from his palace because he would not consent to adopt the national quarrels of France. A letter, dated Grenoble, August 1, 1809, appeared a few days later in the *Moniteur*. 'The public here is very much preoccupied by the passage, in the commune of Bornin (the Pope had passed through this commune on his way to Grenoble), of an unknown animal, and judging by the traces which it has left behind, we may conclude that it is a reptile of extraordinary dimensions.' Half a page followed, full of details as to the course pursued by the animal, which, 'after having so much engrossed public attention, ended,' said the paper, 'by losing itself in a torrent.'[9]

It was a low similitude, but 'losing itself in a torrent' was not so far off the mark. Complete solitude and isolation were to do their best to render the Pope a dead letter. For some years Napoleon had his way, he legislated for Church and State, and endeavoured to

[9] *Moniteur*, du 9 août, 1809.

cause that silent reproach at Savona to be universally ignored. But in making for himself a position holding a middle between that of the Anglican Church and the Russian Czar, he found that he had succeeded to many of the thorns which lie hidden in the tiara as the most dolorous of crowns.

If we care to seek a perfect contrast to the dream of universal empire as realized by Napoleon when he had attained the height of his glory, we find it at the town washed by the Mediterranean where the Sovereign Pontiff 'possessing his soul in patience,' was calmly accepting his captivity—Savona. Pius VII., who had known only the tears, never the luxuries of a diadem, here betook himself once more to the cenobitical life now imposed by his misfortunes, but which had been the peaceful vocation of his youthful days. He occupied a small suite of apartments where confinement seems not to have hung heavily on his hands. His food consisted almost entirely of vegetables and a little fish. Air and exercise he had none beyond an occasional walk in the garden belonging to the episcopal palace (the house where he was confined), which was very small and surrounded by high walls. Many times he was pressed by his guardians to consent to sing High Mass at the Cathedral of Savona, but such a step would have been an act of weakness incongruous with his state of captivity. The domestic chapel sufficed for his daily Mass, and the hidden God there often received his secret and tearful prayer, not only for the oppressed and persecuted Church, but for the man who caused her suffering which was his own.[10] All natural means of resistance had been taken away. The Holy Father saw himself isolated from his counsellors, the Sacred College, from theological books and documents, to which

[10] Italian MS. British Museum, n. 8,389.

he might have referred in the absence of the Cardinals; no ecclesiastical dignitaries were to have access to him, but strictly and solely he was to be confined to the divine consolation which came to him undoubtedly from the tabernacle of that still, silent chapel in his prison. Solitude, however, to a Pontiff of Pius VII.'s character was not in itself an evil, and it is impossible to realize Savona without reproducing in some measure the nature and disposition of the men appointed by Napoleon to act as his gaolers. The first and the principal of these was the Prefect of Montenotte, the Comte Chabrol de Volvic. He was scientific and full of capacity, in spite of which qualities, he bent with perfect docility to the unlawful will of the Emperor with regard to the Holy Father. He was considerably strengthened in his servile submission by the Comte de Salmatoris, who arrived from Paris for the avowed purpose of organizing the pontifical household on a footing splendid enough for a reigning prince of the first rank. Expense, indeed,. was no object in Napoleon's eyes, if he could only succeed in destroying the universality of the office of the Vicar of Christ, and in rendering him second in rank, a vassal, in fact, to the French Emperor. Liveries,. carriages, horses, and a monthly allotment of one hundred thousand francs were offered by the Comte de Salmatoris as an allurement to Pius VII. An attempt, too, was made to gain the members of the Holy Father's household by the promise of a salary equal to that they had formerly received at Rome, but it is immaterial to a prisoner that the walls which he must hourly contemplate should be gilded. The offers availed nothing, and another course of seduction was employed by Napoleon, who certainly possessed the capability of thinking of everything. The mission of the Comte César Berthier (brother of the Prince of Wagram) at Savona, was

M

perhaps the most delicate of all. He possessed a great reputation for spending money magnificently, and this propensity was to gratify itself under the eyes of the Holy Father, without, however, imposing upon him anything contrary to his habits. Berthier was charged to keep open house, to show great hospitality to those connected with the Papal household, and to prove to the public, as far as he could, that the Pope was no prisoner at all. At the same time, he was to execute a minute inspection over all doings within the episcopal palace, which inspection he was recommended to dissimulate as much as possible. He served a difficult master, for in his unfortunate person he was bound to unite the obsequiousness of an inferior with the severity of a gaoler.

At the time of the Concordat, Napoleon had said that 'if the Pope had not existed, he must have been created for the occasion.'[11] The same cry would have been legitimate in the mouth of the Church of France from 1809 to 1814, for the article in the Concordat relating to the confirmation at Rome of bishops nominated by the First Consul was rendered null and void by the violence employed against the Holy Father. A contract ceases to be valid when one of the parties concerned infringes its conditions. In this point then, the moral importance of the Holy See became strikingly manifest. It was easy to impose confinement, with all the accessories we have mentioned, upon Pius VII., but he still continued to be the Keeper of the Keys, he, who alone on earth has supreme power to bind and to loose, and one of whose most precious prerogatives it is to guide and to direct the appointment of truly apostolical pastors over the lambs of his flock. He could legitimately refuse to confirm the bishops named by Napoleon. More than this, he

---

[11] *Mémoires de Napoléon.*

owed it to justice and to his own dignity. The position was embarrassing for the Emperor. He had caused the Pope to be confined in an obscure town of his Empire, and now he discovered, that, powerful and magnificent sovereign though he was, the machinery of the spiritual kingdom over which he longed to reign, stopped as if of itself, without the weak old man to set it in motion, whose supposed incapacity had called forth his contempt. The situation necessitated a move in the direction of the Prisoner of Savona, but the initative must not come from Napoleon himself. In July, 1809, he recommended the highest dignitaries of the French Church, Fesch, Caprara, Maury, and several other bishops, to write to Pius VII. *as if from themselves*, and to represent the grievous results of his refusal to confirm the subjects honoured by the Emperor's choice. To command and to be obeyed was one and the same thing. The docile bishops immediately conformed themselves to Napoleon's wishes, but a striking difference marks their several letters. Fesch expressed great sympathy with the trials of the Holy Father, and Maury alluded to them in becoming terms, but others who were afraid so to commit themselves, passed over in silence the indignities offered to Pius VII., and expatiated upon the actual evils of the French Church which he fostered by his resistance.[12] Caprara was one of those who were thus dead to all honourable and noble sentiments of loyalty and justice. The Holy Father's reply addressed to his former legate, is remarkable by its calm firmness. It perhaps somewhat opened the eyes of Napoleon to the nature and quality of the combat he was waging against a spiritual kingdom, and to the character of Pius VII., who, alone and uncounselled, could produce such an uncompromising, yet gentle answer.

[12] *L'Eglise Romaine et le Premier Empire*, t. iii. p. 401.

'However little, my Lord Cardinal, you reflect upon this proposition, it is impossible that you should not understand that We cannot acquiesce in it, without acknowledging in the Emperor the right of nomination, and the faculty of exercising such right. You say that our Bulls would be accorded not to his instances, but to those of the Council and of the Minister of Worship. First of all, the Catholic Church recognizes no Minister of Worship having authority in virtue of the secular power; then, this Council and this Minister, are they not one and the same thing as the Emperor himself? Are they not the organ of his commands, and the instruments of his will? After so many innovations fatal to religion which the Emperor has allowed himself, and against which We have so long and so uselessly protested, after the vexations imposed upon so many ecclesiastics of our States, after the exile of so many bishops and of the majority of our Cardinals, the imprisonment at Fenestrello of Cardinal Pacca, the usurpation of St. Peter's patrimony, our own violent arrest in our own palace, our peregrinations from city to city, where We were watched so closely that bishops of several dioceses traversed by Us, could not approach Us nor speak to Us without witnesses, after all these and numerous other sacrilegious attempts, which it would take too long to enumerate, and which both general councils and the apostolic constitutions have anathematized, have We done anything but render obedience to these constitutions, as indeed our duty compelled Us to do? How then now could We recognize in the author of these violent measures, the right in question? how consent to his exercising it? Could We do this without rendering ourself guilty of prevarication, or making our conduct a contradiction of itself? Should We not disedify the faithful, causing it to be believed that, broken down by so much suffering and dreading still greater anguish, We are weak enough to betray our conscience and to approve what it compels Us to forbid? Weigh all these reasons, my Lord Cardinal, not indeed in the measure of human wisdom, but in that of the sanctuary, and you will feel their force. In spite of such a state of things, God knows whether We ardently desire to find pastors for the vacant sees of that Church of France, which We have always cherished so especially, and to discover an expedient to accomplish this in a fitting manner. But are We to act in an affair of such importance without consulting our natural counsellors, the Sacred College? And how can We consult them, when violence has been used to prevent all communication between Us, and to take away from Us all means of despatching similar business? Hitherto We have been unable to obtain even one of our secretaries.' [13]

The concise nature of this reply rendered the Emperor delighted with an expedient suggested by Maury, for at least momentarily dispensing with the desired Bulls. Louis XIV., said the Cardinal, had contrived on a somewhat similar occasion, to cause his dioceses to be administered by bishops elect who had not received the customary and necessary Bulls from Rome. The same plan was adopted by Napoleon, though if we may believe M. Bigot (who had succeeded M. Portalis as Minister of Worship), the bishops, at an earlier period, had expressed great unwillingness to undertake episcopal functions without the approbation of the Holy See. Now, however, he remarked, as soon as they learned his Majesty's will on the subject, they would hasten to prove their devotion and gratitude! [14] Napoleon's heightened irritation dated

---

[13] Bref du Pape au Card. Caprara, 25 août, 1809.
[14] Lettre de M. Bigot de Préameneu à l'Empereur, 7 xbre, 1809.

from the course pursued by Pius VII. on the 10th of June, 1809. The Bull *Quum Memoranda* had made a profound impression upon him, which he endeavoured to dissimulate by an openly-expressed contempt in the presence of Cardinals and bishops who did not refuse to communicate with him *in divinis*. The wording of the Bull, which did not name the Emperor personally, rendered this communication possible, although Napoleon feigned to ignore the license and ridiculed it. That it was but an assumed insensibility is fully proved by the orders issued at the time of the arrest of the Holy Father, namely, that the secret of the excommunication was to be rigorously kept under pain of the severest punishment. One of the Pope's valets, mysteriously asked at Avignon whether Napoleon had really been excommunicated, replied, that it was as much as his life was worth to answer.[15] Gallicanism once more offered its services to the Emperor at this period of his combat with the Sovereign Pontiff. M. Bigot de Préameneu was a faithful representative of the tendency of the French magistracy and of that parliamentary influence which had usurped, in a measure, in France, the authority of the Roman See. Owing to national and hereditary prejudices, his mind was predisposed to sympathize with Napoleon, whilst he sought to modify what seemed excessive in the Emperor's manner of showing anger to Ultramontane Cardinals and bishops. The comte Bigot succeeded M. Portalis as Minister of Worship, and resembled him in that strange capacity for forming a one-sided appreciation of the state of the question, and causing the balance always to weigh heaviest on Cæsar's side. This new functionary was charged to examine the Bull and to see how far it touched or affected the Emperor. The result went to prove against the logic of the argument brought

---

[15] Italian MS. at British Museum, n. 8,389.

forward by Bigot. Because the Pope had not mentioned Napoleon, his intention had not been to excommunicate him personally, *therefore* the wiser plan would be to bury the whole matter in oblivion, and to let it die from inanition. An honest mind seldom, if ever, fears open daylight; a secret then, and very deeply felt misgiving lurked at the bottom of Napoleon's affected disdain, when he said that, 'the Bull of Excommunication was a document so ridiculous that it did not deserve the smallest attention.'[16] The same sensitive apprehension led to the suppression of missionary priests in France, who by the very nature of their attributions seemed more likely to escape the vigilance of the police, and thus, possibly, might divulge the secret. Spiritual conferences at St. Sulpice were, on similar grounds, pronounced dangerous, and prohibited. It was impossible for priests to meet without falling immediately under the suspicion of 'plotting,' which was a general term employed by the Emperor to signify anything he did not like.[17] His resentment was, moreover, carried to the head-quarters of all the mischief—Rome. He ordered the departure within twenty-four hours of the Cardinals still there, especially designating Cardinal di Pietro (who had worked at the Bull), and of those prelates possessing faculties for spiritual affairs, 'which are no longer to be treated at Rome.'[18]

About this time may be placed an important interview between Napoleon and the Superior of St. Sulpice. M. Emery is known to us chiefly as a French ecclesiastic who had the singular merit of speaking the truth to the Emperor in his dissensions with the

---

[16] Lettre de l'Empereur à M. Bigot de Préameneu, 3 juillet, 1809.
[17] Lettre de l'Empereur à M. Fouché, 15 7bre, 1809.
[18] Lettre de l'Empereur au Comte Bigot, 18 7bre, 1809. *Not* inserted in his correspondence.

Holy See, and what is more strange, of calling forth in consequence, sentiments of admiration and esteem in Napoleon. Author of a book treating the question of the Declaration of 1682, he was accused of *Ultramontanism*, and sent for to Fontainebleau, to render an account of himself. He did not know what the Emperor had in view in wishing to see him, but he was determined to tell Napoleon his mind upon Roman affairs, and had prepared a little speech to this effect: 'I am on the borders of the grave, no human interest can have any weight with me, but the pure interest of your Majesty obliges me to tell you that it is most important for you to become reconciled to the Pope, and that otherwise you will subject yourself to great misfortunes.' After waiting three days at the Palace of Fontainebleau, M. Emery was at last admitted to an audience. Napoleon began by speaking of the *opuscules* (small treatises of Fleury, which Emery had been editing). 'I have read your book,' he said, 'Look, it is on my table. Certainly, there is something in the preface not quite *franc du collier*, but on the whole, there is not wherewith to *fouetter un chat.*' With this, the Emperor pulled M. Emery's ear, a movement which indicated special favour, and then plunged immediately into the great question—his disagreement with the Pope, *whose spiritual power he respected, but whose temporal power did not come from Jesus Christ, but from Charlemagne.* He, Napoleon, wished to deliver the Sovereign Pontiff from the anxiety of material things that His Holiness might thus have more leisure for spiritual matters. M. Emery objected that Charlemagne had not given the Pope all his temporal possessions. In the fifth century, they were already considerable; let the Emperor, therefore, at least respect such as had not entered into Charlemagne's gift. Napoleon, whose knowledge of Church history was very slight, as we have seen, found no reply to this representation. He thought it was surprizing that those who had studied theology all their lives could discover no method of *arranging* him with the Pope. 'As for me,' he said, 'if I had studied theology for six months only, I should soon have made all things clear, because (with his hand on his forehead) God has given me intellect. I should not certainly talk Latin as well as the Pope. Mine might be dog Latin, but soon all would be settled.' During the interval, three kings were announced. Napoleon had made them, and could afford to keep them waiting. M. Emery, seeing that he was not sent away, took occasion to present another edition of his work on Fleury, hoping to bring before the Emperor's notice the splendid testimony—which had been introduced into the supplement—of Bossuet and Fénelon, in favour of the Roman Church. It appears that Napoleon *did* read the book, but it was a case not of invincible, but of wilful ignorance, for a few days later, M. Emery's latest work was seized by the police and condemned. It thus shared the fate of all, that, with the innate strength of truth and honesty, excited the Emperor's suspicions.[19]

The *sénatus-consulte* which made Rome the second city of the Empire, and imposed upon each Sovereign Pontiff at his succession the oath of fidelity to the Four Propositions of the Gallican Church, with two million francs for revenue, and a palace wherever he might choose to reside, was no fiction. The decree passed without raising any protestation of indignation from the European Cabinets. Nations had ceased to be Catholic, but individuals proved that fidelity to lawful authority was still to be found in the continent whose representatives had succumbed to less noble passions. The Italian clergy in the mass refused alike the oath and the gold of the new

[19] *Histoire de Pie VII.* t. ii. p. 257.

Government. After the Peace of Vienna, in October, 1809, all the Cardinals, except a very small number whose age or ill-health rendered the journey impossible, were summoned to Paris, to grace the Imperial instead of the Papal Court. Of these a certain number, afterwards known as the Red Cardinals, showed in Consalvi's opinion too easy a condescension in taking part in worldly dissipation at a time when their Chief was suffering a dreary imprisonment.[20] A few months later, February, 1810, the Penitentiary and Datery Tribunals were transferred to the French capital,[21] so that it is true to say that the Roman Court was bodily removed to Paris, whilst by the mercy of God it is plainly proved to those who have discerning eyes, that even the Court of Rome is wholly powerless without its Head. It was as the Kingdom of France without the French King, or the Empire of Russia without the Czar. Napoleon could at least satisfy his ardent desire to rule. Some of his directions to M. Bigot about this time would call forth a smile, were not the subject so serious. He says to him on 13th August, 1809, 'At no price will I tolerate payment for Bulls, dispensations, &c. . . . It is a profanation of sacred things.[22] Has the Minister of Worship sent a circular to the bishops, ordering them to suppress the prayer to St. Gregory VII., and to substitute another feast for that of this saint whom

---

[20] *Mémoires*, t. ii. p. 167.

[21] Lettre de Napoleon à M. Bigot, 4 février, 1810.

[22] Whatever is paid at Rome for this kind of dispensations, is a very small and legitimate indemnity for the cost of sending them, and the salary of those employed in the work. Simple common sense, and a natural feeling of justice, have introduced emoluments into every court in the world. If Protestants maintain the contrary, they on their side have no right to enjoy any living, or to receive any fee for baptisms, marriages, or funerals. The same principle would render *any* salary or indemnity unlawful, for every man being capable of doing service to his neighbour without money, he is bound to do it without money (*Histoire de la Révolution Religieuse en Suisse.*—Haller).

the Gallican Church cannot recognize.' [23] Napoleon, who professed a great horror for the *profanation of holy things*, did not show any scruples of conscience when it pleased him to diminish the number of Italian bishoprics, and to confiscate their revenues and those of all religious houses. Until, however, his marriage with Marie Louise was finally settled, he maintained a certain regard for appearances, although with the secret resolution of pushing State intrusion into the new departments of Rome and Thrasimene. During his honeymoon he found time to write to M. Bigot, that things were 'to be organized as if no Pope existed.' The number of bishoprics was to be diminished, and all foreign religious at Rome were to return to their native country. No priest was to be ordained in the new departments without Napoleon's permission; the oath was to be imposed on the bishops, but it was a matter of small importance to the Emperor whether they all accepted it, as he purposed only keeping three or four sees in Rome and Thrasimene. All religious corporations were abolished.[24] Two solid advantages resulted from these measures. The revenues of the bishoprics suppressed in the two departments went to augment Napoleon's treasure, and the refusal of the oath by the clergy enabled him to reproach the Holy Father with the widowed condition of so many dioceses, as well as the poverty of a great number of unfortunate priests, who were thus thrown upon the world. It is hard indeed to imagine anything more desolate than the religious aspect of Italy at this time. Armed force was employed to bring about, if possible, the submission of the Church to the arbitrary secular power, represented by a despot of Napoleon's calibre. Nineteen bishops in

---

[23] Note dictée par l'Empereur au conseil des ministres, le 18 janvier, 1810. *Not* inserted in his correspondence.
[24] Lettre de l'Empereur au Comte Bigot, 7 mai, 1810.

the Roman States had refused the oath. The alternative was beggary or imprisonment. The second order of the clergy followed the example of the bishops. What was to be done with these refractory priests? Napoleon solves the question after his fashion. 'Give orders to the prefect of the Taro Department to choose fifty of the worst priests at Parma, and fifty of the worst at Piacenza. . . . Let them embark for Corsica.' As to the priests Boni, Ascensi, and Toni, who have refused the oath, send them to Toulon, and only there, inform them that they are bound for Corsica.' [25]

It may be remembered by readers of the memoirs of Napoleon written at St. Helena, that he there mentions fifty-three as the number of priests imprisoned in consequence of discussions with Rome, for a legitimate cause. Here, as in other matters, his own correspondence gives him the lie. The only way to account for such proceedings is to try and form an idea of the ambition of Napoleon. It was so great as to render lawful all means whatever as steps to attain an end which is gigantic, indeed, but not novel, in the strife between God's kingdom on earth and the material power of Cæsar. He aimed at the suppression of the temporal power of the Holy See, to make Rome the second city of the Empire, and to establish a Papacy dependent on the new Western Emperor, with residence at Paris or Avignon, the enjoyment of splendid palaces, and a revenue of two million francs, besides many other advantages. In return for these benefits the Pope would be required to acknowledge himself the first among the subjects of Napoleon, in the same way as the Holy Synod of the Russian Church recognizes the supreme authority of the Czar, and the Scheik-el-Islam that of the Sultan. In February, 1811, a year after the promulgation of the *sénatus-consulte*, which

---

[25] Lettres de l'Empereur au Comte Bigot, 3 et 17 février, 1810.

decreed sovereign power to Napoleon for spiritual legislation with as much right as our own Parliament possessed for legitimatizing and dissolving the successive marriages of Henry VIII., these were the results obtained by the intrusion of the head of the State in ecclesiastical affairs. Thirteen Cardinals had been degraded from the outward marks of their dignity, and were confined in various provincial towns under the strict supervision of the Imperial police. Nineteen bishops of the Roman States had been sent to France under escort, to live under the same conditions. A multitude of canons and vicar-generals, whose number it is impossible to fix, had fallen victims to similar measures, and more than two hundred priests had been banished to Corsica.[26] But this result belongs to a more advanced period of the history of Pius VII. It is now necessary to speak of the new triumph of Napoleon—his marriage with the Archduchess Marie Louise, a daughter of the house of Hapsburg-Lorraine, and to see how it affected the prisoner at Savona.

[26] *L'Eglise Romaine et le Premier Empire*, t. iii. p. 375.

CHAPTER IX.

Strife through Woman.

'He will arm the creature to be avenged upon his enemies.'—
Wisdom v. 18.

THE domestic life of Napoleon with Josephine, and the nature of his relations with her, seemed to partake of the strange character of his own lot. If it is true that he was a man who set his mark upon his century, it is no less so that he was as a husband very original. On both sides there were wrongs which neither cared to dissemble. Josephine ardently loved Napoleon, but she could afford to play at loving others and did do so. He looked upon her as a kind of good genius. With Josephine at his side, his star had risen in the firmament of human glory, and her personal influence had been used to raise it still higher in the social heaven. As the widow of a nobleman, she had conciliated to him in the early years of her new marriage the proud hearts of the old French aristocracy. A careful study of human nature seems to prove that few can love, in the high and true sense of the word; but how many who are capable of the affection, can also wisely fix their choice upon its object? But Napoleon was incapable of true affection, since his mind owned an illegitimate king, a despot of one idea—ambition, the passion to reign. Truly his 'error was his God.'[1] He did not and could not return Josephine's ardent affection, because all the powers of his heart were

---

[1] St. Augustin, *Confessiones*, lib. iv.

concentrated on that dream of his life—the foundation of a Western Empire—to which he shaped both men and events. His divorce from a wife who could no longer entertain hopes of giving him an heir need cause no surprize, if we only follow what must have been the natural promptings of the thirst after fame and domination in Napoleon. Sooner or later he would discover that the glory of a royal alliance, with the prospect of leaving a son whom he might call King of Rome, was alone wanting to him. Where was peace for the modern Western Emperor who could say—there is still more that I might have, and have not got? Other obstacles had stood in the way of his triumphant career and had been swept ruthlessly away. The woman, who had shared his fortunes, and who of all others had inspired him with something *akin* to affection, this woman would meet with no softer fate. Her claims would yield before zeal for the welfare of the Empire. It is impossible to say definitely how long the mind of Napoleon brooded over the thought of a new marriage or when he came to the ultimate determination thereon, but this much is certain, he would have allowed Pius VII. to crown a concubine as his wife, and the Empress had incurred his severe displeasure for that trembling confidence which had been poured into the Holy Father's ear in December, 1804. At that period, he had not *matured* his plan for divorcing Josephine, but it is pretty evident that it occupied a place as an unfledged hope in his mind. In 1808, on his return from Bayonne, he sounded in a characteristic conversation the sentiments of the clergy and Archbishop of Bordeaux, Mgr. d'Aviau. He began to discuss with them the propriety of divorce. An honest old doctor of the Sorbonne, M. Thierry, immediately quoted the passage. 'No man can separate what God has put together.'

'That is very well in ordinary life,' replied the Emperor, 'without it marriage would possess no character of indissolubility; but it cannot be applied when important reasons intervene, or the good of the State.'

This argument was not accepted by Thierry. 'The Gospel precept,' he said, 'admitted of no exceptions.'

'What, Monsieur l'Abbé,' exclaimed the Emperor, 'are you a Protestant?'

It was a strange accusation under the circumstances. The Superior of the Seminary of Bordeaux when asked by Napoleon to decide the question, whether or not tradition was not for him in the matter, very properly sided with Thierry. The Emperor summarily sent away Mgr. d'Aviau and his clergy. He was red with anger, but this was not the sole result of the interview. A few days after reaching Paris, he sent orders through M. Bigot, to remove M. Thierry from his post of Vicar-General, and M. Lacroix from that of Superior of the Seminary. When once he had fully determined to contract a new marriage, he did not delay to broach the subject to Josephine. One day, after a very silent repast alone with her, he brought about an explanation of his wishes. The Empress fell fainting on the floor, and to avoid raising a commotion in the palace, Napoleon, grieved and distressed at her state, summoned the chamberlain in attendance, and asked if he would undertake to carry Josephine to her apartments. But it seems that she too possessed the art in which Napoleon excelled,—she could act a scene. As the chamberlain, whose legs had for a moment entangled themselves in his sword, was conveying her up a very steep staircase, he was astonished to hear the Empress say in a very low tone, 'Take care, Monsieur, you are squeezing me too much.'[2] The

---

[2] *L'Eglise Romaine et le Premier Empire,* t. iii. pp. 201, 207.

religious marriage alone presented a difficulty; the civil contract was easily annulled, although divorce had been strictly prohibited to all members of the imperial house. Josephine's consent was tearfully given, but in descending to private life she retained her household and the title of Empress, and was to enjoy (it was Napoleon's express wish) the greatest consideration. Her adieu to sovereignty was effected under trying circumstances, but she passed through the ordeal with perfect grace. A grand reception took place at the Tuileries on the evening of her departure. For the last time she was empress to the world, and on such an occasion the courtiers did not disguise the curiosity which they felt to watch her playing her strange part. Napoleon showed evident embarrassment and constraint. On that memorable evening a condemned empress assisted at the funeral of her worldly greatness, and Divine Providence, who was preparing a downfall for Napoleon proportionate to the splendour of his triumphs as a soldier and an Emperor, ruled future events unto this end by a few words spoken in the hurry of departure from the Tuileries by two courtiers. Napoleon had caused a violent hand to be laid upon the Vicar of Christ, and utter ruin was coming to him with the daughter of Cæsar, out of that Austrian alliance which he regarded as the most precious trophy won by his sword. Negotiations for his marriage with the Grand Duchess Olga of Russia were all but concluded. In the crowd which issued from the imperial reception rooms that night two men met and exchanged a few words on the all-engrossing topic—the approaching marriage of Napoleon with the Czar's sister. M. de Sémonville, without being a statesman, was learned in diplomacy, and enjoyed the confidence of the Duc de Bassano, then Minister of the Exterior. He found himself side by side with M. Floret, First Secretary of the Austrian Embassy, as they both descended to the hall to wait for their carriages.

'So,' exclaimed M. de Sémonville, 'the deed is done, and we have no more to say. Why did not you (Austria) come forward?'

'Who told you we might not have been willing?'

'So people say. Could it possibly be true?'

'Very possibly.'

'What! you really would agree . . . *You* might, that is, but the Ambassador?'

'I will answer for Prince Schwarzenberg.'

'But Prince Metternich?'

'There is no difficulty from that quarter.'

'But the Emperor?'

'Nor from the Emperor.'

'And the Empress who hates us?'

'You don't know her; she is ambitious, and she would have been induced to like it.'

M. de Sémonville took care to sow the good seed, by immediately communicating his conversation to the Duc de Bassano. The next day, it was Napoleon's turn to listen to it with a face beaming with joy. From that time, he secretly determined that Marie Louise should have the honour coveted by Europe, though outwardly a little hesitation on his part was becoming and pleasing to his imperial vanity. The marriage of crowned heads is not an affair of sentiment but of policy, and in this circumstance it was all-important to consolidate his influence both at home and abroad. We are struck by the wonderful perspicacity manifested on the change of the Emperor's plans by the Arch-Chancellor Cambacérès. Of all the Court he alone remained favourable to the Russian alliance, and when asked for his reasons he replied with a forethought which succeeding events fully justified, 'You will see that my reason is so good that one single sentence suffices to prove its weight. I am morally certain that before two years are over, we shall have war with that sovereign of the two whose daughter the Emperor has not married. War with Austria does not cause me the least alarm, but war with Russia makes me tremble; the consequences are incalculable. I know that the Emperor can find his way to Vienna, but I am not so sure of St. Petersburg.'[3]

Since, however, the Emperor was resolved to marry a daughter of a house so Catholic as Austria professed to be, the duty of proceeding with all necessary formality in the annulment of the religious bond which united him to Josephine was more than ever imposed upon him. A difficulty met him at the very outset, for such cases as his have always been referred to the Sovereign Pontiff, who alone can decide matrimonial questions between crowned heads. No other authority, Cardinal Fesch declared, would be otherwise than 'uncertain or dangerous' on the subject. But moral impossibility, as we have so often said, was an unknown region to Napoleon. Since he chose not to have recourse to the Pope, a tribunal was created expressly for the circumstances, consisting of three different officialities, diocesan, metropolitan, and a third, under the immediate presidency of Cardinal Fesch, Primate of France. About as little liberty of decision was left to the unfortunate priests who composed these several officialities as that granted to Josephine when she was called upon to descend from the throne and to sacrifice her rights as a wife, to the good of the State. Four of the chief members of the diocesan officiality, who went to learn formally the Emperor's determination from the Arch-Chancellor, exclaimed at once that it was a case falling under the immediate province of the Sovereign Pontiff, and that

[3] *L'Eglise Romaine et le Premier Empire*, t. iii. p. 223.

consequently, they could do nothing until the officiality, presided over by Fesch, should have pronounced them competent. But Cambacérès was determined that matters should be speedily resolved; 'formalities are injurious to the subject treated.' A few days after this interview the written consent of the higher ecclesiastical officiality was procured, without, however, the signatures of the president Fesch, or of M. Emery (who was likewise on the commission). The Cardinal Primate was personally interested in a marriage he had had extraordinary faculties to bless, and pending the final judgment he intervened uncomfortably more than once, to destroy the best arguments of Cambacérès. Thus the Arch-Chancellor had informed the diocesan officiality, that the marriage of 1804 had taken place in the Emperor's room, without curé, witnesses, or deed. But Fesch could affirm that he himself, after drawing up the deed, had confided it to Josephine, who, foolishly enough, had parted with it at the *indirect* solicitation of the Emperor. Another alleged cause of non-legality was the absence of the parish priest and witnesses, but the extraordinary faculties conferred upon Fesch by Pius VII. might serve to cover this want of formality. The third argument was one that caused great astonishment. Napoleon was not ashamed to say that he had never given his consent to the religious marriage. The indelicacy of such an affirmation is easily discerned. The Emperor who could condescend to acknowledge that he had deceived his wife, Cardinal Fesch, and the Sovereign Pontiff, embittered by a stinging profession of indifference the misfortune of Josephine, whom, according to himself, he had never wished to marry. Probably this want of moral consent had never existed; but Napoleon was anxious to find a legitimate plea, no matter at what price, for the dissolution of the religious bond. The diocesan officiality was menaced with the anger of his Majesty, if its decision kept him waiting beyond a certain day. As may be premised, the Emperor had his way with the religious tribunal which had been set up only to do his bidding. The marriage was dissolved on the plea that it had not been validly contracted, and for a moment, at least, Napoleon entertained the extravagant idea of assigning to the Holy Father, his prisoner, a part in the approaching nuptial ceremony. It is most important to note that Pius VII. was entirely outside the whole question of the marriage. Napoleon never attempted to make even a semblance of consulting him on the subject; but we may suppose, with very good grounds, that the Holy Father who had so nobly defended the rights of Protestant Miss Patterson, would have equally maintained the sacred character of a valid marriage authorized by his express command in the case of Josephine.

What position at this time could have been more delicate than that of the Primate, Fesch? He had blessed the first marriage, where absence of the parish priest had been alleged as a reason of nullity, in spite of faculties derived immediately from the Holy Father, and it would devolve upon him to perform the second ceremony, whilst at the same time he saw himself exposed to the irritation of Napoleon on account of partiality for the Sovereign Pontiff. Constantly, when Fesch would have discussed a point of ecclesiastical discipline, he was silenced by the Emperor with: 'Where did you learn that? I don't care for what you think; I wish for the advice of M. Duvoisin (Bishop of Nantes) and M. Emery. It is quite right that they should give their opinion: they are men that understand what they are talking about.'[4] Mgr. Duvoisin, who belonged also to the ecclesiastical tribunal, was a Gallican prelate, who laid all his theo-

[4] *L'Eglise Romaine et le Premier Empire*, t. iii. p. 256.

logical science at the feet of Napoleon. M. Emery, 'the only man whom the Emperor feared,' had done what he could to escape belonging to the commission, but in vain. He used his influence generally to combat the projects of the Government; for now that Napoleon counted upon a long peace, he would have desired nothing better than to arrange the affairs of the French Church as summarily as he had resolved the question of his divorce. Whenever in the Senate Rome was discussed it was always with the bitterest invectives, but Pius VII. was not mentioned by name. It was Napoleon's will that he should be universally ignored; for between a sovereign in possession, 'walking in glory,' to use an expression of Cambacérès, and a sovereign dethroned to live as if not living, apart from all he loved, save the Eucharistic God, in an obscure town of the conqueror's dominions, the contrast was too striking in favour of the persecuted and oppressed Holy Father. Conscience would have its own way with Napoleon, to the extent of palliating the joy of his approaching triumph, by an indefinable irritability in the face of small events which in any way recalled to him the existence and the actual position of the Prisoner at Savona. He would not allow his people to draw their own comparisons between the Pontiff and the Emperor; but in the depths of his soul he was constrained to draw them himself. He came forth lessened in his own eyes, and this produced an impatient dissatisfaction, the burden of which fell on those who happened to recall the unpleasant thought. Satisfied pride! Is it not a commonplace phrase that awaits its realization with as little chance of reaching it as a dwarf who undertakes to combat a giant need hope for victory? At this period, Napoleon determined not to leave stone upon stone of the Roman Court at Rome. Cardinals di Pietro and Consalvi yielded at last to main force, and arrived in Paris in

February, 1810. We have seen enough of Consalvi to appreciate the nobility of his demeanour at Paris. Unlike the other Cardinals, he was personally known in all the great circles, and proportionately loved and valued. As Secretary of State, he had been brought into contact with different members of the imperial family, and they would vie with each other, he felt, to try and make him forget his dearly-loved sovereign at Savona. Most of all, he dreaded the Emperor's advances. It was peculiarly painful to Consalvi to respond to kindness with coldness and apparent incivility; but there was one thing stronger in him than any other sentiment—devotion to duty, so that he can say with truth in his memoirs: 'With the divine assistance I triumphed over human respect, and during my stay in Paris I acted, I consider, in a manner befitting my dignity.'[5] The other Cardinals, who had preceded him in Paris, had made no difficulty in accepting the yearly allotment of thirty thousand francs, offered by the Government. It is true that some of the number received it as a compensation for the privation of their Italian benefices, and later on, better informed of the Holy Father's wish, refused to accept it any longer.[6] At the outset, however, Consalvi had other notions, which were shared by Cardinals di Pietro, Saluzzo, and Pignatelli, who arrived almost at the same time. These members of the Sacred College, having refused the allowance, lived a retired life, according to the injunctions of the Holy Father. This course was easily adopted by di Pietro, Saluzzo, and Pignatelli, who were personally unknown in Paris; but the same cannot be said of the Cardinal who had negotiated the Concordat, and long held the post of Prime Minister of the Holy Father. He was seen nowhere, and he owns that it cost him a great deal to appear to be wanting in

[5] *Mémoires*, t. ii. p. 169. [6] Pacca, *Memorie*, t. ii. p. 129.

politeness. He could not give the real cause of his absence from all gaiety without incriminating other Cardinals, whose consciences opposed their acceptance neither of the allowance made by the Government, nor of the invitations which at that time were numerous in proportion to the great events constantly succeeding each other on the French panorama. Six days after his arrival he presented himself at the Tuileries, together with four other members of the Sacred College. Cardinal Fesch introduced each by name to the Emperor, as they stood in order of rank. Napoleon passed over the first four with little comment; but before the Primate had named Consalvi, he exclaimed, in a kind tone: 'Oh, Cardinal Consalvi, how thin you have got! I should hardly have known you.' As if to explain what the Emperor remarked, the Cardinal replied: 'Sire, years succeed each other so fast. Nearly nine have gone by since I have had the honour of speaking to your Majesty.' 'That is true; it will soon be nine years since you came for the Concordat, which we effected in this very room. But of what use has it been? It has ended in smoke. Rome has lost everything. It must be owned that I did wrong to cause your resignation. If you had continued to occupy your post, things would never have come to such a pass.'

This was just what Consalvi feared, but he had not imagined that Napoleon would have gone so far. He could not let a similar assertion remain undenied before the public; so consulting only his 'honour and the truth,' and seeming to ignore all that such an acknowledgment signified in the mouth of the Emperor, he undauntedly replied: 'Sire, if I had remained Secretary of State, I should have been faithful to my duty.'

Napoleon looked at him fixedly, and going the round of the room from right to left, he began a long string of complaints against the Pope and Rome, which he finished by once more stopping before Consalvi and repeating: 'No, if you had remained at your post, things would never have come to this pass.'

And once more, Consalvi contradicted the assertion: 'Let your Majesty be persuaded that I should have done my duty.'

Napoleon seemed not to tire of the subject. A second time, he went the round of the audience, uttering the same complaints against Rome. Then addressing di Pietro, so as to be heard by Consalvi, he said for the third time: 'If Cardinal Consalvi had remained Secretary of State, things would not have gone so far.' The indefatigable Consalvi moved from his place at this third accusation, and taking hold of the Emperor's arm exclaimed: 'Sire, I have already assured your Majesty, that, if I had remained at my post, I should most certainly have done my duty.'

'I repeat it, your duty would not have allowed you to sacrifice spiritual to temporal interests.'[7] It was Napoleon's last word.

The Emperor's attempt at courtesy was beyond a doubt well-timed, for it was exceedingly important that the Cardinals, especially Consalvi, the best known of them all, should assist at the religious ceremony of his marriage with Marie Louise. Moreover, Consalvi was at the head of a party amongst the Cardinals, who declared themselves incompetent to arrange ecclesiastical affairs as long as they were cut off from their chief. What Consalvi terms his 'great catastrophe,' was the conduct pursued by him in the affair of the marriage, for it became necessary to determine at once upon the course to be adopted by the Cardinals, and he was the soul of the opposition which conscience represented as a

---

[7] *Mémoires*, t. ii. p. 177.

necessary struggle. Fourteen Cardinals, without including Fesch and Caprara, who was feeble in mind and dying, gave it as their opinion, that the dissolution of the religious marriage was valid. Thirteen others rightly asserted that such causes between crowned heads could only be resolved by the Sovereign Pontiff, or by a legate or bishop deputed by him. Of this number were Cardinals Mattei, Pignatelli, della Somaglia, di Pietro, Litta, Saluzzo, Ruffo Scilla, Brancadoro, Galeffi, Scotti, Gabrielli, Opizzoni, and Consalvi. They strove vainly to bring the fourteen with Cardinal Fesch to see the force of their reasons, and it is important to note this, for after the event the Red Cardinals accused the dissidents of having, in the matter of the marriage, made a secret of their opinion.[8] The Dean of the thirteen, Mattei, formally communicated the decision to the majority of the fourteen Cardinals, adding that, to save making a great commotion, the narrow space allotted for the celebration of the marriage would seem of itself to cover their absence. The whole proceeding was inspired by that wonderful tact which was so eminently the gift of Consalvi. To use his expression, it was a question of wounding the Emperor 'in the apple of his eye,' and a step which could only have been dictated by the imperious voice of conscience. The middle course suggested by Consalvi to Fesch would have been the non-invitation of the thirteen, but the bare idea of their resistance threw Napoleon into a terrible fit of anger. 'Bah, they will not dare,' he had exclaimed to his uncle.

The fourth audience at the Tuileries, which Consalvi mentions as taking place eight days before the marriage, is particularly significant. The Emperor, apprised of the Cardinal's view as to the approaching alliance, sought to

[8] *Mémoires*, t. i. p. 421.

intimidate him with the dreadful looks of which his imperial eyes possessed the secret. 'He, Napoleon,' Consalvi says, 'came expressly to the place where I was standing. Without addressing me the smallest word of courtesy, . . he stopped in front of me, and gave me a thundering look. Then to make me perfectly understand that *I* was the person in fault, he turned immediately with a cheerful face to Cardinal Doria (one of the fourteen) by my side, and talked most amiably with him. Then he walked about, addressing other Cardinals pleasantly too, and came suddenly back, stood straight in front of me, and looked at me most ferociously as he had at first.'[9]

Of the four invitations of which the imperial marriage was the occasion only two were accepted by the thirteen Cardinals. The four were, first, a reception at St. Cloud, where the great bodies of the State were to be presented to Marie Louise. The second regarded the civil, and the third the religious marriage, which the thirteen could not acknowledge. The fourth, the most splendid of all, was a full Court reception, the sovereigns being seated on their thrones. The Cardinals resolved to go to the first and to the last. Waiting for the Emperor and Empress at St. Cloud, Consalvi was taken aside by his friend, Fouché, Minister of the Police, and compelled to listen to the propounding of certain wise ideas, of which the main drift was this. Fouché could hardly believe that a man of Consalvi's good sense could refuse to be present at the marriage. He was capable of fetching the Cardinal in his own carriage, for the non-appearance of so marked a personage would produce terrible consequences, and for what good? The imperial marriage had been already effected by proxy at Vienna, the rest was pure formality. This logic failed

[9] *Mémoires*, t. ii. p. 195.

to convince Consalvi, although the conversation produced on him 'a mortal sweat.'[10] The Emperor appeared leading Marie Louise by the hand. He was all smiles and affability, and designated Consalvi as the Cardinal 'who had negotiated the Concordat.'

On Monday, April 2nd, the religious ceremony took place at the Louvre in the grand reception room, temporarily and magnificently arranged as a chapel. Passing slowly through the picture gallery, which immediately precedes the grand *salon*, the imperial pair riveted all eyes. Napoleon wore an extraordinary air of triumph, which became visibly overcast when he reached the chapel, for his quick eyes could only count fourteen Cardinals.

'Where are the Cardinals?' he asked in an irritated tone of the Master of Ceremonies.

'A great number are here;' was the reply. 'Many of them, besides, are infirm and old, and the weather is so bad.'

'Ah, the fools! but they are *not* here,' said Napoleon, with another glance at the empty seats. 'The fools, the fools.'

The Emperor somewhat contained his anger during the ceremony, for he could well reserve his revenge till the next day, when a public, consequently a more striking humiliation, should punish the refractory Cardinals. As for the thirteen, they remained for two days in the seclusion of their houses, as 'victims destined for sacrifice.'[11] On Tuesday, which was fixed for the grand State reception, Consalvi and the others who had not assisted at the religious ceremony awaited the audience at the Tuileries, in a state of mind easily to be conceived. After three hours of anti-chamber an order was suddenly brought from the Emperor to the effect that the thirteen Cardinals must leave the palace

[10] *Mémoires*, t. ii. p. 198.   [11] *Mémoires*, t. ii. p. 202.

immediately, because he would not see them. What was still more important was the degradation which he imposed shortly afterwards upon them on the ground that, it being his intention to cause the *resignation of these individuals*, they were henceforth to be deprived of the Purple. The title of Black and Red Cardinals arose from this extraordinary usurpation of power, which divided the Sacred College into two camps. Furthermore, the property, both private and ecclesiastical, of the degraded Cardinals, was seized, and their income went to augment the public treasure. They were obliged to live on the alms which charitable persons never failed to bestow, and were exiled to different provincial towns, care being taken here that those who sympathized with each other the least should be thrown together.[12] But they were happy at least to attain by these measures a closer resemblance to their suffering head. He who is not with Peter is against him.

The punctiliousness of Napoleon on this question of the marriage was further proved by the severe treatment inflicted on M. Emery, whose only crime had been the counsel which he had given to a perplexed prince of the Church. Cardinal della Somaglia consulted the Sulpician as to whether he could assist at the religious ceremony. 'I myself,' was Emery's reply, 'should have no objection to go there if my rank obliged me, because I think that the dissolution of the first marriage is valid. But if, in the sanctuary of your conscience, you have a contrary opinion, you will perhaps do better not to go, because conscience obliges us.' Napoleon possessed only one arm against moral resistance—the employment of force. The Sulpicians were declared to be 'people who made a great deal out of nothing,' and suppressed.[13]

[12] *Mémoires*, t. ii. p. 215.
[13] *L'Eglise Romaine et le Premier Empire*, t. iii. p. 298.

Whatever indiscreet, not to say highly unlawful means the Emperor used to punish and to humiliate those who in any way acknowledged openly the Pope's authority, he could not absolutely create bishops. The expedient suggested by Maury was after all but a temporary way of facing a difficulty. A General Council *without the Pope* had for a moment been thought of, but in truth the Sovereign Pontiff was found practically (we do not say avowedly) to be indispensable, and before long, in May, 1810, a new method of indirect communication with Savona was devised. Prince Metternich, who had manifested great zeal for the Austrian alliance, applied to Napoleon about this time for permission to depute an agent to Savona for the determination of certain ecclesiastical matters. The Emperor agreed the more readily in that he tacitly understood that the envoy of Austria would be disposed to improve the occasion to settle French affairs as well as those of his own Court.[14] M. de Lebzeltern, who was the chosen deputy, had formerly acted as Austrian Ambassador at the Court of Rome. Pius VII. was pleased and touched to see him again. The sight of a friendly face was an event at Savona. He spoke kindly of Napoleon, and his partiality was remarked by the Austrian, who plainly perceived that it was always the French and not his own sovereign, that occupied the best place in the heart of the Holy Father. When he spoke of the dangers which menaced the Church, and asked Pius VII. if he would do nothing to get out of his dependent and effaced state, this was the reply. 'We had foreseen this state of things, and it is the only matter which preoccupies Us. This interruption of all relations with the clergy of various nationalities, the difficulty of our intercourse with the French bishops, cause Us the deepest

[14] *L'Eglise Romaine et le Premier Empire*, t. iii. p. 415.

grief. Although confined here without the liberty of free epistolary correspondence, without news, except the very vague statements which We gather from a detached page or two of the *Moniteur*, which the General (le Cte. César Berthier) has the goodness to send Us, We have been able to form an idea of the difficulties of the bishops, and We continually complain to him (Berthier) of our position in this respect. It is a real schism for all practical purposes. We ask for nothing for ourself from the Emperor, We have nothing more to lose. We have sacrificed all for our duty. We are old and want for nothing. What interested consideration, then, could dissuade Us from following the line that our conscience points to Us to follow? Personally, We desire absolutely nothing. We wish for neither pension nor honours. The alms of the faithful are enough for Us. There have been Popes poorer than We are, and We dream of nothing beyond the narrow space where you see Us; but We *do* ardently desire that our intercourse with the bishops and the faithful be re-established.' [15]

Pius VII. then told M. de Lebzeltern that Mgr. Menochio, his confessor, and the Secretary of Briefs, Mgr. Torsa, were not allowed to approach him. He was obliged in consequence to employ the pen of one of his servants whose writing was legible, and had thus been able to despatch five hundred dispensations for which the French bishops had asked. Upon the suggestion of the Austrian envoy that the Pope would do well to break the silence, and to inform the Emperor of his wishes with regard to spiritual matters, Pius VII. replied: ' He (Napoleon) is well aware of our complete isolation. The continual complaints and remonstrances which We have addressed to the Prefect and to the General are certainly known to him.' The Holy Father only alluded

[15] Lettre de M. de Lebzeltern au Cte. de Metternich, 16 mai, 1810.

indirectly to his temporal sovereignty during the conversation. His words are remarkable. 'When opinions are founded on the dictates of conscience and of duty, they are irrevocable, and be assured that in the long run, *no material force in the world can combat a moral force of this nature.* What We said concerning the sad events which have befallen the Apostolic See was prompted by this conviction, and We can never, consequently, express ourself otherwise on the subject.'[16]

The immediate result of M. de Lebzeltern's account of the Holy Father, (which had been drawn up as much for the benefit of Napoleon as of the German Emperor), produced the secret and non-official visit to Savona of Cardinals Spina and Caselli. The Emperor still hoped to bring the Pope to adopt his views, and in the meantime two Cardinals, who had become French in all the strictness of the term, could open the way to the negotiations which were to remedy the condition of the French Church. Their mission was to present every appearance of a casual encounter, for Spina, as Archbishop of Genoa, naturally passed by Savona on the way to his diocese. That Caselli should accompany him, and that they both should stop to see the Holy Father, was also perfectly comprehensible. Pius VII. was not slow to guess the object of this visit from two Cardinals. He felt they had come to sound his dispositions and to make them known to Napoleon. Through a natural diffidence produced by this intuitive conviction, he manifested no desire to enter upon negotiations. Spina and Caselli passed two days at Savona before they were admitted to an audience, and when at last the Holy Father broke through his legitimate reserve he gave them perfectly to understand, that before ecclesiastical matters could be arranged he expected to have the

[16] Dépêche de M. de Lebzeltern au Cte. de Metternich, 10 mai, 1810.

choice of two Cardinals for counsellors. He expressed himself strongly against a residence at Avignon. If he left Savona at all, it must be for Rome. Under any other circumstances, he preferred to remain where he was. He would be very much grieved to be taken to Paris, but would always seek to prevent the outburst of popular feeling on his account. Perhaps, however, if they constrained him to perform a public function, he would not be capable of controlling his feelings sufficiently to prevent a great scandal.[17] The Cardinals erroneously concluded from the conversation of the Holy Father that he might be induced to agree to the nomination of bishops, but that he would do nothing without the impartial counsellors for whom he seemed to yearn.

The Emperor speedily made up his mind as to his course of action upon learning the result of the visit of Spina and Caselli. We have said that, until his marriage with Marie Louise was effected, he kept up what were certainly very empty appearances of deference for the Holy Father. He had rendered Pius VII. a close prisoner, but still from time to time he seemed to be taken with an involuntary need of communicating, however indirectly and for whatever ostensible purpose, with the spiritual Head of the faithful. Thus, twice in less than a year he had been the real cause, first of the letters in August, 1809, of the principal dignitaries of the French Church, and secondly, in May, 1810, of the visit of Cardinals Spina and Caselli to Savona. He had gained nothing by these steps, and now the Sovereign Pontiff, so far from being disposed to adopt his ideas, named conditions which must necessarily be complied with before he could consent even to treat of spiritual affairs. Napoleon, with his Empire of sixty millions and

---

[17] Lettre de M. le Cte. de Chabrol à M. le Cte. Bigot de Préameneu, 11 juillet, 1810.

the Austrian bride whom he had won with his mighty sword, was weary of struggling with a moral difficulty. He would add one more faculty to the astounding list which he had already attributed to himself, and dispense, in the nomination of bishops, with the Papal confirmation. The nature of the combat became graver from day to day, but Napoleon, in assuming illegitimate authority, helped to build with his own imperial hands that fortress of moral strength which encircled the prisoner of Savona with power, not from man, but from God.

CHAPTER X.

The Ring of the Fisherman.

'Go to the sea, and cast in a hook, and that fish which shall first come up, take; and when thou hast opened its mouth, thou shalt find a stater. Take that, and give it to them for me and thee.'

GALLICANISM, in its partiality for subtle arguments, for a long time discussed the important point, whether the authority of the Pope surpassed that of a General Council, or the authority of a General Council that of the Pope. The question is best answered by another. Where, in the intervals of the convocation of a General Council, is the Church? History and tradition both prove that the government of the Church founded by our Lord, so far from constituting a democratical, or even an aristocratical republic—which the absence of any singular and central authority would render it—is essentially monarchical; that is, it is to present, through all ages, the perfect union of the Body under one Head; it is to carry on and to develope the teaching of the One Teacher, Christ, Who, whilst investing His Apostles with authority to preach, gave but to one the mission of Supreme Pastor—the keys of the kingdom of heaven. The nature and the quality of the Pope's office are best proved to be a necessity in the world by the fact, that when powerful efforts are made to release the Successor of Peter from his formidable sovereignty, they do not tend to abolish the position altogether, but only to transfer it to another, to an illegitimate successor of Peter. There have been anti-popes, and there have been monarchs and emperors who contested the authority of the Sovereign Pontiff, only that they themselves might usurp his place. The beginning of schism discovers in Napoleon's words, that the 'triple crown is a monstrous abuse of the Court of Rome.' The logical carrying out of the reproach would therefore be to employ the resources of sovereignty to abolish an usurpation of power destined to produce disastrous effects on countries and nations, but here it is a case of scandal taken at a right, and that by an Emperor. They who in daily life have this propensity are in general men and women with false consciences, who judge their neighbour with a measure which they never dream of applying to their own actions. What is a crime in others is a virtue in themselves. The admonitions of history ought not to be given in vain. It tells us in the early years of this century that no despotism is so over-bearing as that produced by a system of state-usurpation over the consciences of men, a system tyrannically imposed and timidly accepted by the spiritual authorities of a nation. Material interests are far from remaining unimpaired in the question, for even glory and fame which lend their support to despotism may have been bought at too dear a price. Nations suffer for their magnificence as individuals for the acquisition of a large fortune, which in this world of burdens adds a fresh responsibility. In 1810, a certain number of French bishops, in soliciting of Pius VII. the right of granting marriage dispensations on their own authority, brought forward the rarity of marriageable men in France owing to the number of violent deaths on the field of battle, and a general mistrust which attached itself to the possible opinions of those who were outside the circle of family relations.[1]

[1] Lettre des cardinaux et évêques à Sa Sainteté, Pie VII.

If Napoleon had hitherto tolerated a certain amount of vagueness in the avowed sentiments of the French clergy, no such licence would henceforth be conceded. After the visit to Savona in 1810 of Spina and Caselli, he summoned them all, with Fesch at their head, to give an open preference to his pretensions. The time for compromises and half-measures was past. They must sanction his system of public defiance of one already so weak in power of material resistance as the Holy Father, or accept the terrible consequences of non-submission. In the mass the French clergy was undoubtedly compliant, but we must not forget that prisons reduced to silence the generous voice of confessors. More than ever now, Napoleon counted upon the zealous cooperation of the Primate, but Cardinal Fesch, who had not demurred to accept the *title* of Archbishop-Elect of Paris (being already Archbishop of Lyons), flatly refused to *take possession* of a second see without the papal confirmation. His answer in reply to the Emperor's summons was the innocent cause of the election which ensued.

'I can force you to obey me,' said Napoleon to his uncle. 'Sire, *potius mori.*'

'Ah ah, *potius mori*, rather Maury. Be it so. You shall have Maury.'[2]

Cardinal Maury, who accepted the position, although already attached to the Church of Montefiascone, manifested a strange joy at the Emperor's choice of him, which we are at a loss to comprehend. At the same time Napoleon was anxious to provide for the vacant arch-diocese of Florence. His design in choosing for the post the actual Bishop of Nancy, Mgr. d'Osmond, was the same as that which had actuated Maury's promotion. Two important dioceses of his empire would

[2] *Vie du Card. Fesch.* Par M. l'Abbé Lyonnet, t. ii. p. 174.

be thus governed in open defiance of the Holy Father, and to attain this end he was not above deceiving Mgr. d'Osmond, whose conscience would not allow him to take possession of a new diocese without the papal confirmation. The departure of the prelate was pressed forward with the promise that he should receive his Bulls at Lyons. It is needless to say, that in spite of three successive halts which he made on his way to Florence, too confident in the Emperor's word, his hope proved an utter fallacy.

But for Maury, as for Mgr. d'Osmond, the new position was far from being a bed of roses. Both archbishops found in their chapter one priest at least bold enough to consult by letter the advice of Pius VII. as to whether or not the bishops imposed upon them by Napoleon were to be obeyed. At Florence, a certain Canon Muzzi declared, upon receiving the Holy Father's negative reply, that in 'such matters he acknowledged the sole authority of Pius VII.' His uncompromising attitude procured for him condemnation to imprisonment at Porto Ferraio, whilst three others who had published the Papal Brief were conducted to Fenestrello.[3] Cardinal Maury was subjected to more tiresome contradiction in Paris. The Abbé d'Astros, nephew of M. Portalis, formerly Minister of Worship, defied Maury in his cathedral-church of Notre-Dame. Once at an ordination, as the Cardinal exacted the promise of obedience to himself from the priest before him, the Abbé d'Astros exclaimed in an audible tone, ' My lord, let me remind you, for the instruction of this young priest, that you have not the right to demand this promise.' On another occasion, the intrepid Vicar-General ordered the cross-bearer, who was about to precede Maury, to go back to the sacristy, for the Cardinal's dignity of Archbishop had not been canonically conferred. Pius VII. did not fail to protest

[3] *Vie épiscopale de Mgr. d'Osmond*, pp. 565, 570.

against the intrusion. He addressed a Brief to Maury, which was officially ignored as long as possible in Paris. Napoleon and Napoleon's Government, which was identical, simply shut their eyes to anything they were afraid to look in the face. But the Abbé d'Astros would not be a party to the unlawful vagueness that reigned in the chapter of Notre-Dame. He applied directly to the Holy Father for instructions, and received in reply a Brief, which, falling into the hands of the Government, served it with precisely the arm that it coveted—the ground for convicting him of intercourse with Savona. Napoleon, whose anger was fully roused by the way in which the Vicar-General had defied the Archbishop of his creation, determined to take strong measures. It is curious that imprisonment alike in Italy and in France was the only device for silencing honest and noble resistance. At a reception at the Tuileries on January 1st, 1811, M. d'Astros learned that in the French empire he had the honour of attracting before all others the imperial suspicions; but Napoleon had armed force on his side, and threatened a poor defenceless priest with its application.[4] The menace only proved an excessive dearth of moral strength. Threats were, however, followed by their realization. Maury proposed to the Vicar-General, before leaving the Tuileries, that they should both go together to the Minister of Police. M. de Rovigo, he said, had some questions to put to M. d'Astros, but there was nothing to fear; an explicit protestation of attachment to Gallican liberties would be required—that was all. The Cardinal, in fact, did not hesitate to deliver his Vicar-General over to secular and arbitrary injustice. M. d'Astros suspected no foul play and went with him. The interrogatory of M. de Rovigo was short and to the point.

[4] Mémoire Manuscrit de l'Abbé d'Astros.

'Do you not entertain a correspondence with the Pope at Savona?' he asked the Vicar-General. 'Have you seen a Brief from the Pope to Cardinal Maury? Resign, and there will be an end of it.'

'I cannot.'

'Resign, I say, or you are my prisoner.'

'I *am* your prisoner, then.'

Artifice was furthermore employed to discover the unfortunate accomplices who had shown d'Astros the Papal Brief to Maury. He had refused to implicate his cousin, Portalis, in the affair, for it was at the house of the ex-Minister's son that he had produced the document. But now M. de Rovigo assumed the fact, adding that M. Portalis had told him. The Vicar-General fell into the snare, and confessed his crime without difficulty. He had consulted his cousin as to what course he should pursue, seeing that the Pope condemned Maury's election, whilst at the same time, he, d'Astros, had only seen the Brief, as it were, by chance, and could not therefore claim to know its contents officially.[5] A few hours later d'Astros was taken to Vincennes, that dungeon of evil fame, and there he remained till the fall of the Empire. Napoleon had first resolved to have him shot, but mercifully commuted the sentence into imprisonment for life. About the same time, Vincennes opened its gloomy gates to Cardinals di Pietro and Gabrielli. The purple of Gabrielli had not saved him from a fortnight's confinement at *la Force* with two public criminals who were condemned to capital punishment later on.[6]

Whilst at a distance the smallest homage rendered to the spiritual authority of the Holy Father met with such terrible consequences, Savona itself was subjected

---

[5] *Vie du Card. d'Astros*, pp. 197, 183.
[6] *Notice historique* sur le Chevalier de Thiusy.

to the strictest inspection. Pius VII. was never suffered to give private audiences, and even to approach him at all, the Emperor's permission was necessary. Some priests from Marseilles had been thrown into a filthy dungeon for simply defying Napoleon's unreasonable orders in this respect. On the other hand, such overbearing tyranny met with its natural consequences. Secret committees were organized both in France and in Italy to facilitate spiritual communication with the Holy Father, and his apparently weak cause could count upon a certain number of devoted persons, young men especially, who held themselves in readiness at all hours of the day and night, to seek out the destination of Papal missives, which, in spite of his vigilant guards, they had succeeded in obtaining. In this way, the Holy Father still reigned: he reigned in the strength of a righteous cause, with the further immense power of suffering for justice. The list of those, for instance, who lent their names and their purses at Paris, towards supplying pecuniary aid to the Black Cardinals, contained the titles of some of the noblest houses in France, and strangely enough, the Cardinal Primate was implicated in the charity.[7] In after years, Napoleon bitterly complained of a captivity whose hardships cannot in any way be likened to those which he had inflicted upon the Sovereign Pontiff. But in 1811 the imprisonment of Pius VII., severe as it was, appeared to him to call for still greater restrictions. 'Write to the Prefect of Montenotte,' these are his orders to M. Bigot, 'to inform him of the letter which the Pope has written to the Vicar General at Paris (M. d'Astros), and to enlighten him as to the insincerity of the Pope, who, under pretext of conciliation and charity, secretly excites discord and rebellion. Give him orders to prevent

L'Eglise Romaine et le Premier Empire, t. iii. p. 448.

couriers from being received or sent with letters for the Pope, or for his household. The post must neither take out nor bring in letters for him. For this the prefect must be able to dispose of the director of the post. You will inform him that I am causing the removal to Paris of the Bishop of Savona, who might have kept up secret intelligences with the Pope. You must give orders to the prelate to come to Paris, where I wish to see him. You must insist that M. de Chabrol hold a firmer tone in his conversation, and that he represent to the Pope the evil that His Holiness is doing to religion; that he seeks to sow trouble and division; that he disregards conciliation and moderate measures which might have had a chance of success with me; that he will obtain nothing by the means he uses, and that the Church will end by losing the remains of her temporal power; that those who are ignorant and foolish enough to listen to him will lose their place, and that it will be his fault. This must be vigorously told him. It is useless for the Pope to write. The less he does, the better it will be. It is necessary, first, that the prefect send an account of the persons who surround the Pope, designating those of the number who are capable of the most work, in order that I may send them away, and take from the Pope the means of writing and of propagating poison; secondly, that you order the prefect to send no more letters of the Pope to the kingdoms of Italy and Naples, to Tuscany, Piedmont, or France, and to give him no letter, but to send them all hither. Cause all letters which the Pope may write, or have written to him, to be sent to you. Generally speaking, the less that which he writes reaches its destination, the better it will be. Inform the prefect and Prince Borghese that I desire my displeasure to make itself felt on the interior arrangements of the Papal household, so that from henceforth a sum of from twelve to fifteen thousand francs a month may suffice for its needs. The carriages which were put at his disposal for himself and his household (the Pope had never used them) are to be sent back to Turin. Recommend M. de Chabrol to let nothing fall from his lips which may tend to make the Pope believe that I wish for an arrangement. . . . I trouble myself very little as to what he may do. We are too enlightened not to distinguish between the doctrine of Jesus Christ and that of Gregory VII. The prefect must let the Pope know, that all the canons and all the theologians of France and Italy are indignant at the letters he has addressed to the chapters; that by his behaviour he was the cause of the arrest of three canons at Florence, and of the confiscation of their benefices, and of a similar severity exercised towards the chapter of Asti, of the arrest of Cardinal di Pietro, of Canon d'Astros, the Abbés Fontana and Gregori, who have all been sent to a distance, to keep them from evil doings; that these dark actions are unworthy of a Pope, that he will be the cause of the misfortunes of all those with whom he corresponds. Since he is a declared enemy of the Emperor, and says himself that he is a *prisoner*, he must conduct himself as such, and cease to correspond either with his agents, or with those who have created an intercourse with him. Let him be told that it is distressing for Christendom to own a Pope so ignorant of what is due to sovereigns, but that the State will not be disturbed, and good will be effected without him.'[8]

It is painful to record such language used towards a Sovereign Pontiff, but when that Sovereign Pontiff called himself Pius VII., whose whole career as a Pope

---

[8] Lettres de l'Empereur au Cte. Bigot de Préameneu du 31 xbre, 1810 et du 17 janiver, 1811.

had been full of especial predilection for Napoleon, who had long shut his eyes to humiliation and indignity, and who had only protested in the face of positive wrongs and principles sacrificed, we may conclude what proportions in the mind of Napoleon the fixed idea of universal empire had taken. It was against the *office* of the Pope that he directed all his efforts, but the bitterest drop in Julius Cæsar's cup of death was that stroke from the hand of his friend. The Papacy has other elements of stability than that presented by Cæsar's empire, but the individuality of the man may suffer and smart from the blows directed against the tremendous authority with which he is invested. We know that Pius VII. would have resisted unto blood, and then what would have followed, and where would have been the compensation of Napoleon? He might destroy with ill-treatment the man who had loved him, but he could never annihilate the Sovereign Pontiff. An echo of that cry of the old French monarchy would have resounded through the air of the Catholic world—*Le Pape est mort! Vive le Pape!*

On the 8th of January, 1811, in accordance with the Emperor's orders, a strict search was made at the episcopal palace at Savona of the Holy Father's correspondence and papers. Some men from Paris, expert at the trade of forcing open doors and drawers, came expressly for the purpose of invading his prison at an hour when all the household was buried in sleep, and of unsewing the very clothes of its members—a measure from which Pius VII. himself was not excepted—in order to light upon suspicious information. A little later in the day, whilst the Holy Father was taking a walk in the garden, his desk was broken open, and the books which were thus found, besides even his pens, blotting book, his breviary, and an Office of our Lady, were confiscated. The produce of a collection, the offering of one of the secret committees of which we have spoken, consisting of some pieces of gold, was discovered in Mgr. Doria's apartment. Pius VII., when he heard of the proceeding which had signalized his momentary absence in the garden, remarked simply: 'Let them take the purse, but what will they do with my breviary and the Office of our Lady?' The hardest infliction on a prisoner is to deprive him of a familiar face or object, which recalls to him his home, his country, and happier times. Those members of his household, to whom the Holy Father was particularly attached, were sent off to Fenestrello.[9] Another comparison is suggested by Napoleon's order to divest Pius VII. of the Ring of the Fisherman. In after years at St. Helena Sir Hudson Lowe, who refused the title of sovereign to an illustrious captive, never went the length of imposing upon him the ignominious deprivation of his sword. Yet much more than his victorious sword could ever have been to Napoleon was his humble ring to Pius. It should be taken from him. This was the one act of tyranny which ruffled the gentle composure of the Holy Father. In the face of other humiliations he had manifested, according to M. de Chabrol, an extraordinary indifference. Such a state of things, he knew, would only last as long as Providence willed it to last: as for him, he was prepared for all. The crown that was surely awaiting him in the world beyond the tomb was the consolation for which he looked in the absence of all temporal blessings. The Holy Father might justly suspect that his ring was required of him for fraudulent purposes. With a dolorous emotion he broke it in two, and gave it in this state to the officer of Napoleon. Between taking away the Ring of the Fisherman and seeking to depose

[9] *L'Eglise Romaine et le Premier Empire*, t. iii. p. 479.

the Sovereign Pontiff, the distance it seems would not be great, and this notion did for a moment cross Napoleon's mind, but when, in his sagacious moods, he meditated on all the resources of the Papacy, the project of rendering it a dependance of the French Imperial crown became more and more a fixed idea. Pitt, in his shrewd political foresight, had wished to oppose the power of the Pope to that of the Revolution, as the only efficacious rampart against an overwhelming torrent. The same tacit homage to the moral strength of the Successor of Peter was the motive for Napoleon's course, but perhaps he never stopped to consider that if he indeed fulfilled his great dream, he would destroy, by the very fact, the wonderful prerogatives of an office which in its spiritual character can yield to no man, and never descend to the rank of a mere tool or plaything in the hands of secular power. A moral terror hung over the religious world in Paris. It was impossible to oppose Napoleon's will and still retain freedom, his will, that is, as far as it concerned the Holy Father, and his revenge pursued even charitable ladies who had interested themselves in the Black Cardinals. Unhappily, whatever resistance was made to tyranny in France proceeded rather from the mass of the people than from individuals of ecclesiastical mark. Napoleon was absolute master of the Senate, and of the Chapter of Notre-Dame. Cardinal Maury imposed upon himself the mission of allaying the fears of his canons, for naturally no man could witness acts of violence such as that which had been perpetrated on the Vicar General, M. d'Astros, without suspecting his own turn might not be far distant. A despot who is answered by quaking submission only becomes a still greater tyrant. The Cathedral Chapter concerted an address, or rather, Maury drew it up with the connivance of Napoleon. The theme was its alleged right to institute bishops without the Papal confirmation. A single sentence will tell us to what lengths the Emperor with a docile clergy might have gone, and whether after all, what he was doing was not essentially Gallicanism, that is, the Gallican idea produced with somewhat novel forms, tending to its extreme realization. 'According to the principles of the clergy of France, there being in the Church no power *independent of the canons*, none exists, which by measures contrary to the canons, has the right to oppose this prerogative or rather this duty of the Chapter'[10] (the exclusive nomination of bishops). When this was read in Notre-Dame, M. Emery alone conscientiously remonstrated with Maury. Bossuet's example had, as usual, been cited in the matter against the Holy Father, and Emery, who was thoroughly grounded in such matters, summoned the Cardinal to prove that Bossuet had really counselled Louis XIV. to dispense with Papal confirmation from 1682 to 1693. The answer was that, 'since Bossuet had been consulted by the King on all ecclesiastical matters of his day, he must necessarily have counselled *this* step.' In spite of the plainly trifling character of this and other assertions in the address, Maury was particularly anxious to gratify the Emperor, by causing it to be read at a Court reception in January, 1811. An unfortunate canon, M. Jalabert, who only received a copy of what he was to read when already before the Emperor, was so far acted upon by the presence of the Imperial Court, as to neglect to restore to the text the assurances of esteem which the Chapter had bestowed upon poor M. d'Astros, or to rectify what M. Emery had marked as erroneous. It mattered very little to Napoleon, whether the Chapter of Notre-Dame either spoke the truth, or gave him a

[10] *L'Eglise Romaine et le Premier Empire*, t. iv. p. 18.

disloyal servility instead of what might have been its true sentiments. But he *did* care that the nation should accept the address as the opinion of the metropolitan canons, and it was carefully inserted in the *Moniteur* of January 7th. Napoleon's answer must have tended to open the eyes of the Chapter as to the gravity of the step which it had taken in siding officially with him, rather than with its spiritual head. It brought out clearly that his sole aim in causing the Address was to proclaim officially that the Chapter of Notre Dame was hostile to Pius VII. The canons were told that the unity of Italy had been necessary to ensure success to the Emperor in the strife which he had undertaken against *heretical England*. For this end, to conquer a nation entirely given up to maritime commerce, he needed to be absolute master of the Adriatic. But these powerful considerations had had no influence with the Pope. He had declared that he had no motive for declaring himself against the English, he was the common Father of all the faithful, and could not deprive himself of the means of corresponding with English Christians. Here the Emperor remarked with consideration, that he could not, however, leave the Holy Father to the mercy of England. Negotiations had followed, but the Pope had preferred the annihilation of his temporal sovereignty. He had acted in the same way in spiritual affairs. Bishoprics had become vacant, and he had obstinately refused canonical confirmation.[11]

The idea of capitulary addresses, drawn up after the model of Maury and his imperial assistant, was, however, much too brilliant to be allowed to drop. From all parts, Napoleon elicited similiar assurances, which he caused the *Moniteur* to publish, less with an eye to the instruction of his people, it must be admitted, than

---

[11] *L'Eglise Romaine et le Premier Empire*, t. iv. p. 18.

to induce Pius VII. in his solitude at Savona to believe that those who should have upheld the Papal cause were proving false. For several months the pages of the *Moniteur* were full of these addresses, great preference being shown for the Italian Chapters. This paper constituted the only reading of the Holy Father, and his sole relaxation besides the very small garden of the episcopal palace. Painful doubt was probably uppermost in his mind, as to how far such protestations were spontaneous, and how far an evil which the spiritual members of his flock had judged a necessary concession to peculiar circumstances. But he was certainly not blind to the fact that they differed from each other so little, that the idea and tone of each were precisely the same. Savona signalized itself in the competition of addresses, and its bishop received in consequence a reward of six thousand francs from imperial gratitude.[12]

In the dark labyrinth which oppression had spread round the person of the Sovereign Pontiff, Napoleon perhaps instinctively felt that the sympathies of rational as well as generous men, belonged to the helpless sufferer rather than to the mighty monarch. He reduced all resistance to silence, he ruled with armed force. For a man to speak officially of the excommunication of the Emperor, or of the Papal Brief annulling Maury's election, would have been as much as his life was worth. It is a curious sign of the times, this quiet acquiescence in a servitude so great as that imposed in the pursuit of a chimera by Napoleon. He himself observed, with regard to the Brief to Maury, the same attitude as that he had formerly adopted with the Bull *Quum Memoranda*. Before a few sure and familiar courtiers, he asserted that the Pope had been thus guilty of a very dangerous act of authority, but with members of the clergy, he was careful

[12] Lettre de l'Empereur Cte. Bigot de Préameneu, 10 Mars, 1811.

P

to express himself with a sovereign contempt, or a great vagueness on the subject. The Council of State assumed in the case of these uncomfortable Briefs, an arbitrary power which is proper to all usurpations of jurisdiction either in the spiritual or in the temporal order. It annulled the Papal missive to Mgr. d'Osmond on account of abuse, and from its silence on the question of Maury, the public were to conclude that no such Brief had ever been penned. But the most successful production of Napoleon had been the creation in 1809 of an ecclesiastical commission, which he called together again in the beginning of 1811. It presents the ludicrous spectacle of an attempt to legislate, when its sole possible course of action was to follow, in all things, the will of Napoleon. It put itself, as it were, in presence of imaginary difficulties, which it sought to solve in any but the only right way—reconciliation with the Pope. M. Emery (a member of the Commission) had, with his sound good sense, put his finger on the real evil, 'Let the Emperor leave the Church in peace,' he wrote to a friend, 'let him restore the Pope, the Cardinals, and the bishops, to their functions; let him give up his extravagant pretensions: the rest will soon arrange itself.'[13] But it is hard to speak truth to a despot. The Commission had originally been composed of Cardinals Fesch and Maury, Mgr. de Barral, Archbishop of Tours, Mgr. Duvoisin, Bishop of Nantes, the Bishops of Trèves, Verceil, and Evreux, M. Emery, and Father Fontana, General of the Barnabites. Of these ecclesiastics, Pius VII. could only thoroughly count upon two, M. Emery and Father Fontana, and their practical withdrawal from all doings of the first Commission, goes to prove the fact. Fesch was blamed for his Roman sentiments, and they were scarcely more than sentiments, for he was still faithful to his character of

[13] *L'Eglise Romaine et le Premier Empire*, t. iv. p. 69.

playing two parts, breaking neither with Pope nor with Emperor, yet not pleasing either, and spoiling the good he might have done by his want of tact. Maury's influence was small. Napoleon ruled him, and at the bottom despised him for being ruled. Mgr. de Barral and Mgr. Duvoisin, were courtier bishops, but possessed great theological science, which they proved quite unable or unwilling to use in the right direction. Of the two, Mgr. Duvoisin was the Emperor's favourite, and sometimes in the stormy bursts of imperial anger, he drew forth such speeches as, 'Do not imagine, Monsieur, that what I say applies to you.' 'M. Duvoisin,' Napoleon further remarked, 'is one of those bishops who could make me do all he wished, and perhaps more than I ought.' There was some truth in the imputation, only it was Mgr. Duvoisin who met the wishes of Napoleon half-way, which in itself constituted the capability of doing far more than his conscience could have approved. The questions submitted to this Commission in 1809 had been such as to cast the shadows of future responsibilities before them. The whole argument had been in plain English, *how can we best get on without the Pope?*' The sentence had been given in Napoleon's mind, but he wished his Commission to pronounce it. In January 1811, it finally declared that, 'after protesting its inviolable attachment to the Holy See, and to the person of the Sovereign Pontiff, after imposing the observation of actual discipline, seeing the impossibility of convoking an Œcumenical Council, and the immense peril to which the French Church was exposed, the National Council could declare that the confirmation temporarily given by the metropolitan bishop to his suffragan, or by the oldest amongst the suffragans to the metropolitan bishop, should take the place of the Pontifical Bulls, until such time as the Pope or his successors had consented to the execution of the Concordat.' As for the Bull *Quum Memoranda*, this obliging Commission declared that it was null and void, and binding on no man's conscience.[14] The plea of the condemnation was that the Bull had been published *because* of the invasion of the *Papal States*, and that the Faith does not essentially repose upon the Temporal Power. It is certainly proved by the whole cast of events in this long conflict, that the Holy Father's spiritual jurisdiction rested for its practical exercise upon the liberty which he enjoyed as a temporal sovereign. Napoleon had a system, and insisted upon drawing the Pope into it and under it, and when he had reached the height of his glory, he could devise nothing wiser to solve the spiritual difficulties which he had created, than to call an assembly whose very reason for existing was a fallacy. In the government of the Church, no important act can be effected without Peter. Napoleon had caused the imprisonment of Pius VII.; the abnormal state of things which followed merely existed because he willed it. His ambition formed the real obstacle against which the decisions of the National Council came and broke as waves against a rock. Its task was one that could only have been imposed by the will of a despot. In the same way as everything else which encountered Napoleon's victorious course, it was to become his instrument, to be allowed no liberty in speech, to fall completely under his system. As a figure in a puzzle, the Emperor understood that he was to fit it in to the magnificent frame of events which he intended placing in history's picture gallery. For the bishops in the Council to rebel against being made into a puzzle was an intolerable audacity. Napoleon enforced silence in this circumstance by the same means that he had hitherto employed. He was faithful to his own policy unto the end, and having expressed his wishes,

---

[14] *L'Eglise Romaine et le Premier Empire*, t. iv. p. 62.

he demanded from them a kind of spiritual consecration. Father Fontana, who had been sent to Vincennes, as we have seen, was replaced in the Commission by Cardinal Caselli, and the Bishop of Verceil, who had died, by M. de Pradt, Archbishop Elect of Malines. The cause of Pius VII. gained in no particular by these changes.

The National Council was called upon to decide upon these questions: (1) All communication between the Pope and the Emperor's subjects being for the present interrupted, who is to furnish the dispensations which were formerly accorded by the Holy See? (2) When the Pope constantly refuses to give Bulls to bishops nominated by the Emperor to vacant sees, what is the canonical means of their confirmation?[15] These points raised some discussion, and M. Emery, who was forced to take a part in the second Commission, left the council-room, where they had been exposed, with a sorrowful heart. He energetically represented to Fesch that Napoleon was asking an impossibility of the bishops, and declared to the Cardinal that, as Primate of France, it was his personal duty to resist even unto blood.[16] If such measures were pushed farther, the Emperor must expect to make martyrs. It was too great a presumption. Subsequent events proved the illusion of a generous soul, and Emery, who ennobled himself by a conscientious and loyal resistance, came too late to exert a powerful influence over the mind of Napoleon, over the feverish genius that imagined his will would place him at the summit of the spiritual as it had of the temporal power. Gallican capabilities are proved by the answer of the Commission to the propositions which were later to be laid before the National Council; but Gallicans and Ultramontanes, in the strife with an overbearing State or monarch, need before all things an

---

[15] *L'Eglise Romaine et le Premier Empire*, t. iv. pp. 74, 75.   [16] *Ibid.*

austere love of duty, an uncompromising devotion to principle. After all, it is duty in daily life which makes saints, and duty in death which fills heaven with martyrs. No man ever became a hero through half measures. The first question, relating to dispensations, met with the reply that 'if unhappy circumstances temporarily prevented recourse to the Pope for dispensations, the bishops could temporarily bestow them.' The second, regarding the nomination of bishops, was answered, that, 'as the Pope refused the Bulls without alleging any canonical reason for his refusal, the wisest means of proceeding would be to add a clause to the Concordat, stipulating that the Pope should be bound to give the confirmation in a determined space of time. If he refused, the right of confirming should devolve upon the Provincial Synod, and the best course of action for insuring the enforcement of this modification of the Concordat, would be to re-establish, as far as the bishops were concerned, the regulations of the *Pragmatique Sanction*.' [17] Before calling the National Council, however, the Commission thought it desirable to send a deputation to Savona. What, under the circumstances, it could have had to say to the Holy Father, is unintelligible. 'All difficulties would be smoothed,' the bishops said, 'if this deputation meets with the success for which we hope. But if, contrary to our expectation, this last effort proves useless, the people who witness our deliberations with a troubled mind, would acknowledge that we have in no sort of way neglected the respect which we owe, as bishops, to the Head of the Universal Church. Their confidence and the authority of our ministry would

---

[17] The *Pragmatique Sanction* was the work of a King of France (Charles VII.). Its aim was to dethrone the Pontifical power in favour of civil legislation. As an inspiration of Gallicanism, it was jealous of the supreme jurisdiction of the Holy See, the subjection of which to the temporal power is a destruction of its character.

not thus become weakened, and they would exhibit less repugnance for a new order of things, which imperious circumstances and the necessity of providing for their spiritual needs would have forced upon us.'[18]

Before the final determination was taken for the convocation of the National Council, it pleased Napoleon to call an extraordinary sitting of the dignitaries of the Empire at the Tuileries, in March, 1811. M. Emery, the hero of the occasion, and whom, strangely enough, the Emperor took a certain pleasure in confronting, was conducted almost by force to the palace. Two bishops appeared at the last moment, just as he was setting out for the country, and declared that Fesch had charged them to bring the Sulpician in his own carriage. Emery was very much against appearing. He had never, he said, had a deliberative voice in the Commission, and its assembly did not regard him. For the honour of the French Church, he bethought himself of his oratory. Prayer should decide his course. When he rose from his knees, he submitted with calm resignation to be taken by the two prelates to the Tuileries. After causing himself to be waited for during the space of two hours, and declaring those who waited to be wanting in common sense for their pains, Napoleon opened proceedings by one of his violent diatribes against the Pope. It was received by the assembly in a frightened silence, and to create a diversion, as it seemed, Napoleon addressed M. Emery, to know what he thought upon the subject. Not a single bishop present had ventured to contradict the Emperor's untruthful assertions. This was a perilous glory reserved to M. Emery. 'Sire,' he answered, 'I cannot on this point own a different opinion to that which is contained in the catechism taught by your orders in every church of the Empire. I read in this

[18] *L'Eglise Romaine et le Premier Empire*, t. iv. p. 79.

catechism that *the Pope is the visible Head of the Church.* Now, can a Body exist without its Head, without him to whom it owes obedience by Divine right? We are obliged in France to uphold the Four Articles contained in the Declaration of 1682, but we must accept the doctrine in its entirety. In the introduction to this Declaration we read that the supremacy of St. Peter and of the Roman Pontiffs was instituted by Jesus Christ, and that all Christians owe obedience to this supremacy. Nay, more. The Four Articles, it is added, were judged necessary in order to prevent, that, under pretext of the liberties of the Gallican Church, this supremacy might suffer infringement.' The logical conclusion of M. Emery's speech, which, as a deeply felt conviction, should have been in the mouth of every prelate assembled at the Tuileries, was, that 'a Council convoked without the Pope would be utterly powerless.'

'Well,' replied the Emperor, displaying no sign of anger at being thus thwarted by a simple ecclesiastic, 'I do not contest the spiritual power of the Pope, because he received it from Jesus Christ. But Jesus Christ did not give him the temporal power. It was Charlemagne who gave it to him, and I, as successor of Charlemagne, mean to take it away, because it is an obstacle in the way of his spiritual functions.'

'Sire,' replied M. Emery, 'here again I can have no other opinion but that of Bossuet, whose great authority your Majesty respects, and whom you are pleased often to quote. This great Prelate, in his *Defence of the Declaration of the Clergy,* expressly states that the independence and the entire liberty of the Sovereign Pontiff *are* necessary for the free exercise of his spiritual authority in all the universe, and in such a multiplicity of kingdoms and of empires.' Here M. Emery, whose memory where Bossuet was concerned was particularly keen, quoted verbally the testimony of the Eagle of Meaux in favour of the temporal power of the Holy See: 'We congratulate not only the Apostolic See on account of the temporal sovereignty, but the Universal Church, and we desire with all our heart that this sacred dominion may retain its independent character in every particular.'

Nothing could be more irrefutable than this argument. Napoleon listened patiently. On his side he opposed a different actual state of things in Europe. Once more he said what was practically false,' I do not refuse the authority of Bossuet. All that was true in his time, when Europe owned several masters. It was not fitting *then* that the Pope should be under the thraldom of any particular sovereign. But what impropriety can there be that the Pope should acknowledge my authority, now that Europe owns no other master but me?' The personal nature of the remark was embarrassing to M. Emery. How could he satisfactorily answer the Emperor without wounding the very sensitive imperial vanity. He objected the unstable nature of human fortune. What actually existed did not form an exception to the rest, and in any case why subvert a wise and established order of things.'[19] Napoleon passed on to the clause which the bishops had proposed to add to the Concordat, to the effect *that His Holiness should give the canonical confirmation in a determined time, without which the right of confirming would devolve upon the Provincial Synod.* Was this a concession to which the Pope would be likely to agree, the Emperor asked. M. Emery unhesitatingly answered that it was a most improbable concession, seeing that it would annihilate the Sovereign Pontiff's right of confirmation. So it was a *pas de clerc*[20] that his bishops would have imposed

---

[19] *L'Eglise Romaine et le Premier Empire*, t. iv. p. 85.
[20] 'Vous vouliez me faire faire un pas de clerc.'

upon Napoleon, and which he resented before the lucid and noble language of M. Emery. Unfortunately, the impression produced by this conversation on the Emperor's mind was momentary. It increased his esteem for the Sulpician, for in leaving the room of the debate he bowed most graciously in passing M. Emery, and pretty well ignored the other members of the Commission who had so perfectly drilled themselves to silence. A few days afterwards, when Cardinal Fesch was entertaining him with theology, he exclaimed, without ceremony, 'Be quiet, you are an ignoramus. Where did you learn theology? It is with M. Emery, who knows it, that I wish to talk upon such matters.'[21]

The question naturally suggests itself here, whether, if Napoleon had met with a few more possessing, as M. Emery did, the courage of their convictions, he would still have attempted, in the same audacious way, to despatch the spiritual affairs of France, and called together a National Council, whose insufficiency and powerlessness without the cooperation of the Sovereign Pontiff had been fully pointed out by the one ecclesiastic of his empire, whose theological science he so perfectly respected? Would his passion have proved stronger than his good sense? It is a question whose answer we may not give, for it lies between Napoleon and God, the King of the human heart and conscience, Who, in pronouncing judgment on His creatures, rewards and punishes with a balance as unknown to us as it is mysterious. He asks a rigorous account of evil committed; but has He not also a regard for the attenuating circumstances of sin, so tender and so loving that our own harshness terrifies us when it is confronted with the mercy of an infinitely holy God? We may not say how Napoleon would have acted if he had encountered

[21] *Vie de M. l'Abbé Emery*, p. 311.

a courageous resistance from his clergy. We see that, in spite of M. Emery's protestation, he actually did convoke the National Council, that by some unaccountable hopefulness, little warranted by the Holy Father's whole demeanour, he still imagined that he should bring the Apostolic See under his system. The consequences of a passion that directed its efforts against the Spiritual Power were for him, even on earth, a downfall as complete as his glory had been stupendous. Strong in his weakness, the Sovereign Pontiff conquered the greatest son of the Revolution, the democratic beginning of whose empire ended in a fierce despotism, which called its subjects to distant battle-fields for flimsy and unprofitable fame, and substituted the rule of a Minister of Worship devoted to its cause for the Catholic Voice of the great Chair of Peter. It is a saying the best known perhaps and the least practised of all contained in the range of Gospel teaching: 'He who exalteth himself shall be humbled, and he who humbleth himself shall be exalted.' Providence was biding its own time to humble Cæsar and to loosen the chains of one who, in order to attain the crown, was first to taste of the chalice of his Lord.

CHAPTER XI.

A Gallican Council.

'La violence prouve bien la volonté de celui qui fait trembler, mais nullement celle de celui qui tremble.'—Joseph de Maistre.

THE sitting at the Tuileries of March 16th, 1811, had been for M. Emery the flame's expiring flicker. There he had spoken his last word as a champion of Catholic rights. He died on the 28th of April following, carrying with him to the tomb both sorrow and joy. He had fought his fight and won the crown, but it needed no great perspicacity to perceive that the Church of France was on the borders of a dark abyss, that it threatened to become truly a Gallican Church under the despotism of Napoleon, or rather more even than this, for the idea of Gallicanism would be to set up a limited monarchy in the Church; but not to submit blindly in religious matters to the will of a tyrant. It would be rather a genteel sanctioning of State usurpation than base servility to a system where Cæsar reduces the claims of Almighty God to a practical nonenity. Napoleon's efforts fast tended to produce schism, but when we consider the keen good sense which he had manifested on the outset of his power with regard to religious matters, how fully he had grasped the great fact that religion is necessary for the material as well as for the moral prosperity of a nation, we may be disposed to question whether he really possessed full and entire consciousness of the subversions which he was effecting in its domain? Was it not rather with a view to putting the Holy Father into a still more unfavourable position that he called a National Council? Pius VII. refused to confirm the bishops of his nomination. He would bring about a state of things which should oblige the Sovereign Pontiff to yield, were it only to spare the Church greater trials. This policy was not novel with Napoleon. In the Concordat, it was precisely the argument which had been instilled into the ears of Consalvi and Caprara, with what success we have seen. The Papal Legate had consented to be imposed upon, and had earned for himself the Emperor's most profound contempt. Consalvi, who avoided the snare, had been through Napoleon's intrigues obliged first to resign his post of Secretary of State, and then, because he would not lend his purple to assist at a mere 'formality,' which however possessed curiously enough the charm of averting further evils from the Church, he was now confined at Rheims, degraded outwardly, and in a state of evangelical poverty. Cardinal Consalvi would certainly not have willed it otherwise. No doubt he esteemed it a privilege that his own life should be shaped after the model of his imprisoned Head at Savona.

The National Council, convoked in June, 1811, wonderfully illustrates the impotence of a great body without a head, obeying or indeed striving against an unlawful authority, which had violently imposed its will upon the assembly. Nothing is more natural than a council headed by the Pope. It is its normal state to be ruled by the Spiritual Legislator to whom Jesus Christ gave the Keys, and the charge of feeding His flock with the care of providing for His children lest they should faint in the way. All things are in their place. If in the Church the choice of a ruler were optional, so that it might be for instance allowable, in the case of an extensive empire, to vest secular and religious power under one head, history would give us a very different experience. A general council may or may not be a mark of the true Church, but it is at least a very remarkable fact that only one religion has hitherto produced an Œcumenical Assembly of its members, and that the Pope alone, whatever his personal character may have been, has possessed the necessary faculties and qualities for presiding over the bishops. All such attempts made without the cooperation of the Apostolic See have proved abortive. Hence we may gather which, the General Council or the Pope, is the most important. The one is a rare creation to meet special and peculiar needs. The other is at once the head and soul of the body, and this is so true that the impossible event or state of things, which could erase the Pope from the world and from society, would destroy by the same stroke the very existence of the Church. Napoleon's National Council must call forth these reflections, but strictly speaking, it can have no claim to the title even of *national*, since not half the sees recently united to the French Empire were represented. It was a great manifestation which the Emperor exerted his utmost to impose upon the Holy Father as an expression of spontaneous feeling on the part of the French Episcopate against the authority of the Apostolic See, and against the lawful resistance which its occupant was offering to himself. The French bishops were for the most part entirely ignorant of the state of the question between Pope and Emperor. Innocently they obeyed the summons to Paris to form an assembly which, they imagined, would provide a remedy against existing evils, which concerned ecclesiastical jurisdiction, under the sanction of Pius VII., but in reality they came to solve an impossible riddle, and one which has defied the efforts of eighteen centuries, simply because what God has ordained cannot be subjected to change by the mere will of man. The end of the Council, as Napoleon intended it, would be fully realized if it could produce one conviction on the mind of the Sovereign Pontiff; that the French bishops, summoned to take a side in the quarrel, would unhesitatingly pronounce themselves for Napoleon. This was the all-important point, which once attained could not fail to bring about an end to the serious embarrassment arising from the dearth of bishops. The Holy Father seeing himself alone would certainly yield, and not only consent to confirm the bishops but accept the cherished dream of Avignon or Paris, where with a revenue of two million francs, he would become the first subject of the French Emperor. The National Council formed a link in the chain which was called universal empire, and as such Napoleon meant it to prove no exception to the rule. It was to fall under the supervision of the secular power, to own himself as president, and his wishes as law. In the mass, as a council that is, it resisted and thwarted him, but the strength which had been manifested by the body, did not exist in the individual members. When coercion was exercised upon them separately, they made no difficulty in accepting what they had considered impracticable when united in council, but this submission following upon violence and the employment of Napoleon's usual arms—arbitrary imprisonment—after too the formal dissolution of the body, was quite worthless as a result. The Emperor cloaked the whole proceeding with religion, but when once he had built up an idea in his mind, we know that he used all means indifferently to carry it into effect, that, if he allowed it to slumber for a time, it was only to produce a more completely developed maturity. The very nature of things called upon him to make a final stand against the Pope. The ground for the Council ostensibly was the imaginary grievance that he so often imputed with anger to his adversary. viz., that Pius VII. had proved faithless to the Concordat which required his confirmation of the bishops nominated by Napoleon. But by what right had the Sovereign Pontiff been driven from his palace, dragged in a state of great suffering from one place to another, and at last strictly imprisoned at Savona, where he was deprived not only of books and counsel, but of the simplest knowledge of outward events. Clearly, he could not consent blindly to confirm whatever bishops might be imposed upon his good faith. 'First,' he said, 'allow us the liberty of choosing impartial counsellors amongst the Cardinals, then we will consider what we can do.' Nothing could be more just than the demand, and when Napoleon turned a deaf ear to solicitations so conscientious, the extent of his folly in convoking a council to meet a difficulty of his own creation, and of which his will alone constituted the obstacle, is almost inconceivable. Before the opening of the Council, which was convoked for June, 1811, four bishops calling themselves a deputation from the French Church were to visit Savona, and to 'negotiate' with the Holy Father. The term is a wide one. Here it meant that, forgetful of their duty as princes of the Church, they were to act the part of tempters towards their Spiritual Head. These prelates were Mgr. de Barral of Tours, Mgr. Duvoisin of Nantes, and Mgr. de Trèves, to whom was adjoined later the Patriarch Elect of Venice. They were authorized to treat separately the affair of episcopal confirmation, and the general state of ecclesiastical matters. These had for three years been thrown into confusion, and Napoleon could allow no pretence whatever to stand in the way of a disentanglement so indispensable. The malice of the deputation was that, presenting to the Holy Father the appearance of a national and religious expression of feeling, it in reality emanated entirely from the Emperor, and did not disdain to receive its instructions from a functionary whose office was obnoxious to all Catholic feeling—from M. Bigot de Préameneu, the Minister of Worship. This being the true state of the case, it was Napoleon's aim to affect indifference in the business. If he allowed it at all, he was sinning by excessive courtesy. A letter preconcerted with M. Bigot was addressed to the Holy Father by the deputation in the name of all the bishops. Pius VII. was therein intreated to be assured that the whole Gallican Church was speaking by its mouthpiece.[1] It seems as if Napoleon took a certain pleasure in imposing his will upon consciences, which, as far as human wisdom is able to pronounce a judgment, fully merited the reproach of being neither 'hot nor cold.' When a man tries to play two parts, the chances are that he will play both badly. Because Fesch could bear to lose his standing with neither Pope nor Emperor, he submitted to write a confidential letter to Pius VII., urging him to a prompt arrangement 'which the state of the Church justified.' Napoleon required the principal ecclesiastical personages in France to support the step of the deputation with a letter coming, as it were, from themselves, so as to throw in their weight with the Holy Father against all idea of resistance. If nineteen bishops were weak enough to yield to the imperial wishes, we must not forget a greater number of noble voices which Vincennes and other State prisons had inevitably prevented from reaching the ear of Pius VII. Truly it was no time for half measures,

[1] Lettre citée par Mgr. de Barral, *Fragments Historiques*.

however Fesch might seek to silence his conscience by compromises. In whatever light his actions appeared to his own eyes, history has given us his true standard. He was not morally courageous or unworldly enough to side with the right. 'If,' as the bishops expressed it in their letter, 'the answer of the Holy Father did not reach them, they would be under the necessity by the very nature of things, of allowing dispensations by their private authority. He would not surely persist in an impossible resistance.'[2] To possess a true notion of what was taking place at Savona, it is necessary to examine closely the nature of the negotiations which were employed to force the Holy Father's conscience. Two distinct batteries were thereunto directed by Napoleon. The deputation of the bishops had religious questions for its field of battle, but under the strict supervision of the State, and the obligation of secrecy, a restriction which did not touch the Emperor. The second was a political negotiation headed by M. de Chabrol, whose moral descent (seeing that he was gaoler-in-chief to the Sovereign Pontiff) we could hardly have thought possible without this new feature in his service. Pius VII.'s health was in a very precarious state. His doctor, Porta, was bribed by M. de Chabrol to serve the Emperor against his own master. Gold is the great conqueror, but for the honour of human nature let it be said that it has never reigned over a noble heart. The services of those so bought, must in the main, prove utterly worthless, and history in recording the fact, puts its stigma alike upon the man base enough to offer and the man whose sense of honour is so completely dead as to accept.

'Send word to Dr. Porta,' Napoleon wrote to M. Bigot, on November 1st, 1811, 'that you have brought his

[2] *Fragments Historiques*, p. 316.

letter under the Emperor's notice; tell him that his Majesty remarked in a margin contained in his Amsterdam letter, that whatever discussions there may have been between the Pope and his Majesty, and however violent they may have been, his Majesty will always consider the *personal service* rendered to the Pope as if rendered to himself. Dr. Porta has only to name his terms, and his allowance will be paid to him as when the Pope was still in Rome. A sum of twelve thousand francs yearly is allotted to him, and it shall be continued to him as long as he remains with the Pope.'³ 'The Pope's doctor, M. Porta,' wrote M. de Chabrol, in May, 1811, 'serves us admirably. He has immense confidence in the commander of the palace (M. La Gorse), who is a worthy man ... All is going on smoothly in a way to promise support to reason and the good cause. ... Thanks to these fortunate circumstances, we heard yesterday morning that the Pope did not reject the overtures made to him, that he was thinking seriously about them, but that he raised the difficulty that honourable concession was impossible so long as he was deprived of liberty, and did not possess a counsel strong enough in the public opinion to overcome his resistance, and powerful enough to justify his adhesion. ... We and their lordships the bishops, determined that we would use all suitable means to persuade the Pope of the uselessness of counsel to help him to decide. What more worthy influence need he acknowledge than that of three bishops sent by the authorization of their Sovereign and by the whole Church, which awaits the end of this dispute in tearful suspense. They possess the public confidence and have already suffered for the Church.⁴ The kind of treatment which is implied in M. de Chabrol's despatches, joined to com-

---

³ Lettre de l'Empereur au Comte Bigot de Préameneu, 1 9bre. 1811.
Lettres de M. de Chabrol au Ministre des Cultes, 12 mai 1811.

plete isolation had had its effect on the Holy Father. It was now four months since he had been deprived of his papers, books, and writing materials, and of the familiar and cherished servants who had contributed a little towards softening his imprisonment. He had been kept in complete ignorance of political events which touched his own feelings the most strongly, as for instance, the fate of the Cardinals whom he best loved. When on the 9th of May 1811, he was officially told of the arrival of the bishops deputed by the French clergy, he had the notion that they had come to receive his depositions for the Council which was, he imagined, convoked to judge him. It had, indeed, been the Emperor's aim to foster so preposterous an idea. In this particular episode of Savona it seems to us that Napoleon surpassed himself in unjust treatment of him whom he had made his adversary. As usual, with an eye to the end, he was blind or indifferent to the means employed for its attainment. Was he unmindful of the all but eternal record of history, or did he hope to bury this page of the conflict in the disloyal hearts of those who had served his iniquitous designs? But long ago, as a warning to men who are more especially prone to do evil, apparently for the furtherance of their own interests, our great poet wrote:

> The evil that men do lives after them,
> The good is oft interred with their bones.[5]

The whole question as it lies before us at Savona during the month of May, 1811, amounts in reality to this: Napoleon, who represents the power of the State, had assumed an arbitrary authority over the Church, and he now called upon the spiritual Head of that Church to sanction officially his pretensions with regard to his usurpations. *Ostensibly*, the ground of the quarrel was the Holy

[5] *Julius Cæsar*, Mark Anthony's Oration.

Father's refusal to give the Bulls of confirmation, or to sign a promise that he would respect the Declaration of 1682, but the evil lay in the disposition of mind in Napoleon which would have remained dissatisfied with the greatest concessions. Vainly might Pius VII. have hoped to prevent, as the Deputation expressed it, further trouble from befalling the Church by an acquiescence which would have stained his memory in Catholic hearts. The Pope is the great rampart of the world and of society. It is his office to protect the friendless and the persecuted, to uphold the right against triumphant and prosperous iniquity, to oppose encroachment, and most of all that State-usurpation, which, if it had not played so conspicuous a part from the very beginning of the sensible action of the Church, we might almost imagine to belong especially to latter times. In accepting this mission, the Vicar of Christ embraces not peace but strife, a conflict righteous because indispensable, not only in the circle of religious interests, but in the political and social fabrics which need to repose as to their ultimate basis upon the rock, not to quiver and snap through the flickering and unstable course of human events. Now that a suitable distance of time separates us from the sad days of Savona, let us see what was the real attitude of Pius VII. with regard to the Deputation, whether he conceded anything at all, and if so, taking into consideration all the accompanying circumstances, whether such concession was valid, that is, a result of unbiassed conviction freely and willingly expressed. For the first few days of the stay of the bishops at Savona, from the 9th to the 16th of May, the Holy Father invariably replied to their remonstrances that 'he could and would do nothing without counsellors.' The prelates for one moment entertained the extravagant thought of taking the place of the much desired Cardinals, and made the proposal to the Pope, who, however, eluded it as politely as possible, saying that he did not consider them disinterested enough. This supposition was less than the truth, since they were actually governed by the secret instructions of Napoleon, communicated through M. Bigot. One day, when according to custom, the bishops were expatiating to the Holy Father on the troubles which his resistance was bringing upon so many persons devoted to his cause, Pius VII. raising his eyes to heaven, exclaimed: '*Pazienza.* I am without counsel, and the Head of the Church is in prison. *Plus vident oculi quam oculus.*'[6]

The bishops were discouraged, and already thought of returning to Paris and having to confront Napoleon after an unsuccessful mission. But if they showed signs of weariness, not so M. de Chabrol. On the 13th of May he had a long interview with the Holy Father, and did ample justice to the full confidence reposed in him by the Emperor. He feigned immense astonishment at the refusal of Pius VII. to meet the demands of the bishops. The Council, he said, was prepared to pronounce sentence against the Sovereign Pontiff, and to take away altogether a right of which he could still dispose. As for the advice solicited, it should be conceded when the Pope had decided one way or the other. M. de Chabrol was gently answered that, in the case of opinions touching upon conscience, Pius VII. would refer against the judgment of men to that of God. The Prefect of Montenotte could obtain nothing of this 'incomprehensible obstinacy.' Meantime he learned from Porta, that the Holy Father's health was suffering cruelly from the fatigue and anxiety caused by the discussions. He could hardly sleep or eat; he was sad and downcast, and troubled at the terrible respon-

[6] Troisième lettre des Evêques députés, au Ministre des Cultes, 13 mai, 1811.

sibility which was forced upon him. He knew nothing of the outer world. He lived, as it were, in presence of his conscience and of the embarrassed state of the Catholic Church. No mental solace, no recreation was ever provided for him. By day he was wearied with remonstrances; by night he was restless and troubled with the fear of compromising things still more through his own fault. It was too much. M. de Chabrol profited by a disposition of mind which a few days later amounted to *temporary insanity* to pay another of his over-bearing visits to the Holy Father. 'Doctor Porta,' he remarks, 'has been of great service to us.' This service consisted in warning the Prefect of the favourable moment to approach the unhappy prisoner. The result of the interview was a desire expressed by the Pope to see the bishops immediately, and to examine once more if anything could be arranged. On the 17th they had submitted a note to the Holy Father, which he read and kept, but in their letters they gave little hopes of being ultimately successful. On the 18th, thanks to M. de Chabrol's stormy visit, which, owing to the sinful intelligence entertained with Dr. Porta, he had so prudently timed, the Deputation found the Holy Father more disposed to concession; but according to his own statement, his head was too tired to attend to business, and he adjourned their meeting till the evening. This last effort was the crowning point of the negotiation. The bishops drew up in the Pope's room a rough copy of that which they had directions to demand of him. After Pius VII. had suggested a few not very material corrections, the Deputation left the memorandum, with his consent on the mantel-piece, and the next day set off early in the morning for Paris. This constituted in its entirety their feeble victory (if indeed it was one) over Pius VII., whose moral sufferings, anxiety, privations, and peculiar—indeed, alarming—state of health must all be taken into due consideration. During the night preceding their departure, a valet who slept in a room near to that of the Pope heard him accusing himself audibly in the most contrite terms for having prevaricated. In a state of extreme agitation he sent the following morning, first for M. La Gorse, to know if the bishops had already gone, and then for M. de Chabrol, to whom he represented with the deepest emotion, that he had been surprized the day before, and could not accede to the memorandum. The last words involved a touch of heresy, and he would rather die a thousand times than consent to such a scheme. But it had only been a scheme, a preliminary to a treaty, and this, with the knowledge that he had signed nothing, consoled the Holy Father. It is not quite clear how he could have protested had Napoleon used the document against him; but this is what he threatened to do.[7] The state to which bad treatment had reduced Pius VII. exactly proves the truth of his own words: he needed counsel to strengthen him in that weary struggle which was consuming him. For some days those who surrounded the Holy Father were able to attest the presence of all the symptoms of madness. Extreme mental concentration produced a fixed look which expressed outwardly the disposition of his mind. This rigid look, it was the thought or the fear of the troubles of the Church which had brought it to the calm, sweet face of Pius VII.; but as in the days of St. Peter, when it is recorded that the whole Church prayed without ceasing for the loosening of his chains,[8] so now strength was given to the Sovereign

---

[7] Lettres de M. de Chabrol au Ministre des Cultes, du 22 et du 23 mai, 1811.
[8] Acts c. xii.

Pontiff to triumph over the greatest evil which can befall man. If we have touched upon this question, it has been solely to prove the full extent of Napoleon's tyranny, which is only grasped by arriving at the result produced. M. de Chabrol was able to write to M. Bigot at the end of May: 'You will have seen by my last letters that the uncertainty of the Pope when he is left to himself goes to the length *of affecting his reason and his health.* At present the *mental alienation has passed off,* and the physical indisposition is less grave, but everything warns us that support (counsel) is indispensable to a mind that is weakened, and to a sensitive conscience.'[9]

What, then, in one word, had been the results attained by the Deputation sent by the Emperor to Savona? They were utterly worthless. If the plan of a scheme for concession (it was nothing more) had been torn from Pius VII., it possessed no official value without a signature, and was openly protested against by the Holy Father, who declared what was only plain truth, that he had been surprized into yielding, not to say forced, and that if the document were produced against him, he would use those spiritual arms which could never be taken from him. The general situation of the religious world was furthermore falsified by the convocation of the Council for the 17th of June, since there was no cause for delay after the termination of the negotiations at Savona. If it were needed, another proof of their non-success would be the complete silence which was thrown over the whole proceeding. Napoleon was too ready to take hold of the shadow of concession in the Holy Father not to have speedily published a triumph effected at any price over his weakest yet his strongest opponent. No such anxiety, but its exact contrary, is manifested in

[9] Lettre de M. de Chabrol au Ministre des Cultes, 30 mai, 1811.

the Emperor's injunction to the bishops of the Deputation to preserve the strictest reserve on the subject of the visit to Savona. On their side they obeyed so well, that during the conferences preliminary to the council no single bishop present could arrive at a fair conclusion as to what they had really done. Napoleon, who delighted in any unusual pomp which could add to the lustre of his name, probably took a certain pleasure in calling together a meeting of so highly respectable a body of men as the French bishops. He liked the outward splendour of the thing, but he loved the surreptitious wielding of the Keys which he promised himself from a council whose every member was placed under his control, and where an opposing voice fell as a drop of water into the ocean. He was its secret yet powerful president. Fesch only assumed the title by courtesy, for in truth the Primate was nothing more than presiding prelate, still wavering between conscience and regard for his imperial nephew. As an example of the unceremonious way in which its true president (Napoleon) was disposed to treat the princes of the Church on the eve of the council, we may quote his very strange behaviour to the Bishop, and to M. le Gallois, the Vicar General of Séez. The crime of the bishop was twofold: he had prepared a circular to his curés, recommending them to sing vespers in their church on the feasts suppressed by the Emperor, and his too frequent absence from the marriages of the *rosières* of Séez with retired officers had been remarked. In this there was the very slightest disregard for Napoleon's character of spiritual legislator, and under the First Empire an example must be made of such open indifference for the sake of edification. On a journey to Normandy, in May, 1811, the Emperor passed by Séez, and remembered that he had a bishop to punish. He sent for the unfortunate prelate one morning, and the following conversation took place between them :

'Are you the Bishop of Séez?"

'Yes, sire.'

'I am very displeased with you. You are the only bishop of whom complaint has been made to me. You keep up party spirit here. Instead of uniting different parties, you still make a distinction between constitutional clergy and non-constitutional priests. You are the only person in France that still acts in this way. You wish for civil war. You have already caused it; you have stained your hands in French blood. Your diocese alone is in a disordered state.'

'Sire, everything is in the best order.'

'You wrote a very bad circular.'

'I changed it.'

'I sent for you to Paris to show you my displeasure, and nothing does you any good. You are utterly good for nothing. Resign immediately.'

'Sire!'

'Let his papers be seized!' exclaimed the Emperor to M. Rœderer, who was in the room. The Chapter and Canons of Séez, who presented themselves in the formidable audience chamber after the bishop had retired, received, in their turn an explosion of imperial wrath, or rather, it seemed to condense itself for the benefit of an honorary vicar general, M. le Gallois, an exemplary and much respected priest in the province. The canons had hardly appeared before Napoleon shouted out rudely: 'Which of you is it that leads your bishop, who is after all but a simpleton?"

Here somebody not very charitably designated M. Le Gallois.

'So it is you,' continued the Emperor. 'Why did you advise him not to be present at the marriages of the *rosières?*'

'Sire, I was absent at the time of these marriages.'

'Why did you counsel your bishop to write that circular about the suppressed feasts?'

'Sire, I was absent then too, and to speak truth, as soon as I knew about it, I came to Séez expressly to advise an entirely different circular.'

'Where were you then?'

'With my family.'

'How could you absent yourself so often with a bishop that is such a simpleton? Who governed the diocese? And why did you come to your bishop in that way to become his vicar general?'

'Sire, I obeyed my superiors; every priest owes them obedience.'

'Are you a good Gallican?'

'Yes, sire, and perhaps one of the sincerest in your empire.'

The nature of the last reply did not conduce to alter the fate reserved for M. Le Gallois. Forty-eight hours later he was arrested in the episcopal palace, taken between two policemen to prison at Alençon, from thence to *la Force* in Paris, on to the straw still warm that had been used by a criminal condemned to capital punishment. After eleven days passed here he was sent to Vincennes, as a canon 'possessing too much intelligence, and consequently dangerous.' His sufferings alone caused a commutation of the prison, and he was transferred to a milder form of confinement, where he remained till the fall of the Empire.[10] As in the case of Pius VII. himself, it may be seen that Napoleon joined to outward coarseness of language the further insult of feigning to believe that his victims were not capable of opposing him *motu proprio*, but that they must needs have been counselled.

[10] *L'Eglise Romaine et le Premier Empire*, t. iv. pp. 177—183.

By a strange and not a fortuitous arrangement, Napoleon chose to open the session of the Legislative Body on the 16th of June, the eve of the Council. The simple people of those days (if they existed) who founded all their hopes of the day's news on the *Moniteur*, as we are accustomed to do with the *Times*, must have gathered a very inadequate conclusion of the importance of that imposing Assembly which occupied the Cathedral of Notre Dame on the 17th of June. The *Moniteur* was the *official newspaper of the French Empire*, and in this capacity shared the honour of all other public organs devoted to the new imperial dynasty, that of having neither will nor voice of its own. Although the National Council was a novelty that Napoleon appreciated, he would not have been content if it had proved too engrossing to his people. After all, it was a religious business, and it was highly necessary to prevent in bishops and priests an overbearing notion of their own importance. The *Moniteur's* assertions, or rather the scantiness of its details on this point, are not to be taken as the actual appreciation of the French nation. The vision of ninety-five bishops in cope and mitre in a cathedral so grand as Notre Dame, presents an unusual and imposing spectacle; but what from a moral point of view cannot fail to strike us forcibly, giving us as it does the general feeling and tone of the religious element of the French people, is that natural craving for the Pope which even the National Council of 1811 knew how to manifest, or rather manifested in spite of itself, and in spite, too, of the Emperor. But it is often said of individuals that they have not the courage of their opinions. This is the verdict which an impartial jury would probably pass upon the Assembly in question. It had generous impulses, it had moments when the tide of Catholic and Roman feeling seemed to promise to bear all before it, and to force the prison at Savona. Oh, that these, instead of proving transitory bursts of mere emotion and sentiment, could have constituted its normal state! The bishops, with a few happy exceptions, give us rather the notion that they would have done the Emperor's bidding in all points if they could, but that, as princes of the Catholic Church, they were impelled by the very force of their position to render a tacit homage to their imprisoned Head. Many of them came no doubt in ignorance as to the sufferings of Pius VII., but we cannot be blind to the fact that Gallicanism and its sensitive liberties had somewhat prepared the situation, and rendered Napoleon's pretensions less preposterous in their eyes, while it facilitated the part which he intended to play. The prelates who especially distinguished themselves by a noble resistance in the Council, were the Bishops of Bordeaux (Mgr. d'Aviau), Ghent (Mgr. de Broglie), Troyes (Mgr. de Boulogne), and Tournai (Mgr. Hirn). Opened on the 17th of June, the Council was prematurely dissolved on the 12th of July, by the will that ruled all its proceedings. It did indeed struggle into an attempt at resurrection, but it was a feeble effort not blessed with any great or even satisfactory result. During its bare month of existence, did it contribute to elucidate the question pending between Pope and Emperor, or does it not rather prove the utter impotence of State legislation in religious matters? It is not saying too much to assert that the Catholic Church, as a sound creation of God, needs the air and liberty of a healthy organization. She is no weak or ailing temperament which requires the best endeavours of science and worldly prudence to keep up the life of a valetudinarian; but strong and vigorous, she pines and wastes, where others, not possessing her superhuman force might live such a life as belongs to them. A State hot-house, under a king or Emperor, is no place for her. The first and only Session of the Council denied more powerfully than mere words can ever do the statement which Napoleon had tried to impose on the credulity of Pius VII. The French bishops had been represented to him as ready to side with Napoleon, should matters come to a crisis, but here in the midst of Notre Dame, the orator of the day, Mgr. de Boulogne, alluded in elegant and burning terms, 'to the supreme Head of the Episcopate without whom it could only resemble a branch separated from its trunk and withered, or be tossed by the waves as a vessel without rudder or steersman. Whatever vicissitudes the See of Peter may experience, whatever the state and condition of his successor may be, we shall always be united to him by the ties of filial respect and veneration. This See may be removed, but it cannot be destroyed. Its magnificence may be taken away, but never its strength. Wherever this See shall establish itself it shall draw all others round it. To whatever place it may go, all Catholics will follow it, because everywhere it must continue to be the representative of the Succession, the centre of government, and the sacred deposit of Apostolical traditions.[11]

Napoleon had foreseen what might be made of the opening discourse, but unfortunately, when Fesch had taken him the manuscript, he had relied upon his uncle to efface the doubtful sentiments relating to the imprisoned Head of the Church. Both Fesch and Mgr. de Boulogne had promised that nothing should be uttered from the pulpit that could admit of mischievous interpretation; but in the ardour of his oratory the Bishop of Troyes allowed himself to be led away; his words fell as burning coals in the midst of the learned assembly, and produced wonderful emotion. The effect

[11] *Œuvres complètes de Mgr. de Boulogne, Evêque de Troyes.*

had not died away when the Bishop of Nantes rose to fulfil a necessary formality in asking each prelate individually whether it pleased him that the Council should be opened. Mgr. d'Aviau answered the question by a condition : 'Yes, saving the obedience due to the Sovereign Pontiff, to whom I bind myself, and whom I swear to obey.' As in the inaugural oration, it was again the movement of the bee seeking its flower, the river its sea, for every Catholic bishop must of necessity tend to union with the centre of spiritual repose. But now Cardinal Fesch, with that singular inconsistency which characterized him, was preparing to ascend a raised platform placed in the middle of the choir, from whence he read in a loud tone of voice the oath prescribed by a Bull of Pius IV. As officiating prelate, he might be thought to express the feelings of the Assembly when he said : 'I acknowledge the Holy Catholic, Apostolic, and Roman Church to be the mother and mistress of all other churches ; I promise and swear perfect obedience to the Roman Pontiff, the Successor of St. Peter, Prince of the Apostles, and Vicar of Jesus Christ on earth.' This oath was repeated by every bishop in the cathedral in the hands of Cardinal Fesch. One by one they bound themselves irrevocably to the cause of Pius VII., and if it happened that any one of them articulated feebly the words of the formula, the Primate required a repetition, and manifested additional anxiety in the case of former constitutional bishops, or of those who were suspected of unorthodox views.[12]

A session whose principal features were an eloquent sermon containing expressions of inviolable attachment to Pius VII., and an oath imposed upon each prelate present to render him perfect obedience, did not certainly possess the questionable merit of squaring with

[12] *Vie du Card. Fesch par l'Abbé Lyonnet*, t. ii. p. 329.

Napoleon's views. The services of the *Moniteur*, which might have proved invaluable if the occasion of the opening had been utilized in his favour, were now uncalled for. It would never do to let it convey to the Holy Father the true statement of the case, after all the false assertions of the Emperor as to the sentiments of the Episcopate. A dead silence, then, was once more the course imposed upon it, as formerly in the case of the coronation, when Napoleon had crowned himself, but had been prevented by the Pope's remonstrances from telling his people the fact. If, however, the bishops imagined that they had been summoned to Paris to proclaim the supremacy of St. Peter's See, they were woefully mistaken. Napoleon lost no time in destroying such an illusion. Angry as he was with Fesch for 'making one of his scenes,' he was determined to tell the Council his mind in terms clear enough to cause 'foolish attempts' at opposition to fall. The expedient which he invented, to be all but present at the sittings of the Council, was the intervention of two functionaries whose office he had created—the respective Ministers of Worship for France and Italy, M. Bigot de Préameneu and M. le Cte. de Marescalchi. At the first General Congregation, which was held at the Archiepiscopal Palace, these Ministers of the State appeared in official costume, one on the right the other on the left of Fesch. It was the beginning of disenchantment for those bishops who were not in the secret; but when M. Bigot read an Imperial Decree, signifying (1) that Napoleon acknowledged Fesch as President; (2) that a Committee should be formed, intrusted with the State supervision of the assembly, of which the Ministers of Worship would indispensably form a part,—one of their number judiciously observed that by such a measure the Head of the Government obviously aimed rather at *influencing the decisions of the Council than at protecting its deliberations.* Napoleon did not aim for nothing. All that could be obtained by the bishops was to nominate by secret vote the members of the strange committee, which, in common with civil officers (M. Bigot and M. de Marescalchi), was to be charged with State supervision in a so-called ecclesiastical assembly. They pursued the same course in nominating the various Commissions for the preparation of the work of the Council, amongst others one (and it was a deplorable waste of time) to answer the Imperial Message with which M. Bigot had had the goodness to acquaint them in this first congregation. It was a violent tissue of lamentations and complaints against Pius VII. and against his office, of the evil counsels to which he had listened, and of his 'dark designs.' Of his sufferings, his imprisonment, his illness, or the miserable means which the Emperor had used to alienate the members of his household, there was naturally not a word. How different had been the Holy Father's protestations! They had breathed, it is true, abomination of unrighteousness, but compassion for individuals; he 'hated the error, but loved the man.' The message reduced the work of the Council to a miserably weak bending to the designs of Napoleon, who had insured the success of his plans by a long-sighted and delicate attention. A note addressed by him to M. Bigot reveals its extent: 'His Majesty's intentions are (1) that following upon the reading of the message by the Ministers, and upon the proposition to demand an audience of his Majesty by the Council in a body, a committee be nominated to draw up the address, in which committee the four prelates who went to Savona may be placed; (2) that a copy of the address, as well as the Pastoral and opening discourse, be laid before his Majesty; (3) that the Sessions be private. . .'

A little later he wrote again: 'Be careful that nothing is printed without my knowledge. The Pastoral even must not be printed before you have submitted it to me. See that no reporter or foreigner be admitted into the assembly. Bishops alone must be present. As for the priests proposed for admission, I will sanction in this respect, if it is absolutely necessary, the presence of a dozen ecclesiastics, whose names and qualifications you must give me beforehand. They must be virtuous priests, not reactionists. The report which you are to write at the Council must not be printed. You must simply give it after reading it to the Committee of the Council. The Committee is not authorized to print its report till I have approved it, nor to join thereunto other matter than such as has been agreed upon.'[13] The President of the Council here paints himself in his true colours. Cardinal Fesch, on the other hand, floated between the small number of courtier prelates and the majority who were more frightened than potent, but whose conscience refused to accept the Emperor's will without a struggle. As long as Napoleon addressed himself to the Council, to the body, he encountered this resistance, because the absence of individual force is sometimes atoned for by collective strength. But it was he who had weakened the power of the episcopacy by endeavouring to render bishops merely public functionaries presiding over the *Religious Department*, which owned his control to the same extent as the other details of material administration. It was almost natural to him, and the propensity savoured of paganism, to treat men, whatever may have been their intrinsic value, as things, to ignore, that is, the presence of the soul. But free will, the soul's essential attribute, constitutes the difference between Christianity and modern Rationalism, Pantheism, and Materialism, which

[13] Note de l'Empereur au Cte. Bigot de Préameneu, 20 juin, 1811.

are only other words for a paganism worse than the old, though they may express various degrees of intensity. As to the body, Napoleon came finally to employ his usual arm—imprisonment. With it and by it he did not disdain a pitiful victory over individuals, too strong in the mass to yield, too weak personally to resist. In one of the familiar conversations which Cardinal Fesch was wont to have at St. Cloud with the Emperor after the work of the Council was over for the day, Napoleon had produced a mature idea with regard to the nomination of the various commissions. Aided by such bishops as Mgr. Duvoisin and Mgr. de Barral, he aspired to be in very truth the instigator and theologian of the Council by causing them to choose the several members who should form these commissions. Fesch too ardently responded to a plan which would have reduced to nought the small amount of liberty possessed by the unfortunate assembly. In this way, no resolution would be proposed for acceptance that had not been previously discussed with the Emperor under all its aspects in private conferences. Fesch had proved too servilely sanguine, and we have seen how the notion was rejected, the assembly having opined for secret vote in its first General Congregation. But Napoleon, with an impatience which threatened occasionally to subvert his own plans, acted immediately in accordance with his idea. For the moment, setting aside the important answer to the Imperial Message which plunged into the subject-matter of the Council, it devolved upon the bishops to draw up an address to the Emperor, in itself an easy formality, if he could only have consented to leave them alone. When the Commission (for this is the form adopted in a council for the transaction of business) intrusted with this naturally easy work, met for deliberation, Mgr. Duvoisin, who was on it, produced a memorandum which he had previously drawn up, and which he read to the seven assembled bishops. Instead of constituting the mere formality that is customary on such occasions, it was a treaty of State theology, and spoke in a very pointed way against the Bull *Quum Memoranda*. The Bishop of Nantes ingenuously confessed its whole meaning, when he answered loudly-raised objections by saying 'that his work had been laid before the Emperor, whose entire approbation he had already received.' The example of Bossuet, who has been raised to the doubtful dignity of a Gallican champion, was alleged by the Bishop of Ghent. Louis XIV. had required the bishops to submit their pastorals to his royal self, excepting from the measure, *as a favour*, the Bishop of Meaux. Bossuet refused the distinction which he claimed for all the episcopate, and Louis XIV. thought better of his tyrannical decree, and withdrew it.[14] The discussion which followed was stormy, but it was rather directed at persons than at questions. Mgr. Duvoisin had made a revelation, and in some measure he attained the wished-for result. The address which he had penned in connivance with Napoleon was not retained in its primitive state, but it influenced the form finally adopted in such a manner as to render this unsatisfactory to all parties, and the Bishop of Ghent declared that he would never sign it. The effect which it produced when read at the congregation of the whole Council was one of those irresistible and generous movements whose presence we are happy to signalize, although, after all, they were nothing more than impotent manifestations of feeling in favour of Pius VII. A bishop requested that the 'liberty of the Pope' should be demanded. The motion was taken up and covered in a confused murmur of approbation, and Mgr. de Chambéry rose to put into words the

[14] *Journal de Mgr. de Broglie, Evêque de Gand.*

evident sentiments of the assembly. 'How, my lords, is there no question of the liberty of the Pope in the address which has just been read to us? What are we doing here, we Catholic bishops, assembled in a Council without the power of communicating with our Head? It is an obligation for us to demand the Pope's liberty of the Emperor. It is our right, and it is also our duty. We owe it to the Catholics of Europe and of the whole world. Let us not hesitate to go and throw ourselves in a body at the Emperor's feet to obtain this necessary deliverance.'[15] The enthusiasm of the Fathers was indescribable. A courtier prelate, wishing to distract public attention, objected the impropriety of a council going in a body to kneel before a prince. 'I can truly appreciate the episcopal dignity,' was the noble answer of Mgr. de Chambéry, 'whose rights I respect and could defend as well as any man; but believe me, bishops are well able to fall on their knees before their temporal sovereign to obtain the liberty of their spiritual Head; and is it not the time, in so great a cause, to follow the advice of the Apostle, who says: "*Be earnest in season and out of season; correct, supplicate, threaten.*" How shall it be said that the Chapter of Paris was able to solicit the pardon of M. d'Astros, one of its members, and we have not the courage to ask for the liberty of the Pope! Why should the Emperor be angry, my lords? Even Almighty God consents to be supplicated and importuned by our prayers. Sovereigns are the images of God upon earth; by what right should they complain if we treat them in the same way as our Father in heaven?' The Napoleonic minority in the Council began to tremble, and one of them said in an undertone to his neighbour, 'Alas, I had foreseen we should come to this.'[16] Now

---

[15] *Journal de Mgr. de Broglie.*
[16] *Ibid.*

or never Cardinal Fesch might have turned the scale irrevocably in favour of the Holy Father, and what might have followed if the Council had actually gone in a body to the Emperor to solicit his deliverance, we cannot tell, but it is improbable that Vincennes and other State prisons could have expanded to receive the whole episcopacy. The Primate, however, used consummate worldly tact on this occasion. The sentiments of Mgr. de Chambéry, and of those who had supported the motion raised by this prelate, he said, were his own, but the time was inopportune, as if the first and primary duty of a Council did not concern the Pope. To retain his own favour at Court, he smoothed down the element of opposition, and conquered the promptings of justice by a cold-blooded prudence. M. Bigot, who assisted at the congregations, without, however, joining in the debates, was performing despairing gestures for the benefit of the Primate during the speech of Mgr. de Chambéry. He, M. Bigot, had received particular injunctions from Napoleon against the propriety of the Council ever presuming to come to a resolution on its own authority, or addressing him by such a motion as the one in question. What a dilemma for an unfortunate Minister of Worship! But the words, and still more the policy, of Fesch, instead of nourishing the only safe course of acting, replunged the assembly into the discussion of such impossible questions as to whether the Pope possessed, or not, authority to change established discipline in a Church; if he could revoke what his predecessors have granted: if his censures with regard to temporal matters were not, *ipso facto*, null and void. The importance which the Emperor himself had attached to the address, in his impatience, was short-sighted, in that upon a matter of mere formality he evoked all manner of burning questions. It seemed as if the bishops never would come to an understanding as to how much or how little they would insert. Once, in discussing the Bull *Quum Memoranda,* Cardinal Maury declared that the Holy Father had, on the occasion of its promulgation, gone beyond his powers. He was peremptorily silenced by Mgr. d'Aviau, who was blessed with a deafness which rendered impervious the timid remonstrances of his neighbours. 'How can you say that the Holy Father exceeded his powers? You have not, then, read the decree of the Council of Trent, Session xxii. Chap. xi.? Is it not clear and precise enough? *Si quem clericorum aut laicorum, quacumque in dignitate, etiam imperiali aut regali, præfulgeat,* &c.

'This is true,' answered Maury somewhat dumbfounded, 'but we must understand each other. It is meant in the case of notorious sin or proved crime. Otherwise, where would be the independence of crowns?'

'Who will pronounce, then,' asked the Archbishop of Bordeaux, 'on the culpability of the act which has called forth the censure?'

'Opinion,' answered Maury.

Mgr. d'Aviau, who could no longer contain his feelings, threw upon the table, at which he sat as secretary of the Assembly, a copy of the Decrees of Trent, open at the page which acknowledges in the Popes the right of excommunicating sovereigns, exclaiming, 'Well, then, judge the Pope if you will, and condemn the Church if you can.'[17]

In spite of the assurance of Mgr. Duvoisin that the Emperor had 'seen the address and approved it,' the bishops finally determined to adopt one which was meant to have the effect of a middle course on the different parties concerned, for they neither withdrew all that

---

[17] *Vie de Mgr. d'Aviau, Archévêque de Bordeaux.*

their conscience did not approve, nor accepted completely what Napoleon would have imposed upon them. This was signed by the Presiding Prelate and by the secretaries. But the bishops had reckoned without their host: they were very much mistaken if they imagined that they were to have the last word in the matter. The Council was to understand once for all that its assemblies and discussions were to be submitted to the head of the State, and that nothing was to be done without his authorization. For the present, he required it to put an end to its 'idle debates,' and to find an answer to the Imperial Message, that is, to discover an expedient for providing bishops for the vacant sees. The Emperor put a term of eight days upon these weighty proceedings. A sensible mark of displeasure was his refusal to receive the Council officially at one of the Sunday receptions at the Tuileries. Several bishops went nevertheless to the palace, and met with a careless indifference or a studiously forced kind of courtesy. One of them spoke with emotion of the sufferings of Pius VII. 'Yes, he is a simple man,' said Napoleon. 'More than simple, he is a saintly man,' answered the Bishop of Como. Some of the Italian prelates loudly complained to the Emperor of the falsification of the famous addresses from their Chapters, which had covered the *Moniteur's* columns a few months previously. But the desired effect had been thereby obtained, and true to his ordinary tactics, the Emperor cared little about the rest. Perceiving a group of bishops in one of the drawing-rooms, he approached and said, 'It has been my will to make you princes of the Church, it is your duty to see that you are not mere beadles. The Pope refuses to execute the Concordat. Be it so: I care nothing for the Concordat.'

'Sire,' exclaimed Mgr. d'Osmond, 'your Majesty will

not tear up with your own hands the most beautiful page in your history.'

The bishops, was Napoleon's answer, had 'acted as cowards.'

'No, sire, for they have upheld the cause of the weakest.'

When Fesch objected to the unceremonious freedom of his reply to Mgr. d'Osmond, he silenced the Primate with the observation, 'that his only offence had consisted in his saying what his Eminence should have said.'[18]

The Council then was required to find an expedient to confer canonical confirmation without the Pope. It was a task for which it was wholly incapable, and after three sessions devoted to the question, the Commission of the Message (as it was called) acknowledged its own impotence in these words. 'The Congregation nominated by the Council to answer the message of his Majesty, is of opinion that the Council before pronouncing on the questions submitted to it, acting in accordance with the Canons and that which has constantly been the practice of the Church, must solicit of his Majesty permission to send a Deputation to the Pope, which shall expose to him the deplorable state of the churches of the French Empire and of the Kingdom of Italy, and be allowed faculties for conferring with His Holiness on the means for remedying such a state of things.'

On the 5th of July, Fesch carried this declaration, signed by himself and the members of the Commission, to his imperial nephew. He was received with an outburst of anger, and as for the bishops, Napoleon would soon show them their place. When the Primate alleged canonical reasons in defence of their conduct,

[18] *Vie de Mgr. d'Osmond*, p. 587.

the Emperor rudely answered, 'What! theology again! Where did you learn it? Be quiet; you are an ignoramus. In six months I should know more than you do.'

In this interview, he for the first time threatened to dissolve the Council, and why indeed should it be tolerated, if it defeated the sole end for which it had been convoked—the rendering of blind obedience to the imperial will. The Prefects should henceforth nominate to bishoprics, and organize a system of State religion, which, however, is only a natural consequence of the absence of the Pope. It was on receiving this intimation from Napoleon that Fesch is said by his biographers to have replied: 'If you wish to make martyrs, begin by your own family. I am ready to give my life to seal my faith. You may be quite sure that as long as the Pope has not consented to this measure, I, as metropolitan bishop, shall refuse to confirm my suffragans. I go further. If one of them in my default were to confirm a bishop of my province, I would excommunicate him on the spot.'[19]

After two hours of angry words between the Emperor and his uncle, Mgr. Duvoisin was announced. Napoleon saw him privately, and we may suppose that what followed was a suggestion of the Bishop of Nantes, acted upon by the Emperor. After saying to Cardinal Fesch, '*Vous*,' the bishops, '*n'êtes tous que des nigauds. Ce cera donc moi qui vous tirerai d' affaire*,' Napoleon called a secretary and dictated its decree to the Council, on the ground that the Concordat no longer held good since one of the contracting parties had broken his engagement, and that the Pope had positively agreed when he had received the Deputation sent by his Majesty, to confirm the bishops in six months. In default of His Holiness,

[19] *Vie du Card. Fesch.* Par l'Abbé Lyonnet.

the metropolitan bishop should have power to give the confirmation. It ran thus. 'The Council decrees: Firstly, That bishoprics cannot remain vacant for more than a year, and that in this space of time, the nomination, consecration, and confirmation shall take place. Secondly, That according to the Concordat, the Emperor shall name to the vacant sees. Thirdly, That six months at most after the nomination of the Emperor, the Pope shall give canonical confirmation. Fourthly, That the term of six months having expired, the metropolitan bishop shall, by the very concession of the Pope, be invested with power to consecrate, and shall proceed to the canonical consecration and confirmation. Fifthly, That this decree shall be submitted to the approbation of the Emperor to be published as a law of the State. Sixthly, That his Majesty shall be supplicated by the Council to allow a Deputation of bishops to visit the Pope, in order to thank him for putting an end, by this concession, to the misfortunes of the Church.' 'Take this, exclaimed Napoleon, when he had finished dictating, 'and now all is smooth.'[20]

The accounts from Savona in no way authorized the statement contained in this imperial bit of theology, and the document did in fact deceive the bishops. M. de Chabrol wrote word that the mental alienation of Pius VII. had indeed passed off, but to it had succeeded a melancholy calmness, and the Holy Father still protested against the concession which the Deputation had wished to enforce from him. It did not therefore seem likely that he would yield, but M. de Chabrol hinted at a probability of this. Napoleon was telling a carriage to move which had no horses. But Cardinal Fesch, who had spoken in a different tone at the beginning of the interview, and had even assured his nephew that he

[20] *L'Eglise Romaine et le Premier Empire*, t. iv. p. 328.

would 'make martyrs' if he sought to enforce his will, now gave another proof of his extraordinary flexibility of views. At its close, he was filled with admiration when he contemplated the Emperor's expeditious mode of despatching a thorny business. It is impossible to account for this change in the Primate, and for the small account which he made of the falsehood of the assertion as to the Holy Father contained in the readymade decree. Fesch probably possessed better than his brethren the secret of what had really passed at Savona, and was by no means ignorant of Napoleon's propensity to depart from the truth when his policy required it. The bishops on the Commission of the Message had no such knowledge. With two exceptions (Mgr. d'Aviau and Mgr. de Broglie) they voted in favour of the decree. They were beguiled at the first moment into doing so by the alleged concurrence of the Holy Father, but a few hours' reflection brought those of the number who were not sold to the Emperor to this logical conclusion : if Pius VII. had really made so great a concession, why were they apprized of the fact so late in the day? It was an awakening for Spina, Caselli, the Bishops of Tournai, Troyes, and Ivrea, and Cardinal Fesch acted so far loyally, that, whilst not retracting himself, he consented to the decree being once more put to the vote. It was then his disagreeable task to carry the new decision to Napoleon, and after he had assured his nephew beforehand that it would certainly pass at a great majority, the step was doubly hard. Their lordships of Tours, Trèves, and Nantes, refused to accompany the Presiding Prelate to St. Cloud, they evidently feared an explosion of imperial wrath. But the Council assembled might possibly admit what the Commission had rejected, and the Emperor made no difficulty in authorizing a General Congregation for July 10th. He wished all matters to be decided for the 14th. 'What is it,' he had asked his uncle, 'that specially displeases the bishops in the decree?' It was the question of making it into a law of the State. 'If it is that which troubles them, we can drop the subject. But nevertheless when it pleases me, I can still make it a law of the State.' This was a novel idea of concession. The Congregation of July 10th was unimportant, or rather it was abruptly brought to a termination by Fesch. The members of the majority in the Commission had decided to accept a very straightforward struggle against the competence of the Council to pronounce at all upon the confirmation of the bishops. But liberty in the combat was to be taken away, and an example after the fashon of Napoleon was to be made upon the prominent leaders of lawful opposition. On the 11th of July the Council was dissolved. On the 12th, at three o'clock in the morning, Mgr. de Broglie (Ghent), Mgr. de Boulogne (Troyes), and Mgr. Hirn (Tournai), were arrested in their beds, and conducted to Vincennes, where solitary imprisonment as severe as that inflicted upon the Holy Father was their portion. An upright conscience in those days was the best guarantee for the production of unlawful measures of compulsion. Mgr. d'Aviau escaped the same punishment on the ground brought forward by the executor of Napoleon's dangerous whims, that 'the Archbishop was a saint, and that all the world would be up in arms if violence were used with him.' It must have been the only case under the First Empire that a reputation of sanctity brought any advantage in a material sense. The same Minister of Police who spared Mgr. d'Aviau on account of his holiness understood immediately the damage which the imprisonment of these bishops would bring to the imperial cause. So with an utter disregard for truth, he actively spread abroad the report that the arrest of the three prelates was in nowise connected with the Council. The Emperor did not lend himself to these artifices, for Vincennes was his great resource, and he counted upon this severe measure for bringing the remaining bishops to reason. A few months earlier, the Chapter of Notre Dame had not feared to solicit the deliverance of its Vicar-General, M. d'Astros, but nobody was found to protest against the imprisonment of the Bishops of Ghent, Tournai, and Troyes. Does not the fact speak for itself, and prove the demoralizing effects on a great nation of a tyranny which forbade men to listen to the voice of conscience or honour? Not in vain has it been said that the Sovereign Pontiff is the guardian of all liberty.

Cardinal Fesch and Mgr. Duvoisin, who were intreated by the relations of Mgr. de Broglie to use their influence with Napoleon to bring about his release, proved inadequate to a task which any noble heart would have joyfully accepted as a refreshing office in the midst of so much ignominy. They feebly rejected the only honourable course which remained, and Fesch declared that if, as it was rumoured, the Council should be once more convoked, he would have to be fetched to preside at it 'between four fusileers,' for he would never consent to go of his own accord.[21] In the meantime, M. de Chabrol's epistolary activity did not diminish. In his letters to M. Bigot, he affected to believe, on what grounds it is impossible to gather, that the Holy Father might still be brought to adopt the Emperor's views, but one bit of good news that he was able to announce was the improvement in the Pope's health. By degrees he had almost regained it, and with a slight return of physical strength that mental calmness and peace which always distinguished Pius VII. in the midst of his greatest

[21] MS. le Madame la Marquise de Murat.

sufferings. Napoleon, supported by these assertions from Savona, actually meditated another edition of the Council. Three of the most tiresome opponents were lodged at Vincennes, and nine of the least obliging of the remaining ninety-two bishops, without counting Mgr. d'Aviau, had left Paris. M. Bigot seconded his master with great alacrity. Having attended at the deliberations of the Council, he had made his own observations as to those who might be brought to dishonest compliance, and acted accordingly. His mode of proceeding was not wanting in energy. After vigorously talking at the bishop whom he entertained with a private conference in his room, he asked his unfortunate guest to sign a formula of adhesion to the Imperial Decree. In most cases consent was given, but there were some noble exceptions. Mgr. Carletti had replied that the Pope alone could confirm bishops, and that he could not accept the decree in his diocese without scandalizing his flock. '*But nobody will know it,*' urged M. Bigot. ' My conscience will know it, and that is enough.'

' Do you think then that his Majesty is to depend upon the Pope for the confirmation of the bishops? It can never be.'

Mgr. Carletti made a movement which meant, ' then schism is inevitable.' The Minister, on the contrary, spoke of the concessions of His Holiness, of which he held the proof in his hand, and which ought to suffice. 'No,' answered the Italian bishop, ' it has neither the form nor authenticity that are indispensable.'

' You will be in a very small minority. The greater number has already signed.'

' In this case you have no need of my signature.' [22]

The success of M. Bigot's operations fully supported Napoleon's determination to reopen the Council, and

---

[22] *L'Eglise Romaine et le Premier Empire,* t. iv. p. 360.

Cardinal Fesch consented to preside over its last and feeble attempt at a Congregation, although contemporary history does *not* record that the 'four fusileers' were ever sent to fetch his Eminence. It took place on the 5th of August, and, for the first time, the negotiations at Savona were officially made known. The Archbishop of Tours read a memorandum on the scheme then deposited by the Deputation on the Holy Father's chimney-piece, from which scheme the Emperor had previously subtracted what displeased him. Cowardly submission was the order of the day. The decree, signed by Fesch and the secretaries, which miserably closed the National Council of 1811, ran thus:

'Art. I. In accordance with the spirit of the holy canons, the archbishoprics and bishoprics cannot remain vacant longer than a year; in this space of time, the nomination, confirmation, and consecration must take place.

'Art. II. The Emperor shall be entreated to continue to nominate to vacant sees in accordance with the Concordat, and the bishops nominated by the Emperor shall seek confirmation of our Holy Father the Pope.

'Art. III. Within the six months following the notice given to the Pope in the customary manner, he shall confer canonical confirmation according to the Concordat.

'Art. IV. The six months having expired without attainment of the Papal confirmation, the metropolitan bishop, or in his default, the oldest bishop of the ecclesiastical province shall proceed to confirm the bishop elect. In the case of the metropolitan bishop himself, the oldest bishop shall confer confirmation.

'Art. V. The present decree shall be submitted to the approbation of our Holy Father the Pope, and to this effect his Majesty shall be entreated to allow a Deputation of six bishops to visit His Holiness, in order to obtain his confirmation of this decree, as the only means of putting an end to the troubles of the Churches of France and Italy.'[23]

Fourteen bishops refused to sign the decree, but what did it signify to Napoleon? He had first created the evil, then convoked a council to remedy it, and because some of its members had resisted him, he had silenced them by arrest and imprisonment. The remedy was hopelessly ineffectual, because it positively added to the gravity of the situation. How could a body torn from its head present anything but a bleeding and mangled spectacle. In short, if a catechism could be written of the Council of 1811, might it not be summed up in these words of the royal Prophet: 'Except the Lord build the house, they labour in vain who build it.'

[23] *L'Eglise Romaine et le Premier Empire*, t. iv. p. 368.

CHAPTER XII.

From Savona to Fontainebleau.

'Et nunc, reges, intelligite: erudimini, qui judicatis terram.'—
Psalm ii.

A SOMEWHAT novel spectacle is offered by the negotiations at Savona which immediately followed the National Council. It is that of five Cardinals and eight bishops, partisans of the State rather than Fathers of the Church, who used all the influence of their position against the conscience of their Spiritual Head. At the first aspect of things, it would seem that Pius VII. had acted weakly, and it is a conclusion which is a general impression rather than an universal conviction. It would be a grateful task to reveal in some measure the disposition of mind of the Pontiff, whose sufferings can only be compared with the extent of his capability for loving. An act of weakness implies a sacrifice of duty, but this was the battlefield where the Holy Father had more than once declared 'that he would not be found wanting.' When his history gives us the notion of mental fluctuations, doubts, and anxieties long sustained, they were occasioned by a double cause; the peculiarly timorous nature of his mind with its humble deference for the opinion of others when he himself had not arrived at the truth in a question, and his critical situation at Savona. As far as might be, Napoleon had consigned him to a living grave, so that in his prison he partook of the state which places itself between earth and heaven. Prisoners are not dead, but can they be said to live when the greatest gift of God after air and sunshine—the liberty of their will—has been taken away. After the event it is easy for those who see debated questions in broad daylight to accuse others who struggled against a dense night of shortsightedness. It is easy to say Pius VII. was pusillanimous because he began by yielding to the solicitations of the Cardinals and bishops, but we are enlightened by the whole disclosure of the National Council, and the resistance of three bishops actually detained at Vincennes at a moment when some of their weak brethren (for here was an instance of real weakness), were trying to persuade the Sovereign Pontiff that he alone caused the troubles of the Church by a persevering opposition to Napoleon. From the day upon which the Holy Father clearly perceived the snare that had been laid for his unsuspicious ignorance, he became inflexible. It is a proof that he sought but knowledge of what was right and strength to do it. Often it was a weary search in a half light darkened by the head of the State and his agents, by Ministers of Worship, and Princes of the Church, and it was in this hour of dim twilight that the reproach of weakness attached itself to the memory of Pius VII. Let us exercise truer discrimination of men, and shrink from adding one drop of unjust blame to the chalice of a prisoner whose sufferings were aggravated by the fraud which was practised upon him to bring about his deviation from the right path. The Holy Father had often complained that he needed the advice of Cardinals to help him in the grave responsibilities which his charge and the nature of the times accumulated upon his head. Napoleon was prepared to grant this demand in the letter, it is true, but not in the spirit. The Council had established the ground of his proceeding, since in its surreptitious re-convocation it submitted its decision to the Papal approbation. To convey this to Savona was the affair of a second Deputation. To the courtier-prelates whose services never failed the Emperor he now adjoined five Cardinals, whose demeanour in the imperial marriage had earned for them the dishonourable appellation of *Red Cardinals*. In the case of the first Deputation in May, 1811, Napoleon had remarked too easy a propensity in the bishops to be moved by the force of great natural attraction united with suffering. They had done their work, but they had been involuntarily touched. In this case, experience made wise to some purpose, and the Emperor and his Minister, M. Bigot, managed so skilfully as to elicit a written promise from the Cardinals that they would not cease to press on Pius VII. an entire adhesion to the so-called Decree of the Council. If they succeeded, they were to remain at Savona as a counsel in further difficulties; if not, they were to return immediately to Paris.[1] The members of the Sacred College who consented to act this false part were Cardinals Roverella, Dugnami, Ruffo, Doria, and de Bayane, and their assistants were the Archbishops of Tours (Mgr. de Barral) and Malines, the Patriarch of Venice, the Bishops of Feltro, Piacenza, Pavia, Trèves, and Evreux. The Archbishop *in partibus* of Edessa, Mgr. Bertazzoli, who possessed the affection of the Holy Father, had been hunted up from a remote corner of Italy, sent for to Paris, the journey thither having been effected by means of policemen and prisons. The step was, as it may be imagined, preconcerted, and it succeeded as Napoleon had shrewdly foreseen. Mgr. Bertazzoli received a fright from which he never recovered, and was quite willing to adapt the influence which he possessed over the Sovereign Pontiff to the Emperor's views. Napoleon paraphrased the Decree in his own sense. It was to include the *See of Rome*, and he was so

[1] *L'Eglise Romaine et le Premier Empire*, t. v. p. 7.

firmly resolved to reduce the Pope to an instrument in his system that no religion, rather than one which owned Pius VII. as its visible Head, appeared to him preferable for France and Italy.[2] The Deputation opposed a feeble resistance to the notion of including Rome amongst the Emperor's prerogatives. He was obliged to yield the point, or at least to seem to yield in a matter which the bishops would not willingly have specified to their Spiritual Head. Beyond this they were to be inflexible, and to show no weakness, but to press for the Pope's entire adhesion, and to rest satisfied with nothing short of it. No detail was omitted by Napoleon, neither Cardinals of intelligence who were to minister in form at least to the often reiterated need expressed, nor the means of insinuation, which is exercised by a constant appeal to the heart and feelings from the mouth of an old friend, for this was Mgr. Bertazzoli's province. His tears and sighs were to reach 'that central seat of affection in the heart,' which the cold reasonings or the wily counsels of the others might have left unassailed. In short, the conscience and feeling of Pius VII. were to be unceasingly worked upon for a period of five months, from September, 1811, to February, 1812. If he resisted the influence of evil, it was surely by a superhuman strength. Physically he must have sunk under the insupportable burden, or a return of the terrible malady which had for one moment threatened him might have too well convinced the world of the extent of his mental anxiety. No familiar servant had been left to refresh his drooping hours, but the bribed doctor whose presence had become indispensable for the realization of Napoleon's plan.[3] His only visitor was M. de Chabrol, the zealous Imperialist, who talked theology after the fashion of his

[2] Lettre de l'Empereur à M. Bigot de Préameneu, 16 août, 1811.
[3] *L'Eglise Romaine et Le Premier Empire*, t. v. p. 21.

master, and brought his particular battery to bear upon the Holy Father when all others had succumbed to fatigue. When the Prefect of Montenotte, never weary of reverting to the charge, reproached Pius VII. with dulness of comprehension in not responding to the magnificent design of the Emperor to establish him at the Imperial Court, the Holy Father gently replied that he felt no vocation for such a position. Was it not possible that M. de Chabrol was himself deluded, for after all, there was perhaps an advantage for religion in persecution rather than in partaking of the splendid fortunes of a second Charlemagne. Rome had been chosen as residence by the Popes in preference to the Holy Land, and when in a vision St. Peter had met his Master and had asked Him whither He was going, our Lord had answered, 'To Rome, where I am to be crucified again.'[4] There was evident connection in the mind of Pius VII. between the Cross and Rome. Rome indeed without the Cross was possible, but the Cross without Rome was almost unbearable.

The Cardinals and bishops left Paris at the end of August, 1811, and purposely followed a different route in order to give the Deputation an appearance of spontaneous action which was to carry conviction to the mind of Pius VII. But the Emperor's agents at Savona, that knot of secret and political negotiators headed by M. de Chabrol, of which we have spoken, lorded it over the Princes of the Church, as if even in these points of detail the religious was always to submit itself to the secular element. Speaking of the tears shed by Mgr. Bertazzoli on seeing the Pope, M. de Chabrol remarked: 'He can certainly do a great deal by prayers and tears. The Pope's doctor shall see him (Bertazzoli), and I myself will cultivate him assiduously.' The Prefect was a gaoler,

[4] Lettre de M. de Chabrol à M. Bigot, 15 juillet, 1811.

and he never forgot his office. He caused Mgr. Bertazzoli to be lodged in a way that the Archbishop of Edessa could never visit the Holy Father without being spied by La Gorse, but which ended in his being summoned whenever his presence 'was required.' At the same time, De Chabrol thought it would not be prudent to allow others of whom he was not so sure to see Pius VII. alone. 'This might be managed without affectation.' Notwithstanding these arrangements, he wondered that two Cardinals (Dugnami and Ruffo) could venture even to remark on the imprisonment of the Sovereign Pontiff. 'What indeed does the Pope mean by liberty when he has kept in the house for a year and a half, being uselessly solicited to go out, knowing that he could, and that all those who wished to see him were free to approach his palace.'[5] It is evident that one of the least harmless effects of tyranny is to cause men to conceive an erroneous notion of liberty. Of the Cardinals deputed, Roverella was perhaps the one who possessed the most theological science. He had hitherto been thought to have thorough Catholic views, and in this respect might expect to win the confidence of Pius VII. 'The children of this world are wiser in their generation than the children of light.' For one moment the Holy Father had guessed the truth, namely, that these Cardinals were not speaking from the abundance of their heart, but that they had been designedly chosen to give him the perfidious counsel which they did. M. de Chabrol, the confidant of the idea, dismissed it summarily, and the attitude of the Cardinals themselves further dispelled all suspicion. They maintained a reserve which had every appearance of modesty, and affected great diffidence as to speaking on official topics with the bishops *sent by*

[5] Lettre de M. de Chabrol à M. Bigot, 1 sept. 1811.

his Majesty. When, in this conspiracy against conscience, they had produced all their prepared answers against the Holy Father's arguments, M. de Chabrol urged that they should leave him a little peace, during which he might fancy that the idea reached maturity in his mind after the 'slow fashion of the Court of Rome.' The Pope's acceptance of the Decree of the National Council was to be notified in a Brief addressed to the Cardinals, Archbishops, and Bishops assembled in Paris. The Deputation triumphed, for it had achieved the end of its mission, and was in comfortable expectation of Napoleon's expressions of gratitude for its services. With our knowledge of events, we possess a true estimation of the intrinsic value of the decree. It had been wrung from some seventy bishops, whose human part shuddered at the prospect of Vincennes, and whose dissolution as a deliberating assembly had been pronounced. The Holy Father was in utter ignorance of all this. He still thought that concession was quite compatible with his conscience, especially as he was falsely given to believe that he alone caused the troubles of the Church. He signed the Brief of adhesion on September 20th, 1811, 'his son, though rebellious, was still his son.'[6] A letter in his own hand to the Emperor accompanied it. Therein Pius spoke the language of happier times, for it was that of affection and gratitude for the counsel obtained. The Holy Father had been completely duped, and he thanked his deceiver with an innocent heart. We wish that we could prove that one faint whisper of sorrow raised its voice in Napoleon's breast when he read the letter, but his demeanour tells us that ambition and pride spoke louder there than contrition, the meek daughter of humility.

[6] L'Archévêque de Tours au Ministre des Cultes, 15 7bre, 1811.

The negotiating prelates and the menials of the conspiracy against Pius VII. might have long and vainly awaited an expression of gratification from the master whom they had thought to serve so well. Now, as in other circumstances of Napoleon's life, just when everybody made sure that things must come to an immediate crisis, the whole question of religion was absorbed by some outer political cause of greater material importance. He was a man of one idea, and threw himself into the interests of the moment which would best further this idea. Spiritual legislator, politician, warrior, simultaneously, he could not practise the functions of each with equal intensity, but at different periods of his career the one or the other qualification appeared uppermost. With the ardour of his genius, he imagined that the conquest of Russia was the event which was finally to triumph over Pius VII. When he once more returned to his people, so his heated imagination reasoned, covered with a glory which would have seemed fictitious, because so tremendous, to any other but Napoleon Bonaparte, how could an old man, weakened by imprisonment and suffering, any longer offer resistance to his notion of an universal Emperor ruling by the side of the universal Pontiff? No terms were good enough for him. He was almost affronted at the Brief, partly because it had been addressed to *his* bishops, the Pope ignoring his pretensions to be an Emperor-theologian; and as for the affectionate letter of the Holy Father, he decided that no answer would be the course best in keeping with his dignity. Forty-eight hours after their reception he wrote to M. Bigot from Flessingue, where he had gone to organize preparations for the fatal Russian Campaign: 'I send you the original Papal Brief. Keep it, and communicate its contents to nobody. I wish to find the bishops in Rome on my return, to see about what we can do. It seems to me that the wisest course would be this: to ignore the Brief entirely (as it is addressed to the bishops, it does not concern me), and to publish as the law of the State the first Decree of the National Council in which it declares itself competent, and the second Decree, causing the insertion of both in the Bulletin of Laws in order to render them obligatory. As to the Brief, it could be sent to the bishops for their administration without the smallest publicity. A Brief, however, cannot be issued unless it has previously been registered by the Council of State. The Council then must register it with the necessary reserve, if occasion offers, for the privileges of the Gallican Church; but as the Pope, instead of simply ratifying the Decree of the Council, has published a Brief after his own caprice, it seems to me that I have a right to add thereunto whatever I please.' Later he wrote again: 'I am in receipt of your letter of October 21, with the projected decree which it contains. I think that this decree would not cooperate towards re-establishing peace, that it would be better to publish the two Decrees of the Council as laws of the State, and to reject the publication of the Brief, that the disapproved passages may be curtailed. The Brief must be sent back to the Pope with a letter from you to one of the Cardinals, or even to Bertazzoli. The Pope must go through this. When the Brief comes back to us corrected, it will be published in its corrected state. It will thus remove all difficulties, but it would be ill-advised to publish a Brief with reserves. In this way division would be fostered. The truth of it is that the Church is experiencing a crisis. . . . Before the Pope is told of the difficulties and impediments which the Council of State raises against the publication of the Brief, care must be taken that he confirms those nominated to the vacant bishoprics. From now, the decrees of the Council shall be published as laws of the State, and the bishops shall receive confirmation. The Pope will be unable to obtain a final arrangement, to defy us, or to exercise any spiritual jurisdiction, unless he approves the Decrees of the Council. His position will be worse in proportion as he confirms all the bishops, and as he sees the decrees published as laws which must necessarily postpone the arrangement of his affairs for many years. I recommend the greatest secrecy. It would be well were the final resolution carried unanimously to proceed from the Council of State.'[7]

Napoleon's mode of attack is always the same, secrecy, and the suggestion of proceedings which were to come, as it were, spontaneously from his Government. But here he seemed to gloat over the aggravated suffering which would accrue to Pius VII. from this system of State religion. Was it a proof of true greatness to dictate conditions to the Sovereign Pontiff before he would condescend to accept the Brief which even in the eyes of the courtier bishops had fulfilled their most sanguine expectations? 'Inform the bishops of the Deputation,' he wrote once more to M. Bigot, 'that I shall answer no letter, nor come to any determination, as long as my bishops are without their Bulls.' As a further ignominy, he added the recommendation that the Pope should be apprized that the Decree was applicable to all bishops of that Empire to which the *States of Rome* belong.' At first sight, it may appear that these details go to disprove the fact that Napoleon's undisturbed attention was no longer given to religious matters. But if he had not already traversed fresh spaces in the flight

---

[7] Lettres de Nap. au Cte. Bigot de Préameneu du 30 7bre et du 30 8bre, 1811.

of his ambition, if he could only have said, 'My power is great enough, I will seek a glorious repose with my Empire of sixty millions of subjects,' must he not at least have rendered homage to the good will of the Holy Father? He wished not for peace or satisfaction. To the end of time, if he could have lived, he would have discovered that an Alexander still ruled in Europe besides himself, and that a Pius VII. exercised an authority over the hearts of men which made him only half a sovereign. His uncontrolled genius goaded him on to the region where Cambacérès had almost foreseen his destruction, and where the arms would literally fall from the hands of his soldiers. On the eve of his departure for Russia, he was not altogether sorry that his new requirements should leave the question between the Pope and himself still an open one. Far-seeing ambition overleaps itself, and Napoleon, whose victory over the Emperor of all the Russias was already an accomplished fact in his imagination, pictured to himself an elysium of earthly glory when he should in very truth reign over Europe. The Pope would be at his side to reproduce a perfect example of the line of conduct perceptible in those bishops and curés who accepted the pastorals and discourses furnished by the Ministry of Worship, praised the Emperor's allies, and execrated his enemies. Where would the Catholic Church have been after ten years of such a system? She would simply have ceased to exist, since truth is defined to be that which is, and error that which is not.

The Deputation at Savona, with a want of stability of purpose, which is a sure accompaniment of servility, after deeming it an indignity to the Holy Father to urge him too much respecting the bishoprics of the States of the Church, could now hardly express themselves rapidly enough in this sense. The situation of the

Church, they represented, was such as to require all possible submission to the Emperor's will: the nomination of a few bishops in the Roman States was not to be compared to the evils of protracted misunderstanding. What would be the consternation of the faithful, said these unworthy bishops, if they learned that the Pope had rejected the only means of putting an end to the troubles of the Church![8] But the cup of concession was filled up, and the Holy Father declared that in doing more he should 'dishonour his character in the eyes of all Catholics.'[9] In a letter dictated by the Emperor to M. Bigot for the Deputation, he declared, in language injurious to the Pope, that the Brief could not be accepted because it infringed the imperial authority, and contained certain expressions with regard to the Catholic Church that displeased his fine appreciation of men and institutions. It was once more the voice 'teaching with authority' that distressed him and upset his equilibrium. In the words of the letter, 'it would be supposing an astonishing inconsistency in his Majesty to imagine that he could allow the Black Cardinals to go to the Pope. If His Holiness wished to take counsel of the Emperor's enemies, even of those who had brought him to his actual pass by their perfidious machinations, there would be nothing more to hope. You can easily understand that under the circumstances it is impossible that the Emperor can answer the Pope's letter. Disputing with him on questions of ecclesiastical discipline, or addressing to him reproaches for the obstacles which he raises against a conciliation, would be at least useless. His Majesty awaits, then, the simple acceptance of the Council's Decree before he can believe

---

[8] Note adresse par M. M. le Cardinaux, 16 9bre, 1811.
[9] *L'Eglise Romaine et le Premier Empire*, t. v. p. 94.

that the first step has been taken towards an agreement.'[10]

Gradually the Holy Father was arriving at the truth in all its crudity, and for him it was peculiarly painful. By degrees he discovered that those who had been sent to counsel him in his hour of mental anguish, when a long imprisonment and its accompanying hardships had impaired his faculties of mind and body, were nothing better than imperial emissaries. The knowledge weakened considerably the concession contained in the Brief of September, for in all probability it would never have been sent if Pius VII. had known then what he knew later. When the Deputation did not disdain to urge the Holy Father, in an audience of December 13th, to compose a new Brief in a 'spirit of perfect conformity to the Emperor's wishes,' the Sovereign Pontiff came to the final resolution to be henceforth guided by his own lights. His path had been strewn for him by Princes of the Church with falsehoods and misrepresentations. A guilty silence had deceived him as to the real demeanour of the Council. He would trust to God and to his own conscience; they, in this dearth of all external help, would never fail him. The effect of the determination proved that it was an inspiration from above. It was with gentle affability that he even now received the members of the deputation and M. de Chabrol, who still tormented him with visits. The Cardinals and bishops had, however, exhausted their resources, and one of them, Mgr. de Barral, announced the application of the only remaining 'bit of artillery in their arsenal.' This was a farewell letter to the Holy Father, which caused him indeed some emotion but no indecision. The Prefect of Montenotte, who visited him whilst still under the impression it had produced, improved the occasion once

[10] Note pour les Evêques députés à Savone, 3 xbre, 1811.

more to tell him that he was making his 'cause odious by a resistance which attracted the sympathies of nobody.'[11] The Pope appeared to be pensive, and to the enlightened eyes of M. de Chabrol was lost in uncertainty, but Pius was in reality meditating an humble appeal to the heart of Napoleon. It was a step in keeping with the rest of his conduct, and humility is sometimes efficacious where all else is powerless. Forgetting the indignities with which his last letter had been met, and that he had vainly counted upon an answer to it, he resolved, if it were possible, to lay hold of any remaining affection and generosity in the Emperor. On the 24th of January, 1812, Pius VII. wrote to him directly in that perfectly loving language of which he possessed the secret. Before all things he demanded disinterested counsellors and free communication with the faithful. If this were conceded, he might agree to reconsider the Brief.[12] The answer, addressed to the Deputation, came from M. Bigot. It is itself its best comment. 'His Majesty deems that it is unfitting to his dignity to answer the letter of the Pope, of which letter I send you a copy. I must own to you confidentially that he deeply regrets having followed a different course in earlier days, and letting himself be drawn into a direct correspondence with the Holy Father. Indeed, all correspondence which falls to his Majesty between crowned heads consists of letters of courtesy and compliment. But letters of discussion and reproach are unworthy of his high rank. The Emperor will write to the Pope when he has compliments to pay; but in the case of painful questions, he prefers to make use of an official hand. It is a pity that the Pope did not follow the same course, instead of addressing his Majesty di-

[11] Lettre de M. de Chabrol au Ministre des Cultes, 16 janvier, 1812.
[12] Lettre autographe de Sa Sainteté Pie VII. à l'Emp. Nap., 24 janvier, 1812.

rectly in a letter, which he might have known beforehand could not be satisfactory in any way. . . . The Pope asks for free intercourse with the faithful; but how has he lost it? He has lost it by violation of all duties of peace and charity. He cursed the Emperor and civil authority by a Bull of Excommunication, of which the original was seized at Rome. Was it to curse sovereigns that Jesus Christ was crucified? . . . But the Emperor has allowed the Pope at Savona to communicate with the faithful. What use has he made of his ministry? He has sent Briefs which have been as remarkable for ignorance of the canons as for the spite therein manifested in order to stir up rebellion in Chapters. . . . He knows that a quantity of priests, otherwise good and honest people, are possessed with the notion of rendering him obedience. Has he taken any steps or showed the slightest inclination to make them cease to oppose their sovereign? Has he, through love of the truth, religion, or humanity, tried to extricate them from a position so painful? No: he has done nothing in this direction. There is consequently no warrant that he would not continue to abuse his ministry. What would be the use of accumulating scandal on scandal, and how can the Emperor be so ill-advised as to allow freedom to one who persists in forbidding Cæsar his rights! . . . It is true that the Pope has written two letters to the Emperor, and we may gather from this that he renounces an excommunication whose substance and form are not accepted by the clergy generally. . . . The only counsels which he demands are those of the Black Cardinals, and these he shall never have. If the Pope imagines that he can decide nothing without them, it is his fault. If, in consequence, he loses irrevocably the right of confirming the bishops, it is also his fault. Religion will be maintained without his help, and every day it is ostensibly proved that his intervention is unnecessary, as in default of bishops, the vicars-capitular administer the dioceses. He wishes to produce troubles. It is an erroneous calculation. The public is too enlightened. This guilty hope, which is proved by men to be a fallacy, and which religion and its Divine Author disavow, will one day be laid to the charge of the Pope. His Majesty pities the ignorance of the Pope, and compassionates a Pontiff who could have played so great a part, but has become the calamity of the Church. He could have retained all the advantages possessed by the Papacy; but owing to prejudices, and in spite of what the teaching of the Church would seem to prescribe, he preferred to break with His Majesty. Within three days of the reception of this letter, secure a simple acceptance, which shall include all bishoprics save that of Rome, or in default of such acceptance, leave Savona. . . . The only course open to the Pope is to be found in simplicity, confidence, and firm trust in the Emperor's loyalty. His Majesty understands these matters of ecclesiastical jurisdiction better than the Holy Father, and too well ever to stray from the path which he has traced for himself. In the false position wherein His Majesty sees the Pope to be, he is indifferent as to the acceptance of the Decree, for if the Pope refuses, he will be enveloped in the shame which is caused by ignorance. If His Holiness imagines that he is not sufficiently authorized nor enlightened by the Holy Spirit and the hundred bishops, why does he not resign, acknowledging himself to be incapable of distinguishing between dogma and the essence of religion, and that which is only temporal? If the Pope cannot make a distinction which is simple enough to be grasped by the most uncultivated seminarist, why does he not voluntarily descend from the

Papal Chair, and leave it to a man who is less feeble in mind and better principled than he, and who may repair at last all the evils which the Pope has brought about in Germany, and in all other countries of Christendom?'[13]

But the Deputation had already left Savona, and M. de Chabrol alone remained to communicate this insulting document to Pius VII. The Prefect proved equal to the task. The Holy Father showed signs of deep emotion when he listened to the invitation to resign. His gaoler says in rendering an account of the interview, "I saw that he was quite disheartened, and so agitated that his hand trembled a great deal . . . He was very much moved, but I do not think that he was shaken.'[14] Surely it was a peculiar and singularly heavy cross to be so persecuted by a man that he had really loved. The word persecution, however, faintly expresses the nature of that cross. Pius experienced every detail of suffering which was capable of wounding him to the very heart's core. Physical and mental privations, rebuffs, lies, and corruption were sorry means indeed to direct against the conscience of a Sovereign Pontiff, but ingratitude was the worst of all, and the sharpest thorn where each was sharp. Nevertheless more ignominy still remained. During the stay of the Deputation the Holy Father had enjoyed comparative liberty, that is, he had been allowed to use his pen, and to consult a few theological books. But now that nothing had been obtained of him, the order was reversed, and he returned to his former state of destitution. We can only say in his own words, that

---

[13] Lettre à MM. les Deputes, dictée par Sa Majesté l'Empéreur à M. Bigot de Préameneu, 9 fevrier, 1812. *Not* inserted in correspondence of Nap. I.

[14] Lettre de M. de Chabrol à M. le Cte. Bigot, 19 fevrier, 1812.

a man who cared not for life, when duty was at stake, attached but small importance to its accessories, even to such accessories as pen and ink, which from a certain point of view constitute actual necessaries, inasmuch as they are the natural means of entertaining that intellectual life, without which material existence is little worth. But such privations, when they are accepted willingly for the sake of conscience, become glorious, for the Cross of Jesus Christ envelopes in its own splendour the struggles which it sanctifies. In all probability, a deep political reason was at the bottom of the imperial order to transfer Pius VII. to Fontainebleau. As the ostensible motive, Napoleon alleged to Prince Borghese the presence of English cruisers at Savona, who were waiting to take the Pope either to Sicily or to Spain. A diligent and conscientious search at the Foreign Office, undertaken by a modern writer of reputation,[15] who has interested himself in the troubles of Pius VII., goes to prove that there were not the slighest grounds for the assertion. Probably it was made to cover the real motive, and this real motive—if we can pretend to any knowledge of Napoleon—was the desire, not subsequently realized, of having the Pope at hand when he returned a more than conqueror from the Russian Campaign. Pius VII. should be overwhelmed by glory, and render tardily, it might be, but still completely, homage to Cæsar, that kind of semi-adoration with which alone the Emperor in his foolish pride was to be pacified. Prince Borghese, whose speed on a former occasion, when the Sovereign Pontiff was concerned, had been excessive, could hardly fail to be equally over-zealous in this case. It was a question of transporting the prisoner of Savona almost through the

---

[15] M. le Comte d'Haussonville. See *l'Eglise Romaine*, &c. t. v. p. 153.

entire length of France. The Prince was ordered to insure two carriages for the Pope and his suite. The inseparable and indispensable Porta was to travel with the Holy Father, and the journey was to be accomplished at the greatest speed with only one stoppage at the Mont Cenis. The large towns, such as Turin, Chambéry, and Lyons were, as might be expected, to be passed through by favour of the night; and at all costs the Pope's incognito was to be preserved. The imperial summons reached the episcopal palace at Savona on the 9th of June, 1812, and found the Holy Father taking his siesta. MM. de Chabrol and La Gorse immediately awakened him with the intelligence that in a few hours he must set out for France. Pius displayed no surprize, and on the representation of the Emperor's officers that there would be some difficulty about his pontifical dress, he submitted to have the embroidered cross taken off his white shoes, and the shoes themselves to be smeared with ink. Quietly and patiently he put them on again still damp from the operation.[16] The gold cross on his breast, another mark of his dignity, was removed. He accepted the hat of an ordinary priest, and a kind of grey overcoat which belonged to him completed this strange accoutrement of a Sovereign Pontiff. In this costume, and still accompanied by his two gaolers, he was obliged to walk through the town of Savona, for only outside its walls a carriage in which Porta was to be his companion awaited him. In order to put the inhabitants of Savona off their scent, the most deceitful appearances were kept up for seven days within the palace. The Pope's dinner was regularly brought up at the accustomed hours, and the candles were lighted for his Mass. M. de Chabrol, moreover,

---

[16] Rilazione della traslazione di Pio VII. nel Castello di Fontainebleau. MS. at British Museum, n. 8,390.

made his special contribution towards the popular delusion by taking the trouble to visit the Papal apartments in his official costume, as if for one of those dreadful interviews which had perhaps not been the lightest infliction on Pius VII. at Savona.[17] For a few days the Holy Father's journey progressed favourably, but just before reaching the Mont Cenis, he fell dangerously ill. As it may be remembered, he was subject to an infirmity, which rapid travelling seriously aggravated. This time his suffering was fearful and evidently dangerous. He seemed to reach the Monastery of the Mont Cenis only to die, and the monks, as they watched him descend from the carriage, might well have thought that his hour had struck. General La Gorse's embarrassment was extreme. Between the serious state of the Pope and the imperative orders which he received to proceed at all costs, he resorted to the expedient of sending for a surgeon, whose appearance called forth the following heartless speech, pronounced in breathless haste: 'You are going to see a sick man, whose sufferings you must alleviate at any price. I need not tell you who he is. You will certainly know him; but, if you publish the fact of his presence here, it is as much as your liberty, perhaps your life, is worth.'[18] The surgeon, whose aid was thus invoked, managed to restore to the Holy Father sufficient strength to bear his misfortunes a little farther. A bed was arranged in the carriage, and he accompanied the Sovereign Pontiff with the instruments which might be called for a second time. Sometimes, out of compassion for his suffering state, La Gorse consented to a few hours' repose at postal relays. When at length Pius VII. reached

---

[17] Rilazione della traslazione di Pio VII. nel Castello di Fontainebleau. MS. at British Museum, n. 8,390.
[18] Lettre du docteur Claraz.

Fontainebleau,[19] he was worn out with fatigue and pain, but after the pattern of his Master, he found not whereon to lay his head at the imperial château. The concierge was wholly unprepared for his visit, and displayed some hesitation about opening the gates; but the worthy man was more humane than the sovereign whose orders he dared not disregard, till he had received further directions. He offered the Holy Father a small house which he owned near the palace, and here Pius VII. passed the first night of those three weeks of helpless pain and illness which followed his arrival at Fontainebleau. Must we not see more than an accident in this reception at the Emperor's château? He feared no army stretched in battle array, but he was afraid and jealous of the enthusiasm that the report of the Pope's coming visit might have caused. To avoid this, he chose to cause a journey so rapid as to endanger the life of his victim, and left the Vicar of Christ to be kept waiting at the door of his house until it pleased him to say, 'come in.' Fontainebleau was a shelter, but no repose beyond the material solace which its master vouchsafed at length to give to a body that was crushed with suffering. M. Bigot de Préameneu was the first amongst the Ministers to hasten to the palace, and the rest of Napoleon's agents did not fail to follow in his steps. They were naturally anxious, not so much to see Pius VII. (who, as we have said, was confined for the first three weeks to a bed of suffering), as to assert by this attention that they had no personal part in the treatment inflicted upon him. Surely no blame could be attributed to them if Prince Borghese and General La Gorse had brought the Holy Father to death's door by the punctuality with which they both had fulfilled the imperial orders. Individually perhaps they were

[19] June 19th, 1812.

not cruel, but must we not say that they were the most arrant moral cowards? How would posterity have viewed their behaviour had the Pope really died on the road? The agents, it seems to us, would have shared in an equal degree the guilt attached to the memory of their sovereign, for it may be questioned whether an ambitious and tyrannical will is much more repulsive than a servile and iniquitous obedience.

A new phase in the chequered life of Pius VII. opens at Fontainebleau. It was a trial of ease and magnificence quite opposed to the isolation and tame respectability of Savona, although the effect aimed at was precisely the same. Much was anticipated from the atmosphere of the place, and what indeed is harder than having many things, to be as having them not? Placed in the midst of splendour, and surrounded by prelates who had imbibed Napoleon's notions, far from disinterested counsels, and from those whom State corruption had not touched, the Holy Father would surely consent at last to fix his residence in Paris, to become in the glorious French Empire the first subject of its ruler. Then the Emperor would lend his sword to fight the battles of the Church, and the Pontiff would be at hand to hold up his arms in prayer over the combat. It was indeed a true picture of the Gallican idea realized, but had it succeeded the Catholic Church would have perished of inanition. Her life would have been pressed out by the weapon which was called hers, but wielded by her tyrant; or if she continued to exist as a mere human society, it would have been by a State mechanism lasting only so long as that which set it in motion. Waiting at the gate for admittance was a beginning worthy of the life to which the Emperor condemned the Holy Father at Fontainebleau. Pius occupied the same rooms (furnished now with great magnificence) as at the time of the Coronation. Mgr. Bertazzoli, Dr. Porta, and his household, were lodged close by, and other apartments belonging to the same wing were destined for Church dignitaries who should come to visit the Sovereign Pontiff. This latter arrangement was perhaps the most important link in the chain. As yet, it is true, no persuasion had been quite efficacious with Pius VII. Time, the sumptuous delights of an imperial residence, and the repeated representations of those who had already acted as tempters that 'present evils demanded a remedy *at any price*,' would doubtless in the end act favourably on the unfortunate Successor of Peter. But already the spectacle of the Pope enjoying the splendid hospitality of the Emperor must, so Napoleon imagined, in the opinion of the mass of the people who judged from superficial appearances, profit his cause to no small extent. He had formed a very erroneous notion of Pius VII., to which he clung with wonderful and incomprehensible tenacity. Cardinal Maury had orders to prepare his episcopal palace in Paris for the Papal residence. The gardens and stabling there were to be enlarged for the monk of former days, who retained under the tiara so much of the simplicity of a son of St. Benedict. A little book, the *Guide of Travellers at Paris*, was published at this time, less probably to direct the steps of wanderers in the great capital, than to apprize the Parisians themselves that they possessed a 'Papal palace' which had formerly been merely the archiepiscopal residence.[20] The Holy Father baffled all these grandiloquous designs. Fontainebleau was no less a prison than Savona had been, and he would never forget the fact. In the midst of

---

[20] *L'Eglise Romaine et le Premier Empire*, t. v. p. 171.

a luxurious opulence he chose poverty, guided by two thoughts—that of the Church which he had a mission to govern, but to govern independently of sovereigns, and the conviction that he must act on all occasions as it befitted a prisoner. Sorrow and love, those inseparable friends, who in their innate sufficiency can vie with the armies and wealth of empires, were at the bottom of his heart as weapons which no human power could ever wrest from him. Carriages and horses were vainly put at his disposal. He declared that he would never use them, nor did he even consent to walk in the gardens of the palace. Every day he said Mass in the room nearest to his sleeping apartment, instead of using the chapel of the château, where a certain amount of ceremony would have been indispensable. He refused no visit, but lent himself with patience to the conversation of all who came to Fontainebleau, save Cardinal Maury, whom he looked upon as an ungrateful deserter from the cause of right and justice. But his demeanour was most significant, and it was full of perfect nobility. The bishops of the Deputation were received with perfect courtesy indeed, but a marked reserve, and they found that they could make no further impression on the Holy Father's mind as to concession. His answer was invariably the same—liberty and counsel were wanting to him. A jeer has attached itself to two circumstances of the Pope's life at Fontainebleau. He was seen sometimes, with the simplicity of his early vocation, to mend his clothes himself; but is not meanness rather in the mind than in the occupation? Great and splendid acts have not made the best men, and the Apostle St. Paul, a man naturally of the most noble soul, did not disdain to recommend us to have an eye to the glory of God even whilst we are eating and drinking. The other foible reproached to Pius VII.

was, that although the palace possessed a magnificent library he never 'opened a book!'[21] First of all, the profane names of Diane de Poitiers and Gabrielle d'Estrées were not likely to awaken a Sovereign Pontiff's literary taste. He went elsewhere for the satisfaction of his mental needs. The successor of M. Emery furnished him with the works of St. Cyprian, a course of canon law, and other works, which happily prove that he had too sound a mind to allow it to be fed by the imperial library.[22]

Whilst the 'lust of the eyes and the pride of life' were applied to undermine the Holy Father's invincible resistance to the Emperor's desires, what was the condition of the Church in France? Naturally enough, it reflected the struggle which was pending, whereof secrecy was the great weapon. For twelve years now France had been borne down by a despot, and whatever opposition greeted the Emperor's interference in spiritual matters partook of the quality of the time. It rather resembled a constant grumble than an outspoken and frank complaint. The existence of the Brief of September, 1811, had been concealed as much as possible from the bishops, even from Cardinal Fesch, and M. Bigot had executed faithfully the Emperor's orders to allow no prelate, whether Italian or French, to remain in Paris. Good sense, after having vainly striven so long to obtain a reasonable hearing in Napoleon's mind, spoke feebly, but plainly enough to tell him that his pretensions were fast taking the proportions of a mania, and that the bishops might well refuse to be duped any longer, and pass over to the injured side. Silence then was the only course, if his ambition was to have full play in bringing immeasurable evils upon

[21] *Mémoires de Duc de Rovigo*, t. vi. p. 73.
[22] *L'Eglise Romaine et le Premier Empire*, t. v. p. 175.

the French Church, and if he was to prevent the fact becoming palpable that the sympathies of its bishops did not belong to him to the extent to which it pleased him to represent to the Holy Father. Indeed, this was so far from being the case, that his fertile brain discovered an expedient for striking a very material blow, not only at the bishops who possessed any tincture of opposition, but also at their subjects. His revenge should fall upon the young seminarists in dioceses where the pastors proved uncompliant, for in that age of flimsy military glory it was a matter of favour to escape the conscription. Wherever then the bishop displeased him, the youths destined to holy orders should be torn from their quiet seminaries and marched to useless battle-fields. He thus apprized M. Bigot of this bright idea: 'In your last memorandum I found requests for exemption from the military service for two hundred and thirty-nine students destined for ecclesiastical orders, and for the nomination of one hundred and forty-nine bourses in the seminaries. I have struck off from the list all demands relating to the bishoprics of Saint-Brieuc, Bordeaux, Gand, Tournai, Troyes, and the Alpes-Maritimes, because I am not satisfied with the principles manifested by the bishops of these dioceses. It is my will that you do *not* propose for these dioceses any exemption from service for the conscripts, nor any nomination for bourses, curés, or canons. Draw up a memorandum of the dioceses which ought to fall under this interdict. This mode of proceeding must be followed with the greatest secrecy. When bishops insist upon their nominations, tell them that I have refused my consent. Henceforth you will be responsible if you ask either for a bourse, or for exemption for a conscript, in a seminary where the principles of the Gallican Church are not carefully taught. Take precautions to be well informed, and begin by finding out what passes at your door in the diocese of Paris.'[23]

In March, 1812, the Sisters of Charity had fallen under the ban of Napoleon's displeasure, or rather, the long-gathered clouds then burst forth into a storm. M. Hanon, General of the Lazarists, had defied the imperial authority to the extent of not consenting to accept a superioress for his spiritual daughters who was imposed upon him. He was expiating his crime at Fenestrello, and the Sisters of Charity, who would have preferred suppression to state servility, fell victims to a wrathful order which Napoleon penned himself to his Minister of Worship: 'It is time to have done with this scandal of Sisters of Charity in rebellion against their superiors. It is my will to suppress those houses which, twenty-four hours after your warning, still nourish a spirit of insubordination. You must fill the suppressed houses not with sisters of the same order, but with another active order of charity.'[24]

It would be almost impossible to exaggerate the gravity of the situation which Napoleon fostered to so great an extent by refusing the Brief of September, 1811. To adopt a high and mighty tone with the Pope was one thing, but to place the French Church in a position which rendered the consecration of bishops an impossibility was quite another. Expedients had been employed, such as that of intrusting to the bishops nominated by the Emperor the administration of the diocese in the capacity of vicars-capitular, but the insufficiency of the measure was palpable. In some dioceses the chapters were divided, and the canons refused to admit the jurisdiction of the nominal administrator. Any man who has fully grasped the idea of

[23] Lettre de l'Emp. au Cte. Bigot de Préameneu, 22 8bre, 1811.
[24] Lettre de l'Emp. au Cte. Bigot de Préameneu, 3 mars, 1812.

government as carried out by the Catholic Church, must admit that this state of things was only the natural consequences of the imprisonment of the Holy Father. The fortunes of the Body which he governs always reflect his own. But what might cause our surprize in the midst of this anarchy and confusion is, that the French clergy did not protest in the mass against the unwarrantable tyranny of Napoleon. The impulse to throw themselves at the Emperor's feet and to demand the Pope's liberty had died away on the lips of the National Council, and that Assembly gives us the measure of resistance of which religion in France was then capable. The courage of the French bishops had failed collectively; what could be expected from them individually, save, as in the Council itself, a few cases of isolated opposition? Besides, it must not be forgotten that Gallicanism had prepared the situation and rendered possible a somewhat servile acquiescence in the whole consequences of the Gallican system. Many of them probably would have been at a loss to give a definition of what was exactly involved in this system, until they saw before them a sovereign who, with the respected name of Gallican liberties always in his mouth, was the greatest despot of modern times. It was a rude awakening for those who had made a pet theory of Gallicanism. In this thorny question of the bishops, the dioceses of Tournai, Ghent, and Troyes found themselves in the most singular position of all. The imprisonment of their bishops at Vincennes had at first been of the strictest kind. For a long time they had been ignorant of the close vicinity of Cardinals Gabrielli and di Pietro, and condemned to entire solitude, but finally, by an effect of imperial favour, they were allowed to meet again and to take exercise in a sort of public corridor. An emissary of the Minister of Worship drew from them a resignation which they had not the option of refusing, and M. Bigot lost no time in writing to their respective chapters that the 'episcopal see being now vacant, they must proceed to a new nomination of a capitulary administrator and of vicar-generals.' The Bishops of Tournai and Troyes had provided against such emergencies, but the Chapter of Ghent ventured to respond by a very concise and true statement to the notice of the Minister of Worship. 'It was not,' it said, 'the resignation of a bishop which made his see vacant, but the acceptance of such resignation by the Sovereign Pontiff. If the canons took upon themselves faculties which did not strictly belong to them, it would cause great disquietude in the minds of the faithful. The clergy of the country, attached as it was to the principles and customs of the Church, would not submit to the measures taken by vicar-generals who were nominated under such circumstances. Disobedience would destroy the authority of the new administrator, and division between pastor and flock would infallibly follow.'[25]

This chapter raised a difficulty which could only be obviated by a personal statement of Mgr. de Broglie. Imperial clemency had commuted Vincennes into exile to a town situated at forty leagues from Paris for the three bishops, and Beaune had been assigned to that of Ghent. Before setting out, the captives were apprized that they must sign a written promise against entertaining any correspondence whatever with their diocesans, and they were obliged to consent. Napoleon hoped by this measure to reduce to silence the tiresome Chapter of Ghent. But the trials of its bishop were not over, for in this strange persecution it was Mgr.

---

[25] Lettre de M. M. les Members du Chapitre de Gand à Monsieur le Cte. Bigot, 27 8bre, 1811.

de Broglie who played the chief part, probably because public opinion attached to him the honour of having led the opposition in the Council. The vigilant Minister of Police discovered that at Beaune a merchant from Ghent had been sent by the chapter to see Mgr. de Broglie. It served as a pretext to banish him outside the pale of human life to the lonely Isles of St. Margaret, where the existence of that mysterious being, the Man of the Iron Mask, had smouldered away in the shroud of secrecy. It was an extraordinary destiny for a bishop, and a peculiarly painful trial for one of Mgr. de Broglie's tendencies. Brimming over with intellectual ardour and life, he possessed that nervous temperament which renders solitude so prejudicial. To languish at forty-five, condemned to entire inaction in the terrible dungeon which had hidden a great and fearful State secret, required all the fortitude which conscience and innocence could supply. The prelate, whose life was thus darkened in that inaccessible rocky fortress, put into practice one of the most difficult precepts of Gospel morality. He not only forgave Napoleon, but he still wished him well in that sweet spirit of charity which knows no wrath.[26]

To counteract measures such as these the Emperor needed to possess a magic sword, for much is overlooked in a man whose banner attracts constant and brilliant success. But Napoleon's glory had reached its culminating point. It waned just when he most required it. On the 18th December, 1812, he returned a fugitive to his capital. Fire and ice were doing their work amongst his soldiers in Russia and Poland, and he himself came back alone. It was the beginning of the end.

[26] Lettre de Maurice de Broglie ancien Evêque de Gand à M. le Cte. Bigot, 11 xbre, 1811.

CHAPTER XIII.

Greatness in Humility.

'Ex petra martyris fortitudo.'—S. Bern. *in Cant.*

THE touchstone of greatness in those who occupy the high places of the religious and social world is perhaps the capability of acknowledging a truth which everybody knows—that they are not impeccable—as often as truth and conscience call for the acknowledgment. Pius VII. went through this ordeal. The struggle against encroachment of the State had been as long as his pontificate. In a moment of physical weakness the pressure exercised by importunate and false representations became too strong, and he said that 'yes' which, if it had been a sustained instead of a momentary acquiescence, would have gone far to sacrifice a prerogative of the Holy See necessary to the Church's independence, and to allow an intruder entrance into her sanctuary. Was not the Concordat of Fontainebleau the last link in the fettering chain which Napoleon sought to hang about the limbs of the Sovereign Pontiff? Pius VII. was not free to accept servitude for the whole Church. His subsequent conduct showed that he felt that in so doing he would have committed a great sin. When in the depths of his physical weakness and discouragement the voice of a true friend pointed out the possibility of making amends for a momentary and unlawful concession, the

Holy Father grasped the hope with all its humiliating consequences, as if it alone could restore him to life.

The hour-glass of Napoleon's glory was fast running down. The result of the Russian Campaign had produced both terror and relief; for if it is strange to class two such different sentiments together, it is no less true that they existed throughout the French Empire. They who had fancied Napoleon to be invincible, and had worshipped him in a measure as a kind of national type of earthly greatness, awakened to the fact that their hero did not possess the magic sword Excalibur after all. But in the annexed provinces the populations probably sighed in secret for deliverance. Their different nationalities had been suddenly swallowed up, and they were added as French subjects to a new and huge empire, the particular quarrels of whose ruler they were expected to adopt with the warmth and zeal which hereditary feuds might have claimed. The Pope had replied to Napoleon's demands by a *non possum* which had cost him years of imprisonment. Nations weak where he was morally strong had no power of resistance, and suffered themselves to fall under the Napoleonic system, simply because they could not help it. Perhaps, too, the aspect of the religious horizon gave them reason to hope for an approaching release. A dark and heavy pall stretched from Fontainebleau over every member of the Catholic Church. Thirteen Cardinals exiled to various provincial towns under the supervision of the police expiated the homage which they had rendered to the prerogatives of Pius VII. Three bishops who had been Fathers of the National Council shared the same fate. A number of priests were detained in Fenestrello and other State prisons on similar pretences, and a great many dioceses languished for want of pastors, because Napoleon willed the evil and would not will the remedy. In Italy things looked even worse. Rome, the centre of the Catholic world, was reduced to the rank of second city in the French empire: the convents and monasteries were despoiled: a large proportion of bishops and ecclesiastics had been carried off by violence to France, because they echoed the *non possum* of the Pope. Some of the number were silenced by Fenestrello; others—and perhaps it was the majority—had been banished to Corsica. The very darkness of the religious atmosphere may have raised hopes that daylight would soon break, for, if we may so speak, Almighty God seems to take a certain pleasure in glorifying His own cause in a manner which impels men to exclaim, Surely His Finger is here. He reduces all things to powerlessness and silence, then He acts. Worldly prudence and State policy had hitherto been the sole guides to Napoleon with regard to the spiritual power, and so it was to the end. The first touches of adversity gave him the measure of the real worth of the men who surrounded him. To be feared and to be obeyed he needed prosperity, for his government was a despotism, whereof all the strength consisted in success. Losses of men and disagreement between generals and soldiers, which had followed upon Napoleon's arrival in Paris, rendered him inclined to use any means of securing for his cause the almost indispensable mediation of Austria. In a word, he, who not a year earlier had fancied it even beneath his dignity to answer one of Pius VII.'s most paternal letters, judged it now politically necessary to re-open negotiations himself with the much-abused prisoner of Fontainebleau. At Dresden, whence he had ordered the translation to France of the Sovereign Pontiff, he had scouted the feeble remonstrances of the Austrian Emperor as to the impropriety of his dealings with the Head of the Church.

The actual crisis, however, was such as to make him sacrifice all personal vanity to his ambition. At any cost the alliance of the Emperor Francis must be maintained. Perhaps, too, in approaching the Holy Father once more Napoleon obeyed that secret instinct in him which was the direct contradiction of his outward conduct. Over and over again he had proclaimed to the world that religion could very well flourish without the co-operation of Pius VII., yet facts and his own sagacity belied the assertion. There were two men in Napoleon; one had profoundly religious instincts, the other assumed indifference and freethought as to any creed. His whole career as a sovereign had been affected by the deep feelings of the first, whilst the superficial language of the second had so made itself heard as to seem even to be predominant.

The insignificant pretext of the beginning of the year 1813 served as an excuse to Napoleon for the renewal of negotiations with Pius VII. In the letter which he addressed to the Holy Father on this occasion, he begged the Pope to believe that his feelings of respect and veneration were independent of any outward event or circumstance. Mgr. Duvoisin was charged to treat with Pius VII. The primary scheme of the Concordat of Fontainebleau was perhaps the most audacious bit of diplomacy ever submitted to the eyes of a Sovereign Pontiff. It is just what we might have expected had Napoleon conquered Alexander; but his glory was now on the decline, success was gradually yet perceptibly leaving his banner. How can we account for the arrogance of the conditions which at this eleventh hour he thought fit to lay before Pius VII.? The presence of the two sides in his character, which we have mentioned, is a little explanation. In accordance with his policy, it would have ill become him, in the face of possible adversity, to come down before men from his lofty pretensions; or rather, was it not worldly wisdom to assume a haughty tone, more especially at that moment when big words were to supply the place of material fortune in a losing game? The principal features of the projected treaty presented by the Bishop of Nantes were these. Before their coronation the Popes would be required to swear that they would neither do nor command anything contrary to the Four Propositions of the Gallican Church. They would only nominate to one-third of the Sacred College. The nomination to the remaining two-thirds would be the right and the privilege of Catholic sovereigns. Pius VII. was to condemn by a solemn Brief the conduct of the Cardinals who had refused to assist at the Emperor's marriage with Marie Louise, but by signing the said Brief themselves they might hope to be taken back into imperial favour. Cardinals di Pietro and Pacca (the author and promoter, be it observed, of the Bull *Quum Memoranda*), were alone to be excluded from the treaty, and banished for ever as counsellors from the Holy Father's side. The Papal residence was to be fixed at Paris, with a revenue of two million francs, raised on his former territory. The Emperor reserved for himself the exclusive nomination of the bishops of the Roman States, and in every case he stipulated that six months should be the extent of delay for Papal confirmation. This period having expired, the metropolitan bishop would have full right to confer it.[1]

Before going any further, let us see what was the exact state, both from a moral and a physical point of view, of the Pontiff who listened in troubled grief to the proposed treaty as it fell from the lips of Mgr. Duvoisin. The imperial palace covered over a new Savona. The Vicar of Christ, who was still to be beguiled, if possible,

---

[1] *L'Eglise Romaine et le Premier Empire*, t. v. p. 216.

into accepting a false position, was there in his strength and in his weakness. Five Cardinals, four of whom had acted as members of the Deputation to Savona in 1811, were there with Mgr. de Barral and the Bishops of Trèves and Evreux. Mgr. Bertazzoli was not wanting, and Dr. Porta continued his paid services. Probably they all knew as well as the chief negotiator, Mgr. Duvoisin, that Pius VII. was physically unfit to sustain much anxiety of mind, and knowing this they still contended for the most favourable moment of obtaining a victory which his weakness would greatly facilitate. The Bishop of Nantes wrote to M. Bigot on January 13th, 1813: 'The Pope is in a very agitated state. He does not sleep. His health is very much shaken. At present I consider that he is not in a state to bear a discussion. He has but small confidence in those who surround him. He persists in saying that his great wish is to satisfy the Emperor, but that his conscience will not allow him to decide by himself, being a prisoner without counsel. But notwithstanding this, I must have an answer. I am watching for the moment when I can ask him for it without causing him too great emotion.'[2]

This was a more important communication than it appears to be at first sight. It proves that Napoleon and his emissaries were resolved to conquer the opposition of Pius VII. by foul means if not by fair, and that it mattered little to them whether he whom they thus persecuted suffered and died under the rack of their importunities. Mgr. Duvoisin still hesitated to request a reply, out of a little remaining feeling of delicacy and consideration for the health of the Holy Father, but no such scruple was shared by the Emperor. Instead of compassionating the weakness which was his own work, he resolved to drag from the Pope's disarmed and feeble

[2] Lettre de l'Evêque de Nantes au Ministre des Cultes, 13 janvier, 1813.

grasp the consent so long withheld, but which now more than ever was indispensable to his scheme for self-glorification. It would not indeed be just to lay all the fault of the Concordat of Fontainebleau on Napoleon, for Pius VII. afterwards admitted that if he had listened faithfully to the voice of his conscience, he would have remained inflexible. The precise point of the question lies in the extent of the physical weakness which, according to Mgr. Duvoisin himself, rendered the Pope unfit to bear a mere discussion. No doubt the Holy Father possessed, strictly speaking, sufficient strength still to bear up against unrighteous demands, for after the event he was able from the depths of his soul to deplore his fault. But who of the two is most worthy of our condemnation, a Pontiff yielding in a great measure from excessive suffering of mind and body, or an Emperor taking advantage of the ravages he had caused to insure the Papal signature to a treaty wherein all forms usual on such occasions were disregarded? Napoleon was aware of the charm which he could exercise over Pius VII. A day or two after the reception of Mgr. Duvoisin's letter, on January 18th, he was hunting in the woods of Melun. Suddenly, in the middle of the day, he announced his intention of visiting the Pope at Fontainebleau, and caused a post-chaise to be brought for the purpose. It was another of the preconcerted scenes which was to have all the appearances of a spontaneous whim indulged in on the spur of the moment, but the presence of Marie Louise, who had been invited beforehand to go to Fontainebleau at the same time, attests the scheme. Eight years before, Napoleon had confronted the Holy Father in a hunting costume, which had spared his pride under its unceremonious and not fortuitous garb. Then it had been the prelude to numberless humiliations and indignities. What would it be now? Did Pius VII. ask himself the question? When the imperial huntsman entered his apartment, night had overtaken the wintry day, and the Holy Father was talking after his evening repast with the Cardinals and bishops who lodged in the palace. He was pleased to see Napoleon, and those who were in the room with him hastened to leave him in undisputed possession of his illustrious guest. Napoleon embraced him with every mark of affection, but all serious discussions were postponed till the next day. The Holy Father was nevertheless gratified by these outward demonstrations, for if the Emperor pretended to attribute his determination to the undue influence of counsels, he quite honestly imagined that the ill-treatment which had been inflicted upon him was in part the work of evil-minded subordinates. This accounts for the pleasure with which he spoke of Napoleon's greeting and embrace. He, indeed, suspected no guile, and did not understand what the visit could mean.[3] The serious work of the business began next day with the harassing private conferences to which Napoleon subjected him. During these interviews the primary scheme of the Concordat of Fontainebleau was considerably modified, not, as it has been popularly reported, at the price of unbecomingly rude usage of the Holy Father. When questioned as to this fact, Pius VII. replied that the Emperor had been 'guilty of no such indignity, but that his tone had been haughty and disdainful, accusing himself, the Pope, of great ignorance on all religious matters.' Though little of what really passed during these five days of incessant private conference is known, the result has transpired, and it is called the fatal Concordat of Fontainebleau. The time that was not occupied by Napoleon's visits was employed by the Cardinals Ruffo, Joseph Doria, Spina,

---

[3] Artaud, *Histoire de Pie VII.* t. ii. p. 320.

Dugnami, de Bayane, as well as Mgr. Bertazzoli, in urging Pius VII. to consent to the Emperor's demands. 'If they were in his place,' was the remark which was always on their lips, 'they would not hesitate for a moment to sign the document, thus by a final concession putting an end to the troubles of the Church.' No doubt this language determined the point. Pius' health was deplorable, and his very physical weakness served the designs of his enemies. Conscious of his want of vital force and energy, he had repeatedly asked for disinterested counsel, for the admonishing voice of one of his true friends to stay him in his hour of need. He foresaw, perhaps, where Napoleon's persecution was to culminate, and the long chain of sufferings which would end by his fall. When the powers of the world had tried his body and soul in the slow fire of deprivation of liberty, with all its accompanying sufferings, they would triumph over their victim by obtaining his signature to the Concordat of Fontainebleau. Did the Holy Father anticipate this when he prayed that he might not be left alone in the fight? His yearning to see his exiled friends once more, the modifications which Napoleon consented to make in the original treaty proposed by Mgr. Duvoisin, together with the understanding that the articles were the basis of a final arrangement rather than that final arrangement itself, and the entreaties of the Cardinals, all these things worked upon the sensibility of the Sovereign Pontiff. After the event, Napoleon proved that whatever he had previously proclaimed as his intentions, his sole aim in the matter had been to possess himself of the Papal signature. He consented, however, to repeal the stipulation concerning Gallican liberties, the intervention of Catholic sovereigns in the nomination of Cardinals, and the very gratuitous and indelicate blame he had attached to the persons of di Pietro and Pacca. Moreover, he left the disposal of the six suburbicarian bishoprics once more in the power of Pius VII. Thus modified, the text of the Concordat was as follows.

'His Majesty the Emperor and King and His Holiness, wishing to put an end to the misunderstandings which have arisen between them, and to provide against various difficulties of ecclesiastical discipline, have agreed to the following articles as the basis of a final arrangement.

'I. His Holiness will exercise the Pontificate in France and in the kingdom of Italy in the same way and external form as his predecessors.

'II. The ambassadors, ministers, and chargés d'affaires of different Powers at the Papal Court, and the ambassadors, ministers, and chargés d'affaires that the Pope may have with foreign Powers, shall enjoy the same immunities and privileges as the Diplomatic Body.

'III. The domains, which the Holy Father possessed, and which are not alienated, shall be exempt from all taxes. Agents or chargés d'affaires shall administer them. Those which are alienated shall be made good by a revenue to the amount of two million francs.

'IV. Within the six months following upon the customary notification on the nomination of a bishop by the Emperor to the archbishoprics and bishoprics of the Empire and of the kingdom of Italy, the Pope shall confer canonical confirmation, according to the Concordats and in virtue of these presents. The metropolitan bishop shall proceed to the preliminary information. The six months having expired before the Pope confers confirmation, the metropolitan bishop, or in his default, or in the case of the metropolitan bishop himself, the bishop of the most ancient see in the province shall proceed to confer confirmation on the bishop elect, so that no see need remain vacant more than a year.

'V. Whether in France or in the kingdom of Italy, the Pope shall nominate to such sees as shall be subsequently established by mutual consent.

'VI. The six suburbicarian bishoprics shall be re-established. The Pope shall nominate to them. Possessions actually existing shall be restored, and measures shall be taken with regard to those that have been sold. On the death of the Bishops of Anagni and Rieti, their dioceses shall be united to the above sees, conformably to the agreement which shall take place to that effect between his Majesty and the Holy Father.

'VII. With regard to bishops of the Roman States who are absent *through circumstances from their dioceses*, the Holy Father shall be free to exercise in their favour his right of giving bishoprics *in partibus*. A pension, equal to the revenues which they possessed, shall be given to them, and they may be nominated to vacant sees either of the Empire or of the kingdom of Italy.

'VIII. His Majesty and His Holiness shall opportunely concert together the reduction to be made, if necessary, in the bishoprics of Tuscany and the district of Genoa, as well as those that may have to be created in Holland and in the Hanseatic Departments.

'IX. The Tribunals of the Propaganda, the Penitentiary, and the Records shall be established wherever the Pope resides.

'X. His Majesty restores his favour to the Cardinals, bishops, priests, and laymen who have incurred his displeasure in consequence of actual events.

'XI. The Holy Father agrees to the above-stated articles out of consideration for the present state of the Church and out of the confidence which he feels that his

Majesty will grant his imperial protection to the numerous needs of religion in these our times.'[4]

A great orator once said that only oaks and monks are eternal.[5] But Napoleon here measured himself with the Church, as if his dynasty, dating from yesterday, possessed the same vital force that she does. On the 25th January, 1813, the formality of signing took place, and the cardinals assisted at this final interview. But it would have been well for their honour had their names been free from all complicity with the Emperor's extravagant demands. Having adopted Napoleon's views with an intensity of zeal which could leave him nothing to desire, they scrupled not to calm Pius VII.'s manifest hesitation by assuring him that the treaty was a mere preliminary, and that it would be kept quite secret till the dispersed Cardinals could meet and discuss the whole matter. Like the Sovereign under whose banner they had passed after deserting the cause of truth and justice, they cared little what arguments they used, provided the desired end was attained. Before apposing his signature to the document, Pius VII. cast a glance full of trouble and disappointed hope at these wretched counsellors. He looked for some one who would echo aloud the secret voice of his heart and conscience, and who would uphold him in that *non possum* of his office which was ready to burst from his trembling lips. In his weary state it was a last appeal to those whom Napoleon had practically made deserters to the kingdom of this world, while they were officially princes of the Church, whose rights they unworthily sacrificed. The Cardinal who occupied the place nearest to the Holy Father silently bent his head; and Pius VII., who saw that his mute language had been understood, as silently

[4] *Histoire de Pie VII.* t. ii. p. 323.   [5] Lacordaire.

accepted the pen from Cardinal Joseph Doria, and signed the Concordat of Fontainebleau. Napoleon, who kept his eye fixed on the Pope, fearing as it were to see his prey escape, together with Marie Louise, was present at the scene. It may be remarked that he attached little weight to formality, and that his victory consisted after all in a treaty wherein, contrary to acknowledged custom, the two sovereigns that were negotiating signed the same document. Even then the Emperor had misgivings that a retractation might follow, and he therefore took steps to prevent this possibility by signing immediately after the Pope, and causing the Concordat to be published almost before it was dry, but in vague terms as an agreement important to religion which had been effected between himself and the Sovereign Pontiff. The Austrian Emperor was apprized of the fact in breathless haste, and M. Bigot received orders to cause the Bishops to sing a *Te Deum* in thanksgiving for the auspicious event.[6] On the day following its consummation, Napoleon, as a public recognition of the services of Cardinals Ruffo and Doria, conferred upon them the decoration of the Legion of Honour, and presented the other members of the Sacred College and Mgr. Bertazzoli, who had proved useful, with a handsome snuff-box, ornamented with his own portrait and enriched with large brilliants. It was another means of proclaiming officially the great importance in his estimation of the act accomplished. For three days after the event of January 25th, during which Napoleon prolonged his stay at Fontainebleau, the Holy Father bore up against his emotion. But when the Emperor had hastened away to bestow his much-engrossed attention elsewhere, a deep and settled melancholy once more became visible in Pius VII. It fast

---

[6] Instructions dictées au Ministre des Cultes, 24 janvier, 1813. *Not* inserted in his correspondence.

took the proportions of the appalling sadness, the presence of which M. de Chabrol had signalized on a former occasion at Savona. With some timorous souls conscience adopts this means of asserting its claims. In the midst of the factitious joy fed by the imperially-ordered *Te Deums*, the Holy Father, the chief actor in the piece, was the prey to mortal anguish. A vista of the consequences of the responsibility which he had assumed was constantly before his eyes. But the new Concordat had opened the iron gates of Fenestrello and Vincennes, as far at least as the faithful Cardinals were concerned, and they hastened to the feet of their Spiritual Head. After the burden of the day and of the heat he had sunk exhausted at the eleventh hour. They would help him to rise again, and to redeem by a touching act of humility the dereliction of duty produced by suffering. Gabrielli, di Pietro, and Litta were the first to arrive at Fontainebleau. The right of remonstrating with the Holy Father was certainly theirs, for they had truly shared his troubles. Their respectful reproaches fell like the voice of God on the expectant ear of Pius VII. What they said was an echo of his own conscience during the sleepless nights which he had passed since the 25th of January. It had told him that he had assumed an unwarrantable responsibility in yielding to concessions destructive of the jurisdiction of Christ's spiritual kingdom, and in renouncing the Patrimony which belonged to Peter and his successors. In his remorse the Pope judged himself unworthy to celebrate the Holy Sacrifice, and added this voluntary privation to all the others which he suffered by the will of another. Is it too bold to assert that, had the mass of the French nation been enlightened as to the particulars of the Concordat of Fontainebleau, the *Te Deum* would have ill expressed the nature of their feelings. The journey of

Pacca from Fenestrello to Fontainebleau seems, by the reception with which he met, and the conversation which he had with fervent Catholics, to prove that they had a suspicion that the new treaty savoured both of foul play and unlawful concession. Although the Cardinal was a State criminal hardly escaped from prison, to use his own words, he met with great enthusiasm, and at Lyons the inhabitants would have wished to keep him longer within their walls, but with a true Catholic spirit they urged that he should join the Pope as speedily as possible, to try and extricate him from his dangerous position.[7] In the same city Pacca mentions, with wonder and admiration, a discourse addressed to him at a time, he says, of persecution in a crowd of people where Government spies must certainly have found a place. 'We kiss your chains,' were the preacher's ardent words. 'We look upon you as a confessor of the Faith, who have suffered for the cause of Jesus Christ. You, a minister of the Head of the Church, will tell him that we wish to live united and obedient to him.' It is true that persecution had strengthened the right, and that the greeting bestowed upon one of its victims surpassed that which a Cardinal arriving at Lyons in the normal state of things could have expected. As Pacca approached Fontainebleau, he was struck by the silence and solitude of the place, which rather resembled, he says, another State prison than a regal palace. In point of fact, it was nothing more. Meeting nobody of whom he could ask an audience with the Holy Father, he sent his servant before him, to try and get some information out of what seemed this deserted residence. Pacca was invited to go in his travelling dress to the Papal audience; and when at last he reached the Pope's apartment, he was shocked to find the change which had come over

[7] *Memorie*, t. ii. pp. 185, 186.

Pius VII. He looked quite broken down, but rather by sorrow than age. The eyes of the Holy Father were sunken, as if neither hope nor energy existed any more for him. Pacca received a formal embrace, accompanied by the observation that he had not been expected so soon. The Cardinal replied that he had hastened to have the consolation of expressing verbally the admiration which the Pope's heroic constancy in so long and severe an imprisonment caused him.

'But finally,' was the Holy Father's cry of grief, 'we have sullied our conscience. Those Cardinals dragged me to the table and forced me to sign.'[8]

The audience ended by a cold intimation to Pacca to retire to make way for the French bishops. He was escorted to the apartment in the palace assigned to him. Here the silence of the place, the sadness which he noticed on the countenances of all, and the melancholy welcome he had received from Pius VII., oppressed his heart almost to bursting.[9] The general constraint which reigned at Fontainebleau was the more remarkable, as the result of a moral conviction that the Holy Father's concession had not improved the situation. Outwardly, since the signature, things had assumed a more cheerful aspect. The Black and Red Cardinals flocked indiscriminately to the feet of Pius VII. The palace was thronged with bishops, the majority of whom unfortunately shared the sentiments of their lordships of Tours, Nantes, and Evreux. A certain exterior pomp was visible in the household arrangements, which were on the footing (if we can imagine such a thing) of a reigning prince owning no kingdom, and this was precisely the state to which Napoleon would have reduced the Pope.

---

[8] 'Ma ci siamo in fine sporcificati. Quei Cardinali . . . mi strascinarono al tavolino e mi fecero sottoscrivere.'
[9] *Memorie*, t. ii. pp. 190, 196.

In the midst of exterior magnificence the place was replete with spies, so that very little real liberty of speech was left to the Holy Father. Before going to his second audience, Pacca was warned to be guarded in what he said. The Emperor had not nominated a governor and chamberlain (La Gorse, the under gaoler of Savona united those qualifications in his person), to do the honours of the château for no purpose. The Cardinal, as a man, keenly felt the coldness of his greeting, but worse than this was the state of the Holy Father. It was such as to inspire fears for his life, or as he said himself, for his reason. 'Like Clement XIV. he would die mad.' The conviction was evidently taking the proportions of a fixed idea, the force of which was increased by his sleepless nights, and by his abstention from all food except what was strictly necessary to keep body and soul together. Continually, in the course of conversation, his countenance assumed that rigid look of absorption in thought, which was produced in him by severe mental anguish, and he would burst out into expressions of intense grief as the thought of the concessions which had been wrung from him forced itself upon his mind. In his second audience, Pacca strove to pour a little consolation into the troubled heart of Pius VII. In a few days all the Cardinals would be once more assembled round their Head, who could count upon their disinterested counsels to draw him out of his present state. At the words, 'find a remedy,' the Holy Father seemed to awake for one moment from his lethargic sadness.

'Do you think the thing is susceptible of remedy?' he asked.

'Most surely it is, Holy Father,' answered Pacca. 'With a good will nearly all evils may be remedied.'

On the evening of the same day he whom Pius VII. called 'our beloved Cardinal' arrived at Fontainebleau

—Consalvi. When the Sacred College again occupied its natural place, the first duty imposed upon it by the Pope was that each of its members should consign to paper his particular opinion of the Concordat. It was not an easy obedience. Theological books were wanting at Fontainebleau, whose library, we have seen, was full of profane recollections of royal lovers, and the Cardinals had no facilities for meeting, or at least, so false was the whole position, that had they done so, they would have been suspected of intriguing. The imperial marriage had divided them into two camps, and hitherto the title of 'Black' or 'Red' had stamped them at once as partisans of the Pope or of the Emperor. But now division introduced itself into the counsels of the faithful Cardinals. A small number, instead of uniting with their natural leaders, Consalvi and Pacca, in judging a retractation from the Pope to be the only means of retrieving his error, weakly proposed that the treaty should be maintained, with the insertion of certain clauses more favourable to the Holy See and to the Pope. Whilst they were discussing the question, the attitude of Pius VII. aroused Napoleon's suspicions, for the first allotment of the imperial allowance had been refused, and objections raised as to the Bulls of Confirmation. It was plain, then, that although the Sovereign Pontiff had signed the Concordat he was in no hurry to execute its articles. The Emperor resolved to nail him to the point by communicating their precise tenure to the Senate, for hitherto he had carefully abstained from publishing officially the terms or the matter of the treaty. This step was impolitic as far as the Black Cardinals, who counselled silence as the wisest course, were concerned. The very argument which they had alleged—secrecy of the negotiation—was withdrawn by Napoleon himself, who thus unconsciously supported those who advocated an entire retractation. The perspicacity of Consalvi did not fail to point out to him in this circumstance the profit which might be drawn from the Emperor's mistake, and it was he who after bringing the others to see the step in its true bearings, announced to Pius VII. the final conviction of the thirteen that he must accept the humiliation of an entire retractation. But this decision presented almost insuperable difficulties, owing to the active measures of espionage which were set on foot within the palace by the Minister of Police, the Duc de Rovigo. Fortunately, the Cardinals proved the truth of Pacca's words, that few evils will resist the battery of good will earnestly directed against them. Cardinal Pignatelli, an old and infirm member of the Sacred College, was one of the number who did not lodge in the palace but in the town of Fontainebleau. His state rendered it difficult for him to leave his room, and partly for his sake, partly to elude the Duc de Rovigo's spies, the chief advocates of the retractation formed a habit of meeting there to consider how the desired consummation could be effected. They finally adopted the form of loyal disavowal of the Concordat, which was suggested by Pacca, and seconded by Consalvi and di Pietro. It was agreed that the Pope should write a letter to the Emperor directly, in which he should entirely retract his consent. To prevent the Papal missive from sharing the fate of some few of its predecessors, which Napoleon had simply ignored, Pius VII. was to present each Cardinal with a copy, and to enjoin each to make his retractation known to the best of his power. It was indispensable that the Pope should write the letter with his own hand to the Emperor, but here came a double difficulty. His physical weakness was so great that he could scarcely hold a pen, and the espionage exercised upon his desk was so unscrupulous, that he could not have made it a receptacle for any important document. Every day an agent of the Duc de Rovigo utilized the time of the Pope's Mass to proceed to a thorough search of his apartment. His desk and cupboard were opened with false keys, and his papers submitted to a keen examination. Under such circumstances how defy bodily infirmity and the Minister of Police? But Consalvi, Pacca, and di Pietro by no means shrunk from the task. Immediately after Mass each morning Consalvi and di Pietro brought the Holy Father the letter already begun, to which he added a few lines. In the afternoon about four o'clock Pacca appeared, and the same operation was repeated; only that the Cardinal took away the unfinished document in the folds of his dress to Cardinal Pignatelli's house. More than once Pius VII. was obliged to recommence his arduous work, and Pacca in carrying off the precious letter went through so much anxiety for fear of a search on his way home that in spite of the 'bitter cold of the season, he felt suffocated with heat.' [10]

During these negotiations under difficulties, the position of the bishops who had been invited by Napoleon to put a finishing touch to the work of the Concordat of Fontainebleau was at least embarrassing. Mgr. Duvoisin especially felt instinctively that something was going on, and that he was excluded from the confidence of the Cardinals. What else could a bishop expect who was in correspondence with M. Bigot? The letter was progressing so favourably that the Minister of Worship wrote to the Emperor on the 14h of March, 1813, that 'all was as quiet as possible; that there seemed to be no intention of troubling the actual order of things *by any correspondence:* that the Cardinals were divided amongst themselves, and those who lodged out of the

L'Eglise Romaine et le Premier Empire, t. v. p. 252.

palace showed no eagerness to pay their respects to the Pope.'[11] So said and so thought M. Bigot! A few days later, Pius VII. asked for the chamberlain, La Gorse, and gave him the letter of retractation finally completed by the arduous process we have mentioned. It was the 24th of March, 1813. The letter ran thus—

'Sire,
    'However painful the avowal which We are about to make to your Majesty may be to our heart, whatever pain it may cause to yourself, fear of the judgments of God, to Whom our great age and declining health bring Us daily nearer, should render Us superior to all human considerations, and cause us to despise the terrible anguish which is bearing Us down at this moment. Impelled by our duty, and with that sincerity and frankness which befit our dignity and our character, We declare to your Majesty, that since the 25th of January, when We apposed our seal to articles which were to serve as a basis to a final treaty mentioned therein, the greatest remorse and the deepest contrition have continually afflicted our soul. We immediately recognised our error. Constant and serious reflection convince Us more and more powerfully of the evil of a concession into which We allowed ourselves to be drawn in the hope of putting an end to the actual troubles of the Church, and out of the desire to please your Majesty. One single thought calmed our affliction. It was the hope of remedying by an act of final agreement the evil which We had just caused the Church by signing these articles. But what was not our grief when to our great surprize, in spite of what had been determined with your Majesty, We saw these same

---

[11] Le Ministre des Cultes à l'Empereur, 14 Mars, 1813.

articles, which were but the basis of a future treaty, published under the title of Concordat. We have deemed that We could find no means more compatible with the respect which We bear towards your Majesty than that of addressing your Majesty directly by writing you this letter. It is in the presence of God, Who will soon demand of Us an account of the power which was conferred on Us as Vicar of Christ for the government of the Church, that We declare in all apostolical sincerity that our conscience is invincibly opposed to the execution of the articles contained in the document of January 25th. . . . With respect to this document, signed by our hand, We repeat to your Majesty the words addressed by our predecessor Pascal II., in a Brief to Henry V., in whose favour he also made a concession which justly caused remorse to his conscience. With him We say to you: as our conscience acknowledges the document to be evil, We too acknowledge it to be evil, and with the help of God We desire that it may be entirely annulled, so that no pernicious results may ensue for the Church, and no prejudice for our own soul. . . . Whilst We obey the dictates of our conscience, which impels Us to make this declaration to your Majesty, We hasten to tell you that We ardently desire to come to a final agreement, whose fundamental basis may harmonize with our duty. . . . We beseech your Majesty to accept the result of our reflections with the same heartiness with which We have written it. We pray you for the love of Jesus Christ, to console our heart, which desires nothing so much as a conciliation that has always been the subject of our prayers. We conjure you to weigh the glory which it would bring to you, and the precious advantages to your States of a final arrangement, that could be maintained by our successors as the token of true peace to the Church. We address the most ardent prayers to God that He would deign to pour down on your Majesty an abundance of His heavenly graces.'[12]

On the same day the Holy Father delivered an Allocution to the Cardinals, in which they were all instructed as to the actual state of things. 'Blessed be God,' were the humble words of the Sovereign Pontiff in terminating his address, 'blessed be God Who has not withheld His mercy from Us. It is He Who chastises and Who quickens. He has willed to humble Us by a salutary confusion, and at the same time has sustained Us by His almighty hand, giving Us the necessary assistance for the accomplishment of our duty in this trying circumstance. As far as We are concerned, We cheerfully accept this humiliation for the good of our soul. To Him be now and for ever all honour and glory.'[13] But Pius was fully aware of the possible consequences of an action which caused Napoleon's cherished dream to vanish into thin air, although the Emperor was indeed no longer a sovereign who could afford to pass over in a disdainful silence whatever did not chime in with his monstrous pretensions. He could not with any political wisdom treat the Pope's letter of March 24th, as he had done the Bull *Quum Memoranda*. But it is almost an impossibility to human nature to unlearn despotism. Napoleon's genius did not enable him to pass through the ordeal, and now at last the greatest of the waves that had menaced Peter's spiritual kingdom with an all-absorbing inundation from the State broke powerless at the foot of the Rock. As an answer to Pius VII., he invited M. Bigot to impose secrecy and dishonesty on such of the French bishops who would still consent to

---

[12] Lettre du Pape Pie VII. á l'Empereur Napoléon, Fontainebleau, 24 mars, 1813.

[13] *Histoire de Pie VII.* t. ii. p. 346.

obey the representative of the State. 'The Minister of Worship will keep the Pope's letter of March 24th as an inviolable secret, as I wish to be able to say that I have or have not received it, according to the turn which circumstances may take. He must write to the bishops that, on account of Holy Week and the duties which call for them in their dioceses, it is fitting that they should return thither with the exception of the Bishop of Nantes and Trèves, who, as Counsellors of State, must go to Paris for consultation.' Once more his notion was to put what should seem to be spontaneous sentiments into the mouths of the bishops, and in dictating their theme, he developed it, as usual, with a 'careful minuteness.' 'The Archbishops and bishops must entirely ignore the Pope's protestation. It must be completely kept from them, but orders should be given to them to go to Fontainebleau the day following this announcement, as if of their own accord. As if from themselves too they will present their address to the Pope, after which they will immediately set off for their dioceses. . . . The address might be drawn up in this strain: "The undersigned, Archbishops, and Bishops of the Empire, and of the Kingdom of Italy, having complied with the orders of his Majesty to congratulate your Holiness on a Concordat which is to bring about the re-establishment of peace in the Church, see with grief that your Holiness has not yet performed any act in execution of this treaty, and that continued disquietude and the widowed state of a great number of churches are the consequences. They flatter themselves that your Holiness will come to their relief. The Concordat of Fontainebleau was inspired by the Holy Spirit to the Head of the Church for the cessation of her troubles. Hence they are pained to think that since the event scruples have been suggested to him on the subject. In their capacity of bishops and theologians they consent unanimously to the Concordat, and beseech His Holiness to come to an agreement with the head of the State for the conferring of canonical confirmation, etc. " ' [14]

But this time Napoleon over-estimated the compliancy upon which he might count in the bishops. M. Bigot's attempts to induce them to undo, if it were possible, the Pope's retractation by their representations proved ineffectual. Cardinal Maury alone consented to go to Fontainebleau, as if of his own accord, to give at Napoleon's dictation a lesson of theology to Pius VII. When the Holy Father confidentially spoke of the letter and Allocution addressed to the Sacred College, Maury feigned ignorance, and urged the importance for himself of a day's reflection in order to form an opinion on the subject, although the answer was mature in his brain when he set out. It had been prepared and was delivered the following day with a due regard to his personal reputation for eloquence. All that he obtained was the humiliation of defeat, and severe words from a Pontiff so tender by nature as Pius VII.[15]

Two weapons were employed by Napoleon to vanquish resistance. First of all he ignored it, then he required the interference of the Minister of Police, or because it became too palpable, he strove to suffocate it with material force. As in the circumstance of the Bull *Quum Memoranda*, the curious way in which his vengeance singled out persons proves that his affected disdain for the Excommunication was merely superficial talk, so now in the case of the Retractation by Pius VII. of the Concordat of Fontainebleau, the sentiment deepest down in his heart with regard

---

[14] Lettre de l'Empereur à M. le Comte Bigot de Préameneu, 25 mars, 1813. *Not* inserted in his correspondence.
[15] *L'Eglise Romaine et le Premier Empire*, t. v. p. 274.

to both one and the other was really fear. After the abortive visit of Maury, Napoleon sent orders to M. Bigot that Fontainebleau was to return to its former state of prison. Nobody was to be allowed access to the Holy Father, and the Cardinals were to be carefully prevented from meddling in the affairs of the State. General La Gorse, who had been transformed for a time into a chamberlain, once more donned his costume of gaoler, and in this capacity signified to them, that if they wished to remain at Fontainebleau, they must consent to total inaction, and content themselves with visits of mere ceremony to the Pope. Cardinal di Pietro, who had again the honour of rousing the Emperor's suspicions, was seized in his bed during the night of the 5th of April, and obliged to set off immediately for Auxonne in a state of double degradation, if degradation it can be called to have twice in those times and in so marked a manner drawn down upon himself the revenge of Cæsar.[16] Upon him, as the Cardinal who had supplied the religious arguments of the Pope's letter, it fell in all its force.

Meantime, it pleased Napoleon to act as if the Concordat of Fontainebleau still existed. His efforts to ignore a step which so completely frustrated his ambitious schemes are rather pitiable, when viewed at our actual distance from events. He caused a decree of the Empire to render the Concordat obligatory on the Archbishops, bishops, and chaplains; and M. Bigot at his demand drew up a list of the vacant sees, with the names of different candidates for nomination. The Emperor immediately nominated to twelve bishoprics, amongst which were Tournai, Ghent, and Troyes, and held out a delusive hope of pardon 'to such individuals in the departments of Rome and Thrasimene as had incurred the penalties

[16] *L'Eglise Romaine et le Premier Empire*, t. v. p. 276.

of the law for refusal of certain oaths which had been required of them.' Notwithstanding the imperial indulgence few ecclesiastics, imprisoned for the conscientious opposition which they had manifested in the combat between Church and State, seemed anxious to profit by the so-called amnesty. Either they felt that it was only a pretence at pardon, or that the walls of a prison were as good as a dubious liberty. At Troyes, the Chapter refused to acknowledge the bishop proposed by Napoleon, for a simple curé had journeyed to Fontainebleau, where he had managed to foil the Duc de Rovigo's agents so far as to learn from the Holy Father's lips that Mgr. de Boulogne and no other was the rightful pastor. At Tournai, Belgian dislike of the French dominion perhaps added fuel to the fire of religious opposition. Some members of the Chapter resigned in presence of a proposed bishop who could be nothing better than a schismatic in their eyes, and the Superiors of the Seminary at Tournai resorted to the expedient of sending off all the students before the end of the scholastic term in order to avoid recognizing an illegitimate administrator of the diocese. News of these steps particularly incensed the Emperor, probably on account of the political feeling which was associated with religious enthusiasm. The ephemeral success of Lützen prompted him to bring the rebellious Belgians to reason by some of those arbitrary measures which really constituted a penal code applied by the State's emissaries against the Church. The prospect which he held out to this tiresome diocese in such fermentation (always through the medium of M. Bigot), was nothing less than its suppression. 'If,' he wrote, 'I have the least indications of further rebellion from them (the canons and principal priests of Tournai) I shall suppress the bishopric, and deprive the town of Tournai of the privilege of a bishop.

I shall unite it to another diocese, or I shall transfer the see to a town in the vicinity of Ancient France.'[17]

As for Ghent, Pius VII. when consulted on the subject of the bishop proposed by Napoleon, replied in favour of Mgr. de Broglie, and the consequences were that the schismatic pastor had great difficulty in rallying thirty priests under his crozier out of twelve hundred that Flanders at that time numbered. The only course open to the Seminarists of Ghent was the acceptance of the profession which was inflicted on all eligible young men of the period—the conscription. 'It was better,' they exclaimed, in the warmth of their Catholic feelings, 'to be good soldiers than schismatic priests.'[18] Those among them whom corporal infirmity disabled for the military career were taken to Paris under the escort of the police, and imprisoned at Sainte Pélagie, whilst those priests of the diocese who had lent the support of their preaching to resistance, being old and physically weak, were also sent to languish in the prisons of France. The condition of the three bishops whose rights caused all this disturbance was, naturally enough, not thereby ameliorated. Mgr. de Boulogne, who had refused to sign a second declaration which would have made him disapprove of the resistance of his Chapter, had been thereupon removed once more to Vincennes, whose gloomy walls seemed to gain in thickness as the reign of the first Emperor of the French approached its violent termination. Mgr. Hirn had submitted to sign the formula, but he could not materially influence the decisions of his canons. The prison of the Man of the Iron Mask had all but destroyed the physical powers of poor Mgr. de Broglie. His keepers had been forced to reconduct

---

[17] Lettre de l'Empereur à Monsieur le Comte Bigot de Préameneu, 14 août, 1813. *Not* inserted in his correspondence.
[18] *L'Eglise Romaine et le Premier Empire*, t. v. p. 285.

him to Beaune, less from a feeling of humanity, he says himself, 'than from a wish to ensnare him afresh.'[19]

This state of things in three dioceses, not to speak of others which were enduring a hopeless vacancy through Napoleon's obstinacy, is the best proof whether a decree of the Empire had succeeded in rendering the Concordat of Fontainebleau a treaty possessing full force of law, in spite of the Holy Father's revocation of it. Napoleon had disturbed the peace and prosperity of Flanders. Its roads were traversed by bands of ex-seminarists going to lay down their lives on his battle-fields, because they might not enrol themselves under the banner of the lawful bishop. Throughout France prisons were peopled by soldiers of the same legion, soldiers of Christ's spiritual kingdom, whose warfare consisted in a passive combat, rendered thus doubly terrible. They indeed were not asked to wield a material sword, but to endure privations which might almost seem to justify the wish to die. Amongst their troubles the sacrifice of liberty, air, and sunshine, and social consolations may be reckoned as the most prominent. After the example set them at Fontainebleau by the Holy Father, they would submit nobly and unrepiningly to the suffering of inactivity, entrusting their cause to God, and awaiting His own time to see their prison gates open, as if by an invisible hand.

The last words written to Napoleon by Mgr. Duvoisin, on the bed where death overtook him in July, 1813, were: 'I beseech you to restore his liberty to the Holy Father. His captivity troubles my last moments. I have had the honour of telling you more than once how distressing this captivity is to all Catholics, and how unfitting its prolongation has been. The return of His

---

[19] Relation Latine addressée au Saint Père par Mgr. de Broglie, Evêque de Gand.

Holiness to Rome is, I believe, necessary for your happiness.'[20] The conviction expressed by the Bishop of Nantes in that half light of eternity which often illumines a death-bed, was silently shared by the mass of the clergy. It quietly fixed its hopes on the only event which could restore things in the ecclesiastical order to their normal state—the fall of the Empire. For a moment Napoleon had entertained thoughts of securing the sympathies of the bishops by describing the actual moment of crisis in all its gloominess, and by appealing to their nationality, which was so soon to be wounded by an invasion of foreign Powers. But if the flatteries of a certain number of the chief pastors of the French Church had not failed him in the days of his prosperity, adversity was soon to test his true friends. In his secret heart he felt that he could place no reliance on courtier prelates, and he rejected the memorandum in which M. Bigot had depicted the social aspect of things under its true colours. By his own fault he had divided the French Church into two camps, one of which had been false to the Holy Father by adopting temporarily material interests; but was such conduct a guarantee of fidelity to the imperial cause in its hour of trial? Napoleon possessed a truer knowledge of men. The other had courageously protested in favour of the most sacred rights upon earth, even unto suffering and imprisonment. What could be expected from it? Either Napoleon must agree to an entire change of policy with regard to the Spiritual Power, or reduced by Providence to powerlessness because he had not the moral strength to retract, his weakness would at length force him to admit that the finger of God was palpable in his own defeat. Cardinal Fesch had said it already. For some time past the Primate

[20] *Mémoires Historiques sur les Affaires Ecclésiastiques de France*, t. ii. p. 527.

had spent his time at Lyons in a kind of exile brought upon him by his fearless predictions of misfortune to the Emperor himself. He contemplated from his retreat the increasing temerity of his imperial nephew with anxiety and dread. 'The Emperor is ruining himself, he is ruining us all,' he would say to Madame Bonaparte; 'I foresee the moment when he will be borne down and annihilated. All who touch the Holy Ark experience the same fate. . . . My nephew is lost, but the Church is saved; for if the Emperor had returned in triumph from Moscow, who knows how far he would have carried his pretensions?'[21] This time Cardinal Fesch was a true prophet.

[21] *Vie du Card. Fesch.* Par l'Abbé Lyonnet, t. ii. pp. 379, 455.

CHAPTER XIV.

The fallen Emperor and the restored Pontiff.

> Ei si nomò : due secoli,
> L'un contro l'altro armato,
> Sommessi a lui si volsero,
> Come aspettando il fato.
>
> . . . . .
>
> Ei sparve: e i dì nell' ozio
> Chiuse in sì breve sponda.—*Manzoni.*

THE patience of Pius VII. was not exhausted. Calmly and peacefully, in a region superior to the emotions which are caused by good or adverse fortune, he awaited the decision of events, shaped out by Providence. The year 1813 witnessed the crowning effort of Europe against the gigantic power attained by Napoleon. A sixth coalition of its peoples, instigated by Russia, rose up against him with that unity of purpose which seldom acts in vain. The secret of its success is not to be sought in the preponderance of material force alone, or in the ability of its warlike tactics. At no time, if we believe the testimony of those who were competent to pronounce a judgment in the matter, had Napoleon's military genius exhibited more wonderfully its astonishing capacity and brilliancy than at the moment when he was unconsciously bidding 'a long farewell to all his greatness.' The Emperor was vanquished in his might, the meek Pontiff triumphed in and by his suffering. We are accustomed to view temporal prosperity as the kind of reward bestowed on the good in the Old rather than in the New Testament, as if the Gospel which said, 'Blessed are they that mourn, for they shall be comforted,' intended the fulfilment of its promises to take place for greater security against the sorrows of time in a world beyond the touch of pain and death. Perhaps the Papacy is the one great exception to the notion which we not erroneously form as to the way and the manner by which the right seldom triumphs visibly on earth. The Papacy partakes of the double nature of its Founder, Whose Person it represents. If our Lord died in fearful ignominy upon the Cross, as it appeared to the mass of beholders, death was overcome by the dazzling splendour of the Resurrection, to those who were privileged to see it. Hardly is the sacrifice consummated on Mount Calvary, when they who have become wise with the wisdom of God begin to look for its fitting consequence (if we may so speak), in the divine plan. God as God must be glorified. Though He Who died was truly God and Man, humiliation and suffering do not constitute the normal state of His Divinity. For love of us He consented that His Humanity should be wounded and pierced, but afterwards comes the retribution of His Divinity. So the Church as the Church, the cause of God and of justice upon earth, must always rise again from the depths of humiliation and weakness with a reflection at least of the day when the heavy stone was removed from Christ's sepulchre by immortal hands, and an angel in white remained to announce His ineffable triumph to His faithful ones upon earth.

Germany was the scene of Napoleon's defeats, as it had formerly been of his conquests. Here, gradually deserted by those whom mere selfish considerations had drawn into his alliance, he found himself alone to meet his overwhelming ruin. Russia, Prussia, England, and Sweden bore down in the European balance the feeble assistance of Denmark, the last ally of greatness which yielded reluctantly before its adversity. The brilliant but in their result not important successes of Lützen, Bautzen, and Würschen by causing the French army to penetrate from Dresden as far as Breslau, rendered Napoleon master of Lusatia. The support of Austria might have outweighed other disadvantages; but about August, 1813, the Emperor Francis announced his intention of siding against the son-in-law whose throne he had once been so eager for his daughter to share. This decision augmented the number of Napoleon's enemies by three hundred thousand men, and so speedily was his star descending in the horizon of nations that the country which proved faithful to him the longest had already paid the penalty of its generosity. Denmark had lost Norway, which Sweden was happy to recover at the easy price of declaring itself hostile to a now universal foe. Austria's determination, morever, rendered the position of the French almost untenable in Germany, when the crushing defeat of Leipsic came in October. Eighty thousand perished in the fight; the Napoleonic yoke over Germany was irretrievably loosened. Nations threw off the dominion of their surreptitious Bonapartist sovereigns, and acknowledged once more that of their hereditary princes, yet not before they could insure themselves against all possibility of Napoleon's vengeance. Those who live with a prince put their own interests before his, and take care not to procure an advantage for him which is only to be gained by a disadvantage for themselves.[1] What Pascal said of persons is true of nations. Napoleon now went through this bitter experience. Later on more flagrant desertions came upon him, as if all men vied with themselves in wounding the fallen lion. In 1814 Joachim Murat, whom Napoleon had made a sovereign, sought to set up his own reign on the ruins of his benefactor's power; but was not the

[1] Pascal, *Pensées*.

King of Naples the link which held together an invisible chain? God's Providence had determined to restore the temporal kingdom of Peter, and the ancient monarchy of Naples, which should henceforth be called that of the Two Sicilies; but Napoleon, to prevent the designs of his brother-in-law from succeeding, when he was no longer powerful offered to make a restitution prompted by necessity. He could better bear to see the Roman States in the possession of Pius VII., than of a prince whose dynasty he himself had founded.

Whilst the year 1813 was drawing its sombre shadow over Napoleon's glory, Pius VII. was, as we have said, calmly awaiting the decision of events, not, as his gaoler La Gorse accused him of doing, in an inactivity worthy of a 'sanctimonious, prattling nun in her cell,' but in that patience which is the best part of fortitude. On the success of Lützen he had received an intimation of the transitory good fortune from Marie Louise, who immediately despatched a page to Fontainebleau with the news. The Empress was persuaded that Pius would rejoice at the intelligence, as she knew 'what affection His Holiness entertained for the Emperor.'[2] In the answer sent to what was a strange announcement under existing circumstances, two difficult things had to be conciliated; courtesy towards the Empress, and just enough reproach for Napoleon's conduct to prevent the Pope's reply from being represented as an official answer, or thought to imply that Pius VII. really had any reason to rejoice. Consequently rather severe complaints were inserted in it as to the actual treatment inflicted on himself, and as to the arrest of Cardinal di Pietro.[3] At the same time the Holy Father composed a vigorous Allocution, nominally addressed to the Cardinals at Fon-

[2] *L'Eglise Romaine et le Premier Empire*, t. v. p. 302.
[3] Lettre de Sa Sainteté Pie VII. à l'Impératrice Marie Louise.

tainebleau, but practically intended for the Universal Church. It was an energetic protestation, and the personal work of Pius VII. against the insertion of the Concordat of 1813 in the *Bulletin des Lois*, and the confirmation of bishops, which might very possibly be conferred through the Emperor's nominations in virtue of its decrees. In July, 1813, the Sovereign Pontiff proved still further the false appreciation of La Gorse by profiting by the Congress of Prague to demand officially the restitution of his temporal power of the Emperor of Austria. But once more Napoleon had need of the Holy Father. From a sure source he received the intelligence that the United Powers would infallibly require the restoration of the States of the Church, and to prevent, if he could, a consummation so painful to his pride, he resolved to reopen communication with Pius VII. before it was too late. Circumstances had altered considerably, but the Holy Father was still Napoleon's prisoner, and in this capacity might consent to prove docile once more. This was the reason and the motive for the singular negotiations which were opened towards the end of 1813 by a great lady of Marie Louise's Court. They ended by submission to a necessity which Napoleon would have averted, if the power of resistance had been left to him. The Marquise de Brignole's mediation was courteously refused at Fontainebleau by Consalvi, on the plea that 'neither time nor place were favourable for a new treaty.'[4] The Bishop of Piacenza, Mgr. Fallot de Beaumont, succeeded the lady negotiator in what was as nearly an official character without being it as possible. He had orders to signify delicately to Pius VII., *as if spontaneously*, that his return to Rome was not out of the range of possibility. The Bishop met with no better success than the Marquise, for if the Holy Father listened to

---

[4] *L'Eglise Romaine et le Premier Empire*, t. v. p. 307.

him patiently, it was with perfect indifference. He was naturally weary of Napoleon's empty words, and had forbidden even the Cardinals to talk to him on the subject. After the fruitless attempt of Mgr. de Beaumont, the enlightened M. La Gorse was convinced that no better negotiator could be found than himself, and he did not hesitate to offer his services as such. In a letter to M. Bigot he expatiated on his singular aptitude for the office, having, he said, become acquainted through long and close observation with the character and habits of Pius VII., who was 'more anxious to acquire the reputation of a martyr than that of a great prince, because it is easier to say prayers than to make treaties.'[5] Whilst M. La Gorse propounded these sentiments, so worthy of the office imposed upon him by the Emperor at Savona, with regard to the Holy Father, Cardinals Pacca and Consalvi endeavoured to set the situation in its true light to Mgr. de Beaumont. After mature deliberation the Pope was of opinion that no treaty made in his actual state of dependence would stand the test of time. For the discussion of spiritual matters to be freely carried on, and in order to come to a final understanding on these points, his position must first be settled. This was indispensable, if he hoped to impart a character of immutability to his decisions. A fortnight later the designs of Murat upon the Roman States, and the seriously aggravated position of Napoleon's army on the Rhine, prompted a last movement on his part in the direction of Pius VII. Mgr. de Beaumont was once more despatched to Fontainebleau. This time he was the bearer of a letter dictated by M. Bassano at the instigation of the Emperor, which itself best explains his conduct. After having despoiled the Pope of his temporal possessions, he now requested the Sovereign Pontiff to take

[5] Lettre de M. La Gorse au Ministre des Cultes, xbre, 1813.

back St. Peter's Patrimony for his own imperial convenience.

'Most Holy Father,

'I approach your Holiness to inform you that the King of Naples, having effected an alliance with the coalition which apparently proposes itself as an end in view the ultimate reunion of Rome to his States, his Majesty the Emperor and King has judged it conformable to the true policy of his empire and to the interests of the people of Rome to restore the Roman States to your Holiness. He *prefers to see them in your hands rather than in those of any other Sovereign, whoever he may be.* Consequently, I am authorized to sign a treaty by which peace would be re-established between the Emperor and the Pope. Your Holiness would be recognized in your temporal sovereignty, and the Roman States, such as they were incorporated in the French Empire, would be restored to your Holiness, or to your agents. The fortresses would be included in the restoration. This convention would treat merely of temporal matters and with the Pope as Sovereign of Rome.'[6]

The interview which consigned this letter into the hands of Pius VII. and which called forth his noble reply, is almost an event in his Pontificate. He refused Napoleon's offers for the same reason that he had already dismissed the negotiations of the imperial desires, because 'the restitution of his States being an act of justice, it could not become the object of a treaty, and that moreover all that he accomplished outside his States would appear to be the result of violence and cause scandal to the Catholic world.'

[6] Projet de lettre au Saint Père, remis le 18 janvier à Mgr. de Beaumont.

His sole desire, Pius observed, was to return to Rome, but he needed nothing, for he trusted to Providence to take him back. He added, 'It is possible that my sins render me unworthy to see Rome again, but be assured that my successors will entirely recover the States which belong to them.' Then, remembering the Sovereign whom he had always and whom he still loved, and fearing to add an apparent forgetfulness to the but too real adversity of Napoleon, he said as a final injunction to Mgr. de Beaumont: 'Assure the Emperor that I am not his enemy. Religion would not allow me to be so. I love France, and when I am in Rome again you will see that I shall not be wanting towards your country.'[7]

The piety that could prompt language so gentle and forgiving was certainly no idle word, and Napoleon might still have acknowledged the long-suffering and loyalty of Pius VII. by giving him in return for his affectionate pardon an easy mark of confidence. But the Emperor thought with La Gorse that it would be a 'dangerous proof of magnanimity' to allow the Holy Father to regain Italy otherwise than as a captive. When Mgr. de Beaumont had accomplished his business, and as he was walking afterwards through Fontainebleau, he saw three carriages driving in the direction of the palace. They were to take the Sovereign Pontiff away from a place which might come into a dangerous contact with the allied forces, not in an honourable state of liberty, which Napoleon's recent offer might have led us to imagine, but as a prisoner with the escort of the melancholy journey which had been effected nearly two years earlier from Savona to Fontainebleau. It would have been easy to retrieve in some measure, though even at the eleventh hour, the ill-usage of so many years by a

---

[7] Relation écrite par Mgr. de Beaumont Evêque de Plaisance, 2 mai, 1814.

final act of generosity. But Napoleon had other views. In submitting to the necessity of changing the Pope's prison, he was already weighing in his own mind the probabilities of that war which was now brought into the heart of France. With all the powers of his military genius he planned and executed the manœuvres of the French Campaign. They profited him not even to check the vast and terrible shipwreck of his hopes and dreams. Once more he listened to ambition, and its programme was, not to fulfil what he had himself proposed concerning the temporal power, but to cause the Pope, after a minute itinerary of France in company with La Gorse, to reach Savona by outlying roads. There an account had been opened with the officials of the Department of Montenotte to insure the payment of the Holy Father's household expenses at the rate of twelve thousand francs a month. The Cardinals were not to accompany Pius VII., but to leave Fontainebleau four days afterwards for a destination which was to be communicated to them later, and by a refinement of bad manners they would be called upon to furnish the money for their journey. All was purposely left vague and indefinite in the eyes of the public, so that however events turned out, Napoleon might have the grace of doing the right thing, if indeed, a repetition of Savona deserves this qualification. Ostensibly, M. La Gorse had orders to conduct the Pope to Rome; but if, as Napoleon dared to hope, fortune were true to him just this once, he would profit by his continued prosperity to retain the Holy Father in his grasp. If then this is proved to have been positively the design of the Emperor (as it is by undeniable contemporary documents[8]), it was clearly not owing to his bounty, if Pius VII. ever saw Rome again. Misfortune irretrievably overtook the Sovereign whom

[8] See *L'Eglise Romaine et le Premier Empire*, t. iv. p. 317.

experience had not taught, and caused that humble carriage which bore away the Holy Father to take the direction of the Eternal City by the impulsion of One Who shapes all human events, 'rough-hew them how we will.' Providence did not fail the confidence of Pius VII. It brought him, when the Emperor had been completely humbled, to the place of his temporal rest—to Rome. He had no difficulty in understanding that the departure from Fontainebleau constituted nothing more than a change of prison, a prudential removal from the theatre of war. In vain he asked La Gorse for the company of two or three Cardinals. No such permission had been accorded in the orders of the ex-chamberlain. The Pope was informed that Mgr. Bertazzoli would travel in his carriage, whilst La Gorse would follow with two valets. It would seem that no event had henceforth any power to trouble the serenity of Pius VII. After calmly saying his Mass on the morning of the 23rd of January, he called the Cardinals together in order, according to all appearances, to address them for the last time. With a simple and touching nobility of language he told them that he was about to set out for an unknown destination; perhaps he might never see them again. But under all circumstances, and in all eventualities, he counted upon their devotion to the cause of the Church. Their whole attitude must reflect her suffering state; they were to be mindful of their mother's tears. He left written directions in case of need with Cardinal Mattei, and above all he enjoined them to turn a deaf ear to any kind of proposition which might relate to a treaty, whether on spiritual or temporal matters. Such he said, and the expression was strong in his mouth, 'was positively his firm and steadfast will.'[9] The Sacred College was much moved.

---

[9] Allocution du Pape Pie VII. aux Cardinaux réunis au palais de Fontainebleau.

The Pope alone was calm before so precarious a future, because his conduct was imprinted with the conviction of his secret heart: 'in pace in idipsum dormiam et requiescam, quoniam Tu, Domine, singulariter in spe constituisti me.'[10] After a short prayer in the chapel of the château, he ascended the carriage, and his last act at Fontainebleau was to bless at the railings of the imperial residence the small group of lookers-on, whose faithful instincts augured no good from the departure of their Holy Father. A few days later war was raging at the very doors of the palace so recently occupied by Pius VII. Its eventualities influenced the fortunes of him who was now once again the Apostolic Pilgrim. The gleam of success which Napoleon experienced in February and March caused him to reject in disdain the proposal of the Congress of Châtillon to confirm his possession of France, such as its boundaries had existed under Louis XIV. So far from accepting conditions, he suggested to La Gorse that the Pope's course should be steered apart from Italy. But the conferences at Châtillon, which never assumed the consistency of a treaty, proved at least the general sentiments of the Allies, with regard to the Temporal Power. They would unanimously have demanded its restitution, and Napoleon, whose banner fortune had at last forsaken about the middle of March, became anxious that himself, rather than events, should undo his own handiwork. On the 10th, he caused the publication of a Decree which restored his dominions to the Pope. He had consented, the Emperor said of himself, to the Holy Father's demand, but he did not add that it was only when he had exhausted all his resources that he yielded to a hateful necessity. La Gorse had been ordered to avoid the large towns with his important charge, for fear, in reality,

[10] Psalm iv.

that the sight of Pius VII. should excite too great an enthusiasm. But each day that confirmed the Emperor's ill-fortune on the battle-fields of Champagne, relaxed necessarily the gaoler's need of vigilance. By slow degrees the Holy Father's progress began to assume the appearance of an ovation much in the same way as his former journeys in the South had done. He had reached Savona when the Emperor's compulsory Decree was made known to him, and for the first time since 1808 he listened to words which spoke of liberty: 'Your Holiness is free, and can start for Rome to-morrow.' But the morrow was the feast of *Our Lady of Deliverance*, and Pius announced his intention of celebrating the Holy Sacrifice in the metropolitan church of Savona, in honour of the day which not fortuitously, as it seemed, placed the loosening of his chains under the protection of the Mother of God. Cesena, Ancona, and Loretto, formed the resting-places of his homeward way. Each of these names has its own significance. During the pontifical stay at Cesena, Joachim Murat requested an audience of the Holy Father. He affected ignorance as to the term of the journey, and when Pius mentioned Rome, asked how it was possible to return thither against the will of the Romans. In proof of this assumed ill-feeling, he produced a memorandum addressed to the Allied Sovereigns by some of the nobles, and containing a request that they might in future be governed by a secular prince. Pius quietly took the document, and threw it still unopened into a stove which was near, where it was speedily consumed. 'Is there anything *now*,' he then asked, 'to prevent Us from re-entering Rome?'[11] At Ancona, whose occupation had been the beginning of his troubles, he received a magnificent compensation for its unwilling co-operation in evil designs. The popula-

[11] Dr. Weathers' *Modern History*, p. 384.

tion hailed his approach with an enthusiasm which bordered on frensy. In the midst of salvos of artillery and the ringing of every bell in the place the Papal carriage drawn by the inhabitants made its entry into Ancona. On the following day, Pius crowned in the Cathedral a statue of our Lady, under the title of *Regina Sanctorum Omnium*. Murat's pretensions to retain the Marches of Ancona might have occasioned the Holy Father some trouble, but he caused the matter to be referred to the Allied Sovereigns. Consalvi, who had lost no time in leaving Fontainebleau together with the other Cardinals, after the departure of Pius VII. was sent by him to Paris to settle the question. The Plenipotentiaries had directed their steps to London, and thither Consalvi followed them. He obtained an audience of each, and saw the Prince Regent, who afterwards expressed the nature of his feelings towards the Pope by a very solid benefit—a blank exchequer bill, which the Holy Father was requested to accept, and to fill up to any amount of which he might stand in need.[12] The crowning triumph, which few in the annals of the Papacy can surpass, was the entry into Rome. They who had shared the perils and sufferings of imprisonment, received together a glory which is rarely in this world the inheritance or result of persecution for justice. The Dean of the Sacred College, Cardinal Mattei, and Pacca, whose merits need no recording here, found a place in the Papal carriage. Monarchs swelled the procession which was bringing back in splendour the humble Successor of Peter; Charles IV. of Spain with his Queen and the Infante Don Francisco, the ex-King of Sardinia, the Queen of Etruria, and other distinguished persons formed part of the procession. It was on the 24th of May, 1814, that the Feast of Our Lady, *Auxilium Christianorum*,

[12] Dr. Weathers' *Modern History*, p. 385.

ushered in a glorious spring day, whose Italian sun lit up the cavalcade which passed through the streets of Rome. It was that of an old man with eyes dim from emotion blessing his people on their knees. A white-robed band of young men and girls met him at the *Porta del Popolo*, bearing palms, which a gentle breeze swayed as the sun's rays touched them with its golden beams. 'Blessed is he who comes to us in the name of the Lord!' It was re-echoed from mouth to mouth, as the Romans looked again upon the Father, whom suffering had not broken because he trusted in God, and whose humility was proof against so great and glorious a triumph, because in the manifestation of popular feeling he saw before all things a homage rendered in his person to the Lord, whose Vicar he was. 'Blessed is he who comes to us in the name of the Lord!' At the Ponte Milvio, thirty young men of the noblest families of Rome esteemed it an honour to replace the horses of the Papal carriage, and thus to draw Pius VII. to the tomb of the great Apostles. In the midst of universal enthusiasm, which suddenly became transformed into deep religious emotion on the part of the crowd of spectators, the Holy Father ascended at last the steps of the Basilica of St. Peter, where the hidden God, from whose mystery of love St. Peter's guidance of his people is drawn, received the first prayer of the Pontiff once more restored to Rome. It was one of heartfelt joy and thanksgiving, and perhaps too there was just one tinge of sorrow mingled with it, for the *Imitation* truly says: 'Sine dolore non vivitur in amore.'[13] Pius VII. had loved Napoleon. But in this hour of the Pontiff's rejoicing, the Emperor was crushed. With the exaltation of the one had come the terrible humiliation of the other. But a short time before the very palace of Fontainebleau, where the

---

[13] Lib. iii. c. v.

seduction of imperial opulence had been employed against the Sovereign Pontiff, witnessed a scene strikingly different in all its details from that which closed the month of Mary in the Eternal City. It was the silent farewell of Napoleon to his dreams of greatness. On the 24th of January, 1813, Pius VII. had signed his forced abdication of the Patrimony of Peter. On the 28th of April, 1814, that is, fifteen months later almost to a day, at the same palace of Fontainebleau, and at the very same table, Napoleon put his name to the Decree which declared his Empire at an end, and he himself to be a fallen sovereign. He passed out once more through the ranks of men he had so often led to battle and to victory. They would willingly have followed him still, even unto death, but general and soldiers were condemned to separate. The veterans of his Imperial Guard were powerless to avert the ruin which was falling on their chief, or, later on, to soothe the bitter hours of the inaction which was in itself a slow martyrdom to Napoleon. Only with their hearts might they accompany him to the island which buried in a premature tomb his hopes and happiness.

> O quante volte al tacito
> Morir d' un giorno inerte,
> Chinati i rai fulminei,
> Le braccia al sen conserte,
> Stette, e dei dì che furono
> L'assalse il sovvenir.
> El ripensò le mobili
> Tende, e i percossi valli,
> E il lampo dei manipoli,
> E l'onda dei cavalli ;
> E il concitato imperio,
> E il celere obbedir. [14]

That his joy might be perfect, one thing was wanting to the Pontiff who came back in the midst of palms and

[14] Manzoni.

hosannas to his capital, one thing by which he might justify his title of Father. If it is natural to a father to love his children, the desire to pour balm upon the wounds of others is perhaps the first craving of a noble heart which is suddenly transferred from suffering to peace and joy. All things are learned best by their contrasts, and who can sympathize with the wonderful vicissitudes of love and its indispensable accompaniment, sorrow, that has not first himself both suffered and loved. The day after his return, a Roman noble who had signed the memorandum presented by Murat at Cesena, sought an audience of the Holy Father to crave forgiveness. 'And We,' was the answer of Pius VII., 'do you think that We are not worthy of reproach in some respects? Let us all forget together what has passed.'[15]

Time did not blunt in the Holy Father the wish to imitate the Divine Master Whose followers should be known by their love one for another, and by their patient rendering of good for evil. We find that he spoke of Napoleon's sorrow in these words to his 'beloved Cardinal' on the 6th of October, 1817.

'The family of the Emperor Napoleon has informed Us through Cardinal Fesch that the rock of the Island of St. Helena is killing him, and that the poor exile is the victim of a rapid decline. We learned this news with very great pain, and you will share it no doubt, for we must both remember that, after God, the re-establishment of religion in the great kingdom of France is principally due to him. The devoted and courageous initiative of 1801 causes Us to forgive and forget all subsequent wrongs. Savona and Fontainebleau were but errors of judgment, or chimeras of human ambition; the Concordat was an act which saved society by its heroic and

[15] *Histoire de Pie VII.* t. ii. p. 381.

Christian nature. The mother and the family of Napoleon appeal to our mercy and generosity; We think that it is both grateful and just to prove that We have heard them. We feel certain of entering into your views in charging you to write from Us to the Allied Sovereigns, and especially to the Prince Regent, who has given Us so many tokens of esteem. He is your dear and good friend, and We expect that you will ask him to soften the sufferings of so formidable an exile. It would be an incomparable joy for our heart to have contributed towards diminishing the anguish of Napoleon. He no longer possesses the means of wronging anybody: We wish him to cause remorse to no man.' [16]

By the side of this letter, is further testimony necessary to tell us that Pius VII. in his prosperity preserved the humble and loving heart which he had in the days of Savona and Fontainebleau, and that he took pleasure in relieving the man the weight of whose former greatness had pressed him down to the depths of physical and mental weakness, which we have seen? If it were needed, a mother's gratitude would be there to record the Holy Father's generous forgiveness. Of all sovereigns of Europe, he had resisted almost singly the power and system of Napoleon. He had not been favoured with a kingdom, with honour or wealth, but he had been imprisoned, he had suffered, and those whom he best loved had been compelled to suffer too, yet Pius VII. alone of all the monarchs of Europe sought to mitigate the pangs endured by his former persecutor at St. Helena, and used his restored power to propagate his own feelings of compassion amongst the men who, possessing an empire which belonged only to this world, had no

---

[16] *Mémoires de Consalvi*, t. i. p. 78. Lettre de Pie VII. au Card. Consalvi.

thoughts but for the passing and worldly interests of the moment. Madame Bonaparte thus thanked Consalvi, and through him the Sovereign Pontiff, for their solitary efforts on behalf of a fallen hero, as deserted and abandoned in his misfortunes as he had been courted and flattered during the short reign of his stupendous glory.

'I listen both to my inclination and to my duty in thanking your Eminence for all that you have done for us since exile has weighed upon me and upon my children. My brother, Cardinal Fesch, has not left me in ignorance as to the generous way in which you received the request of my great and unhappy Proscript of St. Helena. The Cardinal told me that, upon the just and Christian demand of the Emperor, you made haste to intercede with the English Government, and to seek for worthy and able priests. I am truly the mother of all sorrow, and the one consolation which remains to me is the thought that the Holy Father is forgetful of the past and remembers only the affection which he shows to all my family. . . . Under the Pontifical Government alone we find support and shelter, and our gratitude corresponds to the benefit. I ask your Eminence to lay it as a homage at the feet of the Holy Pontiff, Pius VII. I speak in the name of all my family of proscripts, and especially in the name of him who is slowly consuming his life on a deserted rock. His Holiness and your Eminence alone in Europe seek to soften his sufferings and to shorten their duration. I thank you both with all my mother's heart, and I beg to remain,

'Your gratefully devoted,
'MADAME.' [17]

---

[17] Lettre de Madame Bonaparte au Card. Consalvi, 27 mai, 1818, *Mémoires de Consalvi*, t. i. p. 102.

x

CHAPTER XV.

'They who sow in tears shall reap in joy.'
(Psalm cxxv.)

THE Empire of Napoleon, founded as it had been on the undue preponderance of military force, had followed upon a revolution which shook the very basis of the social constitution of Europe. Of its great Powers the thrones of England and Russia alone had escaped the ravages of the overwhelming torrent which threatened, always in the name of liberty, to produce universal destruction. We except the Papacy, the destinies of which cannot be classed with those of nations. The triple crown, somewhat in the same way as a sacrament, marks as an outward sign the presence of the reign of God on earth. England and Russia had remained not unassailed, but inviolate, after having fought hand to hand with the eldest son of the Revolution, transformed into the unsatisfied sovereign of sixty million subjects. For the rest Europe, shaken to its centre and through all its institutions, regained even the appearance of its former state only through many tribulations. Once more the monarchs set up their thrones again over the barely closed abyss opened by a factitious liberty. But of all triumphs that of Pius VII. was the brightest, who returned to Rome in the midst of the acclamations of his people, after a series of sufferings unheard of, at least during many hundred years, in the history of the Papacy.

In his capital, Pius came back to inhabit once more the unostentatious apartments where Radet had assured him that nothing should be touched. This promise had not been kept, for it fell to the Pontiff's lot to inherit the imperial magnificence which Napoleon had prepared for himself in the second city of his Empire. The Quirinal was now a palace dazzling with art and elegance; luxurious and splendid fittings replaced the former simple furniture. One room, however, retained its original aspect; it was the sleeping apartment of Pius VII., with its simple and uncurtained bed, where he who still cherished religious poverty sought repose from his pontifical labours. The act which signalized the restored power of Pius VII. was emphatically one that gave him every claim to be blessed as the Father returning in the name of the Lord. A great Society, the foremost in the body-guard of the Church militant, slept in a premature tomb. The Holy Father bade it arise, unswathed the bands, not of corruption, but of inaction, which had only been accepted at the voice of Peter, and sent forth the sons of St. Ignatius to the thick of the battle, once more to proclaim their device, 'for the greater glory of God,' and to suffer persecution as the inheritance of their founder. The Society of Jesus rose again to resume its special labours in the Church, and to show its old love, zeal, and unflinching devotion for souls. Cardinal Pacca greatly promoted this re-establishment. In the interviews of Fontainebleau he had often spoke to the Pope of the Order of Jesus, and they had deplored together the suppression of its apostolic labours. On the return of Pius, Pacca, who had previously entertained hopes that the actual Sovereign Pontiff would ultimately add the glory of its restoration to the numerous benefits of his reign, ventured, in spite of the sickly state of men's minds, to suggest the step. Towards the end of June, 1814, he says in an unpublished manuscript, 'I remarked to the Holy Father in an audience: "Most Holy Father, we must resume our conversation on the Order of Jesus." Without further comment, Pius replied: "We can re-establish the Society at the approaching feast of St. Ignatius."'[1] On the 7th of August, 1814, the Bull *Solicitudo omnium Ecclesiarum* was published. It restored many apostolic men to their labour of love. The following passage is remarkable in the Bull itself: 'The Catholic world unanimously asks for the re-establishmen of the Society of Jesus. Every day We receive to this end the most pressing demands from our venerable brethren, the archbishops and bishops, and from persons of most distinguished rank, more especially now that the abundant fruits produced by this Society in Russia and Sicily[2] are generally known. The dispersion of the very stones of the sanctuary through recent calamities which it is wiser to deplore than to recall to mind, the annihilation of discipline in religious orders that are the glory and the support of the Catholic Church . . . imperatively require Us to yield to so just and general a desire. We should esteem ourself guilty of a great crime, if, in the immense dangers of the Christian commonwealth, We neglected to employ the means which are afforded Us by the especial Providence of God, and if, placed in the Bark of St. Peter, that is agitated and tossed by continual tempests, We refused to make use of vigorous and experienced rowers who voluntarily offer themselves to stem the tide which threatens Us with shipwreck and

---

[1] Crétineau-Joly, *Histoire de la Compagnie de Jésus*, l. vi. p. 54, note.

[2] In these two countries alone the Jesuit organization had bee maintained by permission of Pius VII.

destruction at every moment."³ Subsequent events prove that the Holy Father did not overrate the services of the Society of Jesus. Since 1814, as before, there has scarcely been a battle in the cause of the right where it has not sustained great and glorious wounds.

The first year which followed upon the return to Rome of Pius VII. was spent by Europe in recovering its old state with its former national boundaries. The Congress and Treaty of Vienna, 1814—1815, , re-established equilibrium in the region which had sustained almost fatal shocks. It gave back what the Revolution had taken away. The Papacy, wearing the first and most sacred of crowns, was naturally not a stranger to its doings. Consalvi presented himself as the champion of rights which might possibly be disputed. His capacity and talent for diplomacy singled him out in a world which was recovering from a moral fever as the man of the situation. At the time of his accession, Pius VII. had been no more than a nominal sovereign. The Treaty of Tolentino, enacted under his predecessor, Pius VI., had in reality despoiled the Church of her temporal possessions. The inheritance which accrued then to her Head at the beginning of this century was doubtful in tenure and beset with material weakness. The reign of Pius VII. as it went on had been in a worldly sense a progression from bad to worse, and at one terrible moment men might almost have feared that they were assisting at the agony of the Papacy as a sovereign power. When due consideration is bestowed upon these facts, the triumphant return to Rome stands out as a wonderful event, since, humanly speaking, nothing seemed further removed from the range of possibilities. But Providence allowed the trials of Pius VII. in order to set up again the Temporal

³ *Histoire de Pie VII.* t. ii. p. 403.

Power by the supernatural force of suffering. The 9th of June, 1815, saw the end of the Congress of Vienna, whereat Austria, England, France, Prussia, Russia, and finally, the Holy Father, were represented. On that day a treaty composed of one hundred and twenty articles was signed by the assembled plenipotentiaries. As far as the Papacy was concerned, it was a thorough compensation for the humiliations which had begun at the Quirinal to end at Savona and Fontainebleau. The amount of territory restored to the Pope by the Allied Powers comprised the Marches of Ancona, Benevento, Ponte-corvo, and the Three Legations. Avignon alone was given up to France. Moreover, the Papal Nuncios recovered the right of general precedence in the Courts of Europe.

But before the happy termination of negotiations another Bonapartist invasion threatened the newly-acquired European peace. Napoleon had left Elba on the 26th of February, 1815, and reappeared once more in France. Simultaneously with his arrival there, Joachim Murat demanded officially of the Pope passage for twelve thousand men through his States. He strove to rally the Neapolitans round his standard with the fallacious cry of Italian unity, but his unimportant successes at Ferrara and Florence were soon covered by the Austrians and the co-operation of the English, who exacted the signing of a convention which would pronounce the deposition of Murat. Joachim's name and dynasty had taken but small root in Neapolitan hearts, and the Pope's attitude expressed this to be his personal conviction. He had refused to temporize, and had preferred to follow once again the path of exile. Surely more than most men he had a special right to trust in Providence. At Genoa, where he had taken refuge, he said by way of consolation to the French Ambassador, who was perhaps too disposed to despond at the dark aspect of events: 'My Lord Ambassador, fear nothing; this is a storm which will last three months.'[4] But those who, unlike the Pope, were little accustomed to the vicissitudes of human fortune, might have feared the realization of their worst surmises. Louis XVIII., momentarily re-established on his throne, had fled to Ghent; Napoleon was issuing proclamations from the Tuileries; and during the three months assigned by the Holy Father as the duration of his enterprize, he found time to write to Pius VII. His letter never reached its destination, though probably the Pope was apprized of the step. The Court of Rome wisely ignored all similar communications, and awaited in confidence the great result which Europe once more referred to the battle-field. Murat was the sole ally of Napoleon on the Continent; his ill-success, therefore, could not fail to reflect dishonour and prejudice on the imperial cause. Then came the crushing defeat of Waterloo, in June, 1815. Napoleon cast himself upon the mercy of England, and was sentenced to a life-long imprisonment on a solitary island of the Atlantic. The harshness of the measure has been reproached to our country, but after all it only involved the punishment of one man. It would have been utterly vain to condemn Napoleon to exile at a place as easily accessible to Europe as Elba. His vicinity would have constantly disturbed the peace of a whole continent, so that it is merely a question whether it was not a wise policy to sacrifice the comfort of one to the safety of many. It does not follow that we must approve of the unnecessary rigour which was displayed by Napoleon's guardians at St. Helena, and of which he complained so bitterly. It is true that the Emperor had

---

[4] *Histoire de Pie VII.* t. ii. p. 416. 'Questo é un temporale che durerà tre mesi.'

treated Pius VII. with a severity never reached by Sir Hudson Lowe; but silence, solitude, and inaction were of themselves sufficient trials for the great dethroned hero. The Holy Father would have been the first to exclaim: 'Let it not be meted to him as it was meted to me at Savona and Fontainebleau.' Murat had retired to Corsica after the Battle of Waterloo, but a thirst for domination foolishly prompted him to descend upon Naples in October, 1815, in the hopes of restoring his throne. He met with repulse, was seized, tried, and shot on the fifteenth of that month.

Pius, on the other hand, was now installed for good in Rome. Consalvi returned from the signing of the Treaty of Vienna in July, 1815. He came back full of honours, for the object of his mission had been completely attained. After an interval of nine years, he resumed his post of Secretary of State, and inaugurated an administration which aimed to produce unity in the government of the Papal States, to applying to them modern ameliorations, and to repair the damages of revolution under the triple head of the public weal, science, and the fine arts. Consalvi delighted in surrounding the Papal throne with men whose genius could reflect upon it the human glory which it does not always care to seek. He was the friend of Canova, Thorwaldsen, and Camuccini; he encouraged the labours of Niebuhr, and smiled at the dawning talent of Rossini. Immense public works were planned and executed, amongst which must be classed the excavations practised at Ostia under the intelligent superintendence of the Abbé Fea. The position of a subterraneous street was discovered which had been inhabited by the former goldsmiths of the place. In Rome itself the work of restoration was vigorously carried on. The monuments of the Eternal City could not be appreciated, surrounded as they were in many cases with dust and rubbish. The Roman Forum, the Piazza del Popolo, and that of St. Peter's especially benefited by the general clearance, whilst the Forum of Trajan was rescued from its ruins, and the Ponte-Molle considerably improved. Pius VII. added new rooms to the Museum of the Vatican, and built the part which is called *Braccio Nuovo;* but the particular glory of his reign, in a scientific point of view, were the literary labours of Mgr. Maï, who was invited by his command to Rome, and encouraged in his work. The Romans were not a little proud of the result of the researches which were stimulated by Pius VII. Mgr. Maï succeeded in discovering many ancient works, and among them part of Cicero's Republic. The public walks and plantations begun under the French administration in the Roman States were also successfully brought to a termination. But if these measures concerned the material prosperity of the Pope's subjects, he was likewise the promoter of very great and beneficial reforms in the legislation which have the moral well-being of a people in view, although they may seem to touch only the circle of exterior interests. Pius VII. and Consalvi have not escaped the reproach of too strong an attachment to old-fashioned notions. The Holy Father's *motu proprio* of July 6th, 1816, is the best answer to the accusation. At the Congress of Vienna Consalvi had pledged his word that an administrative reform should be carried out in the Papal States. Revolutions and change of masters do not come upon a people to no purpose, and for many years the government of the Popes had been most precarious. Their temporal throne had been undermined by the social storm of 1792. Other sceptres shake and quiver at the approach, and long after the departure of similar tempests, and no man pretends to wonder at so natural a fear. But with the

Popes it is otherwise; popular opinion becomes suddenly severe. It has difficulty in understanding that temporal power, wielded even by spiritual authority, must necessarily partake of many of the weaknesses inherent in human things. The *motu proprio* of the Holy Father signified that he had taken cognizance of the various changes which he announced, and that they received his entire approbation. In the first place, the law was strengthened by five new codes. The civil code was the work of a former counsellor of State of Napoleon, who himself had adopted many of the Roman laws. The financial system was refounded on a more perfect basis. The same legislative renovation was applied to the department of inland receipts. The attributions of judiciary and administrative tribunals, as well as those of a Court of Exchequer, were likewise defined. The price of salt and tobacco were rendered uniform in the Roman States. The promises announced by Pius VII. on this occasion were fully realized later.

After giving his attention to the re-organization of his temporal kingdom, it was his especial task to set on a more secure basis the affairs of religion in other nations by conventions between the Holy See and the various Governments. In that age of Concordats, it was once more the turn of France to cause the greatest anxiety to the Holy Father. The Concordat of 1801 had been drawn up under very peculiar and trying circumstances, but such as to render lawful the employment of an extraordinary remedy. The Holy See almost consented to act a secondary part in the celebrated transaction which built up again altars overthrown by the Revolution. Moreover, the state of the French Church at the time of the Restoration necessitated a movement of expansion. In 1801 it had been a question of raising from the ground the edifice of religion.

In 1817 the time seemed come to decorate its walls. For sixteen years the French Church had somewhat resembled the life of a man who struggles to supply his animal wants without power of mental enjoyment. The source of spiritual exuberance and strength had been well-nigh quenched in Napoleon's ambitious grasp. It requires the free working of supernatural power to draw water with joy from the 'Saviour's fountain,' and this power an outward tyranny had cramped. The Holy Father, in a situation without precedent, had made sacrifices also without precedent, and now three different classes of bishops caused him to view the conclusion of a further Concordat as no easy work. There were former titular bishops of the ancient régime, some of whom had not submitted to resign their sees at the invitation of the Holy Father. A certain number of constitutional bishops, after obtaining Papal confirmation, had reproduced errors which rendered them unworthy of their posts. Finally, there were the bishops of the Concordat, and perhaps the National Council of 1811 represents their tone and feeling with sufficient correctness. They would have sided with Pius VII. if they had dared, but in point of fact such daring had been a very solitary exception. Besides difficulties with the bishops, there was a further misfortune which loudly called for remedy, and that was the limited number of dioceses which the Convention of 1801 had permitted. On the 11th of June, 1817, an agreement, known as the Concordat of 1817, was finally signed between Consalvi, acting for Pius VII., and the Comte de Blacas for Louis XVIII. It obviated all religious troubles by restoring the Concordat between Leo X. and Francis I. Its chief articles declared that the Convention of 1801 had ceased to take effect, that the Organic Articles were repealed, inasmuch as they were prejudicial to religion and the laws of the Church. A certain number of suppressed sees were restored, and it was agreed that measures should promptly be taken for the creation of others out of consideration for actual needs. His Christian Majesty pledged himself to concert with the Holy Father for the furtherance of religious interests in France.[5] But it is one thing to talk and another thing to act, or perhaps a monarch cannot always be a man of deeds, even when he has the will. The intrigues of the *petite Eglise*, the dearth of material power and stability in the Government of Louis XVIII. after all the disasters of his dynasty, and other machinations of modern Liberalism, prevented the Concordat of 1817 from taking effect before 1819. When its repeal was solicited of Pius VII., he answered that he would lend himself to all modifications '*salvo il Concordato.*' His experience had taught him only too well that nothing was to be gained by condescension to certain petitions.[6] The hostile feeling to Rome, which had manifested itself in the old French magistracy, reappeared in the Legislative Assemblies of the nineteenth century. They exhibited the strange phenomenon of a daily conflict, not between the Church and avowed Revolution, but between the Church and the prejudicial attacks of a legally constituted power. One of the projected ordinances of the French Chambers was a perfect repetition of the Concordat of Fontainebleau. In point of fact that of 1817 was destroyed by the French Government, although the Holy Father never consented to undo his own part in the matter. He adopted the middle course of a Brief which he addressed in 1819 to all the bishops of France, and thus brought to a termination the opposition encountered by the Concordat. It would be too

[5] See the Concordat of 1817. *Histoire de Pie VII.* t. ii. p. 503.
[6] *Histoire de Pie VII.* t. ii. p. 516.

much to say that it was a happy termination, for religion cannot be said to have flourished under Louis XVIII. Fourteen archbishoprics and sixty-one bishoprics were to constitute the number of French sees. Actually there are seventeen archbishoprics and sixty-nine bishoprics in France. At the close of 1819, Cardinal de Périgord was solemnly enthroned as Archbishop of Paris. It was the end of the seemingly interminable difficulties which a religious convention evidently excited in France, under a monarch whose personal views were not easily ascertained. Whether Louis XVIII. really had the interests of the Church at heart or not, is an open question, but the universal impression of those who have is, that he was a fair type of a Liberal Catholic Sovereign, who tried to earn a certain reputation for decency, whilst he rather disdained treading in the beaten path of Catholic tradition with respect to the relations of Church and State.

Universal solicitude for his flock in the heart of Pius VII. helped on the conclusion of other Concordats. Piedmont, Russia for Poland, Naples, and lastly in 1821 Prussia, manifested a desire to insure the co-operation of the Holy See. When Fredinand I., King of the Two Sicilies, as he was now styled, returned to his hereditary States after the expulsion of Joachim Murat in 1815, he found religion in great straits through the dearth of the monastic life. As at Vienna so at Naples, the spirit of an infidel Minister rested as an evil inheritance on the scene of his iniquitous labours. Tanucci was no more indeed, but his influence was perpetuated through Medici, Ferdinand's chief Minister, and perhaps in the midst of godless counsels it was greatly to the credit of the Neapolitan King that he succeeded in concluding a Concordat in 1818, which restored the Church as a working and vigorous institution, built up again the Episcopate and the religious orders, and conferred upon all Catholics of the kingdom the right of free communication with the Apostolic See in matters pertaining to the Faith. The majority of the bishoprics were vacant. Henceforth, in virtue of the Concordat, one hundred and nine were to constitute the whole number, monastic vows were legally recognized, whilst intercourse with the Holy Father was permitted alike to pastors and flock. The King would nominate the bishops, and the Pope would bestow confirmation.[7] These conditions, with the necessary local variations, were those of the Concordats in general. Nations had experienced the fallacy of all hopes except those that were founded on the Rock. Monarchs had attempted to reduce the Catholic Church to the rank of a national institution in order that they themselves might wield a double sceptre. Joseph II. and Kaunitz, Tanucci, and the great Napoleon, where were they now? In rendering to himself over and above what was his, Cæsar had been unmindful or wilfully neglectful of divine claims. Gradually the storm of European tumult and conflicting passions was subsiding into a temporary calm at the feet of an old man, who legislated for his spiritual children with the mighty powers of Europe. Only the truly humble of heart could have been chosen by God to be exalted as Pius VII. was exalted, but in the glory which was offered to him, he saw nothing but the incense of Faith which Catholic charity burns on the holy altar—a homage rendered to the Divine Emmanuel, God dwelling in and with His Church. A modern writer expresses this when he speaks of the festival of *Corpus Domini* at Rome, and the attitude of the Sovereign Pontiff before his Lord veiled in the Holy Eucharist. 'But high in air, beneath the canopy

---

[7] Möhler, *Kirchengeschichte*, t. iii. pp. 372, 366.

and upon the estrade or small platform borne aloft, is the crowning object of the entire procession. Under a faldstool richly covered stands the golden monstrance, as it was anciently called in England, that contains the holiest object of Catholic belief and worship; and behind it the Pontiff kneels with his ample embroidered mantle embracing the faldstool before him. Thus he is borne along, so that all may see and join him in his devotion, wherein he is undisturbed by even the motion required to walk in a procession. No one who ever saw Pope Pius VII. in this position will easily forget the picture. The hands firmly and immovably clasped at the base of the sacred vessel; the head bent down, not in feebleness but in homage; the closed eyes that saw none of the state and magnificence around, but shut out the world from the calm and silent meditation within; the noble features so composed that no expression of human feeling or an earthly thought could be traced upon, or gathered from them; the bare head scarcely ever uncovered except then, with locks still dark floating unheeded in the breeze; these characteristic forms and appearance of a human frame, unmoving and unwavering as a sculptured figure, might have been taken as the purest and sublimest symbol of entranced adoration. The swelling chorus of the hymns and psalms before him evidently did not reach his ear; the smoke of the fragrant incense just under him did not soothe his nostrils; the waves of a multitude, swayed to and fro with the murmur of a sea, traced not its image on his eyeballs; he was himself abstracted from all that sense could convey and was centred in one thought, in one act of mind, soul, and heart, in one duty of his sublime commission. He felt, and was, and you knew him to be what Moses was on the mountain, face to face, for all the people, with God; the Vicar with *his* Supreme Pontiff, the Chief Shepherd with the Prince of Pastors; the highest and first of living men with the One Living God.'[8]

The life of Pius VII. was a daily repetition of the procession of the Blessed Sacrament in which he bore so sublime yet so humble a part. He carried Jesus Christ into all hearts, and when he spoke, it has been said of him that he 'drew their soul out of his auditors to give them his own.' A voice from St. Helena, as a token that could recall the memory of its great and solitary misfortune, could not fall unheard upon the listening ears of Pius VII. In the deep tenderness of his heart, he was waiting for all such cries as a compensation for the joys with which Almighty God had been pleased to crown his Pontificate. Yet his gladness was not unmixed, for his power as Sovereign Pontiff was very limited as far as it regarded the mitigation of Napoleon's exile. When Fesch announced his intention of coming to live in Rome, Pius answered with his eager and affectionate courtesy: 'You are heartily welcome. I will do all I can to make it agreeable for you here. Rome has always been the country of noble exiles. It will be doubly yours, both as a Cardinal and as the Emperor's uncle.'[9] The mother and the brothers of Napoleon enjoyed the Holy Father's hospitality, for he had maintained in face of the Emperor's power that Rome was neutral ground, and now by a strange subversion, of which human events sometimes present the spectacle, the proscript's family profited by the sufferings which he had caused in his prosperous days to Pius VII. A few years later, a petition still more after the Sovereign Pontiff's own heart came to him from St. Helena. Napoleon wished for the ministry of a priest who might

---

[8] Wiseman, *Recollections of the Four Last Popes.*
[9] *Vie du Card. Fesch.* Par l'Abbé Lyonnet, t. ii. p. 250.

help him to die in the bosom of the Catholic and Roman Church. Whatever infidel opinions have been attributed to him, their presence is not recognizable in the hour which proves the faith of every man—in the valley of death, which is, as it were, the forecast shadow of judgment. His mortal illness began on the 17th of March, 1821. Its progress was tenderly watched by a priest, M. Vignali, who possessed the entire confidence of the Holy Father. Every date and every fortuitous appearance during those last days at St. Helena awakened the slumbering memories of greatness. On the 2nd of April, the anniversary of that imperial marriage which had brought Napoleon more pain than gladness, one of his servants announced the appearance of a comet in the east. 'A comet,' exclaimed the Emperor, who spoke from the abundance of his heart; 'a comet was the precursor of Cæsar's death.' A few days later, M. Vignali was called and addressed by Napoleon in these words: 'I was born in the Catholic religion. I wish to fulfil the duties which it imposes, and to receive the help which it administers.' Strong in death with the presence of the Uncreated Strength, the fallen warrior triumphed over enemies more formidable than those of the earthly battlefields who had trembled at his approach. It is a greater glory to die a Christian death than to reign victorious over a whole continent of foes. The one is a work of human genius alone, the other is achieved by the supernatural efforts of a man who says to all the world in his hour of agony: Now I can do nothing of myself. But by Him, in Him, and with Him Who can do all things, I am made strong. The confession of weakness is true greatness. Napoleon was not ungrateful for the interest which Pius VII. manifested in his welfare. Many times the Holy Father's name had been on his lips; he had spoken of the Pontiff as a lamb who still loved his persecutor. We cannot tell how far the patience of the 'lamb' contributed to the peace of the Emperor's end, but surely it had won an undisputed victory over material power represented by that tremendous empire of sixty millions. 'I should like,' Napoleon said, 'to have seen my wife and my son again; but the will of God be done.' Then as if the long force of habit prevailed over his last conscious moments, he murmured in dying the words: 'Head . . . Army . . . March!'

It was the 5th of May, 1821. From February 2nd, 1808, till March 10th, 1814, Pius VII. had been a captive, first in the Quirinal Palace, and then at Savona and Fontainebleau. From June, 1815, till May, 1821, Napoleon endured an exile which coincided almost to a month with the imprisonment of the Sovereign Pontiff, Did not the lonely rock of St. Helena expiate with a terrible exactness a persecution as cruel as it was gratuitous? But did it not likewise as a most merciful punishment open the gate of penitence and reconciliation? To have imprisoned a blameless Pope may have given six years of thought and recollection to a discrowned Emperor, with the result of forgiveness and peace.

Pius VII. and his minister Consalvi were fast hurrying towards the harbour. The Secretary of State was the victim of an organic disease which caused him to say that the Pope and he were dying together. But his mental activity still supplied the absence of physical strength. Like Pius, he had borne the burden of the day and of the heat, and he had also received a great compensation for his labours even in the worldly sense of the word. Many of Europe's potentates had formed a friendship with the Cardinal, whose cherished reward was the affection which he inspired. His intimacy with our George IV., whom he called 'his prince regent' is interesting to note, if only as a peculiarity of the times, when a ruler of England proclaimed his kindly feelings for a prince of the Church otherwise than by vain words. When Consalvi, after his peregrinations in Europe on the Pope's business, had finally settled down again as Prime Minister at Rome, George IV. who had kept up an interrupted intercourse by means of correspondence, sent him once through Giovannino (Consalvi's valet) a magnificent scarlet robe of Indian produce. The Cardinal followed the rule of genius, that is, he was generally where his spirit rather than where his body led him, and he did not remark the substitution. He appeared at a Papal chapel in his dazzling costume, and the Cardinals after the ceremony gathered round him to express their admiration. Consalvi was far more astonished than they, but he speedily retired, and disposed of his British Majesty's present in favour of a poor church of the *agro romano*.[10] He had been the only member of the Roman Court in office that had really excited the fear of Napoleon, who consequently used every means to try and bring about his retirement from the ministry. In 1814, as the Emperor was forced to turn his steps towards Elba, he met Consalvi, who was journeying back to Italy, after Pius VII., on the road. 'That is a man,' he remarked to his companion in the carriage, General Koller, 'who does not wish to appear *cagot*, but who is in fact *cagot* before all others.'[11] In his will, Consalvi bequeathed his testamentary riches, which comprised handsome presents from the majority of the crowned heads of Europe, to the honour of God and the memory of his friend

---

[10] Crétineau-Joly, *L'Eglise Romaine en face de la Révolution*, t. i. p. 479, note.
[11] Möhler, *Kirchengeschichte*, t. iii. p. 380.

Pius VII. They were to be employed partly in restoring the façade of the principal churches in Rome, partly in raising a monument to the Sovereign Pontiff for whom he had laboured, and by whom he had been so deeply loved. It is to Consalvi that St. Peter's owes the tomb that was executed by Thorwaldsen, and which allegorically resumes the reign of Pius VII. in two figures, one of strength, the other of moderation.[12]

The event at St. Helena in the year 1821 had been a divine retribution, the sufferings caused by which Pius had sought to allay. There was but one death-warrant which he would willingly have signed, that of the Revolution. In our century carbonari and secret societies are its special produce, and against them the Sovereign Pontiff spoke his last protest from the great Chair of Truth. He had restored the foremost champions of the Church Militant; he could not fail to condemn the attempts of evil and the powers of darkness which seek in a mysterious gloom to destroy the Catholic Church by stealth and fraud, because in broad daylight they cannot confront the supernatural force which is in her. At the solicitation of Austria, a Bull dated September 13th, 1821, was published against the carrying out of any such iniquitous designs. It exposed the snare to Catholics by forbidding them throughout the world to hold the principles of the carbonari. Not for the first time did the Holy See signalize with a 'loud and independent voice' the infamy of the secret societies. In this Bull it descended into points of detail, such as the means, the views, the hypocrisy and perjury of the members who authorize lies in order to cover their secret projects, and in whose ceremonies the Passion of our Lord is profaned.[13]

[12] *Histoire de Pie VII.* t. ii. p. 624.
[13] *Histoire de Pie VII.* t. ii. p. 587.

Little less than a month before the death of Pius VII., in July, 1823, the Church of St. Paul beyond the Walls, in whose convent he had passed so many years as a Benedictine monk, was destroyed by fire in one night. A dangerous fall he had experienced a few days previously, in seeking without assistance to reach the bell of his apartment, had obliged him to take to his bed; news of the flames which devoured the church of his former convent probably produced a further shock upon his exhausted frame. The doctors had enjoined that the serious nature of his fall should be kept from him; but how could Pius VII. fear death? Of his own accord he asked for the Holy Viaticum, the stay of the Sovereign Pontiff as It is of the poorest and weakest child of the Church. A few hours before the end, a priest addressed him as *Your Holiness*, and as at the death-bed of St. Helena, approaching eternity brought an increase of humility. 'How do you say Holiness,' replied Pius VII., 'I am only a poor sinner.' Almost the last words he was heard to murmur were: 'Savona . . . Fontainebleau.' Was it a last request for mercy at the remembrance of a momentary weakness? He expired on the 20th of August, 1823, aged eighty-one years and six days, after a Pontificate of twenty-three years and five months.

At the sound of military music, according to custom, and with almost military honours, he was brought to St. Peter's for his last rest. He had suffered and conquered not by shedding the blood of his body, but through a devotion to duty so true and noble that it may be likened to the victorious course of those who bear the martyr's palm. 'The kingdom of heaven suffereth violence.' Contemplating the indignities, humiliations, and imprisonment of Pius VII., may we not view the triumph of the Papacy as their especial reward, and write his own words in our Catholic hearts as encouragement and consolation: 'In this consists the essence of the holy institution of the Church which we acknowledge, that trouble serves but to develop its strength, and oppression but to produce its greater exaltation.'[14]

[14] Allocution of September 26th, 1814.

Quarterly Series.

(CONDUCTED BY THE MANAGERS OF THE "MONTH AND CATHOLIC REVIEW.")

1872.

1. The Life and Letters of St. Francis Xavier.

By the Rev. H. J. COLERIDGE. Vol. I. Second Edition. Price 7s. 6d.

2. The Life of St. Jane Frances Fremyot de Chantal.

By EMILY BOWLES. With Preface by the Rev. H. J. COLERIDGE. Second Edition. Price 5s. 6d.

3. The History of the Sacred Passion.

By Father LUIS DE LA PALMA, of the Society of Jesus. Translated from the Spanish. With Preface by the Rev. H. J. COLERIDGE. Third Edition. Price 7s. 6d.

4. Life and Letters of St. Francis Xavier.

By the Rev. H. J. COLERIDGE. Vol. II. Price 10s. 6d.

1873.

5. Iërne of Armorica: A Tale of the Time of Chlovis.

By J. C. BATEMAN. Price 6s. 6d.

6. The Life of Doña Luisa de Carvajal.

By Lady GEORGIANA FULLERTON. Price 6s.

7. The Life of Blessed John Berchmans.

By the Rev. F. GOLDIE. Price 6s.

8. The Life of Blessed Peter Favre,

First Companion of St. Ignatius Loyola. From the Italian of Father BOERO. With Preface by the Rev. H. J. COLERIDGE. Price 6s. 6d.

1874.

9. *The Dialogues of St. Gregory the Great.*
An Old English version. Edited by the Rev. H. J. COLERIDGE, S.J. Price 6s.

10. *The Life of Anne Catharine Emmerich.*
By HELEN RAM. With Preface by Rev. H. J. COLERIDGE, S.J. Price 6s.

11. *The Prisoner of the Temple; or, Discrowned and Crowned.*
By Mr. O'C MORRIS. With Preface by Rev. H. J. COLERIDGE, S.J. Price 4s. 6d.

12. *The Public Life of our Lord Jesus Christ.*
Part I. "The Ministry of St. John Baptist." By the Rev. H. J. COLERIDGE, S.J. Price 6s. 6d.

1875.

13. *The Story of St. Stanislaus Kostka.*
Edited by the Rev. H. J. COLERIDGE, S.J. Price 3s. 6d.

14. *The Public Life of our Lord Jesus Christ.*
Part II. "The Preaching of the Beatitudes." By the Rev. H. J. COLERIDGE, S.J. Price 6s. 6d.

15. *The Chronicle of St. Antony of Padua,*
"The Eldest Son of St. Francis." Edited by Rev. H. J. COLERIDGE, S.J. In Four Books. Price 5s. 6d.

16. *The Life of Pope Pius the Seventh.*
By M. ALLIES.

IN PREPARATION.

The Sermon on the Mount and *the Lord of the Sabbath.*
Being the Third and Fourth volumes of the PUBLIC LIFE OF OUR LORD.

History of the Suppression of the Society of Jesus.
From Documents hitherto unpublished. By the Rev. A. WELD.

Life of the Blessed Mary of the Incarnation
(Madame Acaria). By EMILY BOWLES.

The Life and Letters of St. Teresa.

BURNS AND OATES, PORTMAN STREET AND PATERNOSTER ROW.

A

Select Catalogue of Books

LATELY PUBLISHED BY

BURNS AND OATES,

17, 18 PORTMAN STREET

AND

63 PATERNOSTER ROW.

LONDON
ROBSON AND SONS, PRINTERS, PANCRAS ROAD, N.W.

Books lately published

BY

BURNS AND OATES,

17, 18 PORTMAN STREET, W., & 63 PATERNOSTER ROW, E.C.

———o———

Sin and its Consequences. By His Eminence the CARDINAL ARCHBISHOP OF WESTMINSTER. Third edition. 6s.

    CONTENTS: I. The Nature of Sin. II. Mortal Sin. III. Venial Sin. IV. Sins of Omission. V. The Grace and Works of Penance. VI. Temptation. VII. The Dereliction on the Cross. VIII. The Joys of the Resurrection.

'We know few better books than this for spiritual reading. These lectures are prepared with great care, and are worthy to rank with the old volumes of sermons which are now standard works of the English tongue.'—*Weekly Register.*

'We have had many volumes from his Grace's pen of this kind, but perhaps none more practical or more searching than the volume before us. These discourses are the clearest and simplest exposition of the theology of the subjects they treat of that could be desired. The intellect is addressed as well as the conscience. Both are strengthened and satisfied.'—*Tablet.*

'Of the deepest value, and of great theological and literary excellence. More clear and lucid expositions of dogmatic and moral theology could not be found. No one can read these very forcible, searching, and practical sermons without being deeply stirred and greatly edified.'—*Church Herald.*

'His Grace has added to Catholic literature such a brilliant disquisition as can hardly be equalled.'—*Catholic Times.*

'As powerful, searching, and deep as any that we have ever read. In construction, as well as in theology and in rhetoric, they are more than remarkable, and are amongst the best from his Grace's pen.'—*Union Review.*

The Prophet of Carmel: a Series of Practical Considerations upon the History of Elias in the Old Testament; with a Supplementary Dissertation. By the late Rev. CHARLES B. GARSIDE, M.A. Dedicated to the Very Rev. JOHN HENRY NEWMAN, D.D. 5s.

'There is not a page in these sermons but commands our respect. They are Corban in the best sense; they belong to the sanctuary, and are marked as divine property by a special cachet. They are simple without being trite, and poetical without being pretentious.'—*Westminster Gazette.*

'Full of spiritual wisdom uttered in pure and engaging language.'—*The Universe.*

'We see in these pages the learning of the divine, the elegance of the scholar, and the piety of the priest. Every point in the sacred narrative bearing upon the subject of his book is seized upon by the author with the greatest keenness of perception, and set forth with singular force and clearness.'—*Weekly Register.*

'Under his master-hand the marvellous career of the Prophet of Carmel displays its majestic proportions. His strong, nervous, incisive style has a beauty and a grace, a delicacy and a sensitiveness, that seizes hold of the heart and captivates the imagination. He has attained to the highest art of writing, which consists in selecting the words which express one's meaning with the greatest clearness in the least possible space.'—*Tablet.*

'The intellectual penetration, the rich imagination, the nervous eloquence which we meet with throughout the whole work, all combine to give it at once a very high place among the highest productions of our English Catholic literature.'—*Dublin Review.*

'Is at once powerful and engaging, and calculated to furnish ideas innumerable to the Christian preacher.'—*Church Review.*

'The thoughts are expressed in plain and vigorous English. The sermons are good specimens of the way in which Old Testament subjects should be treated for the instruction of a Christian congregation.'—*Church Times.*

Mary magnifying God: May Sermons. By the Rev. Fr. HUMPHREY, O.S.C. Cloth, 2s. 6d.

'Each sermon is a complete thesis, eminent for the strength of its logic, the soundness of its theology, and the lucidness of its expression. With equal force and beauty of language the author has provided matter for the most sublime meditations.'—*Tablet.*

'Dogmatic teaching of the utmost importance is placed before us so clearly, simply, and unaffectedly, that we find ourselves acquiring invaluable lessons of theology in every page.'—*Weekly Register.*

By the same,

The Divine Teacher. Second edition. 2s. 6d.

'The most excellent treatise we have ever read. It could not be clearer, and, while really deep, it is perfectly intelligible to any person of the most ordinary education.'—*Tablet.*

'We cannot speak in terms too high of the matter contained in this excellent and able pamphlet.'—*Westminster Gazette.*

Short Sermons preached in the Chapel of St. Mary's College, Oscott. Collected and edited by the President. 6s.

Month of Mary of our Lady of Lourdes.
By HENRY LASSERRE. Translated from the French (twenty-third edition) by Mrs. CROSIER. 2s. 6d.; cloth, 3s.

More than 25,000 copies of the original have been sold. This edition is copyright.

'There is no devotional work with which we are acquainted that can for an instant be brought into comparison with it. The exquisite charm and attraction of this beautiful prayer-book it would be difficult to exaggerate.' —*Weekly Register.*

'An impressive and a wonderful book.'—*Nation.*

'A valuable work conceived in the most admirable spirit of Catholic piety, and expressed in language the most graceful and elevating.'—*Cork Examiner.*

Sermons by Fathers of the Society of Jesus.
3 vols.

Vol. I. Third edition. 7*s.*

CONTENTS: The Latter Days: Four Sermons by the Rev. H. J. Coleridge. The Temptations of our Lord: Four Sermons by the Rev. Father Hathaway. The Angelus Bell: Five Lectures on the Remedies against Desolation by the Very Rev. Father Gallwey, Provincial of the Society. The Mysteries of the Holy Infancy: Seven Sermons by Fathers Parkinson, Coleridge, and Harper.

Also, printed separately from above,

The Angelus Bell: Five Lectures on the Remedies against Desolation. By the Very Rev. Father GALLWEY, Provincial of the Society of Jesus. 1*s.* 6*d.*

Vol. II., comprising Discourses by the Rev. Father Harper, S.J. 6*s.*

Vol. III. 6*s.*

CONTENTS: Sermons by the Rev. George R. Kingdon: I. What the Passion of Christ teaches us; II. Our Lord's Agony in the Garden; III. The Choice between Jesus and Barabbas; IV. Easter Sunday (I.); V. Easter Sunday (II.); VI. Corpus Christi.—Sermons by the Rev. Edward I. Purbrick: VII. Grandeur and Beauty of the Holy Eucharist; VIII. Our Lady of Victories; IX. The Feast of All Saints (I.); X. The Feast of All Saints (II.); XI. The Feast of the Immaculate Conception; XII. The Feast of St. Joseph. —Sermons by the Rev. Henry J. Coleridge: XIII. Fruits of Holy Communion (I.); XIV. Fruits of Holy Communion (II.); XV. Fruits of Holy Communion (III.); XVI. Fruits of Holy Communion (IV.).—Sermons by the Rev. Alfred Weld: XVII. On the Charity of Christ; XVIII. On the Blessed Sacrament.—Sermons by the Rev. William H. Anderdon: XIX. The Corner-Stone a Rock of Offence; XX. The Word of God heard or rejected by Men.

WORKS WRITTEN AND EDITED BY LADY GEORGIANA FULLERTON.

The Straw-cutter's Daughter, and the Portrait in my Uncle's Dining-room. Two Stories. Translated from the French. 2*s.* 6*d.*

Life of Luisa de Carvajal. 6s.

Seven Stories. 3s. 6d.
    CONTENTS: I. Rosemary: a Tale of the Fire of London. II. Reparation: a Story of the Reign of Louis XIV. III. The Blacksmith of Antwerp. IV. The Beggar of the Steps of St. Roch: a True Story. V. Trouvaille, or the Soldier's Adopted Child: a True Story. VI. Earth without Heaven: a Reminiscence. VII. Ad Majorem Dei Gloriam.
  'Will well repay perusal.'—*Weekly Register.*
  'Each story in this series has its own charm.'—*Tablet.*
  'In this collection may be found stories sound in doctrine and intensely interesting as any which have come from the same pen.'—*Catholic Opinion.*
  'As admirable for their art as they are estimable for their sound teaching.'—*Cork Examiner.*

Laurentia: a Tale of Japan. Second edition. 3s. 6d.
  'Has very considerable literary merit, and possesses an interest entirely its own. The dialogue is easy and natural, and the incidents are admirably grouped.'—*Weekly Register.*
  'Full of romantic records of the heroism of the early Christians of Japan in the sixteenth century. Looking at its literary merits alone, it must be pronounced a really beautiful story.'—*Catholic Times.*

Life of St. Frances of Rome. 2s. 6d.; cheap edition, 1s. 8d.

Rose Leblanc: a Tale of great interest. 3s.

Grantley Manor: the well-known and favourite Novel. Cloth, 3s. 6d.; cheap edition, 2s. 6d.

Germaine Cousin: a Drama. 6d.

Fire of London: a Drama. 6d.

OUR LADY'S BOOKS.
Uniformly printed in foolscap 8vo, limp cloth.

No. 1.
Memoir of the Hon. Henry E. Dormer. 2s.

No. 2.
Life of Mary Fitzgerald, a Child of the Sacred Heart. 2s.; cheap edition, 1s.

A Sketch of the Life of the late Father Henry Young, of Dublin. 2*s.* 6*d.*

Meditations for every Day in the Year, and for the Principal Feasts. By the Ven. Fr. NICHOLAS LANCICIUS, of the Society of Jesus. With Preface by the Rev. GEORGE PORTER, S.J. 6*s.* 6*d.*

'Most valuable, not only to religious, for whom they were originally intended, but to all those who desire to consecrate their daily life by regularly express and systematic meditation; while Father Porter's excellent little Preface contains many valuable hints on the method of meditation.'—*Dublin Review.*

'Full of Scripture, short and suggestive. The editor gives a very clear explanation of the Ignatian method of meditation. The book is a very useful one.'—*Tablet.*

'Short and simple, and dwell almost entirely on the life of our Blessed Lord, as related in the Gospels. Well suited to the wants of Catholics living in the world.'—*Weekly Register.*

'A book of singular spirituality and great depth of piety. Nothing could be more beautiful or edifying than the thoughts set forth for reflection, clothed as they are in excellent and vigorous English.'—*Union Review.*

Meditations for the Use of the Clergy, for every Day in the Year, on the Gospels for the Sundays. From the Italian of Mgr. SCOTTI, Archbishop of Thessalonica. Revised and edited by the Oblates of St. Charles. With a Preface by His Eminence the CARDINAL ARCHBISHOP OF WESTMINSTER.

Vol. I. From the First Sunday in Advent to the Sixth Saturday after the Epiphany. 4*s.*
Vol. II. From Septuagesima Sunday to the Fourth Sunday after Easter. 4*s.*
Vol. III. From the Fifth Sunday after Easter to the Eleventh Sunday after Pentecost. 4*s.*
Vol. IV., completing the work. 4*s.*

'This admirable little book will be much valued by all, but especially by the clergy, for whose use it is more immediately intended. The Archbishop states in his Preface that it is held in high esteem in Rome, and that he has himself found, by the experience of many years, its singular excellence, its practical piety, its abundance of Scripture, of the Fathers, and of ecclesiastical writers.'—*Tablet.*

'It is a sufficient recommendation to this book of meditations that our Archbishop has given them his own warm approval. . . . They are full of the language of the Scriptures, and are rich with unction of their Divine sense.'—*Weekly Register.*

'There is great beauty in the thoughts, the illustrations are striking, the learning shown in patristic quotation considerable, and the special applications to priests are very powerful. It is entirely a priest's book.'—*Church Review.*

'A manual of meditations for priests, to which we have seen nothing comparable.'—*Catholic World.*

The Question of Anglican Ordinations discussed. By the Very Rev. Canon ESTCOURT, M.A., F.A.S. With an Appendix of Original Documents and Photographic Facsimiles. One vol. 8vo, 14s.

'A valuable contribution to the theology of the Sacrament of Order. He treats a leading question, from a practical point of view, with great erudition, and with abundance of illustrations from the rites of various ages and countries.'—*Month.*

'Will henceforth be an indispensable portion of every priest's library, inasmuch as it contains all the information that has been collected in previous works, sifted and corrected, together with a well-digested mass of important matter which has never before been given to the public.'—*Tablet.*

'Marks a very important epoch in the history of that question, and virtually disposes of it.'—*Messenger.*

'Canon Estcourt has added valuable documents that have never appeared before, or never at full length. The result is a work of very great value.'—*Catholic Opinion.*

'Indicates conscientious and painstaking research, and will be indispensable to any student who would examine the question on which it treats.'—*Bookseller.*

'Superior, both in literary method, tone, and mode of reasoning, to the usual controversial books on this subject.'—*Church Herald.*

Glories of the Sacred Heart. By HENRY EDWARD, Cardinal Archbishop. 6s.

CONTENTS: I. The Divine Glory of the Sacred Heart. II. The Sacred Heart God's Way of Love. III. Dogma the Source of Devotion. IV. The Science of the Sacred Heart. V. The Last Will of the Sacred Heart. VI. The Temporal Glory of the Sacred Heart. VII. The Transforming Power of the Sacred Heart. VIII. The Sure Way of Likeness to the Sacred Heart. IX. The Signs of the Sacred Heart. X. The Eternal Glory of the Sacred Heart.

Also by the same,

The Love of Jesus to Penitents. Third edition. 1s. 6d.

CONTENTS: I. The Sacrament of Penance the Special Sacrament of the Compassion of Jesus. II. The Sacrament of Penance a Means of Self-knowledge. III. The Sacrament of Penance the Means of Perfecting our Contrition. IV. The Sacrament of Penance the Sacrament of Reparation. V. The Sacrament of Perseverance.

WORKS OF THE REV. FATHER RAWES, O.S.C.

Homeward: a Tale of Redemption. Second edition. 3s. 6d.

'A series of beautiful word pictures.'—*Catholic Opinion.*
'A casket well worth the opening; full to the brim of gems of thought as beautiful as they are valuable.'—*Catholic Times.*
'Full of holy thoughts and exquisite poetry, and just such a book as can be taken up with advantage and relief in hours of sadness and depression.'—*Dublin Review.*
'Is really beautiful, and will be read with profit.'—*Church Times.*

God in His Works: a Course of Five Sermons. 2s. 6d.

SUBJECTS: I. God in Creation. II. God in the Incarnation. III. God in the Holy See. IV. God in the Heart. V. God in the Resurrection.

'Full of striking imagery, and the beauty of the language cannot fail to make the book valuable for spiritual reading.'—*Catholic Times.*
'He has so applied science as to bring before the reader an unbroken course of thought and argument.'—*Tablet.*

The Beloved Disciple; or St. John the Evangelist. Second edition. 3s. 6d.

'Full of research, and of tender and loving devotion.'—*Tablet.*
'This is altogether a charming book for spiritual reading.'—*Catholic Times.*
'Through this book runs a vein of true, humble, fervent piety, which gives a singular charm.'—*Weekly Register.*
'St. John, in his varied character, is beautifully and attractively presented to our pious contemplation.'—*Catholic Opinion.*

Septem: Seven Ways of hearing Mass. Eighth edition. 1s. and 2s.; red edges, 2s. 6d.; calf, 4s.; French Translation, 1s. 6d.

'A great assistance to hearing Mass with devotion. Besides its devotional advantages it possesses a Preface, in clear and beautiful language, well worth reading.'—*Tablet.*

Great Truths in Little Words. Third edition. Neat cloth, 3s. 6d.

'A most valuable little work. All may learn very much about the Faith from it.'—*Tablet.*
'At once practical in its tendency, and elegant; oftentimes poetical in its diction.'—*Weekly Register.*
'Cannot fail to be most valuable to every Catholic; and we feel certain, when known and appreciated, it will be a standard work in Catholic households.'—*Catholic Times.*

Hymns, Original, &c. Neat cloth, 1s.; cheap edition, 6d.

* *The Eucharistic Month.* From the Latin of Father LERCARI, S.J. 6d.; cloth, 1s.

* *Twelve Visits to our Lady and the Heavenly City of God.* Second edition. 8d.

* *Nine Visits to the Blessed Sacrament.* Chiefly from the Canticle of Canticles. Second edition. 6d.

* *Devotions for the Souls in Purgatory.* Third edition. 8d.

* Or in one vol.,

Visits and Devotions. Neat cloth, 3s.

WORKS BY FATHER ANDERDON, S.J.

Christian Æsop. 3s. 6d. and 4s.

In the Snow: Tales of Mount St. Bernard. Sixth edition. Cloth, 1s. 6d.

Afternoons with the Saints. Eighth edition, enlarged. 5s.

Catholic Crusoe. Seventh edition. Cloth gilt, 3s. 6d.

Confession to a Priest. 1d.

What is the Bible? Is yours the right Book? New edition. 1d.

Also, edited by Father Anderdon,

What do Catholics really believe? 2d.

Cherubini: Memorials illustrative of his Life. With Portrait and Catalogue of his Works. By EDWARD BELLASIS, Barrister-at-Law. One vol., 429 pp. 10s. 6d.

Louise Lateau of Bois d'Haine: her Life, her Ecstasies, and her Stigmata: a Medical Study. By Dr. F. LEFEBVRE, Professor of General Pathology and Therapeutics in the Catholic University of Louvain, &c. Translated from the French. Edited by Rev. J. SPENCER NORTHCOTE, D.D. Full and complete edition. 3*s.* 6*d.*

'The name of Dr. Lefebvre is sufficient guarantee of the importance of any work coming from his pen. The reader will find much valuable information.'—*Tablet.*

'The whole case thoroughly entered into and fully considered. The Appendix contains many medical notes of interest.'—*Weekly Register.*

'A full and complete answer.'—*Catholic Times.*

Twelve New Tales. By Mrs. PARSONS.

1. Bertha's Three Fingers. 2. Take Care of Yourself. 3. Don't Go In. 4. The Story of an Arm-chair. 5. Yes and No. 6. The Red Apples under the Tree. 7. Constance and the Water Lilies. 8. The Pair of Gold Spectacles. 9. Clara's New Shawl. 10. The Little Lodgers. 11. The Pride and the Fall. 12. This Once.

3*d.* each; in a Packet complete, 3*s.*; or in cloth neat, 3*s.* 6*d.*

'Sound Catholic theology and a truly religious spirit breathes from every page, and it may be safely commended to schools and convents.'—*Tablet.*

'Full of sound instruction given in a pointed and amusing manner.'—*Weekly Register.*

'Very pretty, pleasantly told, attractive to little folks, and of such a nature that from each some moral good is inculcated. The tales are cheerful, sound, and sweet, and should have a large sale.'—*Catholic Times.*

'A very good collection of simple tales. The teaching is Catholic throughout.'—*Catholic Opinion.*

Marie and Paul: a Fragment. By 'Our Little Woman.' 3*s.* 6*d.*; gilt edges, 4*s.*

'We heartily recommend this touching little tale, especially as a present for children and for schools, feeling sure that none can rise from its perusal without being touched, both at the beauty of the tale itself and by the tone of earnest piety which runs through the whole, leaving none but holy thoughts and pleasant impressions on the minds of both old and young.'—*Tablet.*

'Well adapted to the innocent minds it is intended for. The little book would be a suitable present for a little friend.'—*Catholic Opinion.*

'A charming tale for young and old.'—*Cork Examiner.*

'To all who read it the book will suggest thoughts for which they will be the better, while its graceful and affecting, because simple, pictures of home and family life will excite emotions of which none need be ashamed.'—*Month.*

'Told effectively and touchingly, with all that tenderness and pathos in which gifted women so much excel.'—*Weekly Register.*

'A very pretty and pathetic tale.'—*Catholic World.*

'A very charming story, and may be read by both young and old.'—*Brownson's Review.*

'Presents us with some deeply-touching incidents of family love and devotion.'—*Catholic Times.*

Dame Dolores, or the Wise Nun of Eastonmere; and other Stories. By the Author of 'Tyborne,' &c. 4s.

CONTENTS: I. The Wise Nun of Eastonmere. II. Known Too Late. III. True to the End. IV. Olive's Rescue.

'We have read the volume with considerable pleasure, and we trust no small profit. The tales are decidedly clever, well worked out, and written with a flowing and cheerful pen.'—*Catholic Times.*

'The author of *Tyborne* is too well known to need any fresh recommendation to the readers of Catholic fiction. We need only say that her present will be as welcome to her many friends as any of her former works.'—*Month.*

'An attractive volume; and we know of few tales that we can more safely or more thoroughly recommend to our young readers.'—*Weekly Register.*

Maggie's Rosary, and other Tales. By the Author of 'Marian Howard.' Cloth extra, 3s., cheap edition, 2s.

'We strongly recommend these stories. They are especially suited to little girls.'—*Tablet.*

'The very thing for a gift-book for a child; but at the same time so interesting and full of incident that it will not be contemned by children of a larger growth.'—*Weekly Register.*

'We have seldom seen tales better adapted for children's reading.'—*Catholic Times.*

'The writer possesses in an eminent degree the art of making stories for children.'—*Catholic Opinion.*

'A charming little book, which we can heartily recommend.'—*Rosarian.*

Scenes and Incidents at Sea. A new Selection. 1s. 4d.

CONTENTS: I. Adventure on a Rock. II. A Heroic Act of Rescue. III. Inaccessible Islands. IV. The Shipwreck of the Czar Alexander. V. Captain James's Adventures in the North Seas. VI. Destruction of Admiral Graves's Fleet. VII. The Wreck of the Forfarshire, and Grace Darling. VIII. The Loss of the Royal George. IX. The Irish Sailor Boy. X. Gallant Conduct of a French Privateer. XI. The Harpooner. XII. The Cruise of the Agamemnon. XIII. A Nova Scotia Fog. XIV. The Mate's Story. XV. The Shipwreck of the Æneas Transport. XVI. A Scene in the Shrouds. XVII. A Skirmish off Bermuda. XVIII. Charles Wager. XIX. A Man Overboard. XX. A Loss and a Rescue. XXI. A Melancholy Adventure on the American Seas. XXII. Dolphins and Flying Fish.

History of England, for Family Use and the Upper Classes of Schools. By the Author of 'Christian Schools and Scholars.' Second edition. With Preface by the Very Rev. Dr. NORTHCOTE. 6s.

Tales from the Diary of a Sister of Mercy. By C. M. BRAME. New edition. Cloth extra, 4s.

CONTENTS: The Double Marriage. The Cross and the Crown. The Novice. The Fatal Accident. The Priest's Death. The Gambler's Wife. The Apostate. The Besetting Sin.

'Written in a chaste, simple, and touching style.'—*Tablet.*
'This book is a casket, and those who open it will find the gem within.'—*Register.*
'They are well and cleverly told, and the volume is neatly got up.'—*Month.*
'Very well told; all full of religious allusions and expressions.'—*Star.*
'Very well written, and life-like; many very pathetic.'—*Catholic Opinion.*

By the same,

Angels' Visits: a Series of Tales. With Frontispiece and Vignette. 3s. 6d.

'The tone of the book is excellent, and it will certainly make itself a great favourite with the young.'—*Month.*
'Beautiful collection of Angel Stories.'—*Weekly Register.*
'One of the prettiest books for children we have seen.'—*Tablet.*
'A book which excites more than ordinary praise.'—*Northern Press.*
'Touchingly written, and evidently the emanation of a refined and pious mind.'—*Church Times.*
'A charming little book, full of beautiful stories of the family of angels.'—*Church Opinion.*

ST. JOSEPH'S THEOLOGICAL LIBRARY.
Edited by Fathers of the Society of Jesus.

Vol. I.

On some Popular Errors concerning Politics and Religion. By the Right Honourable Lord ROBERT MONTAGU, M.P. 6s.

CONTENTS: Introduction. I. The Basis of Political Science. II. Religion. III. The Church. IV. Religious Orders. V. Christian Law. VI. The Mass. VII. The Principles of 1789. VIII. Liberty. IX. Fraternity. X. Equality. XI. Nationality, Non-intervention, and the Accomplished Fact. XII. Capital Punishment. XIII. Liberal Catholics.

XIV. Civil Marriage. XV. Secularisation of Education. XVI. Conclusion. Additional Notes.

This book has been taken from the 'Risposte popolari alle obiezioni piu diffuse contro la Religione; opera del P. Secondo Franco. Torino, 1868.' It is not a translation of that excellent Italian work, for much has been omitted, and even the forms of expression have not been retained; nor yet is it an abstract, for other matter has been added throughout. The aim of the editor has been merely to follow out the intention of P. Franco, and adapt his thoughts to the circumstances and mind of England.

Considerations for a Three Days' Preparation for Communion. Taken chiefly from the French of SAINT JURE, S.J. By CECILIE MARY CADDELL. 8*d.*

'In every respect a most excellent manual.'—*Catholic Times.*
'A simple and easy method for a devout preparation for that solemn duty.'—*Weekly Register.*
'A beautiful compilation carefully prepared.'—*Universe.*

The Spiritual Conflict and Conquest. By Dom J. CASTANIZA, O.S.B. Edited, with Preface and Notes, by Canon VAUGHAN, English Monk of the Order of St. Benedict. Second edition. Reprinted from the old English Translation of 1652. With fine Original Frontispiece reproduced in Autotype. 8*s.* 6*d.*

The Letter-Books of Sir Amias Poulet, Keeper of Mary Queen of Scots. Edited by JOHN MORRIS, Priest of the Society of Jesus. Demy 8vo, 10*s.* 6*d.*

Sir Amias Poulet had charge of the Queen of Scots from April 1585 to the time of her death, February 8, 1587. His correspondence with Lord-Treasurer Burghley and Sir Francis Walsingham enters into the details of her life in captivity at Tutbury, Chartley, and Fotheringay. Many of the letters now published are entirely unknown, being printed from a recently-discovered manuscript. The others have been taken from the originals at the Public Record Office and the British Museum. The letters are strung together by a running commentary, in the course of which several of Mr. Froude's statements are examined, and the question of Mary's complicity in the plot against Elizabeth's life is discussed.

Sœur Eugenie: the Life and Letters of a Sister of Charity. By the Author of 'A Sketch of the Life of St. Paula.' Second edition, enlarged. On toned paper, cloth gilt, 4s. 6d.; plain paper, cloth plain, 3s.

'It is impossible to read it without bearing away in one's heart some of the "odour of sweetness" which breathes forth from almost every page.'—*Tablet.*

'The most charming piece of religious biography that has appeared since the *Récits d'une Sœur.*'—*Catholic Opinion.*

'We have seldom read a more touching tale of youthful holiness.'—*Weekly Register.*

'The picture of a life of hidden piety and grace, and of active charity, which it presents is extremely beautiful.'—*Nation.*

'We strongly recommend this devout and interesting life to the careful perusal of all our readers.'—*Westminster Gazette.*

Count de Montalembert's Letters to a School-fellow, 1827-1830. Qualis ab incepto. Translated from the French by C. F. AUDLEY. With Portrait. 5s.

'Simple, easy, and unaffected in a degree, these letters form a really charming volume. The observations are simply wonderful, considering that when he wrote them he was only seventeen or eighteen years of age.'—*Weekly Register.*

'A new treasure is now presented for the first time in an English casket—the letters he wrote when a schoolboy. The loftiness of the aspirations they breathe is supported by the intellectual power of which they give evidence.'—*Cork Examiner.*

'Reveal in the future ecclesiastical champion and historian a depth of feeling and insight into forthcoming events hardly to be expected from a mere schoolboy.'—*Building News.*

'Display vigour of thought and real intellectual power.'—*Church Herald.*

Ecclesiastical Antiquities of London and its Suburbs. By ALEXANDER WOOD, M.A. Oxon., of the Somerset Archæological Society. 5s.

'O, who the ruine sees, whom wonder doth not fill
With our great fathers' pompe, devotion, and their skill?'

'Will prove a most useful manual to many of our readers. Stores of Catholic memories still hang about the streets of this great metropolis. For the ancient and religious associations of such places the Catholic reader can want no better cicerone than Mr. Wood.'—*Weekly Register.*

'We have indeed to thank Mr. Wood for this excellent little book.'—*Catholic Opinion.*

'Very seldom have we read a book devoted entirely to the metropolis with such pleasure.'—*Liverpool Catholic Times.*

'A very pleasing and readable book.'—*Builder.*

'Gives a plain, sensible, but learned and interesting account of the chief church antiquities of London and its suburbs. It is written by a very able and competent author—one who thoroughly appreciates his subject, and who treats it with the discrimination of a critic and the sound common sense of a practised writer.'—*Church Herald.*

LIBRARY OF RELIGIOUS BIOGRAPHY.
Edited by EDWARD HEALY THOMPSON.

Vol. I.
The Life of St. Aloysius Gonzaga, S.J.
Second edition. 5s.

'Contains numberless traces of a thoughtful and tender devotion to the Saint. It shows a loving penetration into his spirit, and an appreciation of the secret motives of his action, which can only be the result of a deeply affectionate study of his life and character.'—*Month.*

Vol. II.
The Life of Marie Eustelle Harpain; or the Angel of the Eucharist. Second edition. 5s.

'Possesses a special value and interest apart from its extraordinay natural and supernatural beauty, from the fact that to her example and to the effect of her writings is attributed in great measure the wonderful revival of devotion to the Blessed Sacrament in France, and consequently throughout Western Christendom.'—*Dublin Review.*

'A more complete instance of that life of purity and close union with God in the world of which we have just been speaking is to be found in the history of Marie Eustelle Harpain, the sempstress of Saint-Pallais. The writer of the present volume has had the advantage of very copious materials in the French works on which his own work is founded; and Mr. Thompson has discharged his office as editor with his usual diligence and accuracy.'—*Month.*

Vol. III.
The Life of St. Stanislas Kostka. 5s.

'We strongly recommend this biography to our readers.'—*Tablet.*

'There has been no adequate biography of St. Stanislas. In rectifying this want Mr. Thompson has earned a title to the gratitude of English-speaking Catholics. The engaging Saint of Poland will now be better known among us, and we need not fear that, better known, he will not be better loved.'—*Weekly Register.*

Vol. IV.
The Life of the Baron de Renty; or Perfection in the World exemplified. 6s.

'An excellent book. The style is throughout perfectly fresh and buoyant.'—*Dublin Review.*

'This beautiful work is a compilation, not of biographical incidents, but of holy thoughts and spiritual aspirations, which we may feed on and make our own.'—*Tablet.*

'Gives full particulars of his marvellous virtue in an agreeable form.'—*Catholic Times.*

'A good book for our Catholic young men, teaching how they can sanctify the secular state.'—*Catholic Opinion.*

'Edifying and instructive, a beacon and guide to those whose walks are in the ways of the world, who toil and strive to win Christian perfection.'—*Ulster Examiner.*

Vol. V.

The Life of the Venerable Anna Maria Taigi, the Roman Matron (1769-1837). Third edition. With Portrait. 6s.

This Biography has been written after a careful collation of previous Lives of the Servant of God with each other, and with the *Analecta Juris Pontificii*, which contain large extracts from the Processes. Various prophecies attributed to her and other holy persons have been collected in an Appendix.

'Of all the series of deeply-interesting biographies which the untiring zeal and piety of Mr. Healy Thompson has given of late years to English Catholics, none, we think, is to be compared in interest with the one before us, both from the absorbing nature of the life itself and the spiritual lessons it conveys.'—*Tablet.*

'A complete biography of the Venerable Matron in the composition of which the greatest care has been taken and the best authorities consulted. We can safely recommend the volume for the discrimination with which it has been written, and for the careful labour and completeness by which it has been distinguished.'—*Catholic Opinion.*

'We recommend this excellent and carefully-compiled biography to all our readers. The evident care exercised by the editor in collating the various lives of Anna Maria gives great value to the volume, and we hope it will meet with the support it so justly merits.'—*Westminster Gazette.*

'We thank Mr. Healy Thompson for this volume. The direct purpose of his biographies is always spiritual edification.'—*Dublin Review.*

'Contains much that is capable of nourishing pious sentiments.'—*Nation.*

'Has evidently been a labour of love.'—*Month.*

The Hidden Life of Jesus: a Lesson and Model to Christians. Translated from the French of BOUDON, by EDWARD HEALY THOMPSON, M.A. Cloth, 3s.

'This profound and valuable work has been very carefully and ably translated by Mr. Thompson.'—*Register.*

'The more we have of such works as the *Hidden Life of Jesus* the better.'—*Westminster Gazette.*

'A book of searching power.'—*Church Review.*

'We have often regretted that this writer's works are not better known.'—*Universe.*

'We earnestly recommend its study and practice to all readers.'—*Tablet.*

'We have to thank Mr. Thompson for this translation of a valuable work which has long been popular in France.'—*Dublin Review.*

'A good translation.'—*Month.*

Also, by the same Author and Translator,

Devotion to the Nine Choirs of Holy Angels,
and especially to the Angel Guardians. 3s.

'We congratulate Mr. Thompson on the way in which he has accomplished his task, and we earnestly hope that an increased devotion to the Holy Angels may be the reward of his labour of love.'—*Tablet.*

'A beautiful translation.'—*Month.*

'The translation is extremely well done.'—*Weekly Register.*

New Meditations for each Day in the Year,
on the Life of our Lord Jesus Christ. By a Father of the Society of Jesus. With the imprimatur of the Cardinal Archbishop of Westminster. New and improved edition. Two vols. Cloth, 9s.; also in calf, 16s.; morocco, 17s.

'We can heartily recommend this book for its style and substance; it bears with it several strong recommendations. ... It is solid and practical.'—*Westminster Gazette.*

'A work of great practical utility, and we give it our earnest recommendation.'—*Weekly Register.*

The Day Sanctified; being Meditations and
Spiritual Readings for Daily Use. Selected from the Works of Saints and approved Writers of the Catholic Church. Fcp. cloth, 3s. 6d.; red edges, 4s.

'Of the many volumes of meditations on sacred subjects which have appeared in the last few years, none has seemed to us so well adapted to its object as the one before us.'—*Tablet.*

'Deserves to be specially mentioned.'—*Month.*

'Admirable in every sense.'—*Church Times.*

'Many of the meditations are of great beauty. ... They form, in fact, excellent little sermons, and we have no doubt will be largely used as such.'—*Literary Churchman.*

Reflections and Prayers for Holy Communion.
Translated from the French. With Preface by His Eminence the CARDINAL ARCHBISHOP OF WESTMINSTER. Fcp. 8vo, cloth, 4s. 6d.; bound, red edges, 5s.; calf, 9s.; morocco, 10s.

'The Archbishop has marked his approval of the work by writing a preface for it, and describes it as "a valuable addition to our books of devotion."'—*Register.*

'A book rich with the choicest and most profound Catholic devotions.'—*Church Review.*

Lallemant's Doctrine of the Spiritual Life.
Edited by the late Father FABER. New edition. Cloth, 4s. 6d.

'This excellent work has a twofold value, being both a biography and a volume of meditations. It contains an elaborate analysis of the wants, dangers, trials, and aspirations of the inner man, and supplies to the thoughtful and devout reader the most valuable instructions for the attainment of heavenly wisdom, grace, and strength.'—*Catholic Times.*

'A treatise of the very highest value.'—*Month.*

'The treatise is preceded by a short account of the writer's life, and has had the wonderful advantage of being edited by the late Father Faber.'—*Weekly Register.*

The Rivers of Damascus and Jordan: a
Causerie. By a Tertiary of the Order of St. Dominic. 4s.

'Good solid reading.'—*Month.*

'Well done and in a truly charitable spirit.'—*Catholic Opinion.*

'It treats the subject in so novel and forcible a light that we are fascinated in spite of ourselves, and irresistibly led on to follow its arguments and rejoice at its conclusions.'—*Tablet.*

Legends of our Lady and the Saints; or
our Children's Book of Stories in Verse. Written for the Recitations of the Pupils of the Schools of the Holy Child Jesus, St. Leonard's-on-Sea. 3s.

'It is a beautiful religious idea that is realised in the *Legends of our Lady and the Saints.* The book forms a charming present for pious children.'—*Tablet.*

'The "Legends" are so beautiful that they ought to be read by all lovers of poetry.'—*Bookseller.*

'Graceful poems.'—*Month.*

The New Testament Narrative, in the Words
of the Sacred Writers. With Notes, Chronological Tables, and Maps. New edition, revised. Cloth, 2s. 6d.

'The compilers deserve great praise for the manner in which they have performed their task. We commend this little volume as well and carefully printed, and as furnishing its readers, moreover, with a great amount of useful information in the tables inserted at the end.'—*Month.*

'It is at once clear, complete, and beautiful.'—*Catholic Opinion.*

QUARTERLY SERIES.

Conducted by the Managers of the 'Month.'

———o———

VOLUMES PUBLISHED.

The Life and Letters of St. Francis Xavier.
By the Rev. H. J. COLERIDGE. Sec. edit. Two vols. 18s.

'We cordially thank Father Coleridge for a most valuable biography. . . . He has spared no pains to insure our having in good classical English a translation of all the letters which are extant. . . . A complete priest's manual might be compiled from them, entering as they do into all the details of a missioner's public and private life. . . . We trust we have stimulated our readers to examine them for themselves, and we are satisfied that they will return again and again to them as to a never-exhausted source of interest and edification.'—*Tablet.*

'A noble addition to our literature. . . . We offer our warmest thanks to Father Coleridge for this most valuable work. The letters, we need hardly say, will be found of great spiritual use, especially for missionaries and priests.'—*Dublin Review.*

'One of the most fascinating books we have met with for a long time.'—*Catholic Opinion.*

'Would that we had many more lives of saints like this! Father Coleridge has done great service to this branch of Catholic literature, not simply by writing a charming book, but especially by setting others an example of how a saint's life should be written.'—*Westminster Gazette.*

'This valuable book is destined, we feel assured, to take a high place among what we may term our English Catholic classics. . . . The great charm lies in the letters, for in them we have, in a far more forcible manner than any biographer could give them, the feelings, experiences, and aspirations of St. Francis Xavier as pictured by his own pen.'—*Catholic Times.*

'Father Coleridge does his own part admirably, and we shall not be surprised to find his book soon take its place as the standard Life of the saintly and illustrious Francis.'—*Nation.*

'Not only an interesting but a scholarly sketch of a life remarkable alike in itself and in its attendant circumstances. We hope the author will continue to labour in a department of literature for which he has here shown his aptitude. To find a saint's life which is at once moderate, historical, and appreciative is not a common thing.'—*Saturday Review.*

'Should be studied by all missionaries, and is worthy of a place in every Christian library.'—*Church Herald.*

The Life of St. Jane Frances Fremyot de Chantal.
By Emily Bowles. With Preface by the Rev. H. J. Coleridge. Second edition. 5s. 6d.

'We venture to promise great pleasure and profit to the reader of this charming biography. It gives a complete and faithful portrait of one of the most attractive saints of the generation which followed the completion of the Council of Trent.'—*Month*.

'Sketched in a life-like manner, worthy of her well-earned reputation as a Catholic writer.'—*Weekly Register*.

'We have read it on and on with the fascination of a novel, and yet it is the life of a saint, described with a rare delicacy of touch and feeling such as is seldom met with.'—*Tablet*.

'A very readable and interesting compilation. . . . The author has done her work faithfully and conscientiously.'—*Athenæum*.

'Full of incident, and told in a style so graceful and felicitous that it wins upon the reader with every page.'—*Nation*.

'Miss Bowles has done her work in a manner which we cannot better commend than by expressing a desire that she may find many imitators. She has endued her materials with life, and clothed them with a language and a style of which we do not know what to admire most—the purity, the grace, the refinement, or the elegance. If our readers wish to know the value and the beauty of this book, they can do no better than get it and read it.'—*Westminster Gazette*.

'One of the most charming and delightful volumes which has issued from the press for many years. Miss Bowles has accomplished her task faithfully and happily, with simple grace and unpretentious language, and a winning manner which, independently of her subject, irresistibly carries us along.'—*Ulster Examiner*.

The History of the Sacred Passion.
From the Spanish of Father Luis de la Palma, of the Society of Jesus. The Translation revised and edited by the Rev. H. J. Coleridge. Third edition. 7s. 6d.

'A work long held in great and just repute in Spain. It opens a mine of wealth to one's soul. Though there are many works on the Passion in English, probably none will be found so generally useful both for spiritual reading and meditation. We desire to see it widely circulated.'—*Tablet*.

'A sterling work of the utmost value, proceeding from the pen of a great theologian, whose piety was as simple and tender as his learning and culture were profound and exquisite. It is a rich storehouse for contemplation on the great mystery of our Redemption, and one of those books which every Catholic ought to read for himself.'—*Weekly Register*.

'The most wonderful work upon the Passion that we have ever read. To us the charm lies in this, that it is entirely theological. It is made use of largely by those who give the Exercises of St. Ignatius; it is, as it were, the flesh upon the skeleton of the Exercises. Never has the Passion been meditated upon so before. . . . If any one wishes to understand the Passion of our Lord in its fulness, let him procure this book.'—*Dublin Review*.

'We have not read a more thoughtful work on our Blessed Lord's Passion.

It is a complete storehouse of matter for meditation, and for sermons on that divine mystery.'—*Catholic Opinion.*

'The book is—speaking comparatively of human offerings—a magnificent offering to the Crucified, and to those who wish to make a real study of the Cross will be a most precious guide.'—*Church Review.*

Ierne of Armorica: a Tale of the Time of Chlovis. By J. C. BATEMAN. 6s. 6d.

'We know of few tales of the kind that can be ranked higher than the beautiful story before us. The author has hit on the golden mean between an over-display of antiquarianism and an indolent transfer of modern modes of action and thought to a distant time. The descriptions are masterly, the characters distinct, the interest unflagging. We may add that the period is one of those which may be said to be comparatively unworked.'—*Month.*

'A volume of very great interest and very great utility. As a story it is sure to give much delight, while, as a story founded on historical fact, it will benefit all by its very able reproduction of very momentous scenes. . . . The book is excellent. If we are to have a literature of fiction at all, we hope it will include many like volumes.'—*Dublin Review.*

'Although a work of fiction, it is historically correct, and the author portrays with great skill the manners and customs of the times of which he professes to give a description. In reading this charming tale we seem to be taken by the hand by the writer, and made to assist at the scenes which he describes.'—*Tablet.*

'The author of this most interesting tale has hit the happy medium between a display of antiquarian knowledge and a mere reproduction in distant ages of commonplace modern habits of thought. The descriptions are excellent, the characters well drawn, and the subject itself is very attractive, besides having the advantage of not having been written threadbare.'—*Westminster Gazette.*

'The tale is excessively interesting, the language appropriate to the time and rank of the characters, the style flowing and easy, and the narrative leads one on and on until it becomes a very difficult matter to lay the book down until it is finished. . . . It is a valuable addition to Catholic fictional literature.'—*Catholic Times.*

'A very pretty historico-ecclesiastical novel of the times of Chlovis. It is full of incident, and is very pleasant reading.'—*Literary Churchman.*

Public Life of our Lord. By the Rev. H. J. COLERIDGE, S.J. 3 vols. published. 6s. 6d. per vol.

The Life of the Blessed John Berchmans. By the Rev. FRANCIS GOLDIE, S.J. 6s.

'A complete and life-like picture, and we are glad to be able to congratulate Father Goldie on his success.'—*Tablet.*

'Drawn up with a vigour and freedom which show great power of biographical writing.'—*Dublin Review.*

'One of the most interesting of all.'—*Weekly Register.*

'Unhesitatingly we say that it is the very best Life of Blessed John

Berchmans, and as such it will take rank with religious biographies of the highest merit.'—*Catholic Times.*

'Is of great literary merit, the style being marked by elegance and a complete absence of redundancy.'—*Cork Examiner.*

'This delightful and edifying volume is of the deepest interest. The perusal will afford both pleasure and profit.'—*Church Herald.*

The Life of the Blessed Peter Favre, of the

Society of Jesus, First Companion of St. Ignatius Loyola. From the Italian of Father GIUSEPPE BOERO, of the same Society. With Preface by the Rev. H. J. COLERIDGE. 6s. 6d.

This Life has been written on the occasion of the beatification of the Ven. Peter Favre, and contains the *Memoriale* or record of his private thoughts and meditations, written by himself.

'At once a book of spiritual reading, and also an interesting historical narrative. The *Memoriale, or Spiritual Diary,* is here translated at full length, and is the most precious portion of one of the most valuable biographies we know.'—*Tablet.*

'A perfect picture drawn from the life, admirably and succinctly told. The *Memoriale* will be found one of the most admirable epitomes of sound devotional reading.'—*Weekly Register.*

'The *Memoriale* is hardly excelled in interest by anything of the kind now extant.'—*Catholic Times.*

'Full of interest, instruction, and example.'—*Cork Examiner.*

'One of the most interesting to the general reader of the entire series up to this time.'—*Nation.*

'This wonderful diary, the *Memoriale*, has never been published before, and we are much mistaken if it does not become a cherished possession to thoughtful Catholics.'—*Month.*

The Dialogues of St. Gregory the Great.

An old English version. Edited, with Preface, by the Rev. H. J. COLERIDGE. 6s.

'The Catholic world must feel grateful to Father Coleridge for this excellent and compendious edition. The subjects treated of possess at this moment a special interest. . . . The Preface by Father Coleridge is interesting and well written, and we cordially recommend the book to the perusal of all.'—*Tablet.*

'This is a most interesting book. . . . Father Coleridge gives a very useful preface summarising the contents.'—*Weekly Register.*

'We have seldom taken up a book in which we have become at once so deeply interested. It will suit any one; it will teach all; it will confirm any who require that process; and it will last and be read when other works are quite forgotten.'—*Catholic Times.*

'Edited and published with the utmost care and the most perfect literary taste, this volume adds one more gem to the treasury of English Catholic literature.'—*New York Catholic World.*

The Life of Sister Anne Catherine Emmerich. Edited, with Preface, by the Rev. H. J. COLERIDGE. 5s.

St. Winefride; or Holywell and its Pilgrims. By the Author of 'Tyborne.' Third edition. 1s.

Summer Talks about Lourdes. By Miss CADDELL. Cloth, 1s. 6d.

Blessed Margaret Mary Alacoque: a brief and popular Account of her Life; to which are added Selections from some of her Sayings, and the Decree of her Beatification. By the late Rev. CHARLES B. GARSIDE, M A. 1s.

A Comparison between the History of the Church and the Prophecies of the Apocalypse. Translated from the German by EDWIN DE LISLE. 2s.

CATHOLIC-TRUTH TRACTS.

NEW ISSUES.

Manchester Dialogues. First Series. By the Rev. Fr. HARPER, S.J.

    No. I. The Pilgrimage.
      II. Are Miracles going on still?
      III. Popish Miracles tested by the Bible.
      IV. Popish Miracles.
      V. Liquefaction of the Blood of St. Januarius.
      VI. 'Bleeding Nuns' and 'Winking Madonnas.'
      VII. Are Miracles physically possible?
      VIII. Are Miracles morally possible?

Price of each 3s. per 100, 25 for 1s.; also 25 of the above assorted for 1s. Also the whole Series complete in neat Wrapper, 6d.

Specimen Packet of General Series, containing 100 assorted, 1s. 6d.

www.ingramcontent.com/pod-product-compliance
Lightning Source LLC
Chambersburg PA
CBHW030603300426
44111CB00009B/1086